Liberty in America's Founding Moment

Doubts About Natural Rights in Jefferson's Declaration of Independence

Howard I. Schwartz, Ph.D.

Copyright © 2010 Howard I. Schwartz

Published by Other Ideas Press. Permission to reproduce or transmit in any form or by an means, electronic or mechanical, including photocopying and recording, must be obtained from the author.
All rights reserved.

ISBN-10: 0982832508
EAN-13: 9780982832509

Printed in the United State of America

Liberty in America's Founding Moment

Doubts About Natural Rights in

Jefferson's Declaration of Independence

Howard I. Schwartz, Ph.D.

Other Ideas Press

TCRMAFGNGNGYMMVHIATLO

Contents

PREFACE AND ACKNOWLEDGMENTS IX

INTRODUCTION. ON NATURAL RIGHTS, HISTORY,
AND THE AMERICAN FOUNDING 1

PART I: THE DECLARATION AND JEFFERSON'S
ALTERNATIVE THEORY OF AMERICAN RIGHTS 13

1. THE DECLARATION, LOCKE, AND CONFLICTS
ABOUT NATURAL RIGHTS 15
    Natural Rights, Locke, and Independence..................................18
    Jefferson's Alternative Theory 26
    Rights and the Allegiance to the Crown 34
    Rights, Territories, and Land Possession 38
    General Ambivalence about Natural Rights 47

2. JEFFERSON'S DECLARATIONS OF INDEPENDENCE 51
    Jefferson's Original Declaration of Independence 53
    No Natural Rights in Jefferson's Original
    Declaration of Independence..56
    Drafting the Declaration of Independence.................................59
    When In The Course Of Human Events 66
    We Hold These Truths 72
    Pursuit of Happiness 75

PART II: PLACING JEFFERSON IN CONTEXT 83

3. EARLY DOUBTS ABOUT NATURAL RIGHTS BEFORE THE REVOLUTION 85
Locke and Natural Rights in Responses to
the Sugar and Stamp Act 87
The Shift to Rights Talk and the Doubts about
Social Contract Theory 94
Social Contract Theory is Metaphysical Jargon 99
The Problem with British Rights 102
The Challenge to British Rights and Arguments
from Birthright 107
James Otis and Doubts about Social Compact 113
Natural Rights and Stamp Act Resolutions 120

4. DIVERGING THEORIES OF AMERICAN RIGHTS BEFORE JEFFERSON 129
Categories of Natural Rights Arguments 130
John Dickinson and the Avoidance of
Natural Rights Arguments 132
The Natural Right to Quit Society and
the New Emerging Theory of the Empire 139
Classic Natural Rights Arguments as
Extensions of British Rights 149
The Law of God and Nature: Christian
Perspectives on Natural Rights 156

5. *A SUMMARY VIEW*: JEFFERSON'S FIRST MAJOR FORAY INTO POLITICAL WRITING 163
A Summary View 164
On the Right to Quit Society 166
On the Conquest of America 168
What Went Wrong? 174

Is Jefferson's Theory Lockean? 177
Jefferson Looks Back 183

6. THE FIRST CONTINENTAL CONGRESS AND THE REJECTION OF JEFFERSON'S PET THEORY 187

Natural Rights, Expatriation, and Naturalization:
The Debates of the First Continental Congress 189
The Galloway Alternative 201
The First American Bill of Rights 211
The American Bill of Rights 214
Jefferson and the Necessity and Causes of
Taking Up Arms 222

PART III: THE PRECARIOUSNESS OF HISTORY 235

7. WHAT DO WE REALLY KNOW ABOUT JEFFERSON ON LOCKE? 237

The Facts of the Case: The Invoice, Letter,
and the Citations of Locke 240
Filling the Gaps in Jefferson's Story 244
Extrapolations from the Events in Question 251
What Can We Infer From the Purchase of
Locke on Government? 253
Jefferson's Commonplace Notes for A Summary View 260
The Locke Citation in the Commonplace Book 264
An Oversimplification of Locke? 268

8. HUME, LOCKE, AND JEFFERSON'S EARLY LEGAL CASES 273

The Fire, the Letter, and the Library 273
What Does a Personal Library Tell Us? 281
On the Possible Influence of Hume on Jefferson 284
Natural Rights in Jefferson's Early Legal Cases 293

The Case of the Mulatto's Grandson:
Howell v. Netherland 294
A Messy Case of Divorce 303

CONCLUSION: DOES IT MATTER WHAT THE DECLARATION MEANS? 309

NOTES 323

REFERENCES 381

Preface and Acknowledgments

Earlier in my life I had no interest in either Thomas Jefferson or the Declaration of Independence. Who cared about early American history anyway? But a change in American political discourse combined with a series of events in my life, and I found myself drawn irresistibly back to the Declaration and its author, Thomas Jefferson, to understand more about the vision with which America was founded.

This was perhaps a natural transition in some sense for a historian of religion and religious studies scholar who spent a good part of his academic life studying religion. After all, the Declaration was the "American Scripture," as Pauline Maier had so aptly called it. And I had already spent a good part of my adult life as an academic studying Judeo-Christian scriptures and their histories of interpretation. It was thus in some sense natural for me to turn to those texts that held mythic significance for Americans and to adopt some of the same skeptical and analytic techniques I had learned in the study of religion.

Yet what drew my attention to these early American texts was a growing awareness of and uneasiness with a new kind of political language that increasingly stressed the importance of individual rights to the exclusion of other values in America. Moreover, the increasingly emphatic language about government infringing individual rights often looked back to and justified itself in terms of the founding documents of early American history. The Declaration of Independence often figured prominently in the stories that Americans were telling about their sacred rights and why those rights must never be infringed. In that story, individuals had rights that transcended government. And the Declaration was often the key document that proved that America had been founded with the vision of protecting our individual rights.

I turned back to the Declaration and Thomas Jefferson to find out if this story was true. Was it the case that America was founded with a vision of individual rights that transcended and always trumped other values, such as community, public good, and responsibility? Did the founders have a fully worked out theory of individual rights? Were individual rights the focus of what they meant by liberty? As I read the literature leading up to the Revolution and delved more into Jefferson's own life and thought, I discovered, as I had suspected, that the answer was more complex. There was no simple and straightforward notion of rights on which the founders agreed. Jefferson, like other writers in the founding period, had read John Locke and was familiar with Locke's theory of natural rights. Most interpreters of Jefferson assumed he was espousing a theory of natural rights and perhaps even relying on John Locke in writing the Declaration of Independence. On that basis, the assumption is often made that America was founded with a vision of natural rights that reaches back to and can be understood in terms of John Locke's *Second Treatise on Government*. But as I discovered, the founders, including Jefferson, had doubts about Locke's notion that government was founded in social contract and had been influenced by other streams of thought that made Locke's ideas about natural rights problematic. These doubts about natural rights led the founders to disagree on which theory of rights actually justified the American Revolution and the War of Independence. These doubts and disagreements, however, are often missing in the histories and stories that are normally told about Jefferson and the Declaration.

As I came to understand these fissures and doubts in the thought leading up to the Revolution and the Declaration, I came to see that there was no single American mind on the matter of rights or at least the foundation of those rights. There were in fact significant disagreements among the pre-independence writers. Indeed, the Declaration's author, Thomas Jefferson, had a theory of rights that had been rejected by most of his colleagues. With this realization, a new way of understanding the Declaration emerged. Instead of seeing the Declaration as a document that unambiguously embraced a theory of natural rights and summarized the American Mind, one can read it as a document that tried to obfuscate and gloss over fundamental disagreements about rights among those who were declaring independence.

In telling this story in the pages that follow, the purpose is ultimately larger than just a reinterpretation of the Declaration, although that is important, too. As a scholar with a background in the history of religion, I have been continually impressed with how history and historical interpretation are often called upon to justify contemporary philosophies and ideologies. In this case, the classic understanding of the Declaration plays a key role in the attempt to justify an obsession with individual rights. But history cannot bear the weight that is too often placed on it. History is itself an interpretive enterprise in which facts are always only partial and interpretation of evidence shapes our understanding of the past. This becomes clear through the interpretation of the Declaration and Jefferson's early writings. We see how difficult it is to really say either what Jefferson himself finally thought or what the Declaration itself was supposed to mean. In this way, the very project of uncovering "the" founders' view of rights is called into question.

In the end, this book is intended to be more than a contribution to the Declaration's understanding and to the early thinking of Jefferson. It is also envisaged as a conversation between history and political philosophy. In this sense, the book is not strictly history though it makes its argument through careful historical analysis and argument. It is also an argument about how little we can rely on the past in making decisions about what values should guide us in the present.

As a scholar trained in the history of religion and religious studies, my methodology and style will be somewhat unfamiliar to many traditional historians. Historians on the whole tend to quote a sentence here and there from a primary source in order to paint a larger picture of a period. Those scholars in the academic discipline of religious studies like me are trained to read texts carefully and pay attention to small variations in language as indications of shifts in thought and larger cultural themes. I was trained to read texts this way as part of my own academic background in religious studies. My conclusions are drawn from such careful textual readings of primary sources that have been often overlooked by a more traditional historical method. Furthermore, traditional American historians do not always delve very deeply into the philosophical sources that the American founders were reading and quoting. They miss some of the nuances of the founders' thinking because they do not always look at the context of those sources that the founders were quoting. I dive deeper than most traditional historians in looking at the ways in which the founding documents quote and use their philosophical sources.

Numerous people supported me and contributed to my thinking during the journey that produced this book. My grown daughter Penina has over the last few years become one of my best interlocutors. I am continually amazed and gratified that she thinks so deeply about many of the same issues that also preoccupy me. Maggie deserves much more than the credit she receives here for putting up with me and supporting me during the years of moodiness that always accompanies creative activity. She gave much more than she received in return. Good friends encouraged me to keep at my intellectual pursuits despite my full-time work in the software industry, which keeps paying the bills. Scott, Ray, and Rick, in particular—thanks for accepting me for who I am.

Introduction

On Natural Rights, History, and the American Founding

It is commonly assumed that Americans as individuals have a set of "God-given" or "natural rights" which are declared in the Declaration of Independence and ultimately embodied in and protected by the Constitution of the United States. It makes sense to call this the founding myth of the United States. It is the story of how the American colonies came to throw off the rule of Great Britain and begin the process of becoming independent and free "united states." It is the story too that Americans tell when defending and arguing over their rights and when protecting themselves against what is viewed as the inappropriate encroachment by government. This founding story, in other words, articulates a political philosophy that justifies the rights and protections that Americans cherish so highly.

But what if part of this story is incorrect or misleading? What if the Declaration of Independence is much more ambivalent about natural rights than has been commonly thought? And what if the Declaration's author, Thomas Jefferson, held an alternative theory of rights that was rejected by the majority of his colleagues? Would these facts matter?

Posed here are two different types of intersecting questions, and both are at the heart of my inquiry. The first group of questions is historical in character and concerns the political ideas held by the leadership in the American colonies in the decade leading up to the Revolution and embodied in the Declaration. This group of questions can be approached through the traditional methods of the historian. The second set of questions is philosophical and political in nature. These questions ask about the relevance of history for deciding questions about how we live, or what some people refer to as "normative" questions. Generally speaking, what impact should history have on questions of political philosophy and rights? More specifically, if the Declaration does not mean what we think it means or does not have a stable set of meanings, does that matter?

I bring both set of questions together in this book and find the intersection of those questions fascinating and interesting. This book is thus in some sense a dialogue between the historian and the political philosopher. It asks whether a historian's revelations about the past should have any relevance to political philosophy and in particular to the American understanding of rights. Ultimately, the larger question at stake is how history should figure into political philosophy. The answer, I suggest, depends on how we understand both history specifically and rights in general. I pursue these questions in two different ways: first, from the side of the historian, doubting the still common and popular conclusion that the Declaration unequivocally endorses a philosophy of natural rights, and second, from the side of the philosopher, who wonders whether it matters what the Declaration means and what value history as a discipline should have in determining how we live and specifically what rights we protect. Let me flesh out both sides of my argument.

The Declaration of Independence is one obvious location to pursue questions at the intersection of history and political philosophy. Historically speaking, the Declaration is an interesting and important historical document that tells us something significant about the views of the colonial leaders at the moment they were declaring political independence from Great Britain. The Declaration thus marked a formal transition from a period in which the colonies fought for their rights within and as part of the British Empire to a period in which they declared Great Britain irrelevant to their rights and declared their own political independence. The Declaration is thus one important statement, although not the only statement, about how what were then "British colonies" understood their rights and the relationship of those rights to their vision of the kind of society in which they wanted to live.

It is important to ask whether this place in history should give the Declaration a "normative" or "prescriptive" claim on the present. Should it weigh in heavily in setting our norms or in establishing what rights we want to protect or even the fact that rights are the "right" language for describing the boundaries of government power and individual freedom? This is not only a question about how Americans understand rights but also a question about the relevance of history to political philosophy. When is history as a discipline relevant to defining rights within political societies?

On the historical side of this investigation, there are a number of interesting questions about the Declaration's meaning and the understanding of rights leading up to its publication. Here I challenge what has become one of the dominant understandings of the Declaration and the idea of rights in that period. In the commonly told version of the story, the leaders of the American colonies came to embrace a natural rights philosophy, and in particular that of philosopher John Locke.[1] According to that theory, individuals are created equal with a set of natural rights to life, liberty and property that cannot be infringed. Although a number of historians recognize other influences on the colonial leaders' thinking, the Declaration's focus on natural rights, and its apparent prominence in the move towards independence, is cited as evidence that a natural rights philosophy is the prominent theory of rights that defines American political philosophy.

In some versions of this story, the Declaration is in fact unique in being the first blueprint for society that is actually founded on a natural rights philosophy.[2] I find both versions of this story too simplistic and misleading in a number of ways that I shall spell out in more detail later. Building on the work of others before me, I shall argue that the story of American thinking about rights and the Declaration's view of rights in particular is much richer, more complex, and more contested than the story that is often presented. I find that fact interesting and probative. I shall argue that the colonial leadership both held diverging and incompatible theories of American rights in the period leading up to independence and had substantive doubts about natural rights philosophy in general and the specific ways in which it should be applied to their own situation in particular. They doubted in fact one of the central claims of natural rights philosophy: that government in general was founded in social contract. This is a stunning fact that warrants attention, both historically as well as for thinking about how rights should be defined in an ongoing way in American society.

The notion that government was founded in a social contract, rather than in other ways, such as by force or by God, was construed by the revolutionary colonial political leaders as both a historical argument about the actual origins of government as a human institution and a normative argument about the way government should rightfully operate. Indeed, the two parts of the theory were intertwined in interesting ways that the colonial political thinkers, like other notable thinkers before them, found troubling and problematic. They were not alone in this worry. It was the link between the historical argument about the origin of government in social contract and what we can refer to as "the normative argument"—that government should be founded on consent—that critics of social contract theory seized upon.[3] At issue was the question of whether the claim that "society should be founded on social contract" was justified by the historical argument that government in fact was a human institution that came about through an actual social contract. And if government was not founded historically in that way, how could one still make the argument that government should be founded that way?

The normative argument that derives from social contract theory is well known and immortalized in the common understanding of the Declaration of Independence.

> We hold these truths to be self-evident, that all men are created equal, that they are endowed by their Creator with certain unalienable Rights, that among these are Life, Liberty and the pursuit of Happiness.—That to secure these rights, Governments

are instituted among Men, deriving their just powers from the consent of the governed...[4]

These words encapsulate social contract theory even as they sidestep and skirt over one of its known major problems, the relationship between the historical origin and character of government (the way government developed) and the normative expectations of it (the way government should operate). We shall see that among writers in the colonies leading up to the Revolution, there were significant and recurring doubts that government was historically in fact founded in social contract. They knew that historically governments often came about through the use of force and an act of conquest. Indeed, the idea that rights derive from conquest was embraced by a number of the colonial thinkers in the period leading up to the Revolution, including the Declaration's author, Thomas Jefferson. Others thought God had much more responsibility in the creation of government as a human institution and doubted the claim that a voluntary social contract was the origin of government. These doubts about the origin of government made colonial thinkers worry that a theory founding government on the "consent of the governed" had to be grounded in some other understanding of government. These doubts caused some to conclude that a natural rights philosophy, or at least parts of it, were unworkable as a foundation for their own political philosophy. In short, while they embraced the notion that government by consent should be the way political societies operated, they were not all of one mind on what reasons could justify that view. The fact that they could not agree on the philosophical and moral justification of the social contract made some of them realize that there was no theory of government's origin on which everyone agreed.

In the historical argument developed in this book, I build on the work of other historians in contending that there was no settled understanding of colonial rights in the decade before the Declaration and that the disagreements and doubts about various aspects of natural rights are evident up to and into the Declaration itself. To unpack this argument, I suggest that it is a mistake to understand the Declaration as a simple and straightforward endorsement of either natural rights philosophy generally or Lockean philosophy specifically. There is no longer any doubt that Jefferson and most of the other colonial leaders read or were familiar with Locke.[5] Yet this view oversimplifies the purpose of the Declaration, which was to state a unified colonial position on independence, despite the fact that there were still some significant disagreements about key elements in natural rights theory. Instead, the Declaration emerges as a document that papers over and hides the substantive disagreements about the nature of American rights that had not been resolved in the period leading up to the Revolution.

It is not widely recognized, for example, that the Declaration's primary author, Thomas Jefferson, held an alternative theory of rights that none of his colleagues actually accepted. While most of his colleagues thought that the settlers brought their "British" rights with them from the "Mother Country," Jefferson argued they had left behind both their country and their British rights to which they had previously been entitled. There was a vast conceptual difference between these views. Jefferson tried and failed to get his colleagues to accept his theory of rights on several different occasions. In this third and final attempt while writing the Declaration, Jefferson tried one more time to smuggle in his alternative theory, only to have his colleagues in the Continental Congress obliterate his theory and leave completely unresolved the actual foundation of American rights. In the end, the Declaration hides as much as it reveals about the understanding of rights held by colonial leadership on its way to declaring independence. In seeing the Declaration this way, I place it into a larger story about the development of American thinking about rights in the period leading up to independence.

We shall see, in fact, that there was not "one American mind" on the question of rights. Instead of seeing the Declaration as a document that unequivocally endorses a natural rights philosophy and possibly even a specifically "Lockean" view, we see the Declaration as ambivalent about the foundation of natural rights and trying to sidestep what are unresolved questions that troubled colonial thinkers before and during the Revolution. Rather than depicting these political leaders as all of one mind on the question of the social contract, I see them hedging their bets and leaving great moral questions unresolved because they could not agree about the foundation of their rights. The details of this historical perspective are developed in the pages that follow.

This reinterpretation of the Declaration brings us to the normative question that hovers always in the background: does it matter what the Declaration of Independence means? Here I am concerned about how history and historical facts should enter into or be used in debates over how people should live their lives and what kinds of rights should be protected. This is a question of how history should intersect with political philosophy. Should it matter, to put it bluntly, if Jefferson or Adams liked or disliked Locke or Hume? How much should that historical issue weigh in our decisions about what limits to put on government or what freedoms to grant individuals? In this stream of my argument, I have constructive goals. History, after all, is only of importance if it illuminates something about the human condition. In this side of my argument, I take up the question of whether the historian has something to say to the political philosopher and social theorist, and if so, what? Here, I argue that because history is an interpretive humanistic discipline, it is problematic as a basis for how a society resolves its view of rights. By this I mean that historians themselves are engaged in an enterprise of continually coming to terms with the past. That enterprise is interpretive. It is always only partial and incomplete and there is no final objective standard for establishing historical truth, once and for all.[6] In this sense, history cannot provide a final answer for resolving questions of how we should live, for history is one way only, and not a privileged way, in which we engage moral philosophical questions. For this reason, the voice of the historian should have no preeminent weight, although it should perhaps have a contributing place, in determining how we understand our rights.

In saying that history should not have a privileged voice, I am taking up a question that is at the heart of American political debate on rights and, in fact, at the heart of social contract theory itself. For American political tradition, building on social contract theory itself suggests that an original contract should be the framework by which Americans interpret the rights by which we are governed. Social contract theory implies that the intentions of the founders as defined in some original contract are binding on the subsequent generations, although subsequent generations become the majority who can change the rules and at least part of the social contract itself. Those who are "contractarians" of this type believe they can resolve the great question of American rights by appealing to the founders' ideas and the meanings in the original texts, whether in the Declaration of Independence, in the American Constitution, or in the political writings leading up to those publications.[7] This understanding of the American founding presupposes a political philosophy in which the intent of the founders or framers should determine how we resolve questions of rights that confront us today. That philosophy of "original intent" or "original meaning," as it is called in discussions of the Constitution, often takes for granted that historical interpretation can be a stable and meaningful foundation for deciding original intentions rights and for settling great questions of political debate.[8] History thus becomes one of the pivotal ways of determining rights, since history helps resolve the question of original intent or original meanings.[9] History, in other words, becomes one of the methodologies of actualizing social contract theory. History is the method that helps reveal the intent of the founders. It is this kind of view that leads some thinkers to turn to the Declaration of Independence as the document by which to clarify the meaning of the original social contract with America. In this view, the Declaration enunciated the political philosophy that led the colonies to declare independence and ultimately provided a vision by which the newly emerging "united states" should be governed.

I argue that these views are problematic for several interrelated reasons. First, as already suggested, the attempt to use the Declaration to settle questions of rights rests on too simple a historical understanding of American thinking about rights leading up to the Declaration. The Declaration does not unambiguously prove that American rights are based on natural rights philosophy in general or the Lockean formulation in particular. I find this point to be interesting and potentially helpful, since many political philosophers would no longer find natural rights arguments compelling, at least in their traditional form.[10] Thus the possibility that the colonial political leaders were themselves in doubt about natural rights opens up a larger discussion about whether there is a defined political philosophy that is embedded in and ultimately endorsed in "an original social contract with America." By contrast, there are enormous implications for us if there are multiple conflicting views in the key founding documents.

Second, even if the Declaration were unequivocal about natural rights—a point I dispute—the question would arise whether history by itself can resolve the great moral questions of rights that face us. I argue that it cannot. And this argument derives from my understanding of how history itself is a constructive enterprise of interpretation. I believe that those who appeal to history and historians to resolve political and moral questions are trying to build a foundation for their house in quicksand. There is no absolute truth in history, and historians' arguments, therefore, should have no more a privileged place in deciding our values and rights than other kinds of arguments. In fact, perhaps historical arguments should have less weight than other forms of arguments that rest on articulated reasons and values.

Political philosophers and politicians, however, often turn to history to save them from what otherwise looks like an ongoing and evolving attempt to define what rights are and which ones should be protected. History, it is hoped, will save us from the messiness of differing views on the various contested values and rights. But history can't save us. Historians are engaged in a constructive humanistic enterprise of trying to understand our past. Their interpretations are always partial, infused themselves with assumptions about human nature and what facts from the past really matters. History itself can never fully explicate the complexity of the past. Information is always missing, and no account can capture the rich complexity anyway.

We shall bring this issue to the fore when we try to pinpoint even something as seemingly simple as what books and philosophies influenced Jefferson's Declaration of Independence. The problem of history, like the problem of original intent, is that the past is always more complex and varied than any historical account can possibly capture. Trying to figure out what ideas influenced Jefferson is enormously problematic and potentially irresolvable. For example, the conclusion that Jefferson was a natural rights thinker or a "Lockean" is an overly simplistic view of both Jefferson and Locke. And the fact that so many historians and interpreters of Jefferson have seen Jefferson that way points to the constructive nature of history as a discipline, too. In showing other influences on Jefferson, and suggesting that he, like other revolutionary political thinkers, had doubts about natural rights philosophy, I want to throw into relief the way that historians sometimes oversimplify the past and assume that there is necessarily a single discernible original intention about rights in the founding documents prior to the Revolution.[11]

This brings me to my third point. Even if the Declaration were clearly endorsing natural rights, and history were clearly an objective discipline, we would still have the problem of knowing whether the Declaration is the core centerpiece of the social contract. While there are good arguments to claim that the Declaration should hold a central place in our understanding of the founders' vision, there are counterarguments about whether the Declaration can bear that weight. The problem of how to locate the essence of the colonial revolutionaries' view is itself inseparable from the historical enterprise and the definition of what the original contract means. All of this is to say that while one argument could put natural rights at the center of the Declaration and the Declaration at the center of the social contract, there are other compelling ways of looking at both of those problems. Thus any attempt to pin down the Declaration's meanings still has to grapple with the many other dimensions of a problem that is always possibly slipping out of our grasp.

On the basis of these different trajectories in my argument, I ultimately tackle the question of whether this reinterpretation of the Declaration matters politically for how we live our lives and shape our political frameworks. From one perspective, one could argue that the Declaration's philosophy should matter simply because it has mattered in the past.[12] If, however, the Declaration does not provide the unequivocal endorsement of natural rights that many suppose it does, then arguments about the nature of the American rights have to rest on some other foundation or source.

That is not to say that the nature of the debate on rights will necessarily change. By its very nature, a philosophy of rights has the power to justify itself in many different ways on historical facts.[13] If the facts or meaning of those facts are perceived to change, the philosophy of rights can shift and find another set of facts upon which to alight. This goes to the larger thesis put forward in this book. History does not and cannot permanently anchor a theory of rights. Or, to put it another way, history can provide only a temporary anchor for a theory of how we should live. But the historical account on which a theory rests is always, by the very nature of historical interpretation, ultimately unstable as a foundation.

There are two ways in which political philosophies can deal with this problem of history. Either they can divorce themselves from history altogether and rest on a philosophical understanding of the human condition in general, a strategy that may have its own problems, too; or they can move on to other historical facts when the ones they rest on become slippery and soft.

This, it seems to me, is the larger, interesting upshot of my study and ultimately led me down the path to tackle the questions that I ask here. It is a myth that the American political framework rests on an original social contract that has a discrete determinate meaning in time that can be discerned. It is this kind of myth, incidentally, that religious traditions presuppose all the time, as I've discussed in my earlier work.[14] A political philosophy of natural rights has the same tendency as religion: to posit some original revelation or contract in which subsequent generations are bound. The debates in American society over the last quarter century are ultimately about whether the original contract that the colonial leaders made should hold sway over our own current understanding of rights. It is that inclination that sees history as the means by which we resolve these debates that I ultimately want to contest. In this sense, I side with David Hume against John Locke, for Hume viewed natural rights philosophy as much a political myth as the royalist theory that the king is God's steward on earth. We shall see in fact that many colonial writers, including Jefferson, seemed to be aware of Hume's critique of Locke and took it seriously.

In this sense, my argument moves on two parallel levels. I'm trying to draw out some of the colonial writers' doubts about Locke's natural rights and their sensitivity to the critique of natural rights philosophy, even as they embraced much that they liked about natural rights philosophy and its emphasis on consent. At the same time, I am endorsing a view that is much more suspicious of history as a source of truth that can pin down a notion of American rights, or any notion of rights at all. My larger goal, which moves beyond the discrete study here and which I have written about elsewhere, is to contest the notion that liberty has a fixed, determinate meaning independent of the particular public values that a society has and adopts.[15] One cannot anchor Americans' conception of liberty and rights, nor that of any society, ultimately on an abstract notion of liberty and rights that does not still need interpretation and engagement with the values of a given society at a given place in time. History is just one fact, among others, that enters into a discussion of how we want to live our lives collectively under this social contract that we call America.

PART I

The Declaration and Jefferson's Alternative Theory of American Rights

1. The Declaration, Locke, and Conflicts about Natural Rights

It is has long been conventional wisdom that the Declaration of Independence is the official and most important American endorsement of natural rights theory. According to this view, the Declaration unequivocally endorses natural rights theory, although there is substantial debate about whether it represents a specifically "Lockean view" of rights and government in particular, a point to which we return below. This reading of the Declaration provides support for the argument that natural rights are the foundation of the American tradition and the basis of rights in the Constitution and the Bill of Rights. Interestingly enough, neither of those other two critical founding documents explicitly endorses natural rights or provides a statement outlining a general philosophy of government.[1] The Declaration of Independence contrasts with these later documents in articulating an explicit philosophy of rights and government. It also represents the culmination of American thinking for the decade leading up to the American Revolution. For all of these reasons, the Declaration has become the source par excellence justifying the view that American constitutional tradition is founded on a natural rights philosophy, even though the Declaration's primary purpose was to justify American independence from Great Britain rather than to serve as a founding document for the new United States.

Against the backdrop of natural rights arguments leading up to the Revolution, this conventional view of the Declaration appears misleading in some critical and potentially troubling ways. To begin with, it is not often realized that the primary author of the Declaration had a different view of rights than is commonly ascribed to the Declaration. Jefferson did not accept the view of rights that had been authorized by the Continental Congress a year and a half before he drafted the Declaration.[2] On two previous occasions, Jefferson had tried to get his alternative view of rights accepted by the Continental Congress, but on both occasions his views were rejected. When he sat down to draft the Declaration, he still held a different view of rights and thus had to make a choice whether to try once again to put forward his own theory of rights or revert to the more traditional theory of natural rights that the Congress had already approved nearly two years earlier. The fact that the primary author of the Declaration disagreed with Congress's official justification of American rights provides a point of departure for rethinking the Declaration's understanding of natural rights and its relationship to American rights and independence. It will also become the point of departure for a much broader discussion of how history and historical analysis relates to political philosophy.

Jefferson was by no means the only thinker with doubts about natural rights theory or the way such theories were used to ground the rights of North American colonies. As we shall see later, in the decade leading up to the Revolution, colonists had expressed some profound concerns about natural rights theory in general and their application to American rights in particular. There was in fact no single monolithic tradition of thinking about natural rights in the decade leading up to the Revolution. And even after the First Continental Congress published its official version of rights in September 1774, doubts remained about the strength of natural rights arguments and about the ways those rights should be used to justify American rights.

Against this backdrop, a more tentative and equivocal reading of the Declaration's statement of rights emerges. Instead of seeing the Declaration as exhibiting a wholehearted embrace of natural rights theory, the Declaration's position on natural rights theory appears much more ambiguous than is often assumed. Because the Declaration was attempting to state a unified colonial position about independence, its language smoothes over and avoids areas of disagreement about natural rights among those favoring independence. On this view, the Declaration's language hides as much as it reveals. It is as if the Continental Congress, through its revision of Jefferson's draft, papered over some of the earlier doubts and disagreements about natural rights theory in an effort to state a unified American view justifying revolution when such a unified theory did not exist. In other words, the Declaration is written in a way that transcends and obfuscates some of the underlying disagreements in American rights theory that had earlier been visible in the writings leading up to the Declaration. That purpose, in fact, may then be one of its effects if not purposes: to try to find common language that could unite Americans across the colonies behind the call for independence. On this understanding, the Declaration's genius is not only in its beautiful language and the powerful way it stated natural rights theory, but also in what it did not say and what opinions it did not take a position on. Its beauty in part is in framing a statement that seemed to justify independence, while avoiding the unresolved question about the origin of American rights. But in its ellipses and language, some of that earlier ambivalence is still evident, and there are major equivocations about just how natural rights can justify the American right to declare independence.

On this view, the foundation of American rights was not, in fact, completely settled, and the meaning of natural rights was more contested than is typically understood. Major questions about the source of American rights vis-à-vis Parliament and the British Empire were left unresolved. Peek below the general language of rights in the Declaration and an alarming number of potentially thorny issues in American political philosophy rise to the surface. The Declaration suppressed and hid these tensions, though at the same time using language that made evident that some of those issues still lay in the background. As a political document, then, the Declaration's effect, if not ambition, was to leave aside philosophical differences and achieve a statement whereby all those who embraced some version of American rights—and the versions were in many ways radically different—could find their voice in the document. In this way, the Declaration is a document that masks differences and complications, even as it points toward and reveals their presence. This alternative account emerges when the Declaration is set against both the background of natural rights arguments leading up to the Revolution as well as Jefferson's own particular views of American rights before the Declaration.

The interpretation of the Declaration proposed here intersects with but diverges in critical ways from recent debates that have taken place about the meaning of the Declaration and its relationship to Lockean natural rights theory. Two key questions have tended to frame that discussion of the Declaration's meaning: The first question, which interestingly enough reaches back to the early 1800s, is whether the Declaration endorses a specific Lockean view of rights. A second and related question is how central is the statement of rights to the Declaration's overall purpose. A brief look at these issues follows below.

Natural Rights, Locke, and Independence

Most interpreters agree that the Declaration contains what is generally regarded as the basic assumptions of natural rights philosophy. There are at least two key passages in the Declaration reflecting these assumptions. The first is the Declaration's most famous passage regarding inherent individual rights.

> We hold these truths to be self-evident, that all men are created equal, that they are endowed by their Creator with certain unalienable Rights, that among these are Life, Liberty and the pursuit of Happiness.

The similarity of this statement in conception and language to passages in John Locke's *Second Treatise on Government* has been remarked on by many interpreters.[3] In addition to this statement about inherent rights, the Declaration articulates a philosophy of government based on consent.

> That to secure these rights, Governments are instituted among Men, deriving their just powers from the consent of the governed,—That whenever any Form of Government becomes

1. The Declaration, Locke, and Conflicts about Natural Rights

destructive of these ends, it is the Right of the People to alter or to abolish it, and to institute new Government, laying its foundation on such principles and organizing its powers in such form, as to them shall seem most likely to effect their Safety and Happiness.

Key assumptions and language from the natural rights tradition are evident in these two famous passages: First, the idea that individuals are created equal and derive inherent rights from the equality of creation is a central contention in Locke's *Second Treatise*.[4] Second, the Declaration clearly articulates the notion that government is instituted to secure these basic rights and that governments in general therefore derive their "just powers from the consent of the governed." Third, we also find present the idea that people have the right—indeed the duty—to throw off a government that attempts to "reduce them under absolute Despotism." So far all of these ideas are key natural rights concepts articulated by John Locke.

While there is a general agreement that the Declaration takes these ideas for granted, there is debate around whether the Declaration's statement of rights and philosophy of government should be considered specifically "Lockean" or whether its source of ideas lies elsewhere. This debate about the Lockean character of the Declaration reaches back to the federalist and republican tensions in 1820 when federalist Thomas Pickering quoted a letter from John Adams to the effect that the Declaration contained no idea "but what had been hackneyed in Congress for two years before." Adams had claimed in essence that the ideas "were in the air" and that all the ideas of the Declaration had been articulated already in the Congress's *Declaration of Rights* of 1774 and by a pamphlet of James Otis.[5]

In response to Pickering and Adams's statements, Jefferson wrote to Madison acknowledging that he had never intended to say anything original but that he had not turned to any particular book or pamphlet. Jefferson also responds to the charge that he had copied from Locke:

> Pickering's observations, and Mr. Adams' in addition, that it [the Declaration] contained no new ideas, that it is a commonplace

compilation, its sentiments hacknied in Congress for two years before...may all be true. Of that I am not to be the judge. Richard Henry Lee charged it as copied from Locke's treatise on Government...I know only that I turned to neither book nor pamphlet while writing it. I did not consider it as any part of my charge to invent new ideas altogether and to offer no sentiment which had ever been expressed before.[6]

Then on May 8, 1825, in a letter to Henry Lee, Jefferson acknowledged multiple sources of inspiration for the Declaration, including but not limited to Locke. The important task in writing the Declaration was:

Not to find out new principles, or new arguments, never before thought of, not merely to say things which had never been said before; but to place before mankind the common sense of the subject, in terms so plain and firm as to command their assent, and to justify ourselves in the independent stand we are impelled to take. Neither aiming at originality of principle or sentiment, nor yet copied from any particular and previous writing, it was intended to be an expression of the American mind...All its authority rests then on the harmonizing sentiments of the day, whether expressed in conversation, in letters, printed essays, or the elementary books of public right, as Aristotle, Cicero, Locke, Sidney, etc.[7]

In many ways, the subsequent debate has merely amplified one or more of the views represented here.

One stream of subsequent thought follows Jefferson's own perspective and argues that Jefferson's genius was in his ability to eloquently capture the American mind or sentiments of the day. For example, Carl Becker, commenting on John Adams's claim that the Declaration was hackneyed, acknowledges that this "is substantially true; but as a criticism, if it was intended as such, it is wholly irrelevant, since the strength of the Declaration was precisely that it said what everyone was thinking. Nothing could have been more futile than an attempt to justify a revolution on principles which no one had ever heard of before."[8] Similarly, Boyd writes that "when he [Adams] said that the Declaration contained only hackneyed ideas, he meant it as criticism, thereby exposing himself to the obvious response: the greatness of the Declaration lay in the very fact that it expressed what Adams himself had said was in the mind and hearts of the people."[9] Indeed, even if Jefferson had copied from Locke or elsewhere "the most that would be proved by this is that he had failed to be original in an enterprise where originality would have been fatal."[10] And Boyd in his opening thus essentially follows Jefferson by stating that "[i]n a broad sense, the author of the Declaration of Independence was the American people...If, as Jefferson intended, the Declaration was 'an expression of the American mind' he was in this sense the inspired amanuensis of the people." And again: "The fact is that these broad concepts, familiar to any reader of Locke or Burlamaqui or Vattel, were so much a part of the air breathed by the patriots of 1776 that Jefferson could not have escaped using them and their more or less fixed phraseology even if he had desired to do so."[11] Similarly, Jefferson's biographer Malone wrote that the ideas of the Declaration "belonged to no single man, but in his opinion, were the property of mankind"; and Merrill Peterson in his Jefferson biography writes that the ideas "belonged to everyone and to no one."[12] Picking up a similar theme, Pauline Maier, in her book on the Declaration, *American Scripture*, comes to the conclusion that the Declaration was "unexceptional in its ideas."[13]

But if one stream of thought claimed that Jefferson's Declaration captured the ideas that were in the air, and thus represents "the American Mind," a second stream of thought has argued the Declaration is most properly described as a Lockean document and owes its largest debt to enlightenment philosopher John Locke.[14]

These two views are not necessarily mutually exclusive. Jefferson's ideas could have been "Lockean" and still have been "in the air." The view that the Declaration is Lockean was put forward most articulately by Carl Becker in his book *The Declaration of Independence*. Becker made at least four different and not necessarily compatible claims, a fact not appreciated by all post-Becker interpreters. Becker argued inconsistently that:

(1) Jefferson copied directly from Locke, (2) Jefferson had read Locke so many times he had memorized Lockean language which he used in the Declaration, (3) Lockean ideas were so much in the air that "where Jefferson got his ideas is hardly so much a question as where he could have got away from them,"[15] and (4) natural rights were compelling to Jefferson and his cohorts because they solved a problem, namely, how to justify independence.

While many have accepted or further developed Becker's assumption of John Locke's direct influence on Jefferson, there has been extensive debate about one or more of Becker's contentions: whether Jefferson knew or read Locke, whether Locke's ideas were in the air in general, whether Jefferson leaned literarily on other American sources of natural rights language, such as James Wilson's pamphlet, *Considerations on the Nature and Extent of the Legislative Authority of the British Parliament*,[16] or George Masons' Virginia Bill of Rights, both of which have strong linguistic similarities to Jefferson's language in the Declaration.[17]

A third and more recent stream of thought, sometimes referred to as "the republican synthesis," has taken a different tact, arguing that the emphasis on John Locke's writings has been overstated in the pre-revolutionary writings in general.[18] Emphasizing the importance of republican ideas and traditions, such as radical Whig thinking, republican views from antiquity or Scottish Enlightenment thinkers, these writers stress how other intellectual traditions beyond that of Locke shaped American thinking. In general, this line of interpretation has argued that Locke's influence has been overstated in the interpretation of the ideas of the revolutionary thinkers. When this perspective is brought to bear on the Declaration, that document appears less like a Lockean natural rights document and instead is thought to have other influences, such as the English Bill of Rights of 1688, which also grappled with the problem of removing the English king, or the writing of the Scottish Enlightenment thinkers.[19]

In response to this republican synthesis, which has downplayed and marginalized Locke, a recent series of important essays and books has reiterated the view that Locke's ideas were very important and influential in the period leading to the Revolution and to the Declaration itself. These responses argue that ideas of Locke were both distinctive in European thought and had themselves already penetrated radical Whig thinking after the Glorious Revolution. Locke's rise to dominance in Whig thinking occurred after the Glorious Revolution and came to dominate and shape Whig radical thinking which influenced the colonial writers and ultimately the Declaration. The Declaration is thus reflecting a view of rights that was new with Locke's *Second Treatise* and thus was "Lockean" whether or not Jefferson ever read Locke. The Lockean character of the Declaration thus differentiates the American Revolution, which was justified by natural rights theory, from the Glorious Revolution, which rested on different assumptions.[20]

In what follows, I offer a different approach to the question of the Declaration's position on rights, arguing that a key aspect of the Declaration's meaning and function has been missed. Instead of asking whether the Declaration is Lockean or what literary documents are the source of its ideas, I will suggest that the Declaration's position on natural rights and independence is much more equivocal than has been typically realized. The question about the source of Jefferson's ideas is less relevant and interesting than the question of what position on rights was getting articulated. The answer to that question is more ambiguous than typically thought. And the equivocation is one part of the Declaration's meaning and function. Indeed, one central purpose of the Declaration was to unite the colonies behind the decision to declare independence. As such, the Declaration had to evade and sidestep any disagreements about rights that might still have lingered. In this sense, the Declaration had to speak as if "debate had ended," to use the words of Thomas Paine in *Common Sense*, when in fact on the matter of American rights, the debate had not completely ended and there remained some significant disagreements about the foundations of and nature of natural and American rights. Jefferson himself did not agree with the view endorsed by the First Continental Congress in 1774, though that constituted the official view endorsed by the Congress on behalf of the colonies. When Jefferson sat down to write the Declaration, he had to find words to unite those who otherwise had diverging views. On this interpretation of the situation, Jefferson's brilliance was not only in his powerful rhetorical performance, but in finding an articulation of rights that would seemingly be amenable to as many parties as possible, including himself. In this sense, "all its authority rests then on the harmonizing sentiments of the day," to use Jefferson's own words, is a more profound and ironic interpretation than anyone has fully appreciated.[21] If Jefferson's Declaration of Independence captures the American Mind, then it does so in all the complexity and disagreement that characterized the "American Mind" at the time. There was arguably no single American Mind on the question of rights.[22] And the Declaration was harmonizing a tradition that did in fact have divergent views and loose ends. This statement on rights would have to speak not just to those who endorsed the position of the First Congress, but also those who did not, including its author. This interpretation of the Declaration thus takes a position that both affirms and criticizes all of the various the positions in the debate. The Declaration does endorse natural rights language and a Lockean-like view but at the same time it exhibits some of ambivalence about natural rights and the way natural rights are linked up to American rights. It thus affirms that Locke's ideas were in the air but also argues that these ideas were contested and doubted. The American foundation of rights was not a settled matter.

In addition to rethinking the meaning and place of rights in the Declaration, the argument here dovetails with the second critical question in the literature: just how central is the statement of natural rights to the Declaration's purpose? It is generally conceded by most interpreters that the central purpose of the Declaration was not primarily to state a theory of rights or of government but to explain to the world why the British colonies were declaring independence from Great Britain and why they deserved to be recognized as independent states among the nations of the world.[23] In fact, we shall see that the colonies had already declared their rights in several earlier documents, in particular in the Declaration of Rights published by the First Continental Congress in 1774. What was new in the Declaration of Independence was not a theory of rights per se, but the justification of independence. As such, the Declaration was making a statement about the right of the colonies to be recognized as independent political entities among the nations of the world. The right to be recognized as a nation or "state" equal with other powers of the world was itself a separate but related question from the matter of the Americans' natural rights. Indeed, it could be the case that an individual or group of individuals could be living in a situation under which their natural rights were being violated without having thereby established a right to set up a separate political entity on a territory and be recognized as a nation of the world. It was one of the central purposes, if not *the* central purpose, of the Declaration to make that latter claim: that the colonies did have the right to *each* become separate nations. From this perspective, some interpreters emphasize that the Declaration thus appears to stand less in a natural rights tradition reaching back to Locke and more in the intellectual tradition reflecting on the *Law of Nations* reaching back to thinkers such as Vattel.[24] In that tradition, key questions include: "When does a political entity get recognized as a state like other nations?" and "What rights do states have vis-à-vis each other?" These are questions that cannot be entirely separated from but also not reduced to individual natural rights. As Vattel put it, for example, "we have already observed, that, in order to form this natural law of nations, it is not sufficient to simply apply to nations what the law of nature decides with respect to individuals."[25]

While most interpreters agree that justifying the independent statehood of the colonies was the overarching purpose of the Declaration, and indeed the understanding of the Declaration in the period immediately after 1776, it is generally conceded that the natural rights language and philosophy of government is critical to that argument.[26] It is the language of rights and philosophy of government that provides the justification for the claim that the colonies should be recognized as independent states. Indeed, the *Law of Nations* tradition was built on and extended the natural rights tradition and was often conflated with it.[27] There is no easy way to extract and separate the stream of thought dealing with the *Law of Nations* completely from the natural rights tradition. The rights language and philosophy of government reflected in the Declaration thus provides the framework in which independence and the justification of statehood makes sense. Without it, the larger argument falls apart.

As we shall see, however, the exact relationship between the natural rights argument and the theory of statehood is one part of what is equivocal in the Declaration. There were two or more very different justifications for statehood among the colonists, and the Declaration equivocates on which one it endorses. That equivocation is key. Jefferson himself had a view that had been rejected by his colleagues on two separate occasions. The Declaration's final language sounds more like the language of the First Continental Congress than it does Jefferson's own view. It thus makes sense that Adams could claim that Jefferson was saying nothing that was not already hackneyed since the First Continental Congress in 1774. From that reading of the Declaration, the very same theory of rights and statehood articulated by Congress was being articulated by the Declaration. And Adams was one of the "Committee of Five" who approved the Declaration and gave Jefferson feedback before it was sent on to the full Congress for final revision and approval. But at the same time the Declaration's language leaves equivocal exactly how the theory of individual rights married up with the theory of the states' rights. That equivocation was useful. It enabled the Declaration to include Jefferson's own theory of rights, which he tried to smuggle into the Declaration. And in this way, Jefferson produced a declaration that transcended but left unresolved some of the underlying disagreements about the natural rights tradition and the American foundation of independence.

Jefferson's Alternative Theory

When Jefferson sat down to write the Declaration of Independence, the "British American" colonies, as they were often called, had already achieved a quasi-official position defining how natural rights would figure into the basis of American rights. That understanding had been embodied in the First Continental Congress's Declaration of Rights in 1774. However, the political philosophy articulated in that document was inconsistent with Jefferson's own personal view.[28]

Jefferson had several times tried to put forward an alternative understanding of rights and political theory. That understanding placed the foundation of American rights on the "right to quit society," or what he later called the "right of expatriation."[29] We shall look at Jefferson's argument in some detail later. Before writing the Declaration, Jefferson had argued that an individual has a natural right to quit one's country. The settlers of North America had exercised this right to quit their country of birth, find new lands, and establish new political entities there that were not subject to the sovereignty of Parliament or under the authority of the king. Jefferson viewed this right to quit society as a natural right and believed it provided the foundation to justify not only the legislative independence of the colonies but the fact that they were independent states among the nations of the world. Jefferson was not the first to put forward this view. Richard Bland, Jefferson's cousin and senior colleague in the Virginia House of Burgesses, had made an almost identical argument in March 1766 near the close of the Stamp Act controversy. Nearly ten years later, in 1774, Jefferson made almost precisely the same argument as Bland, now taking Bland's thinking a step further towards its logical conclusions.[30]

On Jefferson's theory, the settlers had no rights nor obligations derived from the British Constitution when they immigrated to the lands in America. They left those behind. The new settlers, therefore, were not originally "British Americans" in the way that many other colonial writers thought of themselves. After conquering the new lands—and Jefferson did think the settlers had conquered their lands—they set up their own legislatures and freely modeled them after the laws of their mother country and the Anglo-Saxon political tradition. But that decision to adopt the laws of their home country had been done freely and was not mandated by any obligation. Indeed, Jefferson usually avoids the word "colonies" because for him the newly founded political entities always were free and independent states. Jefferson did assume, like many of his contemporaries, that the Anglo-Saxon ancestors were the ones who had brought the traditions of liberty and rights with them to England in the first place.[31] In his view, the various settlers of North America had adopted those laws and traditions of common law by choice. The fact that the settlers had by right quit their country of origin, conquered the new lands in some cases, and set up new political states meant that they were not subject to Parliament's authority. Parliament was simply one other legislature in the empire representing its own people (the English only) and did not have authority over the new political states in America. In this image of a "commonwealth of nations" or "federation of states," multiple political states had autonomy from one another, but were united by a common executive, the Crown, to whom each subject had allegiance.[32] In Jefferson's view, there was no supreme legislature over all the states in the British Empire. It was the Crown alone that held them together and set rules for their interactions.

The Crown in turn was obligated to offer protection to the empire's subjects. In Jefferson's view, the settlers had not only chosen to adopt the British constitution but had also adopted the king as their "chief officer." For this reason, the relationship of the various American states to the British Empire was less of "mother" to "child" (a metaphor many colonial writers used) but something more than simply a contract between equal nations. They were a kind of "league of nations" with separate legislatures united under a common sovereign, whom they had freely chosen to adopt as their chief officer, in order to preserve ties with their country and traditions of origin. Jefferson, as we shall see, had read about earlier European treaties between nations and conceptualized the relationship of the American states to the British Empire in similar ways. In this way, the American political entities called "colonies" had separate legislatures not subordinate to Parliament, yet the individuals were still subjects of the Crown, having made that decision by choice. They were, in other words, under the executive authority of the Crown but not under the legislative authority of Parliament.

Significantly, in Jefferson's view, there was never, ever a need to assert independence as a new state. Independence had already occurred with the emigration of the settlers from England.[33] These new states were independent from the start and never were "colonies." Jefferson outlined these ideas in *A Summary View*, a pamphlet that he wrote as instructions to the

Virginia delegates to the First Continental Congress in 1774. Jefferson himself was too ill to attend the first Congress, but he sent the pamphlet to Patrick Henry and Edmund Pendleton, and the latter "laid it on the table" for perusal by the delegates to Congress. It was this pamphlet which initially gained Jefferson a reputation across the colonies as a strong writer and advocate for legislative independence.[34]

Jefferson's perspective in *A Summary View* could be and often is construed to be based on Locke's view of natural rights. But that picture of Jefferson is arguably an anachronism, projecting the views understood to be represented in the Declaration of Independence back onto his earlier writing, which espoused different views. There are several reasons such a description is problematic, at least without adding substantial nuances and qualifications to the statement.[35]

To begin with, Jefferson's views were rejected by the First Continental Congress, the first official crosscolonial body to approve the use of natural rights arguments as a basis of colonial rights.[36] The published view of the First Continental Congress was much closer to a different and what can be called a more classical natural rights argument as adopted by James Wilson and Samuel Adams, among others. At the very minimum, then, there were several fundamentally different views of how natural rights arguments should justify American rights and independence. And at the heart of the disagreement between Jefferson and Congress were a number of key questions: Do people have a natural right to quit society, and under what conditions? Do they have a right to create new political entities? What conditions must obtain so that conquest of a land should rightfully result in the right to form new states? Did the settlers of North America conquer the land or find it uninhabited? We shall contrast the various views of rights below.

Second, it is at least debatable whether Locke would have agreed with the unqualified statement that people have a right to quit society, as I discuss below.[37] Locke recognized that each individual had a right to consent to (or reject) the social compact at maturity when the parents no longer had authority over their children. In Locke's view, however, a person who had reached maturity and had explicitly consented to live in society could not leave it. For Locke, the right to leave society depended on whether individuals had explicitly consented to live under the compact of a society. Once in, you could not leave without sufficient cause. While Jefferson's right to quit society could be linked back to Locke's philosophy of natural rights, Jefferson nowhere made any argument that would ground his view in Locke or in the natural rights tradition. He offers no recognition of the fact that Locke thought the right to quit society was lost once one explicitly consented to join the social compact. He simply assumed the existence of an unqualified natural right to quit society. Jefferson gives no indication that he cared or understood that this key philosophical assumption may have had no philosophical grounding in Locke.

Third, Jefferson sometimes avoids the use of some classic natural rights language, a point I have developed in much more detail below in an analysis of his *A Summary View*.[38] While he calls the right to quit society a "natural right," there is a marked ambivalence to the use of standard natural rights language in other places in his essay where it would make the most sense. We find nothing in Jefferson's essays like the explicit statement about the nature or origin of government in social compact or an account of original rights in a "state of nature" as found in other writers like Richard Bland, James Wilson, or Samuel Adams, to cite other contemporaries of Jefferson. Although Jefferson makes a statement about "life and liberty" being created by God, there is no general statement anywhere in his earlier essay about the right to "life, liberty, and property," a common refrain in the more classic statements of natural rights found in the writings leading up to independence.

There are other examples where reticence seems to guide Jefferson and a conscious avoidance of natural rights language. He emphasizes "God and the laws" rather than "God and Nature," and he emphasizes God's role in creating liberty, in a way reminiscent of James Otis, discussed in more detail below as well. Moreover, in a passage that deals with the right of the British people to depose their king, and thus a context that would normally seem quite appropriate for a reference to Locke's ideas of natural rights, Jefferson avoids the language altogether: "A family of princes was then on the British throne, whose treasonable crimes against their people brought on them afterwards the exertion of those sacred and sovereign rights of punishment reserved in the hands of the people for cases of extreme necessity." The use of the terms "sacred" and "sovereign," as well as the language "inalienable," are all terms that could just as well refer to rights derived from the common law tradition, the historical tradition of rights reaching back to the Saxons which Jefferson believes the settlers adopted in America.[39]

In *A Summary View*, Jefferson's emphasis is not on general natural rights, but on the right to quit one's society and set up a new political entity. Instead of an argument from general natural rights, there is still a reliance on what looks like a Whig historical argument that links American liberties back to British liberties and ultimately back to Saxons liberties. If one wants to call Jefferson's view a "natural rights" or "Lockean" argument, one at least has to qualify that statement by recognizing that it diverges in fundamental ways from arguments of other colonial writers and thinkers who more explicitly rely on what can be described as a classic Lockean argument. This is often forgotten or not noticed in the general characterization of Jefferson as a disciple of Locke. There were multiple interpretations of natural rights philosophy, and they had fundamental and critical differences between them, differences that ultimately matter in trying to found a theory of American rights.

Even if one still wants to categorize Jefferson's views as a natural rights position, it is evident that it was neither the classic natural rights position nor the one that found the most favor. In fact, the First Continental Congress had rejected Jefferson's point of view when adopting the Declaration of Rights and Grievances published in October 1774, even though Congress endorsed a natural rights argument. Jefferson himself was not in attendance, but views similar to his had been suggested by several of the delegates, such as John Jay and possibly by Richard Henry Lee.[40] One of the key objectives of the First Continental Congress was to publish a statement of rights and this task occupied the Congress on and off for six weeks. Early during the Congress, delegates had debated whether natural rights should be considered a solid or feeble foundation for American rights. In a matter of days, Congress voted to include natural rights as one of the foundations for the colonies' complaints. Like Jefferson, Congress also came to the conclusion that the colonies were independent states. Congress, however, arrived at that conclusion by a very different route and based on very different assumptions than did Jefferson.

Instead, Congress adopted the position that was identical to that of Pennsylvanian lawyer James Wilson, among others. According to that officially sanctioned view, the ancestors of the Americans had no right to quit society, or at least that right was not the basis of American rights. Instead, the emigrants had brought their British rights and obligations with them from the mother country and were as entitled and obligated to them as natural-born British subjects. When they left Britain, therefore, they came as British subjects to the new colonies, obligated to all the duties and entitled to all the rights of people born there. They were thus "British Americans" when they arrived in North America.

This view was shared by many of the delegates to Congress, such as James Duane, John Rutledge, Samuel Adams, John Adams, Richard Bland, and others. Samuel Adams, for example, who endorsed a different kind of natural rights argument than Jefferson had this to say about the subject of quitting society: "All Men have a Right to remain in a State of Nature as long as they please; *And in case of intolerable Oppression, Civil or Religious*, to leave the Society they belong to, and enter into another" [emphasis mine]. For Samuel Adams, the right to quit or leave society was not an absolute right. That right became operable only upon intolerable oppression, and for Adams and many colonial writers, that condition had not obtained in the initial migration of the settlers. The settlers came to the lands in America as bona fide British subjects.

In the view of Congress, James Wilson, and others, a problem emerged for these British American subjects in America because of the colonies' geographical distance from Great Britain, which made it impossible for the colonies to have adequate representation in Parliament. The Continental Congress, of course, took for granted that representation was a key right of British Americans. However, Congress rejected the possibility that the right could be fulfilled simply by adding American representatives to the British Parliament. It also rejected attempts, like that of Joseph Galloway, to construct a new structure of government that would attempt to meet this requirement of representation.

At issue was a broader debate on the nature of representation.[41] Congress, like many colonial and British writers, had come to the conclusion that there was no means possible to satisfy the requirement of British American representation in Parliament. The geographical distance meant that the representatives "there" in England did not live among their constituents "here" in America. By definition, then, representatives in Parliament could not represent the colonies, for a representative, according to one understanding of "representation," had to live with one's constituents and be impacted by the very same laws that were legislated for them. Representatives of the colonies could not both be in Parliament and live at home among the people they represented.

Americans rejected the British claim that representation in England had always been "virtual."[42] British critics had argued that even parts of the English populace did not get to vote or lacked representatives who lived among them. Why should the colonies be any different? The Continental Congress, by contrast, took the position that it was by definition impossible to provide representation to the colonies because of their geographical distance from Parliament. The conclusion followed that the colonists' natural rights were by definition infringed should Parliament legislate for them. On the view of Congress, then, it was this inherent, inevitable, and irreversible infringement of natural rights that justified the colonies having their own separate and independent legislatures. Like Wilson and others, Congress held the view that British Americans' natural rights could be protected in no other way but through their own legislatures. Their British rights came with them as emigrants, but their fulfillment ironically required independent legislatures. Congress thus asserted that the colonies should be supervised by their own legislatures that were wholly independent of and not subordinate to that of Parliament. Had airplanes existed at the time, the argument may have had less weight because American representatives to Parliament could have lived more easily among their constituents.

The position adopted by Congress was thus fundamentally different than that put forward by Jefferson in *A Summary View*.[43] Jefferson did not have to appeal to a theory of representation at all. He understood the initial political independence occurring as soon as the settlers migrated from England. The migration was itself an act of independence. The whole question of representation was thus irrelevant to his theory of independence.

The First Continental Congress was not the only one to reject Jefferson's views. Jefferson tried once again to have his position endorsed when he attended the Second Continental Congress in June 1775. On this occasion, he was called upon to develop the second draft of the *Declaration of the Causes and Necessity for Taking Up Arms* to explain why the colonies were going to war. In his draft of this declaration, Jefferson once again put forward his own theory of rights. But this time his view was rejected by the committee, this time led by John Dickinson and possibly William Livingston. This rejection was not simply a softening of a more radical position, as is sometimes assumed.[44] In fact, Dickinson's version was quite forceful in its own terms. Yet Dickinson's revision was explicitly a rejection of Jefferson's theory of rights. The Declaration of the Causes, published by the Second Continental Congress, was Dickinson's reworked version, which substantially demoted if not obliterated the theory of the ancestors' rights that Jefferson had put forward. Instead, Dickinson's version was much more consistent with the position on rights adopted by the First Continental Congress, a point to which we return.[45]

Rights and the Allegiance to the Crown

In addition to the fundamental disagreement about the origin of the settlers' rights, Jefferson and Congress also diverged on their views of allegiance to the Crown. It is important to separate the question of allegiance from the issue of subordination to Parliament, although today many discussions of the founding period conflate these two issues. On Jefferson's view, the right to quit society implied the right to freely repudiate not just the sovereignty of Parliament but also allegiance to the Crown. This "right of expatriation," as Jefferson later called it, implied that one could leave one's country at will and also leave behind one's status as a subject to the Crown. One's allegiance to and expectation of protection by the Crown did not follow a person who left his or her country of origin.[46] In Jefferson's view, the settlers came to this country with neither a "chief officer" nor an inherited monarchy. They could have elected a different ruler. But they freely chose to adopt the British king as their executive leader once they set up their own political states here.

What is emerging in embryonic form in Jefferson is the notion that the executive officer should be the representative of the people and chosen by them, a view that would become more important as the colonies moved towards independence. A year and a half after Jefferson wrote *A Summary View*, Thomas Paine unleashed a biting critique of monarchy, arguing it was an institution incompatible with natural rights. But that emerging perspective differed from the more traditional view. Natural rights theory, at least as formulated by Locke, had never taken that position. On the contrary, Locke, Montesquieu, and many Americans following the same line of thinking, such as James Otis and others, had assumed that natural rights were compatible with three different forms of government: democracy, aristocracy, and monarchy. As long as the people chose the particular form of government under which they lived, the minimum standard of government by consent had been met. As long as monarchy was not absolute and did not overstep its bounds of power, it was compatible with natural rights and consent. Indeed, Montesquieu, who had tremendous prestige in the colonies, thought the "blended" form of British government, which combined democracy, aristocracy, and monarchy, was the most perfect form of government for achieving and protecting liberty.[47] In the classical understanding of the monarchy, there was a reciprocal relationship between the Crown and the people and each had its own domain of influence. The Crown was viewed as an executive body that played the key roles of protecting the state and the people and balancing the diverse interests of society.[48]

Jefferson initially accepted this view himself. But Jefferson assumed that because the emigrants from Great Britain had a right to quit that society, they no longer were subjects of the British Crown. Once in America, they freely chose to adopt the king as their executive officer. And once adopted, the king had all the executive rights of Crown, such as the "exercise of his negative power" (i.e., veto power), a responsibility Jefferson initially argued that the king had underutilized in controlling the bad behavior of Parliament.[49] In Jefferson's early view, the king's executive role was to mediate between the various states of the British empire for the good of the whole. And the king had been failing to do that, by letting Parliament take powers over the colonies that it did not rightfully have.

It is important to remember that many revolutionary writers thought a pure democracy was potentially dangerous since it lacked the kinds of checks and balances of the English constitution.[50] Jefferson reflected this view when he described the king as "no more than the chief officer of the people, appointed by the laws, and circumscribed with definite powers, to assist in working the great machine of government, erected for their use and consequently subject to their superintendance."[51] Jefferson also understood the king's role "as yet the only mediatory power between the several states of the British empire."[52] This is what it meant to be subjects of the Crown. In return for their allegiance, the monarch was obligated to protect the people and operate the government within the limits set by the people. While natural rights theory had insisted that the Crown's power over the people was balanced by representative bodies, such as the Upper and Lower houses of Parliament, natural rights theory did not initially require an elected *executive* branch.

When Jefferson argued that the settlers had created new political states with the king as their chief executive officer, he made allusion to the possibility that power could revert to the people. What Jefferson's early position in *A Summary View* never makes explicit is, how does one end the relationship with an "adopted" monarch? Can one "unadopt" him, and if so, how? English history had already established a precedent for removing a king from the throne in 1649 with the beheading of

King Charles I and in 1688 with the "abdication" of James II. However, those instances were examples in which an inherited monarch had been deposed. Was the standard the same for removing a "chief officer" one had voluntarily adopted?

Leaving Jefferson's position for now and turning back to the view of the First Congress, a different view of allegiance is evident, more in line with the thinking of Wilson and John Adams, among others. While for Jefferson allegiance to the Crown could be severed by the right to quit society, on the view of Congress the immigrants came to this country with their British rights intact and as subjects to the Crown. Here are two of the first three resolutions adopted by the First Continental Congress in the 1774 Declaration of Rights.

> Resolved, N. C. D. 2. That our ancestors, who first settled these colonies, were at the time of their emigration from the mother country, entitled to all the rights, liberties, and immunities of free and natural-born subjects, within the realm of England.

> Resolved, N. C. D. 3. That by such emigration they by no means forfeited, surrendered, or lost any of those rights, but that they were, and their descendants now are, entitled to the exercise and enjoyment of all such of them, as their local and other circumstances enable them to exercise and enjoy.

In the official view of Congress, the settlers were British Americans initially and came to the American continent subject both to Parliament's authority and as subjects of the Crown. As discussed previously, Congress argued that Parliament could not retain its authority over the settlers, because of the geographical distance that made true representation impossible. Yet the relationship of the settlers to the Crown was of a different nature. That relationship remained intact across geographical distance unless the Crown overstepped its powers or abandoned its protection. James Wilson states this explicitly in his essay, arguing that in the case of Ireland and in the case of the Americas, "[a]llegiance to the king and obedience to the parliament are founded on very different principles. The former is founded on protection; the latter, on representation."[53] Wilson is here reflecting a view at the time that the right of representation was limited to the domain of legislation, and not that of the elected head of state or monarchy.

In the view of Congress, James Duane, James Wilson, John Adams, and a number of others, the settlers of America brought their allegiance to and status as subjects of the Crown with them to America. They were British subjects in British America. That relationship would remain intact across geographical distance, even if legislative representation could not. While for Jefferson that relationship to the "chief officer" was initially a matter of choice, in the view of Congress, the relationship to the Crown already existed at the founding of the American settlements and was obligatory, unless conditions arose for deposing the Crown. One of the conditions for ending that relationship of allegiance was the king reneging on his obligations of protection. The Congress initially did not think the king had reneged on those obligations, and thus natural rights arguments tended to be used more to justify the independence of the colonial legislatures rather than to justify the end of allegiance to the Crown, which was understood as the executive branch.

Rights, Territories, and Land Possession

There was another thorny theoretical problem of rights lurking underneath the surface that differentiated Jefferson's views from some of his colleagues: what right did settlers have to lands in America? The whole issue of how lands were legitimately acquired by states in general and by the settlers of America was a Pandora's box that no one really wanted to examine in too much detail, for good reason. Inside were a number of competing views about how land rights within political entities originated and came about in the first place. The very question was ultimately tied into a much larger question about property rights in general. Indeed, as we shall see, some individuals had argued that natural rights theory was wrong precisely because governments so often were created through conquest, rather than social compact.[54] Locke himself had pondered the question of political territories in quite some detail in his *Second Treatise*, for the question of how social groups acquire land is related to the issue of how individual's consent to live in political groups and how individuals acquire property. For those who thought deeply about the issue of colonial rights, the question of how lands in America were acquired was potentially an embarrassing difficulty and a matter on which not everyone agreed. And it was certainly an issue relevant to the claim of the Declaration—that the political entities on the American lands deserved to be recognized as free and independent states. But what gave the settlers rights to the land in the first place?[55]

Jefferson described the settlement of America as a conquest by the settlers, achieved through their own efforts and blood. That conquest in Jefferson's view gave the settlers the right to the lands that they occupied and thus grounded their right to create political territories on those lands. Their right to found new states thus rested not just on the right to leave their country of origin but on their legitimate claim to the land which they had conquered through their own efforts, without the help of the Crown. Here is Jefferson:

> America was conquered, and her settlements made, and firmly established, at the expence of individuals, and not of the British public. Their own blood was spilt in acquiring lands for their settlement, their own fortunes expended in making that settlement effectual; for themselves they fought, for themselves they conquered, and for themselves alone they have right to hold.[56]

In part, Jefferson is trying to justify his argument that the settlers were not British Americans when they came to America. "For themselves they fought, for themselves they conquered." But at the same time the argument provides the justification for the settlers' claim to land. "From the nature and purpose of civil institutions, all the lands within the limits which any particular society has circumscribed around itself are assumed by that society, and subject to their allotment only."

Jefferson links his view back to the Anglo-Saxon notions of property to argue that the lands in America did not belong to the Crown.

> Feudal holdings were therefore but exceptions out of the Saxon laws of possession, under which all lands were held in absolute right. These, therefore, still form the basis, or ground-work, of the common law, to prevail wheresoever the exceptions have not taken place. America was not conquered by William the Norman, nor its lands surrendered to him, or any of his successors. Possessions there are undoubtedly of the allodial nature. Our ancestors, however, who migrated hither, were farmers, not lawyers. The fictitious principle that all lands belong originally to the king, they were early persuaded to believe real?[57]

Jefferson is arguing here that possession of the land belongs in the hands of the settlers and not the Crown, and that this theory of property extends back to the Anglo-Saxon law which formed the basis of common law tradition. The early settlers, however, were duped into believing the principle that all lands belong originally to the king.

In *A Summary View*, Jefferson did not explicitly acknowledge the presence of natives in America, although at one point he describes the "settlements having been thus effected in the wilds of America" as if to imply that the lands were unoccupied and thus up for grabs, according to natural rights theory. But his claim that the settlers conquered the lands belies that perspective, indicating that he thought there was a right to conquest and a conquest had taken place. The justice of this conquest, and the relationship to rights argument, was a question that Jefferson passed over in deafening silence in *A Summary View*. Congress was also able to sidestep the question of whether lands in America were conquered. But others felt the need to address the question more directly.

James Wilson, whose view was identical to Congress in other respects, took up this question in his *Considerations on the Nature and Extent of the Legislative Authority of the British Parliament*, completed in 1770 but only published in 1774. Wilson considered the view of William Blackstone, the revered British legal scholar, jurist, and philosopher who had pondered the status of the colonies in his majestic *Commentaries on the Laws of*

England (1765-1769). Wilson quotes Blackstone's views on the status of the American "plantations":

> Besides these adjacent islands (Jersey, etc.), our more distant plantations in America and elsewhere are also, in some respects, subject to the English laws. Plantations, or colonies in distant countries, are either such where the lands are claimed in right of occupancy only, by finding them desart and uncultivated, and peopling them from the mother country; or where, when already cultivated, they have been either gained by conquest, or ceded to us by treaties...

> Our American plantations are principally of this latter sort; being obtained in the last century, either by right of conquest, and driving out the natives (with what natural justice I shall not at present inquire) or by treaties.1. Bl Com. 106. 107.

Blackstone's *Commentaries*, published between 1765 and 1769, had become a definitive statement on the rationale of the British Common Law tradition. Blackstone's view of property and of the colonies represents important statements with which colonial lawyers such as James Wilson had to contend. In this passage quoted by Wilson, Blackstone regarded the colonies in America as settlements created through conquest and treaty and thus not necessarily subject to the laws of England. In the extended passage of Blackstone, which Wilson doesn't quote, Blackstone writes:

> And both these rights [the right to claim lands by occupancy and by conquest] are founded upon the law of nature, or at least upon that of nations. But there is a difference between these two species of colonies, with respect to the laws by which they are bound. For it is held, that if an uninhabited country be discovered and planted by English subjects, all the English laws are immediately there in force. For as the law is the birthright of every subject, so wherever they go they carry their laws with them. But in conquered or ceded countries, that have already laws of their

own, the king may indeed alter and change those laws ; but, till he does actually change them, the antient laws of the country remain, unless such as are against the law of God, as in the case of an infidel country.[38]

For Blackstone, different laws apply depending on how the colony came to be acquired. If the lands were uninhabited, then the colonization by English subjects immediately resulted in the imposition of English laws. But in conquered or ceded countries—and the lands of America fell into that category, according to Blackstone—it was up to the king to decide what laws apply. In Blackstone's understanding, then, the American lands were not under Parliament's control but instead under the control of the Crown. The king could set the laws that he liked. It is interesting to note that Blackstone, in passing, raises but does not develop the question of "with what natural justice" the settlers drove out natives.

James Wilson challenged Blackstone's understanding of the facts but not his interpretation of law.[39] In disagreeing with Blackstone, Wilson subtly shifted the discussion away from the conquest of the natives to the question of whether the colonies had been conquered. And in doing so, Wilson articulates a view that differs quite sharply from Jefferson's.

> It will be sufficient for me to show, that it is unreasonable, and injurious to the colonies, to extend that title {i.e., conquest} to them. How came the colonists to be a conquered people? By whom was the conquest over them obtained? By the house of commons? By the constituents of that house? If the idea of conquest must be taken into consideration when we examine into the title by which America is held, that idea, so far as it can operate, will operate in favour of the colonists, and not against them. Permitted and commissioned by the crown, they undertook, at their own expense, expeditions to this distant country, took possession of it, planted it, and cultivated it. Secure under the protection of their king, they grew and multiplied, and diffused British freedom and British spirit, wherever they came. Happy in the enjoyment of liberty, and in reaping the fruits of their toils.

Wilson shifts the question from conquering the natives, as Blackstone framed it, to the question of whether Britain had conquered the colonists. Far from being conquered, he argues, the colonists had come under the auspices of the Crown and settled the lands peacefully. Next Wilson turns to the thorny question of how the settlers had come to have title to the land and whether that should be considered a conquest. If it is a conquest, he argues, it "will operate in favour of the colonists, and not against them," since they came at their own expense, took possession of the lands and cultivated them. The language of "possession" and "cultivation" suggests not an act of conquest, but a settlement of unoccupied lands and the rightful possession by settling and working the land. Wilson here seems to hold the view that the natives were living in a state of nature and that land in such an unoccupied state could be taken for use. This perspective seems to presuppose a view similar to that held by others, such as Vattel, who in 1759 wrote in the *Law of Nations*, for example, that:

> There is another celebrated question, to which the discovery of the new world has principally given rise. It is asked whether a nation may lawfully take possession of some part of a vast country, in which there are none but erratic nations, whose scanty population is incapable of occupying the whole? We have already observed (§ 81), in establishing the obligation to cultivate the earth, that those nations cannot exclusively appropriate to themselves more land than they have occasion for, or more than they are able to settle and cultivate. Their unsettled habitation in those immense regions cannot be accounted a true and legal possession; and the people of Europe, too closely pent up at home, finding land of which the savages stood in no particular need, and of which they made no actual and constant use, were lawfully entitled to take possession of it, and settle it with colonies. The earth, as we have already observed, belongs to mankind in general, and was designed to furnish them with substance: if each nation had from the beginning resolved to appropriate to itself a vast country, that

the people might live only by hunting, fishing, and wild fruits, our globe would not be sufficient to maintain a tenth part of its present inhabitants.[60]

Here Vattel is building on a Lockean style justification of property's origin to justify the European entitlement to American lands. Since God gave the earth to all humans equally, each has an equal right to take possession of parts that can be put to productive use, for his or her own purposes. One people is not allowed to take more than it needs. Since the natives were not making any true use of the land, they cannot be said to possess it, and therefore the peoples of Europe, who needed more land, were lawfully entitled to take possession of it.

Wilson seems to hold a similar view, though he does not make it explicit: the British settlers came to America with British rights, took possession of unoccupied land, and thereby were subject to all the English laws. He thus disagrees with Blackstone on the facts. American lands were not conquered but were uninhabited. But Wilson agrees with Blackstone on the law: as Blackstone put it, "that if an uninhabited country be discovered and planted by English subjects, all the English laws are immediately there in force. For as the law is the birthright of every subject, so wherever they go they carry their laws with them."[61] What constitutes "an uninhabited country," of course, is an interesting question in its own right, but the point here is that Blackstone had assumed that America was "inhabited" and that a conquest had occurred, while Wilson had assumed a rightful possession of unoccupied land, under the auspices of the Crown.

That the issue under debate about land, possession, and conquest touched on and intersected with the question of natural rights was acknowledged by Blackstone in that same passage that Wilson, interestingly enough, skipped. As Blackstone put it: "And both these rights [i.e., conquest or taking possession of deserted land] are founded upon the law of nature, or at least upon that of nations." The equivocation of whether the right of land possession and political territory is a question of natural rights or a law of nations is precisely the same equivocation that arises in the Declaration, as we shall see.

About the same time that Wilson was writing his essay, John Adams offered one of the more profound statements on the moral question at stake in his *Two Replies of the Massachusetts House of Representatives to Governor Hutchinson*, written in 1773.[62] Adams contested Hutchinson's claim that "at the Time that our Predecessors took Possession of this Plantation or Colony, under a Grant and Charter from the Crown of England, it was their Sense, and the Sense of the Kingdom, that they were to remain subject to the Supreme Authority of Parliament."[63] Discussing the original possession of land for the Massachusetts colony, Adams writes that

> We would take a View of the State of the English North American Continent at the Time when and after Possession was first taken of any Part of it, by the Europeans. It was then possessed by Heathen and Barbarous People, who had nevertheless all that Right to the Soil and Sovereignty in and over the Lands they possessed, which God had originally given to Man. Whether their being Heathen, inferred any Right or Authority to Christian Princes, a Right which had long been assumed by the Pope, to dispose of their Lands to others, we will leave to your Excellency or any one of Understanding and impartial Judgment to consider. It is certain they had in no other Sense forfeited them to any Power in Europe. Should the Doctrine be admitted that the Discovery of Lands owned and possessed by Pagan People, gives to any Christian Prince a Right and Title to the Dominion and Property, still it is vested in the Crown alone. It was an Acquisition of Foreign Territory, not annexed to the Realm of England, and therefore at the absolute Disposal of the Crown. For we take it to be a settled Point, that the King has a constitutional Prerogative to dispose of and alienate any Part of his Territories not annexed to the Realm.

Adams makes two points here that differentiate his view from others. In contrast to the view of Wilson (and someone like Vattel), Adams assumes that the "Heathen and Barbarous People" had "a Right to the Soil and Sovereignty in and over the Lands they possessed, which God had originally given to Man." In contrast to Wilson (but like Blackstone and Jefferson), Adams assumes that the lands had been rightfully possessed by the natives.

Did the Europeans have the right to conquer and take away those lands? With obvious sarcasm, Adams questions the doctrine that religious grounds give Christian princes the right to take away lands from pagan peoples. But even if you grant that dubious principle, Adams argues the land would nonetheless be annexed to the Crown and not to the Realm of England, reflecting the view that conquered lands belong to the king. On that view, the king has the right to dispose of land that he had conquered. By implication, Adams is arguing that the king could (and did) grant this land to the settlers, and the settlers would not be subject to Parliament's authority, though they would be subjects of the Crown.

Adams here arrives at a view of a commonwealth of nations like that of Jefferson and Wilson but along a different path than either of them. In his view, the king has acquired the land (whether ethically or not) and could grant those to the settlers without subjecting them to parliamentary authority. This view differed from Wilson who argued that the settlers had peaceably settled unoccupied land and taken possession of the land themselves as British Americans. Jefferson for his part argued that the settlers had conquered the lands but were not British people when they had done so and thus they were never under Parliament or the Crown's disposition. On the moral question involved, Adams acknowledges the problem but places the blame squarely on the shoulders of the Crown. Wilson sidesteps the problem arguing the lands were unoccupied. And Jefferson simply considers the settlement a conquest, without considering the moral question at all.

What we have here are fundamental disagreements about a core and critical issue that ties directly to natural rights theory and the law of nations, and thus ultimately to the question of whether the American settlements were by right free and independent states. Some of these disagreements were partially settled in the First Congress's Declaration of Rights when it sided with the position like that of James Wilson. The Congress held that the settlers settled the lands under the auspices of the

British Empire. The Congress rejected the view held by Jefferson. But the question of conquest and rightful occupation of land was an issue on which there was deep underlying disagreement and on which there had been no real resolution.

In the final analysis, of course, the positions of Jefferson, Congress, Wilson, and Adams ended up in very similar conclusions. From the perspective of the end game, all had argued that the colonies were independent states in the sense that they were not subject to Parliament's authority at all and should be governed only by their own legislatures. In each of these views, moreover, the settlers had an allegiance to the king, who was expected to provide protection and who had executive duties. The similarities in "end state" of the various positions have led many interpreters to conflate these very different positions and assume the Declaration therefore was an expression of a monolithic American Mind and thus expressing ideas that had been hackneyed in Congress for over a year. But the underlying assumptions about rights in general, about how they relate to American rights, and the development of statehood and territory, are quite different.

General Ambivalence about Natural Rights

Jefferson was not the only colonial writer who had doubts about the more classic natural rights position, at least in the version adopted by the First Continental Congress. During the First Congress in 1774, only a year and a half before the Declaration of Independence, there was still substantial debate on whether natural rights provided a solid or feeble foundation for American rights. Reading retrospectively backward from the Declaration of Independence, these doubts about natural rights are often forgotten and portrayed as the opinion of "conservatives" or moderates resisting the momentum towards independence. The story that is often told is that the movement towards independence was tied into an inexorable shift towards natural rights arguments.[64]

But the various positions on natural rights were much more complicated than that story suggests. Not all thinkers who turned to natural rights language agreed on basic assumptions and principles of what natural rights meant. Furthermore, many felt that natural rights simply complemented the argument from British rights (the position of the Congress and James Wilson), but that natural rights arguments could not stand as well on their own. In addition, the embrace or rejection of natural rights did not neatly align with a moderate or radical position. For example, some moderates, such as John Jay, endorsed natural rights arguments quite forcefully, though ultimately siding with those like Joseph Galloway, who wanted to try to preserve the union with Great Britain.

As late as 1774, several delegates were still expressing serious reservations that natural rights arguments constituted a "feeble foundation" for American rights. This was by no means the first time that doubts had been raised about natural rights as a foundation for American rights. In the decade leading up to revolution, several leading colonial writers expressed various doubts about the social contract theory and theory of government's origin upon which classical natural rights theory seemed to rest.[65] Writers like Massachusetts lawyer James Otis, Rhode Island governor Stephen Hopkins, Maryland lawyer Daniel Dulany, and Massachusetts radical Samuel Adams had all expressed serious reservations about some of the central assumptions of the natural rights tradition. In particular, they had doubts the idea that government was itself founded in social compact. This, of course, was a central part of Locke's argument in explaining how individuals consent to give up some of their natural liberties so as reap the benefits of joining society. It was not that these colonial writers doubted the idea that government *should* be governed by the consent of the people or that representation was a critical requirement of a just government. No one doubted those propositions. But they knew that most historical governments were not actually founded in that way, nor were they convinced that the original human institution of government in general originated through a compact. They may even have found evidence of such a doubt in the story of how the British American settlers acquired their own lands, as discussed above. The historical fact that societies may not have been founded in social contract raised doubts for some that natural rights philosophy could justify the fact that political

1. The Declaration, Locke, and Conflicts about Natural Rights 49

society *should* be founded on consent. We shall see, for example, that David Hume, among others, blasted Locke on just this point, poking fun at what he perceived to be Locke's attempt to ground consent in a social contract. This was a critique, moreover, with which Jefferson and other colonial writers were familiar.

A careful reading of Locke's *Second Treatise* would actually have shown that Locke had in fact anticipated this criticism and had made clear that he was arguing, at least at times, that government *should* be founded in natural rights, not that it always was founded that way, although even Locke equivocated considerably on the issue.[66] But the American writers attributed to the natural rights tradition both convictions and assumed that one grounded the other. In their minds, the claim that government should be founded on consent was based on the claim that governments did actually arise that way. If, therefore, that latter assertion was false, then the conclusions of natural rights philosophy—that government should attend to the people's happiness and protect their rights—was theoretically shaky or needed some other foundation. At the very least, other grounds for these truths would have to be found outside of the natural rights tradition.

Noted colonial writers expressed precisely such doubts about the natural rights tradition. Looking back into history, it appeared that governments had often been founded on conquest and colonization and there were few examples of governments that were actually created by people coming together and creating a social compact. To be sure, there were examples of republics in antiquity, and these provided inspiration to the colonial writers. But there were many governments—indeed, possibly a preponderance of existing and historical ones—that had risen by means other than social compact and were ruled by tyrants. On what basis, then, could one argue that the ideal state of society was consent of the governed?

A second and related issue was the purported origin of government as a human institution in general. Natural rights theory seemed to imply that the very beginning of government as a human institution had arisen when some individuals left the state of nature and made a social compact. But that account raised various kinds of difficulties as well.

For more religiously oriented individuals, this account of government's origin seemed to downplay God's role in the creation of government, and appeared to ascribe an inappropriate preponderance of responsibility to the human role in the development of government. This bothered some more religiously and theologically minded writers who thought that the emphasis on the human role in government's origin flew in the face of standard covenantal assumptions. An alternative theory of government's origin attributed the creation of government much more explicitly to God. On that theory, at least the way some writers explained it, government was not a matter of social compact. There was no choice about it. It had been ordained as part of creation itself.[67]

By moving the origin of government back into creation, such thinkers risked undermining the very foundations of the natural rights arguments. After all, Locke understood the individual's decision to submit to government to involve a renunciation of some natural liberties. There was a trade-off, relinquishing some of the freedoms in the state of nature for the benefits of social life. Indeed, it was precisely the view of government as founded in creation that had justified royalist writers such as Robert Filmer in his *Patriarcha* and from whom Locke had differentiated his views. Other writers left the choice of government up to individuals but argued that the state outside of government was not "natural liberty," but a "state of sin." The choice between living under political arrangements and living outside of such arrangements was cast in religious-theological terms. Only by joining a state could one act in accordance with God's will.

2. Jefferson's Declarations of Independence

To understand Jefferson's frame of mind when he sat down to write the Declaration, it is helpful to briefly back up to the moment after the Second Continental Congress rejected his draft *Declaration of the Causes* and adopted Dickinson's reworked version. After writing this draft, Jefferson remained at the Second Continental Congress in Philadelphia, working on committees until December 1775, when he returned home. He did not arrive back to the Congress until May 14, 1776. In the intervening months, Thomas Paine has published his *Common Sense* (January 1776), John Adams had published his *Thoughts on Government* (spring 1776), and several colonies had become ready to declare independence.

We know that in the intervening period since he had left the Continental Congress in December 1775, Jefferson had not yet given up his pet theory about the early settlers' rights. In the period back at home, he was again trying once more to support his theory that the ancestors were entitled to found new states. In an essay that was never published, entitled *Refutation of the Argument that the Colonies Were Established at the Expense of the British Nation*, Jefferson this time turns to a detailed historical argument to prove that the colony of Virginia had no obligation to Parliament.[1] He surveys the various charters that the Crown had made with Sir Walter Raleigh and his predecessors, showing how the lands were granted by the Crown to these early settlers. After surveying the role of Sir Walter Raleigh in founding of Virginia, Jefferson concludes:

This short narration of facts, extracted principally from Hakluyt's voyages, may enable us to judge of the effect which the charter to Sr. Walter Ralegh may have on our own constitution and also on those of other colonies within it's limits, to which it is of equal concernment. It serves also to expose the distress of those ministerial writers, who, in order to prove that the British parliament may of right legislate for the colonies, are driven to the necessity of advancing this palpable untruth that 'the colonies were planted and nursed at the expence of the British nation': an untruth which even majesty itself, descending from it's dignity, has lately been induced to utter from the throne. Kings are much to be pitied, who, misled by weak ministers, and deceived by wicked favourites, run into political errors, which involve their families in ruin: and it might prove some solace to his present majesty, when, fallen from the head of the greatest empire the world has seen, he shall again exhibit in the political system of Europe the original character of a petty king of Britain, could he impute his fall to error alone.[2]

It appears Jefferson was prompted to write this historical essay in response to the start of Parliament in October 1775, when, in a speech, the king declared that the colonies were in a state of rebellion and that too much was at stake "to give up so many colonies which she has planted with great industry, nursed with great tenderness, encouraged with many commercial advantage, and protected and defended at much expence and treasure."[3] Jefferson apparently read the king's speech on January 19, 1776, and likely wrote his response at some point after that time.[4] In this essay, we find Jefferson providing a historical justification for the argument he had earlier made in *A Summary View* and his draft of the *Declaration of the Causes*. It is a "palpable untruth" that the British nation planted and nurtured the colonies. Therefore there are no grounds for arguing that either Parliament or the Crown had authority over the colonies.

What is new here is Jefferson's criticism of the king for being misled and deceived by "wicked favourite" ministers who deceived him into adopting an erroneous political view. Jefferson argues that the consequences will be devastating for the king. His mistaken judgment will cost the British leader his empire, and he will end up being nothing more than a mere petty king of England. Jefferson is clearly implying and threatening that the American states (and perhaps other British dominions) will no longer recognize the king as their sovereign; the result will be that he will rule over England only and no longer be the recognized king of a larger British empire that included the American colonies. The empire in other words will be reduced to just a single state.

By implication, Jefferson is suggesting that the colonies will no longer have any ties left to Great Britain, a clear vision of independence for the American colonies. In *A Summary View*, Jefferson had already argued that the colonies were independent states that had essentially chosen or selected the king as their elected leader. Now he is anticipating that the colonies would repudiate their elected official. The league of nations would be dissolved. Jefferson still does not say here how he envisions putting an end to the relationship with an elected king. But by the time he sat down to write the Declaration of Independence, he had given the question some thought and come up with an answer. The answer is contained in a draft constitution Jefferson wrote for the state of Virginia shortly before he had actually drafted the Declaration of Independence. This document, which was reworked and incorporated into the Declaration of Independence, arguably constitutes Jefferson's original Declaration of Independence and more authentically reflects Jefferson's own views than the Declaration he drafted for Congress, as we shall now see.

Jefferson's Original Declaration of Independence

In June 1776, only weeks before he wrote the Declaration of Independence, Jefferson had written several drafts of a constitution for the state of Virginia. Jefferson's home "state" was in the process of responding to the Congress's call on the colonies to produce their own constitutions. On May 10, four days before Jefferson arrived back in Philadelphia, Congress had approved a resolution recommending that the colonies assume all powers of government.

Resolved, That it be recommended to the respective assemblies and conventions of the United Colonies, where no government sufficient to the exigencies of their affairs have been hitherto established, to adopt such government as shall, in the opinion of the representatives of the people, best conduce to the happiness and safety of their constituents in particular, and America in general.[5]

The resolve essentially recognized the end of all local British authority and that local colonial assemblies now had the authority to establish governments that would "best conduce to the happiness and safety of their constituents."[6] On May 15, Congress, in a divided vote, approved a preamble written by John Adams as an introduction to the May 10 resolution. The preamble was more radical than the resolution, making it explicit that "his Britannic Majesty, in conjunction with the lords and commons of Great Britain, has, by a late act of Parliament, excluded the inhabitants of these United Colonies from the protection of his crown" and that, therefore:

[I]t is necessary that the exercise of every kind of authority under the said crown should be totally suppressed, and all the powers of government exerted, under the authority of the people of the colonies, for the preservation of internal peace, virtue, and good order, as well as for the defence of their lives, liberties, and properties, against the hostile invasions and cruel depredations of their enemies; therefore, resolved, &c.

In essence, Adams's preamble is announcing the end of the colonies' allegiance to the Crown, which according to Congress was the only remaining tie left to Great Britain. Adams recognized Congress's approval of his preamble as an endorsement of independence.[7] That same day, May 15, Virginia adopted its resolution calling on Congress to declare the colonies free and independent states.

Jefferson arrived back in Congress on May 15, one day before both the Virginia resolution and approval of John Adams's preamble. It must have been before or shortly after that date that Jefferson began writing his drafts of the Virginia Constitution, for several drafts were written by June 13, when he sent a copy with George Wythe, who was going back to Virginia.[8] Based on letters Jefferson wrote at the time, it is clear that he actually thought the activity of drafting a Virginia Constitution more important than the activity taking place in Philadelphia at Congress, and he expressed the wish to be recalled. But since he had only recently arrived at Congress, his home colony did not recall him. The result was that Jefferson's drafts of the Virginia Constitution arrived back in Virginia after the shape of the Constitution had been decided, but the committee did alter some of the laws in light of Jefferson's own draft.[9] Jefferson's preamble listing all the various infractions of King George III was incorporated into the Virginia Constitution.

With some revisions, Jefferson's draft of the Virginia Constitution became the basis for the list of charges against King George that appears in Jefferson's first draft of the Declaration of Independence as well.[10] Jefferson took one of his earlier Virginia drafts and made some improvements in style, thus reworking it into one part of the Declaration of Independence. Thus the draft of the Virginia Constitution is an early draft of one part of the Declaration of Independence. But it is more than just that. It arguably actually is Jefferson's original Declaration of Independence. By this I mean that this document, standing on its own, represents Jefferson's first and original Declaration of Independence. For Jefferson understood the Virginia draft Constitution as a document declaring independence for the state of Virginia.[11] He was writing this document, moreover, as an individual and not part of a committee, as he would when drafting the Declaration of Independence for Congress.

Jefferson's first draft of the Virginia Constitution thus provides a window into Jefferson's own political philosophy and conception of independence on the eve of writing the Declaration of Independence. It is illuminating to see which assumptions from the Virginia Declaration made it into the Declaration of Independence and which assumptions did not. While the Virginia Declaration is consistent with Jefferson's own theory of rights, this is not the case with the Declaration of Independence, at least after the revisions by the Committee of Five and Congress as whole. Understanding that Jefferson had to promote a position on rights that he did not fully approve provides a new context by which to understand some of the wording he chose and some of the interesting changes he arguably made to the classic formulation of natural rights language.[12]

No Natural Rights in Jefferson's Original Declaration of Independence

One of the most obvious and important differences between the draft constitution for Virginia and the Declaration Jefferson would shortly write for Congress is the noticeable absence of any natural rights preamble or language. The significance of this difference seems to have been missed by most commentators who have focused instead on how charges against the king were revised and reused in the congressional Declaration of Independence.[13] But the absence of any natural rights statement in Jefferson's first draft of the Virginia Constitution is illuminating. Perhaps Jefferson may have known that George Mason was already at work on such a statement of rights, and perhaps Jefferson had seen it.[14] But there may be another reason Jefferson did not preface his constitution with a statement of rights. In Jefferson's political philosophy, no statement of rights was really needed, since the colonies never were under the sovereignty of Parliament from the very beginning. There was, therefore, no reason for Jefferson to invoke natural rights to justify the colonies' legislative independence. In Jefferson's philosophy, Virginia was legislatively free already because of the original immigration and "right to quit society." Jefferson's view contrasted with most of his colleagues, who understood the new Virginian Constitution to represent a rejection of Parliament's legislative authority. For Jefferson there was no reason to appeal to rights to justify legislative independence. The only tie remaining was between the colonies and the Crown whom the colonies had voluntarily adopted as their "chief officer." The problem of independence as Jefferson framed it was how to remove an elected executive, not a usurping legislature. In looking for a model for that process, Jefferson arguably turned to the English Bill of Rights of 1689, which formally ended the reign of James II.

And that Bill of Rights may have depended on the tradition of ancient Anglo-Saxon principles more than on any philosophy of natural rights.[15]

The focus of Jefferson's Virginia Declaration, therefore, is almost exclusively on the king's misdeeds, consistent with Jefferson's view that the relationship with the Crown was the only remaining connection to the British Empire. Jefferson charges that the king, who was "entrusted with the exercise of the kingly office in this government, hath endeavored to pervert the same into a detestable and insupportable tyranny...." As evidence of this intention, Jefferson cites sixteen violations of his office, such as: vetoing laws of the legislature that were for the common good, stalling the wheels of government, dissolving legislative assemblies, making naturalization of foreigners difficult, keeping standing armies in a time of war, cutting off American trade to the rest of the world, imposing taxes without consent, depriving the right to trial by jury, abandoning the helm of government, and declaring "us" out of his allegiance and protection. Jefferson then provides the theoretical framework for deposing the elected king :

> [B]y which several acts of misrule the sd. George Guelf has forfeited the kingly office, and has rendered it necessary for the preservation of the people that he should be immediately deposed from the same, and divested of all its privileges, powers, & prerogatives
>
> And forasmuch as the public liberty may be more certainly secured by abolishing an office which all experience hath shewn to be inveterately inimical thereto and it will thereupon become further necessary to re-establish such ancient principles as are friendly to the rights of the people and to declare certain others which may co-operate with and fortify the same in future....

And then in the second draft of the Virginia Constitution, Jefferson begins with this shortened introduction, which then appears with a slight revision in the third draft as well.

Be it therefore enacted by the authority of the people that the said, George the third, King of Great Britain...and elector of Hanover be & he is hereby ... deposed from the kingly office... within ys. government. & absolutely divested of all it's rights & powers, & that he and his descendants and all persons claimg. by or through him & all other persons whatsoever shall be & for ever remain incapable of the same; & that the sd. office shall henceforth cease & be never more erected within this colony.[16]

Jefferson here fills out the theoretical position left unclear earlier in his *A Summary View*, explaining how an elected king can forfeit his office by turning it into a tyranny and abusing the prerogatives the people had given him. When this happens, he forfeits his office and the people therefore should depose him. But Jefferson goes further and argues that the very institution of monarchy should cease within the colony. Thomas Paine had already made an eloquent argument to the same effect in his *Common Sense*, and here Jefferson follows in the same path and recognizes monarchy is "inimical to" the public liberty.

It is possible to interpret Jefferson's argument about the king as a natural rights argument. We shall consider this issue in more detail below in our discussion of his *A Summary View*. But consistent with his view in *A Summary View*, Jefferson here appeals not to natural rights in general, but to "ancient principles." Jefferson thus appeals once again to the common law tradition reaching back to the Anglo-Saxons. The settlers came to and conquered new lands, set up new political entities, and chose to adopt the British Constitution and the ancient principles of rights inherited from the Anglo-Saxons. They are preserving the tradition of liberty that reached back to the Saxon ancestors. In Jefferson's Virginia Declaration of Independence there is no preamble appealing to natural rights in general, for in Jefferson's conception of independence, the American states had already established legislative independence from Parliament through the right to quit society. Now, like Parliament before them, they were simply removing the king whom they had originally elected and who had abused his trust. Only in this case, the intent is never to accept a future monarch as an officer over the state of Virginia.

Drafting the Declaration of Independence

Having now looked at Jefferson's Virginia Declaration of Independence, we can turn back to the congressional Declaration of Independence and drafting of that document. The story of the official Declaration of Independence has been told by many other writers in some detail and does not need to be rehearsed in detail here. Briefly, on June 7, 1776, Richard Henry Lee of Virginia introduced a resolution in the Continental Congress proposing a Declaration of independence.

> *Resolved*, That these United Colonies are, and of right ought to be, free and independent States, that they are absolved from all allegiance to the British Crown, and that all political connection between them and the State of Great Britain is, and ought to be, totally dissolved.
>
> That it is expedient forthwith to take the most effectual measures for forming foreign Alliances. That a plan of confederation be prepared and transmitted to the respective Colonies for their consideration and approbation.[17]

On June 10, 1776, Congress decided to delay the vote on independence until July 1, with the hope of achieving a greater consensus from the colonies. On June 11, 1776, Congress appointed a committee "in the meantime" to draft a declaration so "that no time be lost, in case the Congress agree thereto" on the next vote. The committee of five was comprised of Thomas Jefferson, John Adams, Benjamin Franklin, Roger Sherman, and Robert Livingston; Jefferson was selected, for various reasons, to write the first draft.[18] By June 28, the first draft from the Committee of Five was ready and ordered to lie on table for review. This draft already contained some revisions made by Jefferson himself and some recommended by Adams and Franklin.

Based on the preceding discussion, we are now in a position to see that the official, published Declaration of Independence did not represent the way that Jefferson himself thought about independence. Had he had his druthers, he might never have put in the classic statements about natural rights for which the Declaration and Jefferson are so famous. On three other occasions he had passed over the opportunity to insert explicit statements of natural rights in his writing, first in his *A Summary View*, again in his *Declaration* of the *Causes*, and then again in his original Virginia Declaration of Independence. It is reasonable to conclude that Jefferson himself would have happily published a Declaration of Independence with no such statement of rights (as in fact he did in his Virginia Declaration). On his view, a statement of natural rights simply was not needed, and he may have had doubts about natural rights theory anyway, as discussed earlier. What was needed was simply a way to depose the king, the elected official.

But Jefferson had on each of these earlier occasions seen his peers reject his view of rights. The First Congress rejected his view of rights in its Declaration of Rights, which it published in early 1774. Then, about a year before he wrote the Declaration of Independence, Jefferson watched his own draft of the *Declaration of the Causes* be rewritten by John Dickinson. In that rewrite, Dickinson inserted a statement of natural rights before Jefferson's own statement of the ancestor's rights essentially obliterating and reinterpreting Jefferson's own theory.

It is not surprising, then, that Jefferson would try a different tact on his third attempt to draft a document that would be acceptable to his colleagues in the Congress. This time he had learned his lesson. And indeed there was no time to waste since this declaration had to be drafted and approved in haste. Indeed, there is some likelihood that the Committee of Five itself gave Jefferson some instructions about what to say and would likely have instructed him to include a statement of rights, given that two of the members were John Adams and Benjamin Franklin.[19] But even had they not done so, Jefferson by this time knew that his own theory would not pass muster. Jefferson may already have seen the Virginia Bill of Rights by George Mason on June 6 in a Pennsylvania newspaper.[20]

Some have argued that in fact George Mason's language influenced Jefferson, as perhaps it did. But the important point about that influence is often missed. Jefferson would never have added such language to the Declaration of Independence on his own initiative. Wherever he got such language, whether he had Mason's or Wilson's language in mind, or whether he drafted the language from his own muse or remembered language from Locke, he would only have put such language in the Declaration because he was adopting a model of declaration with which he did not fully agree. On this interpretation, what we have is a young man charged with writing a Declaration that did not represent his own political views.

If this line of interpretation is correct, might we not find some linguistic evidence of Jefferson's continued ambivalence towards the classical theory of rights now embodied in the Declaration? Indeed, Jefferson did in fact try "to smuggle" his own theory into his draft of the Declaration.[21] But the very core of Jefferson's theory was deleted by Congress in its review of the document. Here is Jefferson's original passage with the words deleted by Congress marked by square brackets and underscored while the words Congress added are marked in bold.

> Nor we have been wanting in attentions to our British brethren. we have warned them for time to time of attempts by their legislature to extend a jurisdiction over [these our states] **us**. we have reminded them of the circumstances of our emigration & settlement here. [, no one of which could warrant so strange a pretention: that these were effected at the expence of our own blood and treasure, unassisted by the wealth or the strength of Great Britain: that in constituting indeed our several forms of government, we had adopted one common king, thereby laying a foundation for perpetual league & amity with them: but that submission to their parliament was no part of our constitution, nor ever in idea, if history may be credited: and] we **have** appealed to their native justice & magnanimity, [as well as to] **and we have conjured them by** the ties of our common kindred to

disavow these usurpations which were likely to interrupt our correspondence and connection. They too have been deaf to [our] **the voice of justice & of consanguinity,** [& when occasions have been given them, by the regular course of their laws, of removing from their councils the disturbers of our harmony, they have by their free election re-established them in power, at this very time too they are permitting their chief magistrate to send over not only soldiers of our common blood. These facts have given the last stab to agonizing affection, and manly spirit bids us to renounce for ever these unfeeling brethren.] We must [endeavor to forget our former love for them, and to], **therefore, acquiesce in the necessity, which denounces our Separation, and** hold them as we hold the rest of mankind, enemies in war, in peace friends.[22]

Even in this paragraph, buried well towards the end of the Declaration, Jefferson was unable to get his theory by Congress on this his third attempt. Congress deleted the very sections dealing with the settlers constituting several forms of government and adopting one king. One can now understand part of the reason why Jefferson found the editing process by Congress so painful and regarded the changes as "mutilations," as he reported.[23] Indeed, this likely explains why Jefferson forwarded copies of the original with the changes underscored, but not struck out, to colleagues shortly after the adoption. Jefferson in fact wrote that "the sentiments of men are known not only by what they receive, but what they reject also."[24] The changes in the Declaration were, from one perspective, not really that extensive, at least for anyone who has gone through a strong editing process before. And many commentators praise the changes of Congress as improving the document.[25] But from the point of view of Jefferson's own commitments, they were "mutilations" and, once again, obliterated his own understanding of rights. With the removal of this paragraph, Jefferson's pet theory of rights was nearly obliterated from the Declaration.

Commentators such as Becker and Boyd both miss the significance of this deletion. Becker writes, "In cutting out the greater part of the next to last paragraph, Congress omitted, among other things, the sentence in which Jefferson formulated, not directly indeed but by allusion, that theory of the constitutional relation of the colonies to Great Britain which is elsewhere taken for granted."[26] Becker assumes that after this deletion occurred, Jefferson's constitutional theory remained intact and "is elsewhere taken for granted." We shall see that this is not so. Boyd, for his part, passes over this deletion in silence and simply summarizes at the end that "[t]he Declaration implied all the way through, the colonies acknowledged a constitutional tie only with the King and that was the only tie that needed to be severed in so solemn a proclamation."[27]

But by omitting this passage of Jefferson's, Congress threw open the whole question of what theory of rights the Declaration was in fact endorsing. By which of the various theories that we have examined was the Declaration justifying independence from Parliament? We simply do not know, because the Declaration leaves the answer ambiguous. This is why Becker can still think the Declaration reflects Jefferson's theory of rights and contradicts the views of the First Continental Congress.[28] By contrast, Adams thought the Declaration was expressing "but what had been hackneyed in Congress for two years before" implying that the view of the Declaration and the First Continental Congress's view were aligned. What we see evident in these commentators is precisely the ambiguity which was left in the Declaration. For those who held views like Congress, and James Wilson, the Declaration seemed to speak for them, at least in its final form. While much of Jefferson's own theory was obliterated in the editing, the Declaration at least does not explicitly contradict Jefferson's view either. In this way, the Declaration could speak for and to individuals who held very different views of rights. It explains only why the colonies are rejecting the king as their executive officer, but it offers no explicit theory of why Parliament did not hold legislative sovereignty.

A similar set of deletions occurred towards the very conclusion of the Declaration. Again Jefferson's original language which was deleted appears between brackets and underscored; the additions by Congress are marked in bold.

We therefore the representatives of the United states of America in General Congress assembled **appealing to the supreme judge of the world for the rectitude of our intentions** do, in the name & by authority of the good people of these **colonies** [states,] **solemnly** publish and declare **that these united colonies are and of right ought to be free and independent states; that they are absolved from all allegiance to the British Crown, and that** [reject and renounce all allegiance & subjection to the kings of Great Britain & all others who may hereafter claim by, through, or under them; we utterly dissolve] all political connection [which may have heretofore have subsisted] between them [us] & the **state** [people or parliament] of Great Britain **is & ought to be totally dissolved**; [and finally we do assert and declare these colonies to be free and independent states], & that as free & independent states they have full power to levy war, conclude peace, contract alliances, establish commerce, & to do all other acts and things which independent states may of right do. And for the support of this declaration **with a firm reliance on the protection of divine providence**, we mutually pledge to each other our lives, our fortunes, & our sacred honour.[29]

Congress's editorial changes revise Jefferson's language in a couple of significant ways. First, Congress adds in an additional religious reference to God, one that could speak more directly to those who might have liked a more personal notion of God invoked. Similar religious language was added by John Dickinson, for example, at the beginning of the *Declaration of Causes* at the start of the Second Continental Congress.

Second, Congress revises Jefferson's language to be consistent with the earlier Lee resolution: "that these united colonies are and of right ought to be free and independent states; that they are absolved from all allegiance to the British Crown." This language of the original resolution softens Jefferson's strong language towards the monarchy: Instead of "rejecting and renouncing all allegiance" the people "are absolved" from an allegiance for which they were previously obligated. "Absolved" implies that a responsibility that was previously obligatory is subsequently lifted, and the language may have religious overtones as well.

Congress also rewrote Jefferson's language on the connection to the people and Parliament. Jefferson had written "we utterly dissolve and break off all political connection which may have heretofore subsisted between us & the people or parliament of Great Britain." The language "which may have heretofore subsisted" was definitely an equivocation on whether any relationship had ever existed between the settlers and Parliament and the people of Great Britain, a view consistent with Jefferson's own position that the ties had only been established voluntarily by the settlers after they had freely established their own states. Had there been any previous relationship with Parliament, we utterly dissolve it. But in the language of Congress's resolution, the language shifts meaning. Now "in the name & by authority of the good people of these colonies...all political connection between them & the state of Great Britain is & ought to be totally dissolved." Perhaps Congress was being sensitive to the feelings of people of Great Britain, as Jefferson noted in his own account.[30] But there is another significant shift in meaning too: Congress's language "is and ought to be" indicates that going forward the relationship should be dissolved, as opposed to Jefferson's wording ("which may have heretoforward"), language which is more equivocal and reflected doubts that any relationship ever existed at all. Congress's language suggests a connection had been established but now needed to be dissolved. Jefferson's underscores the doubt that any relationship ever existed. Congress's language also substitutes the word "colonies" for "states," the first time the term appears in this paragraph. On Congress's rendition, these united colonies "are, and of right ought to be, free and independent states." The language of Congress and the Lee resolution permits the reading that in the past these political entities were colonies but now are and ought to be free states, a view that was consistent with Congress's view.[31] In Jefferson's language, the states (already in existence) repudiate the monarchy and any relationship which may have existed with the people or Parliament. If there is any remaining doubt about the relationship between the American states and Parliament, we "utterly dissolve" it.

Congress eliminates the reference to "the people or Parliament" and refers instead to the abstract relationship "with the State." Jefferson was trying to leave no doubt that the relationship with Parliament had ended. On Congress's rendition, it is not clear at all what theory of rights ended the control of Parliament.

In another section, Jefferson had written, "he [the king] has erected a multitude of new offices by a self-assumed power...." Congress cut out the phrase "by a self-assumed power."[32] For Jefferson, the king had overstepped the powers given him by the people. For Congress, the king's powers had been already in existence by virtue of the settlers having emigrated under sponsorship of the Crown. They were not "self-assumed" powers. They were legitimate powers. Becker tends to take many of these changes as "stylistic" and claims that the phraseology is "more incisive, and does it not thus add something to that very effect which Jefferson himself wished to produce?" Clearly Jefferson did not think so and viewed the various changes as mutilations to the very theory of rights that he had wanted to articulate. No wonder that Jefferson sent a copy of his original draft to Robert H. Lee showing what Congress had done to it. As he wrote to Lee on July 8, "I inclose you a copy of the Declaration of Independence as agreed to by the house, & also as originally framed. you will judge whether it is better or worse for the critics."[33]

When In The Course Of Human Events

Having suggested that Jefferson was still attempting to reiterate his own theory of rights in his early draft of the Declaration, we can turn back to the most famous passages of the Declaration and now detect some of the ambivalence that Jefferson may have had about the classical understanding of natural rights and its application to American right. Here is the opening paragraph as originally drafted by Jefferson and as revised by the Committee of Five.[34] The words with strikeouts show the deletions and the words in brackets the additions.

2. Jefferson's Declarations of Independence

Jefferson's Original Rough Draft	Rough Draft Presented to Congress as Representing the Committee of Five
When in the course of human events it becomes necessary for a people to advance from that subordination in which they have hitherto remained, & to assume among the powers of the earth the equal & independent station to which the laws of nature & of nature's god entitle them, a decent respect to the opinions of mankind requires that they should declare the causes which impel them to the change.	When in the course of human events it becomes necessary for a~~a~~ [one] people to ~~advance from that subordinateion in which they have hitherto remained, & to~~ [dissolve the political bands which have connected them with another,] and to assume among the powers of the earth the ~~equal & independent~~ [separate and equal] station to which the laws of nature & of nature's god entitle them, a decent respect to the opinions of mankind requires that they should declare the causes which impel them ~~to the change~~ the separation.

In the preamble to the original draft, Jefferson is explaining why the settlers are throwing off subordination and assuming the "equal and independent" status as a nation. They never were under the law of Parliament but had been subordinated without right, as he has argued in *A Summary View*. But in the revision which likely reflects the committee's view, "one people" are not just throwing off subordination but are "dissolving political bands" which had connected them with another.[35] This revision recognizes that the colonies and British people have had political connections and had been "one people." In the postcommittee revision, one people is splitting apart, whereas Jefferson's earlier version assumes the Americans already were "a people" that had been subordinate.

In his first draft, Jefferson describes the new status as "equal and independent," whereas after the committee's revision the status is viewed as "separate but equal." The word "separate" implies that the Americans and British citizens had previously been "one" people and subsequently been split apart. Jefferson's earlier version does not recognize that they were one people who had to separate. Arguably, these are more than just stylistic improvements as Becker suggests.[36] On the contrary, these are substantive changes that alter the theoretical understanding. In Jefferson's draft, they were "a" people asserting their independent status and throwing off subordination; in the postcommittee revision they are originally "one people" (British people) who had to split apart and become separate but equal.

A decent respect to the opinions of mankind, concluded Jefferson, required that Americans "declare the causes which impel them to the change." The committee's revision emphasizes the need to explain causes which impel them *"to the separation."* This revision, like the earlier one, emphasizes that the colonies had to split apart from the entity to which they had been attached; Jefferson's first draft implies they were separate from the start and were simply reasserting their already existing rights, which had been inappropriately taken away and forgotten.[37] Independence to Jefferson meant return to a rightful earlier state, whereas for the committee and ultimately those in Congress, it meant the culmination of an act of separation that had not been inevitable.

This line of interpretation also accounts for why Jefferson sometimes uses the word "states" in his grievances against the king, as in, for example, "he has endeavored to prevent the population [growth] of these states." Jefferson's language indicates they were already independent states, a sentence which was deleted by Congress in its revision.[38] Jefferson also writes that the king "has combined with others to subject us to a jurisdiction foreign to our constitutions" again assuming the existence of multiple state constitutions. This is consistent with Jefferson's view that the colonies had been founded as independent states under their own legislative jurisdictions. Congress changed the word "constitutions" in the plural to "constitution" in the singular. In making the word singular, Congress rejected the view that the various states already had their own constitutions. In the singular, the implication is that the king had subjected the settlements to a jurisdiction foreign to "our constitution," a reference to the British constitution, which they brought with them as British subjects in America.

This introductory passage of Jefferson's draft Declaration, of course, does clearly evoke natural rights language, much more so than either *A Summary View* or his *Declaration of the Causes*. Here Jefferson appeals to "the laws of nature & of nature's god." Although Jefferson was still trying to assert his own views, he was also writing for the committee and ultimately Congress, and thus felt compelled to put natural rights language more boldly in the declaration. The language of rights in Jefferson's first draft is very close to language of his *A Summary View*, but with a small but significant difference. There in *A Summary View*, Jefferson is detailing "many unwarrantable encroachments and usurpations, attempted to be made by the legislature of one part of the empire, upon those rights which God and the laws have given equally and independently to all." The language of "God and the laws" in that context becomes in his draft of the Declaration "the laws of nature & of nature's god."[39] In the Declaration, the word "nature" inserts itself into his earlier phraseology.[40] By the same token, the language of "equal and independent" seen in Jefferson's first draft of the Declaration is interestingly used in *A Summary View* to talk about the relationship of the Parliament to the states in America. When Jefferson writes about "those rights which God and the laws have given equally and independently to all," he may refer to the rights of individuals but could just as easily also refer to the relationship of the rights of all independent states vis-à-vis one another. In other words, there Jefferson may be referring to "natural rights" to justify the right of states rather than individuals, just as he may be doing here.

The appeal to "the laws of nature & of nature's god" in the original draft of the Declaration is clearly a reference to a natural rights conception of God, justifying the "equal and independent station" to which a people are entitled. But what theory is Jefferson appealing to here? The language can certainly fit with Jefferson's own view that the "right to quit society" provides the foundation for the "equal and independent station" of the states. Of course, John Adams reading the same language easily could project into the language the view of the First Continental Congress. Thus Jefferson is deftly using language that could support his own view, while Adams could easily see Jefferson as repeating ideas that had been "hackneyed" in Congress for two years already. Both would be correct, because the language can sustain both views. Indeed, that may be part of its genius. It is somewhat startling then to find an equivocation on the theory of rights in the Declaration, a document many think definitively puts natural rights at the heart of the revolution and the ultimate vision of America. The Declaration thus leaves equivocal precisely which theory of rights provides the basis for American independence. We cannot determine whether the Declaration supports the official view of the First Continental Congress or that of Jefferson. But that ambiguity at least served its purpose. The Congress could find its theories of rights reflected in the Declaration's language, as could Jefferson, though the latter obviously would have been happier had some of his other language not being obliterated.

The ambiguity discussed above is also consistent with the notable fact that Parliament is scarcely mentioned in the Declaration, as Carl Becker and others have noted.[41] This omission is striking given the ten years of debate in which colonial writers argued against subordination to Parliament. Instead, the focus is almost entirely on the grievous acts by the king. Why is Parliament not mentioned? Some interpreters like Becker argue that the Declaration already assumes that settlements were legislatively independent from Parliament but still under allegiance to the Crown.[42] And that is a reasonable conclusion. But what this argument misses is the fact that the Declaration never explains which theory of rights it is embracing to explain the legislative independence from Parliament. Is it assuming a view on the basis of Jefferson's position, Wilson's or John Adams's? Did the ancestors have a right to quit society and found new states or did they become independent states because they could not be represented in Parliament? Or did the Crown own the land and have the right to make charters with the colonies? How did the colonies or Crown acquire rightful ownership of the land? Was it through conquest by the settlers, by Great Britain, or through peaceful occupation of uninhabited lands? If the Declaration is justifying to the world the right of the colonies to be independent states, then surely a "decent respect to the opinion of mankind" would appreciate answers to those questions. Indeed, if Congress was attempting to explain itself to the nations of the world, it would have seemed reasonable to explain the justification of war and independence in terms of the *Law of Nations* tradition, the philosophical tradition that asked about the origin of nations' rights vis-à-vis one another. One of the questions in that tradition was how a people came by rightful occupation of its lands. The Declaration is noticeably silent on the question entirely. Jefferson's earlier draft of the Declaration did emphasize the right of the settlers to quit their land of origin, implying his earlier view that the settlers had rightfully conquered the lands. But after the revision by Congress, that theory of rights was suppressed, making the Declaration's ideas sound more "hackneyed," in line with the original Declaration of Rights of 1774.

Because other interpreters do not recognize or make anything of this ambiguity, they simply assume that the Declaration is reflecting "The American Mind" or reiterating a hackneyed view of Congress. Thus Becker writes that

> Accordingly, the idea around which Jefferson built the Declaration was that the colonists were not rebels against established political authority, but a free people maintaining long established and imprescriptible rights against a usurping king. The effect which he wished to produce was to leave a candid world wondering why the colonies had so long submitted to the oppressions of this king.
>
> The major premise from which this conclusion is derived is that every 'people' has a natural right to make and unmake its own government; the minor premise is that the Americans are a "people" in this sense. In establishing themselves in America, the people of the colonies exercised their natural rights to frame governments suited to their ideas and conditions; but at the same time they voluntarily retained a union with the people of Great Britain by professing allegiance to the same King. From this allegiance they

might at any time have withdrawn; ...The minor premise of the argument is easily overlooked because it is not explicitly stated in the Declaration—at least not in its final form. To have stated it explicitly would perhaps have been to bring into too glaring a light certain incongruities between the assumed premise and the known historical facts.[43]

Becker is correct that Jefferson wrote the Declaration based on his theory of rights. But Becker arguably misses the point when he concludes that this premise is "easily overlooked because it is not explicitly stated in the Declaration—at least not in its final form."[44] Becker assumes that the theory is there, just not articulated. He assumes that Jefferson's view was not stated to avoid the incongruity between the premise and the historical facts. I have suggested another reason: Jefferson's thesis was eliminated precisely because it was not a view on which there was consensus. Becker assumes that Congress agrees with Jefferson's view, when in fact it did not. When Congress eliminated Jefferson's theory of rights, therefore, it simply left no statement in the Declaration that made clear which of the two or three different theories of rights it embraced. The effect is that the Declaration eliminates any link or connection between a specific theory of natural rights and the foundation of the rights of the American states.

We Hold These Truths

Turning now to the most famous passage of the Declaration, the one that is always cited as proof of Jefferson's and the Declaration's endorsement of natural rights, we can see that even some of the wording here may hint at Jefferson's ambivalence about the natural rights traditions. In the left column is Jefferson's wording as it likely was presented to Franklin, and on the right is the "fair copy" as it likely looked later when presented to Congress.[45]

2. Jefferson's Declarations of Independence 73

Jefferson Draft As Likely Presented to Franklin	Rough Draft "fair copy" as it likely looked when presented to Congress.
We hold these truths to be ~~sacred and undeniable~~ self-evident that all men are created equal & independent; that from that equal creation they derive in rights inherent & inalienable (Adams's copy reads unalienable), among which are the preservation of life, & liberty, & the pursuit of happiness; that to secure these ends, governments are instituted among men, deriving their just powers from the consent of the governed; that whenever any form of government shall become destructive of these ends, it is the right of the people to alter or abolish it, & to institute new government, laying it's foundation on such principles & organizing it's power in such form, as to them shall seem most likely to effect their safety and happiness.	We hold these truths to be ~~sacred and undeniable~~ self-evident that all men are created equal ~~& independent~~; that ~~from that equal creation they derive in rights~~ they are endowed by their creator with ~~equal rights, some of which are~~ inherent & inalienable rights (Adams's copy reads unalienable), among ~~which~~ these are ~~the preservation of~~ life, & liberty, & the pursuit of happiness; that to secure these rights ~~ends~~, governments are instituted among men, deriving their just powers from the consent of the governed; that whenever any form of government ~~shall~~ becomes destructive of these ends, it is the right of the people to alter or abolish it, & to institute new government, laying it's foundation on such principles & organizing it's power in such form, as to them shall seem most likely to effect their safety and happiness.

This is one of the most poetic statements of natural rights philosophy found in the literature leading up to the Revolution. But Jefferson's ambivalence about more classical natural rights language is arguably still in evidence. Jefferson regularly prefers the word "sacred" to describe basic rights. Not only does he use the term here in his first composition draft, but also in *A Summary View*. Referring there to what are classically thought to be natural rights, Jefferson writes, "A family of princes was then on the British throne, whose treasonable crimes against their people brought on them afterwards the exertion of those sacred and sovereign rights of punishment reserved in the hands of the people for cases of extreme necessity, and judged by the constitution unsafe to be delegated to any other judicature." There Jefferson is referring to what are classic natural rights par excellence, namely, the right to throw off a government that is tyrannical. Jefferson calls them "sacred and sovereign" rights, not natural rights. He also uses the term "sacred" rights in his draft of the Declaration to describe the rights of slaves when blaming King George for reinforcing the slave trade in America, a paragraph that was deleted by Congress.[46] And in *A Summary View* he calls slavery a violation "to the rights of human nature," another turn of phrase that seems to diverge from more traditional language of "natural rights." While the language of "sacred" and "sovereign" is used by some of Jefferson's contemporaries as synonymous with natural rights, the same language was also used by some to refer to rights from the Common Law tradition and the traditional British rights extending back into the past to the Saxons. The same ambiguous meaning was true of the word "inalienable," which Jefferson also uses here. That term could also refer to either rights inherited from the Common Law tradition or natural rights.[47] At times such language seems to intentionally obfuscate whether the rights in question are "original British rights" or "natural rights." Both were thought to be "inalienable."[48] In fact, Jefferson's use of the term "sacred" and his emphasis on God is reminiscent of other writers, such as James Otis, who attempts to anchor political rights in the act of creation, not in a social compact. We shall look at this tendency in the pre-Jefferson writers in chapters to follow. Jefferson uses similar language in *A Summary View* that seems to resonate with those like James Otis who prefer the theological and religious subtradition: "The God who gave us life gave us liberty at the same time; the hand of force may destroy, but cannot disjoin them." Jefferson emphasizes that liberty was created by God but nowhere talks about a social compact or the rights to "life, liberty and property."[49] Instead he seems to think of rights as inherent in human nature, known intuitively by moral beings, a position that European writers contrasted to classic natural rights formulations such as those of Locke.[50]

Jefferson's avoidance of more traditional natural rights language is evident as well in the body of charges he makes against the king that follow the opening preamble. "He has refused to pass other laws for the accommodation of large districts of people unless those people would relinquish the right of representation [in the legislature], a right inestimable to them & formidable to tyrants only."[51] Here again Jefferson calls the right of representation, which is a natural right par excellence, "a right inestimable to them." There seems to be a conscious and continual avoidance of more traditional natural rights language in the way used by Wilson or Samuel Adams, as contemporaneous examples.

Pursuit of Happiness

We can now turn to one of the most interesting puzzles about Jefferson's language of rights: Why did Jefferson emphasize "life, liberty, and the pursuit of happiness" instead of the more common "life, liberty, and property"? There has been much debate on the question of why Jefferson substitutes happiness for property. In general, the recent consensus seems to be that Jefferson's emphasis should not be all that surprising since "pursuit of happiness" is used frequently in the philosophical tradition of liberty.[52] Indeed, Jefferson may simply have been improving language from George Mason's Virginia Bill of Rights, which used a similar expression.

But this consensus overlooks a couple of important points. Jefferson never uses the expression "life, liberty, and property", not in *A Summary View*, the *Declaration of the Causes*, or here in the Declaration. It is reasonable to assume, then, that this was intentional. Jefferson certainly knew the refrain. The first resolution of the First Continental Congress read: "Resolved, N. C. D. 1. That they are entitled to life, liberty and property: and they have never ceded to any sovereign power whatever, a right to dispose of either without their consent." If Jefferson wanted to stay true to the Congress's earlier intention he certainly could have just as easily adopted that language.

It is true that "references to happiness as a political goal are everywhere in American political writings…as anyone can see who bothers to look," to quote Pauline Maier.[53] But those who emphasize the use of the word "happiness" in fact miss the subtle point that happiness was very frequently thought of as the end or purpose of government and not as a natural right.

The difference between an "end" and a "right" was preserved by many thinkers, such as John Locke, James Otis, James Wilson, and others. On Locke's view, people gave up some of their natural rights and liberties to reap the benefits from society, which include happiness. Happiness, in Locke's view, was not a natural right, but an end for which people joined society. The search for happiness led people to seek political society, form a social contract, and relinquish some of their rights for the benefits of society. The protection of an individual's rights of life, liberty, and property resulted in happiness, but happiness itself was not conceptualized by Locke as a right. This is the more conventional way that happiness was related to natural rights theory. Reflecting this view, for example, James Otis wrote that "[t]he end of government being the good of mankind, points out its great duties: It is above all things to provide for the security, the quiet, and happy enjoyment of life, liberty, and property."[54]

As James Wilson puts it in language that some claim may have influenced Jefferson,

> All men are, by nature, equal and free: no one has a right to any authority over another without his consent: all lawful government is founded on the consent of those who are subject to it: such consent was given with a view to ensure and to increase the happiness of the governed, above what they could enjoy in an independent and unconnected state of nature. The consequence is, that the happiness of the society is the first law of every government. This rule is founded on the law of nature: it must control every political maxim.

Wilson, quoting Burlamaqui, conceives happiness as the end of government, the purpose for which consent was given, "with a view to ensure and to increase the happiness of the governed, above what they could enjoy in an independent and unconnected state of nature." Wilson does not call it a natural right but conceives of happiness as the driving motivation that leads individuals to give up natural liberties in order to enter a state of society under law. This is what he means by happiness is the first law of government.

Similarly, in a passage from section 3 of the Virginia Bill of Rights, George Mason preserves a similar distinction:

> SEC. 3. That government is, or ought to be, instituted for the common benefit, protection, and security of the people, nation, or community; of all the various modes and forms of government, that is best which is capable of producing the greatest degree of happiness and safety, and is most effectually secured against the danger of maladministration; and that, when any government shall be found inadequate or contrary to these purposes, a majority of the community hath an indubitable, inalienable, and indefeasible right to reform, alter, or abolish it, in such manner as shall be judged most conducive to the public weal.

In another section of George Mason's Virginia Bill of Rights, a section that may also have influenced Jefferson, we find more ambiguous language. Mason wrote:

> That all men are by nature equally free and independent, and have certain inherent rights, of which, when they enter into a state of society, they cannot, by any compact, deprive or divest their posterity; namely, the enjoyment of life and liberty, with the means of acquiring and possessing property, and pursuing and obtaining happiness and safety.

The status of "happiness" is ambiguous in Mason's wording here. Is it an inherent right or is it a benefit that derives from the more primary inherent right of "life and liberty"? The ambiguity arises from word "with." On one interpretation, Mason seems to be saying that the inherent rights are life and liberty *and* "the means of acquiring and possessing property, and pursuing and obtaining happiness and safety." That is, on this interpretation the word "with" is intended to be inclusive. Still, if Mason had used the word "and" instead of "with," his intention would have been much clearer. The word "with" makes his meaning ambiguous and could imply that he thought of life and liberty as the primary inherent rights "plus" or "with" benefits or goods that derived from those rights, namely, the means of acquiring property and pursuing and obtaining happiness and security. Mason's language thus leaves ambiguous whether happiness, and the means of acquiring property, are to be treated as inherent rights or derivative social goods. This ambiguity may not matter much in trying to figure out what Mason meant, although the Virginia Bill of Rights was important in shaping the emerging American conceptions of rights.

However, since it is possible Jefferson was influenced by Mason's language, the ambiguity in Mason's language becomes more important.[55] It is possible that Jefferson's first draft of the Declaration may represent an interpretation of Mason's language with adjustments to fit Jefferson's own conceptions or linguistic sense. It may be the case, as Maier suggests, that in avoiding the reference to property, Jefferson simply "sacrificed clarity of meaning for grace of language."[56] But it is possible Jefferson's variation has more deliberation. Not only does Jefferson avoid including property as an inherent right, but he makes explicit that happiness is an inherent right. Here are Jefferson's words again in his first draft of the Declaration: "...all men are created equal & independent; that from that equal creation they derive in rights inherent & inalienable, among which are the preservation of life, & liberty, & the pursuit of happiness."

In this initial wording of Jefferson, there is no ambiguity that pursuit of happiness is an inherent right. Unfortunately, in the very next sentence the ambiguity creeps back in: Jefferson continues "that to secure these ends [i.e., life, liberty, and the pursuit of happiness], governments are instituted among men, deriving their just powers from the consent of the governed." Here happiness, as well as the preservation of life and liberty, is described as an "end" of government, arguably a concept that differs from a right, a distinction that many like Wilson faithfully preserved. Significantly, in the Rough Draft produced by the Committee of Five (see above), the word "end" is replaced by the word "rights" removing the ambiguity altogether and leaving no doubt that the Declaration treats the pursuit of happiness as a natural right.

Would there have been any reason, apart from literary and stylistic, for Jefferson to emphasize that happiness was an inherent right? Indeed there may have been. In two interesting contexts before the Declaration, we find happiness serving an interesting purpose. In Richard Bland's *An Inquiry Into the Rights of the British Colonies*, Bland argues that happiness is not just an end of government but a natural right.[57] Bland makes this argument in the context of arguing that the American rights were based on a natural right to quit society. Bland writes:

> But though they must submit to the Laws, so long as they remain Members of the Society, yet they retain so much of their natural Freedom as to have a Right to retire from the Society, to renounce the Benefits of it, to enter into another Society, and to settle in another Country; for their Engagements to the Society, and their Submission to the publick Authority of the State, do not oblige them to continue in it longer than they find it ***will conduce to their Happiness, which they have a natural Right to promote.***[58] [emphasis added]

As I discuss in chapters below, Bland anticipates most of the core assumptions of Jefferson in *A Summary View*.[59] He evokes a natural right to quit society, and he also associates this with a natural right to pursue happiness. Thus Bland makes the connection that the right to quit society is tied into the natural right to pursue happiness. In *A Summary View* too, Jefferson links the two conceptions, although there he does not call happiness a natural right but sees happiness as the end of government.

> [T]hat our ancestors, before their emigration to America, were the free inhabitants of the British dominions in Europe, and

possessed a right, which nature has given to all men, of departing from the country in which chance, not choice, has placed them, of going in quest of new habitations, and of there establishing new societies, under such laws and regulations as to them shall seem most likely to promote public happiness.

In this quote from *A Summary View*, Jefferson is more in line with Locke and Wilson, seeing the end of political society to promote "public happiness," which is different from an individual's right to pursue happiness, as discussed earlier.

But turning to the Declaration, where Jefferson had to include a statement of natural rights, Jefferson's turn of phrase "in pursuit of happiness" serves an interesting purpose. Now the Declaration's introduction can be read as a good summary of Jefferson's theory set out in *A Summary View*. The pursuit of happiness is what drives men to quit society and look for new habitations. It is not dependent on "intolerable persecution," as Samuel Adams would have it, or the failure to meet the happiness rule, as Wilson proposed. The shift from "life, liberty, and property" to "life, liberty, and the pursuit of happiness" enables Jefferson to slide in a reference to and an argument for his view about the origin of American rights. It was not based on general natural rights, on "life, liberty, and property," as many of his colleagues would and did say, but the right to quit one's society and go in search of happiness. The "pursuit of happiness" for Jefferson is arguably the equivalent of Jefferson's right to quit society. This position differs from that of Wilson, who considered happiness as the key criterion by which to measure government's execution of its responsibility to the people. By making this a natural right, or at least eliminating the ambiguity in Mason's language, Jefferson smuggles in a reference to his own theory and to the foundation for the right to quit society. He said it without saying it. While there is no way to prove that this is the case, it does fit with Jefferson's repeated desire to defend his own theory of rights. And while he may have copied from Mason, he shortened up the language and removed an ambiguity that Mason had left in his language.

Jefferson's statement on rights went through a revision some of which reflect his own changes, some of which are likely from Franklin or Adams. Interpreters debate whether the change of "sacred and undeniable" to "self-evident" was Franklin's, Adams's, or Jefferson's own.[60] "Self-evident" is very close in meaning to "undeniable," but may carry more direct allusion to the self-evidence to reason. Jefferson himself never seems to appeal to reason as a basis of rights, and instead, as he puts it in *A Summary View*, refers to "not only the principles of common sense, but the common feelings of human nature", and then again to "the feelings of human nature." But "self-evident" can also fit in with and support other types of evidence and thus fit within the parallel tradition that was doubting natural rights based on reason. In this way, the language can embrace other means of knowing, such as "common sense," as visible in Thomas Paine and in the young Alexander Hamilton, or even a kind of innate knowing that may have been presupposed by Jefferson.

In his original language, Jefferson writes that "from that equal creation they derive in rights inherent & inalienable." The notion that "they derive" their rights, is certainly more tentative than the claim that they are self-evident to reason, which the natural rights tradition argued, and more tentative than the wording of the subsequent draft: "they are endowed by their creator with inherent & inalienable rights." This latter phraseology, which came from the committee, puts much more emphasis on the active role of God in giving these rights rather than of men deriving their rights from their equal creation.[61] This may reflect some sensitivity to the theological reinterpretation of natural rights theory discussed in more detail below.[62] Interestingly, this revision also breaks the original dependence of rights on human equality at creation in Jefferson's first draft. Now the statement posits two facts at creation: people were created equal, and God conferred inherent rights. Inherent rights are not derived from equality of creation, the way that Locke originally had put it. It also eliminates the word "independent." Perhaps this was just a literary improvement, as Becker suggests, but it could also reflect some sensitivity to the idea that Otis and other religious-minded writers had put forward: that people were created to be in society, and that sociality was mandated by God, a view that religious thinkers had emphasized in their critique of the natural rights tradition.

PART II

Placing Jefferson in Context

3. Early Doubts about Natural Rights Before the Revolution

Interpreters who claim that Jefferson's Declaration of Independence embodies a natural rights philosophy often ignore the complex and conflicted discussions of natural rights in colonial arguments in the decade leading up to the Revolution. It is natural, perhaps, to ignore the earlier period since the Declaration embodies the first consensus of the colonies' justifying independence. Yet it seems problematic to slice the Declaration out of its historical context in this way and not see the Declaration's position on rights within a broader tradition leading up to independence.

There were in fact many individual and official statements on rights by American colonists in the decade leading up to the Declaration. Notable figures such as Steven Hopkins, James Otis, Samuel and John Adams, James Wilson, John Dickinson, and even Jefferson himself drafted earlier statements articulating the colonies' rights before the Declaration.[1] In addition to these individual statements, officially sanctioned statements such as *The Declaration of Rights* of the First Continental Congress and the *Declaration of Causes and Necessity of War* by the Second Continental Congress were among the officially sanctioned statements on rights in the period leading up to the Declaration. It would seem reasonable, if one was trying to ascertain what the Declaration meant, to take account of these other various statements on rights as a context in which to understand the Declaration's meaning. When we do take account of these earlier statements on natural rights, we find that there is more ambivalence about natural rights than many have emphasized. Bringing this ambivalence to the surface, we see that there were significant doubts among pre-Revolutionary writers about whether natural rights arguments were the best foundation of American rights. That doubt provides an important background for understanding some of the ambivalence about natural rights that is reflected in Jefferson's writings and the Declaration itself.

If one set of interpreters views the Declaration in isolation from this background, another group of interpreters oversimplifies the colonists' views of natural rights. These interpreters acknowledge that the colonists did not immediately embrace natural rights arguments, but they assume that there is an almost evolutionary "inevitable" move towards natural rights arguments. The story they tell is that the colonists turned inexorably to natural rights arguments with the Declaration representing the pinnacle, as it were, of that impulse in American thinking. According to this story, earlier arguments about colonial rights proved inadequate, and the growing move towards independence made natural rights arguments nearly inevitable. We shall question and probe this "evolutionary" story as well, for it oversimplifies a much more complex picture. Doubts about natural rights arguments were very strong in the early period and remained a concern up to and beyond 1774. Furthermore, there was no consensus on the meaning of natural rights. And there were serious doubts about what was perceived to be the foundation of natural rights, namely, social contract theory. These doubts were fed by criticisms of John Locke's theory among prestigious European philosophers such as David Hume, whose writings were also familiar to the colonial lawyers and thinkers. A number of colonial thinkers assumed that social contract theory was a weak theoretical basis for natural rights arguments and therefore undermined American rights should they be founded on natural rights arguments. In addition, religious and theologically oriented thinkers fundamentally transformed natural rights arguments in ways that attempted to bring Locke closer to more traditional covenantal language and concepts. This transformation in some ways completely rethought natural rights assumptions and in some cases turned them on their head. When we look back beyond the Declaration, we find a complex and even contradictory tradition in which serious ambivalence about natural rights was expressed.

In this chapter, I explore this ambivalence in the first part of that decade leading up to Revolution, particularly in the colonists' early reactions to the Sugar and Stamp Acts in the mid-1760s. In subsequent chapters, we explore the trajectory of this ambivalence as the colonies moved towards war and eventually the Declaration.

Locke and Natural Rights in Responses to the Sugar and Stamp Act

Two new acts by the British Parliament in the mid-1760s triggered the American colonists to begin thinking more deeply about their fundamental rights and turn to John Locke's natural rights philosophy, among other theories, to justify those rights. Those legislative acts were the Sugar Act (April 1764) and the Stamp Act, announced in 1764 but not legislated until 1765. It was the Stamp Act more than the Sugar Act that prompted the colonists to react by claiming that Parliament was violating their rights. The two acts were proposed under the leadership of George Grenville, who had become prime minister, and who proposed both acts to address a growing problem of national debt in England that had almost doubled in the Seven Years' War.[2]

In early March 1764, Greenville proposed his new resolutions, which included a range of new trade restrictions and duties, including a ban on rum and a new duty on Madeira wine, coffee, foreign indigo, and foreign sugar. All of the resolutions were known as the "Sugar Act," which revived and adjusted an earlier Molasses Act, which had been legislated in 1733 but had never been effectively enforced. The new Sugar Act was intended to reinstate and adjust that earlier law, lowering the duties from six pence per gallons to three pence, but enforcing stricter custom controls to give the law real teeth. New means of enforcing the laws were also proposed, including new procedures for determining what cargo a vessel was carrying and where a ship had previously been. The colonies were troubled by the fact that offenders would be prosecuted in the admiralty courts, which operated without juries and had been deciding maritime cases in the colonies since 1697. The goal of the new regulations was to eliminate the smuggling that had previously been condoned by local judges and friendly juries.

The Sugar Act included a fifteenth resolution that announced an intention to impose a Stamp Duty, a charge on various documents and articles made of paper. The intention of the Stamp Act was to generate revenue by forcing the colonists to buy and use paper that had a tax stamp for any commercial or legal transaction, including all legal documents, permits, commercial contracts, newspapers, wills, pamphlets, and even playing cards. The proposal for a Stamp Act was announced in the resolutions of the Sugar Act but delayed a year, ostensibly to get colonial feedback.[3]

The colonists in general saw these two acts somewhat differently. They saw the Stamp Act as a kind of "tax" and fundamentally different in character than the Sugar Act, which they regarded as at least in part a "duty on trade." The colonists initially had a fundamentally different understanding of their rights with respect to taxes and trade regulations, a distinction that would become more and more blurry over the decade. At this early stage in the debate, colonists believed it was their fundamental right to consent to any taxes that would be imposed on them by Parliament. Since they were not represented in Parliament, and therefore could not by definition consent, they viewed taxes imposed by Parliament as a violation of their fundament rights. Stephen Hopkins, the governor of Rhode Island, citing Sidney on government, put it this way in his *Rights of Colonies*: "For liberty solely consists in an independency upon the will of another; and by the name of slave we understand a man who can neither dispose of his person or goods, but enjoys all at the will of his master....For it must be confessed by all men that they who are taxed at pleasure by others cannot possibly have any property, can have nothing to be called their own."[4]

Initially, the colonists had a contrasting view of trade regulations. They believed Parliament *did* have the authority and right to set trade regulations for the good of the whole empire without consulting the colonies and without granting them representation. Why the colonists distinguished trade duties from taxes is an interesting point to which we return later for it tells us something about their notions of rights.[5]

In response to the Sugar and Stamp Acts, the colonists wrote a series of pamphlets articulating their discontent with the new regulations. In some of these pamphlets, the colonists cite John Locke's ideas to defend their rights against Parliament. It is worth noting the irony of evoking Locke to argue that Parliament had overstepped its power. In the late seventeenth century, Locke was mostly concerned with limiting the power of monarchy and protecting and expanding the control of Parliament so as to protect the rights of the people. In Locke's own historical context of the 1680s and '90s, Parliament's powers were still in danger of infringement by the Crown. Royalists who supported unlimited power in the monarchy still had strong support in the writings of Robert Filmer and others.

In the American context, the British Americans were using Locke to criticize the very institution whose role and power Locke's work had been partially designed to strengthen. But the use of Locke by the colonists was erratic. Not only was Locke cited inconsistently, but the colonists relied heavily on several other arguments to justify what they regarded as their fundamental rights. Moreover, when they did cite Locke, he was used for various purposes and sometimes not to justify the notion of natural rights at all. Indeed, we see evidence that the colonists were not fully comfortable with the idea of natural rights, although not always for what we might take to be "good reasons."

In fact, the appeal to Locke in this first phase of resistance was potentially risky for the colonists because it arguably even weakened their arguments. American loyalists poked fun at their fellow colonists for basing arguments on "metaphysical jargon." They also charged the colonists with sedition and desire of independence, which was not really on the colonists' minds initially, but could be inferred from their use of rights arguments. Furthermore, Locke's ideas may have had a more radical edge than colonists were willing to articulate or even completely realize this early in the game. As the colonial arguments unfolded, the use of Locke's natural rights ideas becomes more radical, which explains in part the growing use of natural rights arguments as the resistance unfolds.

Let us look first at the place of Locke in the early set of pamphlets written by Stephen Hopkins, James Otis, and Oxenbridge Thatcher as well as some of the responses elicited to their pamphlets.

Stephen Hopkins, governor of Rhode Island and leader of a local political faction, wrote two pamphlets that are of interest in this early phase of the resistance. In the first, *An Essay on the Trade of the Northern Colonies*, published in February 1764, Hopkins summarizes the reactions of his constituents in Rhode Island to the announcement of the Sugar Act. Basing his reasoning on strictly economic grounds, Hopkins argues that the act would hurt both the colonies as well as the British Empire.[6] As in other pamphlets written at this early stage, the argument is economic and pragmatic in orientation and makes no use of Locke or rights language at all.[7] We shall consider in a moment why this is so.

In the essay, Hopkins gives a detailed look at "principal branches of commerce" of the northern colonies, making observations about how the soil and climate shape the region's commerce and increase the need for colonial consumption of British manufactures. At the heart of the essay is the question of what types of economic activities should be regulated, or, as he puts it, his purpose is to determine "whether this commerce, taken together, or any branches of it, be detrimental to the true interest of Great-Britain, or in any degree injurious to the British sugar colonies..."[8] Hopkins then goes on to express a sentiment that would be echoed throughout the early colonial debates: "And first we shall acknowledge, that whatever business or commerce in any of the northern colonies interferes, or is any way detrimental to the true interest, manufactories, trade or commerce of Great Britain, we reasonably expect will be totally prohibited."[9]

Hopkins has no objections to Parliament forbidding trade activities that are detrimental to the best interests of Great Britain, such as the colonial fishing trade with Spain and Italy in which the colonies buy those countries' manufactures and not those of Great Britain. Parliament has the power and right to regulate commerce that undermines British commercial interests.

But there are some types of trade regulations that rest on a mistaken analysis and basic lack of information. For example, the trade of the colonies with North Africa may appear to Parliament to compete with the trade of Great Britain. On deeper analysis and with more knowledge, Hopkins argues, Parliament would realize that this American trade actually has long term benefits for Great Britain. Parliament makes bad trade laws when it lacks sufficient information and arrives at faulty economic interpretations. The fault of Parliament is poor economic analysis and a lack of information, not a violation of the colonies' rights.

With regard to the Sugar Act, however, Hopkins argues there was no doubt about the disastrous economic consequences that would ensue. Using strictly economic style arguments, and appealing to early mercantile concepts of supply and demand, monopoly, and pricing fluctuations, Hopkins argues that the Sugar Act would produce detrimental economic consequences that backfire. The new duty on sugar import would result in the colonists being unable to buy as much sugar. Rather than generating more revenue, which was its ostensive purpose, it would actually depress trade volume.[10]

The Sugar Act, therefore, will have unintended consequences, forcing the northern colonies to abandon or reduce their current forms of economic activity and develop their own manufactures. Hopkins is implying that if Parliament was not careful, the colonies would no longer be a good market for British goods. Such veiled threats about the development of American manufacture appear in many subsequent pamphlets. In fact, the colonists would embargo the importation of British goods in October and November 1765, causing significant hardship to British merchants, who pressured Parliament to repeal the Stamp Act.

It is interesting and significant for our purposes that Hopkins never argues in this pamphlet that the rights of the colonies have been violated. His argument is framed in strictly pragmatic economic and what ethicists would call "consequentialist" reasoning: Instead of serving the best interest of the colonies and Great Britain, the Sugar Act would be detrimental to all. One might see in arguments such as these an early American tendency towards "free trade" arguments. But Hopkins and other writers to follow in this early phase generally do not link the argument against trade restrictions to liberty or freedom, with some exemptions. Liberty and economic arguments over trade regulations have not yet fused here in these early American writings.[11]

Hopkins's pamphlet is of interest in the present context precisely because of the absence of rights talk. The lack of rights language may be because it was early in the debate. As Bailyn notes,

> Yet in the overall development of the Revolutionary movement, these statements of colonial opinion, written before the passage of the Sugar Act, are of considerable importance. For not only do they express the colonists' objections to the economic reorganization of the empire, but they mark the last point at which objections to Parliamentary action affecting them could generally be voiced without reference to ideology. The most striking fact about these addresses and petitions is their entire devotion to economic arguments: nowhere do they appeal to constitutional issues; nowhere was Parliament's right to pass such laws officially questioned. But ideological questions were just below the surface.[12]

Some American commentators have tended to see the development of rights talk beyond this stage as almost "natural" or "inevitable." Morgan, for example, writes, "Undoubtedly the drastic economic effects the colonists anticipated from the Sugar Act prompted the alarm they felt, but it was natural for them to inquire into the right of the matter."[13]

But the move away from strictly economic arguments towards rights language seems more than simply an ordained shift. It is also likely the result of the fact that the Sugar Act, which was the first focus of colonial attention, was more of an ambiguous violation of rights as the colonists understood them than the Stamp Act, which had been announced but not yet approved. In the early years of the resistance, the colonists recognized that Parliament had an undisputed right to regulate trade for the benefits of Great Britain's interests as a whole. To be sure, the colonists did not always believe Great Britain understood its own best interests economically or fully appreciated the outcome of its economic policy. The colonists would therefore challenge trade regulations on economic and pragmatic grounds initially, as was the case with Hopkins.

With respect to taxes, however, the colonists believed that Parliament had no rights without their consent. They considered their right to consent to taxes a fundamental right. The problem of differentiating between a tax and a trade duty would emerge shortly in the debate.[14] And the Sugar Act was at least partly ambiguous. On the surface, the Sugar Act looked like a traditional trade regulation since it imposed duties on imports and forbade certain types of trade between parts of the empire. But the language of the resolutions made it clear that the intention of the law was to raise revenue. "And whereas it is just and necessary, that a revenue be raised, in your Majesty's said dominions in America, for defraying the expences of defending, protecting and securing the same; we, your Majesty's most dutiful and loyal subjects, the commons of Great Britain...have resolved to give and grant unto your Majesty the several rates and duties herein aftermentioned."[15]

The Sugar Act thus raised an ambiguity. Could trade duties be in effect taxes? The Sugar Act, therefore, was a kind of "wolf in sheep's clothing." It was "betwixt and between," to borrow a term of anthropologist Victor Turner, for all intents and purposes a tax masquerading as a trade protection. Should the colonists fight the regulation on the basis of rights or on the basis of economic arguments and justice? In general, the colonists chose to fight the Sugar Act on economic and pragmatic grounds although they worried it violated their rights but were not yet ready to say so as explicitly.[16]

There was no ambiguity at all, however, with regard to the Stamp Act, which clearly was not a regulation on trade between parts of the empire. In fact, the Stamp Act imposed a direct tax on the colonists through a method the colonists had used earlier to tax themselves.[17] As the colonists began to shift attention from the Sugar Act to the Stamp Act, their language expanded from strictly economic and utilitarian arguments to broader rights language. Some strictly economic essays would continue to be written much later.[18] But in the future the economic arguments were typically blended with and complementary to rights claims.

The Shift to Rights Talk and the Doubts about Social Contract Theory

To gauge this shift in perspective, we can turn to another essay written by the same Stephen Hopkins seven months after he penned his earlier essay. Now his focus has shifted to include the Stamp Act in an essay entitled *The Rights of the Colonies Considered* (December 1764).[19] This was not the first response to the Stamp Act. However, it provides an interesting measure of the shift in orientation that had occurred in only seven months' time for the same writer.

With the prospect of the Stamp Act coming into focus, the language of rights has now moved to the fore. The Stamp Act, Hopkins writes, "hath much more, and for much more reason, alarmed the British subjects in American than anything that had ever been done before."[20] Interestingly enough, for our purposes, Hopkins does not appeal at all to Locke. And in avoiding Locke, we find our first clue why the colonists felt ambivalent about natural rights. At the start of the essay, Hopkins writes:

> Liberty is the greatest blessing that men enjoy, and slavery the heaviest curse that human nature is capable of. This being so makes it a matter of the utmost importance to men which of the two shall be their portion. Absolute liberty is, perhaps, incompatible with any kind of government. The safety resulting from society, and the advantage of just and equal laws, hath caused men to forego some part of their natural liberty, and submit to government. This appears to be the most rational account of its beginning, although, it must be confessed, mankind have by no means been agreed about it. Some have found its origin in the divine appointment; others have thought it took its rise from power; enthusiasts have dreamed that dominion was founded in grace. Leaving these points to be settled by the descendants of Filmer, Cromwell and Venner, we will consider the British

constitution, as it at present stands, on Revolution principles, and from thence endeavor to find the measure of the magistrates' power and the people's obedience.[21]

Hopkins is here appealing initially to and signaling agreement with a Lockean-like conception of rights, although he nowhere mentions "natural rights" or Locke by name. But he alludes to "natural liberty" and the impulse to forgo some natural liberty because of the advantages of submitting to government. This is a good short summary of natural rights and social contract theory. Hopkins regards this as the "most rational account of" government's beginning.

But Hopkins acknowledges this account of government's origins is not unanimously accepted and that there are other competing theories. Some argue that government was established by God, arose from power, or was founded in grace. Similar doubts about government's origins are expressed by other writers such as Maryland lawyer and politician Daniel Dulany, for example, in his *Consideration on the Propriety of Imposing Taxes in the British Colonies for the Purpose of Raising a Revenue* (August 1765). Dulany, like others in the colonies, based colonial rights on the charters "founded upon the unalienable rights of the subject and upon the most sacred compact, the colonies claim a right of exemption from taxes *not imposed with their consent*. They claim it upon the principles of the constitution, as once English and now British subjects, upon the principles on which their compact with the crown was originally founded." Dulany goes on to explain basing American rights in charters is not vulnerable to the criticisms of social compact theory generally. "The origin of other governments is covered by the veil of antiquity and is differently traced by the fancies of different men; but of the colonies the evidence of it is as clear and unequivocal as any other fact."[22] Below, we shall look at the same kinds of reservations in an essay by James Otis, another prominent colonial writer, who put forward a similar view some months before Hopkins.[23]

Hopkins is reluctant to base his argument on natural rights and social compact theory precisely because there is lack of consensus on the historical origins of government. He therefore appeals to a different foundation for American rights which he believes is incontrovertible, namely the British constitution and the original compact of the British people.

> The glorious constitution, the best that ever existed among men, will be confessed by all, to be founded by compact, and established by consent of the people. By this most beneficent compact, British subjects are to be governed only agreeable to laws to which themselves have some way consented; and are not to be compelled to part with their property, but as it is called for by the authority of such laws. The former, is truly liberty; the latter is really to be possessed of property and to have something that may be called one's own.[24]

The "glorious" British Constitution was thus founded by a historic compact and creates fundamental rights ensuring that subjects are to be governed by laws to which they in some way consent and that they do not have to part with their property except as "called for by the authority of such laws." For Hopkins, herein lies the protection against taxation without consent:

> For it must be confessed by all men, that they who are taxed at pleasure by others, cannot possibly have any property, can have nothing to be called their own. They who have no property can have no freedom, but are indeed reduced to the most abject slavery; are in a condition far worse than countries conquered and made tributary...[25]

This quotation could have been lifted almost word for word from John Locke. And the statement seems to suggest that the right to consent to taxes is universally "confessed by all men", though Hopkins never tries to anchor it in natural rights and instead links it only to the original British compact.

Given what Hopkins assumes to be widely shared premises about the origin of British rights, the "chief point examined" in his essay considers "whether the British American colonies on the continent are justly entitled to like privileges and freedom as their fellow subjects in Great Britain."[26] Not surprisingly, Hopkins comes to the conclusion that British Americans are entitled to all the rights embodied in the British constitution. The arguments to justify that position are similar to ones repeated throughout colonial writings.

Hopkins, then, is appealing to a notion of social contract and common law that does not depend on natural rights theory. British rights, as distinct from natural rights, are provided by a specific and historical compact (the glorious constitution) which itself embodied an ancient tradition reaching back to the Anglo-Saxons. This theory of the "common law" or "ancient constitution" was in fact a standard English understanding of contract before Locke's rise to prominence after the 1680s and inspired by the Dutch writer Grotius.[27]

We see here, early in the colonial reactions to the new British policies, that Hopkins considers it far safer to work off agreed, uncontested assumptions about the British historical tradition of rights than contested notions of universal natural rights. Since Hopkins regards the origin of government to be debatable and historically obscure, he wants to avoid using natural rights theory as the basis of his argument. He clearly is partly concerned about reaching his more religiously oriented readers who might favor a theory of government originating in divine appointment, or his more empirically oriented readers who might argue that historically government was founded by power.[28] It is as if to say, whatever our beliefs about government's origin in general, we can all agree that there are specific historic rights to which British subjects are entitled. *The origins of government as a human institution are beside the point.*

As an aside, it is important to note that Hopkins' reservation about natural rights theory stems from what is possibly a misunderstanding of Locke, by today's intellectual standards. Hopkins is worried that the theory of natural rights and social compact essentially rests on a particular historical understanding of the government's origin. Locke can legitimately be read that way.[29] But Locke never entirely rested his argument about the social contract or the state of nature strictly on historical evidence alone. For Locke, the social compact also appears at times to be an ideal agreement or construct that *should* structure the relations between individuals and society. Although Locke believed there were historical examples of social compacts and cited examples of some, and although he identified the state of nature with the description of creation in Genesis, as did his contemporaries, he also conceived of natural rights as moral obligations that should structure any relationship between individuals and government. Locke, however, did not fully develop this argument and left it in a footnote. In most compelling contemporary readings of Locke, Locke's theory of government is taken not as an actual description of how government developed, but as an ideal set of rights that should be protected by government.[30] But Locke can also be read as making an argument about the actual origin of government, which gave rise to the doubts about natural rights arguments among Locke's critics, such as Hume, and the colonial writers who were familiar with similar types of critiques.[31]

Hopkins's reservations about natural rights and social compact theory thus rest on a then current (and possibly although not self-evidently mistaken) reading of Locke. It is also interesting that Hopkins is worried that natural rights would seem problematic to those of a more traditional religious orientation who believe government was "appointed by God." This worry, as we shall see, was on the mind of other colonists as well. Although Locke himself was clearly anchoring rights in the law of nature and the law of reason, which he equated with God's law, some colonists saw a tension between Locke's view and a more traditional religious perspective.[32] And Locke himself was subjected to criticism by more traditionally theologically oriented thinkers. Hopkins clearly assumes that some of his religious readers would think Locke's natural rights account placed too much emphasis on the consent of human beings, and not enough on God's role in the origin of government. Below, we shall see that James Otis worries about precisely the same issue.

From Hopkins's early essay, we now have a working interpretation of why American writers felt more comfortable arguing from British rights than natural rights. The colonists did not want to be sidetracked debating contested theories about government's origin or the existence of the state of nature. They wanted to start from a well-accepted point of departure, and they felt that arguing from the origin of British rights was a far safer and more compelling starting point than natural rights. They would soon learn otherwise.

Social Contract Theory is Metaphysical Jargon

Hopkins was not the only writer to express ambivalence about natural rights theory and social compact. Similar but more detailed reservations are expressed in an essay by James Otis, written five months prior to Hopkins's essay. Otis was a well-respected Boston politician and lawyer famous already for his role in a legal case defending Boston merchants against the "writs of assistance," which were in effect search warrants that enabled customs officials to enter businesses and homes in the hope of finding vaguely defined contraband. In arguing the case, Otis delivered a lengthy oral argument in which he maintained that the writs were a violation of the colonists' natural rights. After the announcement of the Sugar Act, Otis went on to write what was one of the most well-known and widely read pamphlets in the colonies, entitled *The Rights of the British Colonies Asserted and Proved* (July 1764).

In this essay, Otis expresses his reservations about social compact theory and the question of government's origin:

> What shall we say then? Is not government founded on grace? No. Nor on force? No. Nor on compact? Nor property? Not altogether on either. Has it any solid foundation, any chief cornerstone but what accident, chance, or confusion may lay one moment and destroy the next? I think it has an everlasting foundation in the *unchangeable will* of God, the author of nature, whose laws never vary.[33]

We shall explore Otis's "alternative theory" of government later, for at first blush it does not seem all that different from Locke's. But it actually represents an attempt of sorts to reconcile more traditional Christian religious thought with Locke's natural rights thinking and shows that not everyone saw social compact theory as completely compatible with more traditional religious perspectives. In quite some detail, Otis lays out the problem with "social compact theory." It is worth quoting Otis at length on this point.

> On the other hand, the gentlemen in favor of the original compact have been often told that their system is chimerical and unsupported by reason or experience. Questions like the following have been frequently asked them, and may be again.
>
> "When and where was the original compact for introducing government into any society, or for creating a society, made? Who were present and parties to such compact? Who acted for infants and women, or who appointed guardians for them? Had these guardians power to bind both infants and women during life and their posterity after them? Is it in nature or reason that a guardian should by his own act perpetuate his power over his ward and bind him and his posterity in chains? Is not every man born as free by nature as his father? Has he not the same natural right to think and act and contract for himself? Is it possible for a man to have a natural right to make a slave of himself or of his posterity? Can a father supersede the laws of nature? What man is or ever was born free if every man is not? What will there be to distinguish the next generation of men from their forefathers, that they should not have the same right to make original compacts as their ancestors had? If every man has such right, may there not be as many original compacts as there are men and women born or to be born? Are not women born as free as men? Would it not be infamous to assert that the ladies are all slaves by nature? If every man and woman born or to be born has and will have a right to be consulted and must accede to the original compact before they can with any kind of justice be said to be bound by it, will not the compact be ever forming and never finished, ever making but never done?..."
>
> I hope the reader will consider that I am at present only mentioning such questions as have been put by highfliers and

others in church and state who would exclude all compact between a sovereign and his people without offering my own sentiments upon them; ...Those who want a full answer to them may consult Mr. Locke's discourse on government, M. De Vattel's law of nature and nations, and their own consciences.[34]

Otis concludes:

"And say the opposers of the original compact and of the natural equality and liberty of mankind, will not those answers infallibly show that the doctrine is a piece of metaphysical jargon and systematical nonsense?" Perhaps not.[35]

Otis here articulates a number of known reservations about social compact theory. There is a worry that the historical social compact is "chimerical" and "metaphysical jargon," lacking evidence to support it. But we see other probing questions as well, some of which have a more philosophical bent and touch on points that Locke actually dwelt on in quite some detail in his *Second Treatise*. Whether such doubts reflect the fact that critics had not read Locke in depth, did not understand his full argument, or simply didn't agree with him is not apparent here.

That colonial critics did indeed think rights theory was "metaphysical jargon" is evident in an early response to Hopkins's and Otis's essays by Martin Howard, a lawyer in Newport, Rhode Island, and key spokesperson for a group of men who were critical of Rhode Island's independent political bent. Howard was one of the early American colonists to reject colonial rights arguments, and his ideas were repeated by later loyalists. In August 1765, his effigy was dragged around the streets of Newport and then hanged and burned. His house was also destroyed, and he fled to the safety of a British ship in the harbor.[36] Here is how Howard explains it in his first response to Hopkins and Otis:

The honorable author has not freed this subject from any of its embarrassments: vague and diffuse talk of rights and privileges, and ringing the changes upon the words liberty and slavery only serve to convince us that words may affect without raising images or affording any repose to a mind philosophically inquisitive. For my own part, I will shun the walk of metaphysics in my inquiry, and be content to consider the colonies' rights upon the footing of their charters, which are the only plain avenues that lead to the truth of this matter.[37]

From Howard's reaction, we can understand why Hopkins and other colonial writers were hesitant to criticize the Stamp Act on the basis of natural rights argument or what critics called "metaphysical jargon." As Hopkins puts it, "Leaving these points to be settled by the descendants of Filmer, Cromwell and Venner, we will consider the British constitution, as it at present stands, on Revolution principles, and from thence endeavor to find the measure of the magistrates' power and the people's obedience."[38] This was a known empirical point of departure and thus much safer and stronger a starting point for the rights of the colonists who thought of themselves as British Americans.

The Problem with British Rights

If British rights were thought to be a less problematic foundation than natural rights, the colonists would soon discover otherwise. In basing colonial rights on the British constitution and the rights of British subjects, the burden for Hopkins, and other pamphleteers who followed the same route, was to demonstrate that American colonists shared fully and equally in these British rights. This turned out to be a thornier problem than the colonists expected and explains in part why the colonists would rely more heavily on arguments from natural rights as the debate proceeded. At issue in this early stage of the debate was the status of "British Americans" with respect to British rights. Everyone agreed that British subjects had rights from the common law and that those rights included protections on life, liberty, and property. But did these rights apply to the settlers in the colonies? Were they included, and on what basis?

The core of the problem was the status of colonies. What are colonies? Are colonies part and parcel of Great Britain or unique in some sense? Do colonial subjects enjoy the same rights as subjects living in the mother country? Are they still "part of the people" who made the original English compact, just as British subjects? Were colonies included in the original British compact, or were they special in some sense and not covered by the original constitution? Who inherited the original compact anyway? How did such rights get transferred to and remain with the colonies? Would rights apply to colonists who were not British in origin? And how did various British historical events (such as the English Civil Wars, the development and fall of the Commonwealth, and the Glorious Revolution) affect British American rights? Did the colonists bring their rights to America when they came there, and if so, did they retain them through these events? These were the kinds of issues that came up and had to be addressed in arguments that based colonial rights on original rights from the British and Anglo-Saxon tradition. The answer to these questions turned out to be as contentious as the "origin of government" and in some sense analogous to that question. And this was the burden of the argument for writers like Hopkins who hoped to base colonial rights strictly on British rights.

To explain why the colonies were entitled to British rights, Hopkins makes a number of arguments familiar throughout later colonial writings. He argues that the first settlers never would "leave their native country and go through the fatigue and hardship of planting in a new uncultivated one for the sake of losing their freedom...." Moreover, the "terms of their freedom" were fully settled before they left the mother country: "They were to remain subject to the king, and dependent on the kingdom of Great Britain. In return, they were to receive protection and enjoy all the rights and privileges of free-born Englishmen." Thomas Fitch, the governor of Connecticut, made a similar argument: "Though the subjects in the colonies are situated at a great distance from their mother country, and for that reason cannot participate in the general legislature of the nation...it may not be justly said they have lost their birthright by such their removal into America."[39]

As evidence of this agreement, Hopkins appeals to the charters provided to the colonies of Massachusetts, Connecticut, and Rhode Island.

Fitch makes similar appeals to the Connecticut charters. And in the Stamp Resolves that followed later, each colony would trot out its rights based on its own charters. Since each colony had its own charter, however, arguments from charters tended to undermine a unified response across colonies, an issue that became more important as the resistance developed. Hopkins's argument from the Massachusetts charters could not help Fitch, who had to argue from Connecticut charters. The appeal to natural rights thus became more appealing over time in part to find a ground for rights that the colonies could share equally.[40]

But there were other problems with basing arguments on rights on charters, too. A charter could be interpreted as granting a privilege, rather than a right, and could be theoretically revoked or taken away. Indeed, as one British writer would write under the pen name of William Pym: "Let me inform my fellow subjects of America, that a resolution of the British parliament can at any time set aside all the charters that have ever been granted by our monarchs."[41] Furthermore, some charters were granted before the English Civil Wars and Glorious Revolution. The question naturally arose as to how those grants of rights, if they were rights at all, were affected by these fundamental changes in the British constitution. If they had been granted by earlier monarchs, did the force of those charters stay in place?

This may explain why Hopkins says he is basing his argument on "revolution principles," referring presumably to the Glorious Revolution of 1688, and trying to get around the question of how the Glorious Revolution or English Civil Wars impacted the early American migration or the "British birthright." There was, however, a question lurking hidden here. For if Americans brought rights with them originally when they migrated, what ensured those rights stayed with them as the English government went through the political upheavals of Civil War, Commonwealth, Restoration, and then Revolution?

As if sensing this vulnerability in the appeal to strictly British rights and charters, Hopkins appeals to general historic evidence as well, trying to ground the rights of colonies in something more than just the British compact. "There is not any thing new or extraordinary in these rights granted to the British colonies; the colonies from all countries, at all times, have enjoyed equal freedom with the mother state."[42] Here Hopkins attempts to find an anchor for American rights beyond just British rights, turning to what he considers real historical precedent as if to find some more universal or general footing for the colonies' rights. This same impulse to look beyond British rights accounts for the reliance on natural rights arguments as the debate unfolds. Summarizing his position, Hopkins writes:

> From what hath been shown, it will appear beyond a doubt, that the British subjects in America, have equal rights with those in Britain; that they do not hold those rights as a privilege granted them, nor enjoy them as a grace and favor bestowed; but possess them as an inherent, indefeasible right; as they and their ancestors, were freeborn subjects, justly and naturally entitled to all the rights and advantages of the British constitution.[43]

It is important to note the use here of the language of "inherent, indefeasible rights" to describe rights that are based, not on natural rights, but on the common law. Rights from the British constitution were also thought to be "inherent," "inalienable," "indefeasible," and "indubitable." The fact that the language of inherent rights can describe rights that originate in either common law or from other sources is significant. We shall see that the colonists sometimes prefer the language of "inherent" rights to "natural rights" and seemingly take advantage of the ambiguity about which type of right they are talking about. A possible example of such ambiguity in Jefferson's own language in the Declaration of Independence has already been discussed, and we will see other examples in the Stamp Act Resolves.

Having established that Americans have equal rights with the English, and therefore the right not to be taxed without representation, Hopkins goes on to consider the respective orbits of Parliament and local American legislatures. Parliament has supreme authority to regulate "things of a more general nature, quite out of the reach of these particular legislatures, which it is necessary should be regulated, ordered and governed. One of this kind is the commerce of the whole British empire, taken collectively, and that of each kingdom and colony in it as it makes a part of that whole."[44]

By contrast, Hopkins argues Parliament has no right to tax the colonies because it does not represent them.

> If the British house of commons are rightfully possessed of a power to tax the colonies in America, this power must be vested in them by the British constitution, as they are one branch of the great legislative body of the nation. As they are the representatives of all the people in Britain, they have, beyond doubt, all the power such a representation can possibly give; yet, great as this power is, surely it cannot exceed that of their constituents. And can it possibly be shown that the power in Britain have a sovereign authority over their fellow subjects in America? Yet such is the authority that must be exercised in taking people's estates from them by taxes, or otherwise, without their consent. In all aids granted to the crown by the Parliament, it is said with the greatest propriety, "We freely give unto Your Majesty;" for they give their own money and the money of those who have entrusted them with a proper power for that purpose. But can they with the same propriety, give away the money of the Americans, who have never given any such power?[45]

Now if this argument and position sound confusing and inconsistent, some American and British readers of Hopkins thought so, too. Hopkins is arguing that the colonies are part of the historic social contract for the purposes of British rights, but with respect to taxes they were not represented by and thus not subject to the supreme authority of Parliament. Yet the colonies are subject to parliamentary authority for the purposes of trade regulations and other laws which are necessary for the good of the whole. Governor Fitch struggles to express the same point in his essay.[46]

How is it that the colonies can be subject to Parliament's authority on one set of matters but not another? Are the colonies subordinate to Parliament or not? In attempting to answer this question, Hopkins offers an early version of the "hub and spokes" vision of the empire in which the colonies are each independent spokes with equal rights.

> In an imperial state, which consists of many separate governments, each of which hath peculiar privileges and of which kind it is evident the empire of Great Britain is, no single part, though greater than another part, is by that superiority entitled to make laws for, or to tax such lesser part; but all laws, and all taxations which bind the whole must be made by the whole.[47]

In this view of the empire, the house of commons, though part of Parliament, was really just another separate legislature (or spoke) parallel to the legislatures of other parts. This was a fairly radical reinterpretation of Parliament, as critics would shortly point out. Hopkins is here anticipating a view of the empire that is developed in more detail by Richard Bland in his pamphlet *An Inquiry Into the Rights of the British Colonies* and Thomas Jefferson in his *A Summary View*.[48] Other colonial writers, like Fitch and James Otis, did not venture as far as Hopkins, acknowledging instead that the colonial legislatures were subordinate to Parliament and the House of Commons. Yet even in this subordinate position, writers like Fitch argued that the House of Commons still did not have a right to tax the colonies.

The Challenge to British Rights and Arguments from Birthright

So far we have seen that one group of colonial writers ignored natural rights arguments, believing that their arguments for colonial rights would be more readily accepted when starting from an uncontested foundation in British rights. They soon learned that their extrapolations from that starting point too were hotly contested by critics both at home and abroad. The criticisms of the "British rights" or "birthright" argument encouraged some colonial writers to look for a grounding of rights outside of the British constitution and common law.

It will be helpful to take a brief look at some early responses to Hopkins and Fitch, by critics such as Martin Howard, Soame Jenyns, and Thomas Whately in England. These critics tended to concede the fact that Americans had British rights. Yet they drew very different conclusions. They argued that since Americans enjoyed British rights, they were also subject to parliamentary authority for all matters, including taxes. As Howard puts it, commenting on Hopkins' essay:

> However disguised, polished, or softened the expression of this pamphlet may seem, yet everyone must see that its professed design is sufficiently prominent throughout, namely, to prove that the colonies have rights independent of, and not controllable by the authority of Parliament. It is upon this dangerous and indiscreet position I shall communicate to you my real sentiments.[49]

It is not exactly true that Hopkins appeals to rights independent of and not controlled by Parliament. Hopkins did not appeal to natural rights. But Hopkins did think there was a limitation on parliamentary power to act without the consent of the people. He saw that limitation deriving from the British original contract itself, not from natural rights per se. Whether this meant that "the colonies have rights independent of, and not controllable by the authority of Parliament" would not have been the way Hopkins would have said it.[50] But Howard characterized Hopkins position this way and thus drew a line in the sand that said "no rights limit Parliament's power." Howard thus accuses Hopkins of being a hypocrite. As Howard put it:

> Can we claim the common law as an inheritance and at the same time be at liberty to adopt one part of it and reject the other? Indeed we cannot. The common law, pure and indivisible in its nature and essence, cleaves to us during our lives and follows us from Nova Zembla to Cape Horn; and therefore, as the jurisdiction of Parliament arises out of and is supported by it, we may as well renounce our allegiance or change our nature as to be exempt from the jurisdiction of Parliament. Hence it is plain to me that in denying this jurisdiction we at the same time take leave of the common law, and thereby, with equal temerity and folly, strip

ourselves of every blessing we enjoy as Englishmen: a flagrant proof, this, that shallow drafts in politics and legislation confound and distract us, and that an extravagant zeal often defeats its own purposes.[51]

The assumption here is that the status of British subject will follow a person across geographies, an assumption accepted by many colonial writers. The common law "cleaves to us." And as it cleaves to us, it gives us both rights but also subjects us to the power of Parliament. With respect to the colonists' core claim that "they can't be taxed without representation," Howard offers an alternative view of "representation." In his view, the House of Commons by definition represents all British subjects everywhere.

> It is the opinion of the House of Commons, and may be considered as a law of Parliament, that they are the representatives of every British subject, wheresoever he be. In this view of the matter, then, the aforegoing maxim is fully vindicated in practice, and the whole benefit of it, in substance and effect, extended and applied to the colonies…
>
> In truth, my friend, the matter lies here: the freedom and happiness of every British subject depends not upon his share in elections but upon the sense and virtue of the British Parliament, and these depend reciprocally upon the sense and virtue of the whole nation.[52]

Howard does not quite claim that the colonists are "virtually represented" which is the way Thomas Whately, the official spokesperson of Lord Grenville, later describes it in the spring of 1765 in his famous *The Regulations Lately Made*. Here Howard essentially says the same thing. The House of Commons is by definition or in fact the representative of the British people. By being elected, the members become representatives of the people as a whole, whether those people voted for representatives or not. Moreover, he argues that "freedom and happiness" rely not on representation per se but on the virtue of those who govern for the good of the whole. We see then that Howard agrees that representation is important but redefines what counts as a fulfillment of that requirement.

Soame Jenyns, a member of Parliament and member of the Board of Trade for ten years before the Stamp Act controversy, takes a different tack with regard to representation. In the spring of 1765, he wrote a pamphlet entitled *The Objections to the Taxation of our American Colonies by the Legislature of Great Britain, briefly consider'd* which was reprinted almost immediately in colonial newspapers. Jenyns in effect argues that there is no guarantee of representation in the British constitution. Individuals never consent to taxes, nor do all individuals have representatives in Parliament,[53]

> for every Englishman is taxed, and not one in twenty represented: copyholders, leaseholders, and all men possessed of personal property only, chuse no representatives; Manchester, Birmingham, and many more of our richest and most flourishing trading towns send no members to parliament, consequently cannot consent by their representatives, because they chuse none to represent them; yet are they not Englishmen? or are they not taxed?[54]

In Jenyns view, representation is not given to every town or every category of person. Yet they still remain Englishmen and subject to the authority of Parliament. Anticipating that the defenders of colonial rights might appeal to thinkers such as Locke and Sydney in their arguments about rights and liberty, Jenyns has this to say:

> I am well aware, that I shall hear Locke, Sidney, Selden, and many other great names quoted to prove that every Englishman, whether he has a right to vote for a representative, or not, is still represented in the British Parliament; in which opinion they all agree: on what principle of common sense this opinion is founded I comprehend not, but on the authority of such respectable names I shall acknowledge its truth; but then I will ask one question, and on that I will rest the whole merits of the cause: Why does not this imaginary representation extend to America, as well

as over the whole island of Great-Britain? If it can travel three hundred miles, why not three thousand? if it can jump over rivers and mountains, why cannot it sail over the ocean? If the towns of Manchester and Birmingham sending no representatives to parliament, are notwithstanding there represented, why are not the cities of Albany and Boston equally represented in that assembly? Are they not alike British subjects? are they not Englishmen? or are they only Englishmen when they sollicit for protection, but not Englishmen when taxes are required to enable this country to protect them?

This statement is interesting precisely in showing us how one British Parliament member misconstrued the potential implications of an American argument from Locke or natural rights. Jenyns assumes that if Locke or Sydney were evoked, they would be used to justify the idea that British subjects are represented in Parliament even without sending representatives to Parliament. If that is the case of subjects living in England, couldn't the same be true of subjects living in America? But that, of course, is precisely the opposite of what the colonists were arguing. They were arguing that one had to have representatives in Parliament. And they argued that representation could not reach across the ocean, as geographical distance did undermine the ability to be represented by people not subject to the laws they were legislating.

These critical responses by British and British American contemporaries of Hopkins help us understand the place of Locke and natural rights arguments in the early resistance literature. First, they show that the early champions of colonial rights were correct in expecting push back on natural rights arguments from their British and local colonial critics. These early defenders of parliamentary authority—both in the colonies and England—argue that there is no source of rights outside the British common law tradition. But they go further. Since rights and parliamentary authority both derive from the common law tradition, they argue there can be no source of rights that supersede Parliament's authority. If you build your case on British rights, you are completely subservient to parliamentary authority.

The critics' arguments about representation further underscored the need for some set of rights that could be anchored outside of the British constitution. That some critics like Soame Jenyns could even argue that "representation" was not even a right at all, or, like Howard, that the colonies were by definition represented in the Parliament even though they had no representatives, underscored the growing need to look for secure footing for rights elsewhere. After all, representation was arguably core to Locke's arguments about natural rights. Locke had argued that the whole people had a right to vote. But due to the inconvenience of gathering everyone in one place for a vote, the consent of the majority should be received as the act of the whole.[55] Locke's statements imply that everyone should be represented, but he did not give details on how that representation should be worked out in practice.[56] At issue in the debate between advocates of colonial rights and their critics is precisely the question of what constitutes adequate representation.

It is now understandable why, over time, an appeal to rights outside of the British common law may have looked more appealing to some colonists. It was not just the growing impulse towards independence, as some historians have suggested. If British rights do not limit Parliament's authority, then surely natural rights, which exist outside of and prior to common law, can. The colonists needed to find some grounding for rights outside of British common law to limit Parliament's authority.

In sum, the colonists were caught on the horns of a dilemma. They thought the appeal to Locke's social compact theory and natural rights was fraught with problems since the origin of government was contested and "chimerical." Some of them also worried that natural rights were not sufficiently religious. But their attempt to ground American rights in common law did not provide them with sufficient grounds to justify a limitation on Parliament's authority. Some set of rights was needed that derived from sources beyond the constitution which was the source of Parliament's own power and right.

3. Early Doubts about Natural Rights Before the Revolution 113

James Otis and Doubts about Social Compact

While Stephen Hopkins appealed to British rights to avoid the doubts about natural rights and social compact theory, James Otis is one of the first colonial writers who tries to navigate the horns of the dilemma in a different way. Recall that Otis offered an extensive list of potential criticisms of Locke's social contract theory. But instead of turning away from natural rights, the way Hopkins and others did, Otis offers an alternative theory of government's origin, basing it on human nature and the will of God. "I think it has an everlasting foundation in the unchangeable will of God, the author of nature, whose laws never vary…Government is therefore most evidently founded on the necessities of our nature. It is by no means an arbitrary thing depending merely on compact or human will for its existence."[57]

In Otis's view, there is no social compact or contract where people leave nature and enter society. *In fact, there is no state of nature at all*. This is a very significant deviation from Locke's conceptions of natural rights. In Otis's conception, we are born as sexual creatures.

> "The same omniscient, omnipotent, infinitely good and gracious Creator of the universe who made it necessary that what we call matter should *gravitate* for the celestial bodies to roll round their axes…has made it *equally* necessary that from *Adam and Eve* to these degenerate days the different sexes should sweetly *attract* each other, form societies of *single* families, of which *larger* bodies and communities are as naturally, mechanically, and necessarily combined as the dew of heaven and the soft distilling rain is collected by the all-enlivening heat of the sun.[58]

> Government is founded *immediately* on the necessities of human nature, and *ultimately* on the will of God, the author of nature; who has not left it to men in general to choose whether they will be members of society or not, but at the hazard of their senses if not of their lives?[59]

What is interesting about Otis's theory of government is that it does not seem all that far from Locke's theory, at least with respect to its implications for natural rights. Otis trots out all many of the familiar principles of natural rights: there needs to be a supreme power over society which can adjudicate law, and this supreme authority is originally in the people. The people can never renounce this divine right. This power is given in trust to government, which should incessantly consult the people's good. When the size of the people becomes too large or dispersed to consult, they have a right to representation. All of this sounds very much like Locke and other writers in the natural rights tradition.[60] Otis even praises Locke favorably on several occasions and denigrates Grotius and Pufendorf, though one might argue that his theory sounds more like Grotius's than Locke's.[61] In all of these ways, Otis seems to fit within a Lockean tradition. But it would be problematic to simply characterize him that way without qualification.[62]

There are significant points of departure from Locke in the idea of the "social compact," the state of nature, and the religiously tinged language that Otis uses. Otis abandons Locke's assumption that people have a choice about government. They do not live in a state of nature and do not consent to enter government. Government is a necessity, as much a part of our natures as the need to procreate. There is no state of nature prior to society. Government emerges with human life, and thus is not an arbitrary decision or choice.[63]

These are a significant departure from Locke and indeed, one could argue, revert to the very position that Locke was criticizing. For Locke formulated his *Second Treatise* principally as a refutation of Sir Robert Filmer's *Patriarcha,* which had argued that government had been instituted by God at creation.[64] Filmer argued that government was not by choice, that there was no original liberty, and that the original father of humankind, Adam, had regal powers which were inherited by later monarchs. This royalist argument denied that "all people were created equal" and also that government occurred through a social contract. A principle aim of Locke's *First and Second Treatises on Government* was to refute Filmer and to argue that government was not founded at creation,

3. Early Doubts about Natural Rights Before the Revolution   115

that people were born into a state of natural liberty, and that government came about only when individuals chose to renounce some natural rights and enter into political societies. The position of Otis, ironically, almost amounts to a reversal of the Lockean position and a return to the position of the royalist Filmer.

Nonetheless, Otis does attempt to secure American rights in what he also calls "natural rights," but he has reinterpreted what natural rights means and tries to avoid some of the problematic challenges that he knows have been leveled against Locke's social compact theory. For the more empirically oriented readers who may doubt the historical origin of government in social compact, Otis dispenses with that problem by anchoring government in human creation. There never was or needed to be a historical social compact. Don't bother looking for one. Government is founded in our natures.

And for the religious readers who preferred a theory of "divine appointment," Otis puts much more emphasis on God's role in creating government and anchoring it in human nature. Government is not an arbitrary decision or choice by human beings but was created by God. In doing so, Otis is reaching out to more traditionally religious Christian readers. Indeed, what Otis has done, essentially, is provide a justification of "natural rights" with a different more religiously tinged account of government's origin. Now government is given by God. That Otis is trying to reach more religiously oriented readers is evident by the religious and theological rhetoric in which he couches his theory. "I think it has an everlasting foundation in the unchangeable will of God, the author of nature, whose laws never vary."[65]

> We have a King who neither slumbers nor sleeps, but eternally watches for our good, whose rain falls on the just and on the unjust: yet while they live, move, and have their being in Him, and cannot account for either or for anything else, so stupid and wicked are some men as to deny his existence, blaspheme his most evident government, and disgrace their nature.[66]

Locke, of course, also believed natural rights were founded in God's law (in contrast to Grotius, for example, who did not).[67] But Locke never used this kind of theologically tinged language, at least in his *Second Treatise*. The difference is one of both tone and substance. Locke was actually breaking free from more traditional theological ways of describing God and God's law and moving towards a new understanding of religion founded in reason. His *Second Treatise*, though quoting scripture occasionally, is noticeably light on scriptural interpretations, in contrast, for example, to his *First Treatise*, which was a direct refutation of Filmer and represents a natural rights reading of Genesis. Locke was writing at the beginning of the great deist critique of religion, which fundamentally subjected the notion of revealed religion to criticism by appeal to the religion of reason. Though Locke never went as far as many deists, and ultimately believed the religion of reason and revealed revelation were compatible, some colonists wanted a more theological tone and emphasis than Locke had provided.[68]

That American colonial readers found some tension to resolve between Locke's theories and their religious sensitivities is already evident in writings prior to the Stamp Act controversy. In 1762, several years before the Stamp Act controversy, Abraham Williams reflected on the origin and end of government in "An Election Sermon," those sermons given on election days in the colonies. For a sermon to his Congregationalist pulpit in Sandwich, near Boston, he writes:

> As to the origin of civil Societies or Governments; the Author of our Being, has given Man a Nature fitted for, and disposed to Society. It was not good for Man at first to be *alone*; his Nature is social, having various Affections, Propensities, and Passions, which respect Society and cannot be indulged without a social Intercourse. The natural Principles of Benevolence, Compassions, Justice, and indeed most of our natural Affections, powerfully incite to, and plainly indicate, that Man was formed for Society.[69]

Here, and in Otis, too, Locke's main ideas are being affirmed, but in religious overtones and language that make Lockean ideas seem more

3. Early Doubts about Natural Rights Before the Revolution   117

traditionally religious than Locke's own writing in the *Second Treatise*. And there is much more emphasis placed on God's role in creating government than in the notion of social compact or consent.

> And Government is a divine Constitution, founded in the Nature and Relations of Things,—agreeable to the Will of God,—what the Circumstances of his Creatures require:—And when Men enter into civil Societies, and agree upon rational Forms of Government, they act right, conformable to the Will of God, by the Concurrence of whose providence, Rulers are appointed.[70]

When "men enter into civil societies," they are conforming to God's plan and will. In Locke, by contrast, it is entirely up to people whether to choose society, although there are good reasons for doing so and people are inclined to do so because of their natures.[71] A similar shift in emphasis occurs here with regard to elected officials. "In all Governments, *Magistrates* are *God's Ministers*, designed *for Good to the People*. The end of their Institution is to be Instruments of Divine providence, to secure and promote the Happiness of Society."[72] The notion that magistrates are described as God's ministers, rather than as elected officials of the people, if not a complete substantive change, at least represents a significant shift in emphasis.

These statements are arguably reinterpretations of Lockean theory. We are both within a Lockean milieu and outside it. The attempt here is clearly to bring ideas of government much closer to traditional religious language, wrap religious texts and language around natural rights ideas, and ensure that God's role in the creation of government is underscored. Otis's account of government's origin moves in much the same terrain. But in the process of "theologizing" Locke and natural rights, something different emerges, not quite a theory of natural rights as propounded by Locke, but not entirely different either.

The upshot is that one can read Otis as attempting to save core Lockean ideas of consent, natural rights, and right to representation, by jettisoning the historically problematic assumptions of social compact and shoring up the religious overtones. Now Otis has a theory of natural rights that should appeal to his more traditionally Christian-minded readers and that escapes the criticisms of his empirically oriented readers—those who may been persuaded by Hume—and who are skeptical about the historical origin of social compact. Otis, in other words, has tried to solve the same problem that Hopkins had described in the start of his essay.

With this philosophical backdrop in hand, Otis turns to the rights of the colonies. Like Hopkins and Fitch, he too argues that Americans have British rights derived from the common law. But he does not rest his whole argument on British rights alone. He also argues that the colonists have "natural rights." Natural rights, in Otis's terminology, mean rights given by God and embedded in our natures, not a law of nature, which was known by reason.

Otis acknowledges that his own theory of government might not be accepted. Be that as it may, if not everyone can agree on the origin of government, they can at least agree on its end. "The end of government being the good of mankind points out its great duties: it is above all things to provide for the security, the quiet, and happy enjoyment of life, liberty and property."[73] Locke too spoke often about "the end of government." Here in the context of the American scene, the use of the word "end" carries additional overtones, as discussed earlier. By emphasizing the end of government, dispute or worry about the uncertainty of government's beginning is ignored. As Otis puts it, "But let the origin of government be placed where it may, the end of it is manifestly the good of the whole."[74] The colonial emphasis on government's "end" is therefore language that helps justify the commitment to individual rights while setting aside the problematic question of how historical governments began. This approach was one way of splitting the question of right (the normative question) from the question of historical origin.[75] By agreeing on the end of government, the colonists could paper over their differences on how government began. But they would have to do so by ignoring the fact that they disagreed about how to justify what the "end" of government really was.

Having explicated his notion of natural rights, Otis repeatedly ties together British rights and natural rights. "Every British subject born on the continent of America or in any other of the British dominions is by the law of God and nature, by the common law, and by act of Parliament (exclusive of all the charters from the crown) entitled to all the natural, essential, inherent and inseparable rights of our fellow subjects in Great Britain."[76] Based on these assumptions, Otis keeps repeating that Americans are not just "subjects" but also "men", meaning entitled to rights that belong to human beings in general and not just British subjects.[77]

Because the colonists have rights in their nature, their rights don't depend on the colonial charters, as Hopkins and Fitch, among others, argued. For Otis, it did not matter, therefore, if the charters were or had been declared void.

> What could follow from all this that would shake one of the essential, natural, civil, or religious rights of the colonists? Nothing. They would be men, citizens, and British subjects after all. No act of Parliament can deprive them of the liberties of such, unless any will contend that an act of Parliament can make slaves not only of one but of two millions of the commonwealth.[78]

Because natural rights originate in nature and not in the British constitution, they do serve as a source of right and wrong, independent of Parliament's own discretion.

> Parliaments are in all cases to *declare* what is for the good of the whole; but it is not the *declaration* of Parliament that makes it so. There must be in every instance a higher authority, viz., God. Should an act of Parliament be against any of *his* natural laws, which are *immutably* true, *their* declaration would be contrary to external truth, equity and justice and consequently void. And so it would be adjudged by the Parliament itself when convinced of their mistake.[79]

Natural rights, which are God's law, exist outside of the British constitution and thus serve as a standard against which the justice and right of Parliament's decisions can be measured. Otis does not take the final step and argue that Parliament's authority over the colonies is limited. He draws back from crossing that line and leaves that for others to do. But he does argue that Parliament can be wrong, even though the colonies must obey Parliament until it is brought to its senses. Thus natural rights serve as a standard by which to measure the rightness of Parliament's decisions. But they do not limit Parliament's authority. All the colonies can do is point out the mistake and hope Parliament is brought to its senses.

Critics of Otis, such as Martin Howard, discussed earlier, accused Otis of crossing the line and claiming that Parliament's authority was limited. And one can see why critics would read Otis that way. For even if Otis did not quite go there, it would not be a difficult next step to use natural rights to justify a limitation on Parliament's authority and to make claims for independence. In a later essay penned by Otis in response to Howard's criticisms, Otis himself does seem to back down from his claims somewhat, but he does not renounce the use of natural rights as a source of right and wrong.[80]

Natural Rights and Stamp Act Resolutions

The Stamp Act was passed into legislation by Parliament in March 1765, one year after the original announcement, ignoring all the colonies' petitions and protests in the intervening year. In response, many of the colonies came out with various Stamp Act resolves. Symptoms of the colonies' continued ambivalence towards natural rights is evident in the various Stamp Act Resolutions adopted by many of the colonies and the Stamp Act Congress, in which the colonies came together in New York to provide a united response.

In May 1765, the first set of resolutions, proposed by Patrick Henry, was adopted by the Virginia House of Burgesses in a controversial meeting after part of the assembly had already recessed. Only four of Henry's original resolutions were adopted, and Henry was apparently accused of sedition for some of his statements, although it is not entirely clear what the grounds of this charge were, and they may possibly have been an innuendo suggesting revolution.[81]

The Virginia Resolves make no mention at all of natural rights and base the colonial rights, in order of the resolutions, on the facts (1) that the early Virginia settlers brought their rights with them, (2) that their rights were affirmed in two Royal Charters of King James, (3) "[t]hat the Taxation of the People by themselves, or by Persons chosen by themselves to represent them" are the "distinguishing Characteristick of British Freedom, without which the ancient Constitution cannot exist," and (4) "[t]hat his Majesty's liege People of this his most ancient and loyal Colony have without Interruption enjoyed the inestimable Right of being governed by such Laws...and that the same hath never been forfeited or yielded up..."[82]

Even after the Boston riots in August 1765, some of the colonial resolves still make no mention of natural rights. For example, no mention of natural rights is made in the Rhode Island Resolves (September 1765) nor in the Maryland Resolves (September 28, 1765).[83]

Given that some colonial Americans were ambivalent about the use of natural rights, it is not surprising that no mention of natural rights is made in the Declaration of Rights of the Stamp Act Congress, published in October 1765. The idea for the Stamp Act Congress seems to have been suggested by James Otis who, in early June, asked the Massachusetts legislature to send a circular to invite all the colonies to a congress in New York.[84] Representatives from nine colonies attended, though only six were empowered to sign the resolves. The resolves rest primarily on British rights, with a hint of more universal rights:

> 1st. That His Majesty's subjects in these colonies owe the same allegiance to the crown of Great Britain that is owing from his subjects born within the realm, and all due subordination to that august body, the Parliament of Great Britain.
>
> 2d. That His Majesty's liege subjects in these colonies are entitled to all the inherent rights and privileges of his natural born subjects within the kingdom of Great Britain.

3d. That it is inseparably essential to the freedom of a people, and the undoubted rights of Englishmen, that no taxes should be imposed on them, but with their own consent, given personally, or by their representatives.

4th. That the people of these colonies are not, and from their local circumstances cannot be, represented in the House of Commons in Great Britain.

5th. That the only representatives of the people of these colonies are persons chosen therein, by themselves; and that no taxes ever have been or can be constitutionally imposed on them but by their respective legislatures...[85]

It took the Stamp Act Congress twelve days to come to the wording of its resolutions. There was debate over how much of Parliament's authority to acknowledge and a general consensus that Parliament had a right to regulate trade, though some of the participants did not want to make such an explicit acknowledgement.

Morgan notes that there were two drafts of the resolves that tried out different language regarding the colonists' subordination to Parliament and the basis of rights.[86] The first stated that "all Acts of Parliament not inconsistent with the Rights and Liberties of the Colonists are obligatory upon them." Here the language of "rights and liberties" is completely equivocal as to whether natural or British rights are being discussed.

A second draft tries a more universal approach: "all Acts of Parliament not inconsistent with the Principles of Freedom are obligatory upon the Colonists." This wording may allude to general principles of freedom that apparently are not dependent on any specific British constitution or colonial charters. This phrasing, however, was also abandoned for the final wording of the first resolution that his Majesty's subjects owe "all due Subordination to that August Body the Parliament of Great-Britain."[87] "All due Subordination," of course, equivocates completely on the question of what type of rights the colonists stand on and whether they limit at all Parliament's authority.

But the appeal to general rights did make it into the third resolve. Here the statement that "it is inseparably essential to the freedom of a people" is an allusion to rights outside of strictly British rights. It is the freedom of "a people," not just "the British people." One could infer that natural rights were being addressed here. But the language clearly leaves open the question as to the source and character of those rights. Are they from nature, from divine appointment, human nature, or some other source? Are they discerned by reason or written on the heart? By not specifying "nature" as the source, the resolves equivocate on what theory of rights lies behind the general claims about freedom. It is not surprising that the emphasis in the first few resolves is on British rights, not these general essential freedoms. Since the Stamp Act Congress had to speak for a broader audience and a consensus across colonies, it opted for the "lowest common denominator" and based the colonial claims primarily on British rights.

During the Stamp Act Congress there was discussion of adding in more general rights language but this was rejected. In a letter after the Congress, Christopher Gadsden of South Carolina reflected on the discussion.

> I have ever been of opinion, that we should all endeavor to stand upon the broad and common ground of those natural and inherent rights that we all feel and know, as men and as descendants of Englishmen, we have a right to, and have always thought this bottom amply sufficient for our future importance...There ought to be no New England men, no New Yorker, &c., known on the Continent, but all of us Americans; a *confirmation* of our essential and common rights as Englishmen may be pleaded from the Charters safely enough, but any further dependence on them may be fatal.[88]

Gadsden puts his finger on one key reason why natural rights might be a stronger foundation of argument than colonial charters. Natural rights are common rights that are shared across the colonies and thus enable each colony to be united in its joint claims. They would enable the colonies to argue, not as members of individual colonies, but as Americans or "men" in general. Unification of identity across the colonies in a common cause was one reason why natural rights arguments began to take on more prominence.

If the Stamp Act Congress remained somewhat equivocal in its use of natural rights, some individual colonies were willing to be bolder, signaling a shift in attitude towards natural rights arguments.[89] On September 21, 1765, the Pennsylvania Assembly added an appeal to natural rights to its list of resolves alongside of an appeal to an inherent birthright:

> Resolved, N. C. D. 3. That the inhabitants of this Province are entitled to all the Liberties, Rights and Privileges of his Majesty's Subjects in Great-Britain, or elsewhere, and that the Constitution of Government in this Province is founded on the natural Rights of Mankind, and the noble Principles of English Liberty, and therefore is, or ought to be, perfectly free.

> Resolved, N. C. D. 4. That it is the inherent Birth-right, and indubitable Privilege, of every British Subject, to be taxed only by his own Consent, or that of his legal Representatives, in Conjunction with his Majesty, or his Substitutes.[90]

The Massachusetts Resolves (October 29, 1765) take this line of thinking even further. Instead of just setting universal rights and British rights claims side by side, as do the Pennsylvania Resolves, the Massachusetts Resolves implicitly argue that the latter are derived from the former:

> Resolved, That there are certain essential Rights of the *British Constitution* of Government, which are founded in the Law of God and Nature, and are the common Rights of Mankind—therefore

> II. Resolved,—That the inhabitants of this province are unalienable entitled to those essential rights in common with all men: and that no law of society can, consistent with the law of God and nature, divest them of those rights.

III. Resolved,—That no man can justly take the property of another without his consent; and that upon this original principle the right of representation in the same body, which exercises the power of making laws for levying taxes, which is one of the main pillars of the British constitution, is evidently founded....[91]

The first three resolves anchor essential rights of the British Constitution in more general universal rights. Nothing can divest anyone of those rights since they are based on the law of God and nature. After arguing that the British Constitution is founded in these general rights, the resolutions go on to make arguments from other sources of rights as well, including, charters and equity.

It is interesting to note that these Massachusetts Resolves do not use the expression "natural rights," preferring the expressions "common Rights of Mankind," "essential rights in common with all men, and "original principle" "which are founded in the Law of God and Nature."

As noted earlier, it is possible the expressions "common rights" and "inherent and unalienable rights" are simply an alternative equivalent way of saying "natural rights." That is how most people interpret comparable language in the Declaration of Independence, for example. But it depends on how one construes the statement "founded in the Law of God and Nature" which appears in two of the resolves. As we have seen, natural rights theory was troubling to some precisely in the role of God and humans in the creation of government. We have seen in writers like Otis and Williams a desire to more strongly emphasize the role of God in creating society and government. Beyond these two writers, moreover, there was in fact a rich American literature of "political sermons" that brought Christian theology, scriptural exegesis, and theory of government much more evidently together. The effort to bring together and intertwine these theological conceptions with classic Lockean ideas of consent, the law of nature and liberty at a minimum, transformed and in some cases arguably fundamentally changed the natural rights tradition. We shall see some further examples of this theological discourse on rights below.

It is possible, although not provable, that the expression "founded in the Law of God and Nature" really equivocates to some extent on the origin of rights and attempts to be much more inclusive and open, leaving ambiguous the precise origin and nature of these common rights. The appearance of and priority given to "God" in the expression "God and Nature" in these Massachusetts resolves, and the avoidance of the term "natural rights," therefore may signal a kind of distancing from traditional Lockean natural rights theory, or at least a move to be more inclusive of more religious-oriented conceptions of rights, liberty, and political society.[92] This language possibly symbolically strips natural rights theory of its problematic Lockean historical assumptions and tries to appeal to a broader audience that sees God and Christian concepts as much more central to the origin of society, rights, and government. It is as if the resolves want to argue for general human rights, without making a specific commitment to which theory of rights they rely on. The language enables both the more Lockean oriented theory and the religiously oriented theory of rights to be embraced in this general allusion to rights.

At the same time, another set of colonial resolves makes one of the most radical uses of natural rights thus far examined. The Connecticut Resolutions of December 10, 1765 appeal to natural rights to justify the dissolution of society and armed revolt.[93] In linking natural rights to revolt, these resolves signal a shift in the debate and in the use of natural rights, now referring not to rights to be equal with British subjects, but rights to leave and abandon British society. In making this link, these resolves go where Otis was not yet willing to go and anticipate more detailed arguments of the same type in a pamphlet by Richard Bland, which would follow in the spring.

> Resolved, 1st. That every form of government rightfully founded, originates from the consent of the people.
>
> 2d. That the boundaries set by the people in all constitutions are the only limits within which any officer can lawfully exercise authority.

3d. That whenever those bounds are exceeded, the people have a right to reassume the exercise of that authority which by nature they had before they delegated it to individuals.

4th. That every tax imposed upon English subjects without consent is against the natural rights and the bounds prescribed by the English constitution.

5th. That the Stamp Act in special, is a tax imposed on the colonies without their consent.

6th. That it is the duty of every person in the colonies to oppose by every lawful means the execution of those acts imposed on them, and if they can in no other way be relieved, to reassume their natural rights and the authority the laws of nature and of God have vested them with.[94]

Here the Connecticut resolves make one of the most explicit and radical uses of natural rights theories examined so far. We see an explicitly Lockean view that governments "rightfully founded" derive from the consent of the people. The people's consent, represented in the constitution, sets the limits on authority, and "the people" can take back that authority "which by nature they had delegated" to authorities. This is not merely a right. It is a duty to oppose laws that infringe the boundaries set by the people in their constitution. If there is no legal way to ensure that those boundaries are preserved, they must "reassume their natural rights and the authority the laws of nature and of God have vested them with."

Not coincidentally, this more radical use of natural rights appeared about the same time that the Sons of Liberty groups began to formally constitute themselves as distinctive groups and began to announce their willingness to resist by force.[95] Yet interestingly enough, even the charters of the Sons of Liberty, who organized specifically to offer resistance, did not consistently appeal to natural rights.[96] Here again we see that that the impulse towards resistance did not inevitably lead to a use of natural rights arguments.

To sum up our findings in this chapter, we have explored colonial ambivalence towards parts of natural rights theory in the early part of the decade before the American Revolution. The grounding of natural rights in the social contract was viewed as problematic for two reasons: first, because it rested on a purported historical origin of government that was unproven, and second, because it did not seem "religious enough" to those who argued government was appointed by God, not the outcome of human choice. There were several different responses to this dilemma. Hopkins chose to avoid using natural rights completely, though he acknowledged finding it the most rational explanation of government's origin. Otis tried a different route, repudiating both the dependence of natural rights on a historical social compact and renouncing the social compact part of Locke's theory, thereby "theologizing" Locke for more traditionally religious oriented readers. Whether one wants to still call this Lockean or natural rights theory is an interesting question, but if we choose to do so, we at least have to see that Locke has been transformed and changed. This ambivalence towards Locke that we have just reviewed is evident in 1764, more than ten years before Jefferson writes the Declaration of Independence. As we shall see in the next chapter, such ambivalence continues to animate colonial discussions in some ways even as new theories of rights are worked out.

4. Diverging Theories of American Rights Before Jefferson

By the time of the Stamp Act controversy discussed previously, Jefferson (born in 1743) was already twenty-two years old. He had already graduated from the College of William and Mary (1760–62) and studied law with his mentor, George Wythe. Jefferson took his bar exam in 1765 and was studying for the bar at the same time as the Stamp Act Controversy.[1] We know very little about how Jefferson reacted to the colonial writings and events surrounding the Stamp Act Controversy, as we shall see in a later chapter. He may have witnessed Patrick Henry give his famous speech in the Virginia House of Burgesses. And we know he was in Maryland when that colony published its Stamp Act Resolves.[2] But much about Jefferson's own reaction to the Stamp Act Controversy is unknown. While Jefferson kept journals or what are called "commonplace" books with notes on his readings, he did not keep reflective notebooks the way that other colonial writers, such as John Adams, did. Jefferson's letters during this time are noticeably silent on the major events of the day, being preoccupied more with other matters, such as his love life. One has to extrapolate from his reading, and guesses about the timeline of his reading, what his reactions were to these early colonial controversies. We shall look in more detail at this young Jefferson later, when we go backward and try to make sense of what he thought before his first major foray into political writing.

Jefferson would only write his first major theoretical piece on political rights in the summer of 1774, some nine years after the Stamp

Act controversy had subsided. By then most if not all the major theoretical positions on colonial rights had been articulated by leading colonial leaders and writers. In this chapter, I look first at several types of theoretical positions that had developed in the colonies during this period as a backdrop against which to situate Jefferson's first major piece of political writing: *A Summary View*. The goal is to place Jefferson in the broad spectrum of thinking on rights that had developed in the colonies since the end of the Stamp Act controversy. A number of questions preoccupy us in this effort.

First, what happens to the early ambivalence towards natural rights evident in the first writings of colonial writers in response to the Stamp Act controversy? Does this ambivalence persist or is there an almost natural, inexorable move to natural rights arguments, as some theorists suggest?[3] Second, are there any signs that this early ambivalence towards natural rights influenced Jefferson's own thinking in his first major writing on political rights? Third, among those who turn to natural rights type arguments, was there a consistent, monolithic view of rights or a conflict of views? Finally, what position did Jefferson lean towards in this spectrum of American colonial thinking?

To frame our discussion of Jefferson's essay, we look first at the various types of theories that had bubbled to the surface in the period following the Stamp Act crisis. The goal is not to be exhaustive but to point to certain "ideal types," to invoke a Weberian concept, to illustrate the various tendencies and impulses in the colonial writing and to situate Jefferson among other kinds of responses.

Categories of Natural Rights Arguments

By the end of the Stamp Act controversy, colonial positions on rights had been staked out in major outline, but there was by no means a consensus on whether natural rights arguments were considered a solid or feeble foundation for colonial rights. Instead there were various inconsistent positions or "fault lines" that remain visible into the late 1760s and into the 1770s leading up to the Revolution. The Declaration of Independence both nods towards and papers over the differences of several of these various positions on natural rights.

Depending how one counts them, there are four or five fairly defined positions on natural rights arguments in this period of colonial writing. First, some writers avoid natural rights arguments completely, suggesting continued ambivalence towards these kinds of arguments. Other writers appeal to some form of natural rights. But among these, there are several different and arguably conflicting ways in which natural rights get developed.[4]

One strand of writing that appeals to natural rights relies on what can be thought of as a more classically Lockean style version of natural rights. These writers appeal to and utilize traditional concepts from that tradition, including the idea of an original state of nature in which all individuals are equal and the idea of a social contract by individuals to leave that state and enter into a political community. Typically, this Lockean style argument is combined with and is used to complement arguments from British rights and colonial charters. These other rights are thought complementary to natural rights, which typically are thought to be the most fundamental source of rights. The exact prioritization of these arguments vis-à-vis each other is sometimes left unclear and at other times made explicit. This view of natural rights is often thought of as "the" colonial view of natural rights. And it is often associated with Jefferson.

A second strand of writing invoking natural rights tends to follow focus on the specific right to quit society.[5] In contrast to the first use of natural rights, which buttresses and complements the claims to British rights, this strand of thinking treats the colonies as essentially independent political states that created new social compacts with Great Britain. While these social compacts were modeled on British rights, the original "settlers" (not "colonists" in this view) have British rights because they chose them, not because they inherited them as a birthright or brought them as British settlers. Neither of these lines of argument immediately calls for a revolution, and both are used to argue that Parliament lacks authority over the colonies, including the right to regulate trade. We shall see that Jefferson's first political writing falls more into this stream of thinking than into the first classically Lockean style argument.

A third strand of natural rights arguments ponders and blends the traditional Christian religious concepts with Lockean notions. This strand of rights thinking sometimes sounds very much like a classical Lockean theory. But at other times, these religious political writings articulate a theory of society, consent, and human freedom that produces something new in both language and concept. And in producing something new, it actually departs in some quite interesting ways from a classically Lockean argument.

All of these arguments aim at the same result: to deny Parliament the power to tax the colonies and, in some cases, to regulate the commerce of the colonies. All of these arguments in the future would be used to justify a right to revolt. But these various versions of natural rights arguments were not all consistent or necessarily compatible with each other. Papering over some of the differences in theories would be one achievement of the Declaration of Independence.

John Dickinson and the Avoidance of Natural Rights Arguments

There is evidence beyond the Stamp Act controversy that some colonists still had qualms about relying on natural rights arguments. One excellent example of this impulse was the widely read set of "Farmer's Letters" penned by John Dickinson in response to a new set of British regulations, the Townshend Acts.

The repeal of the Stamp Act in March 1765 had certainly ended the immediate controversy, but the Declaratory Act, issued at the same time, had insisted that Parliament still had full authority to make any laws whatsoever for the colonies. In late spring 1767, a new set of acts proposed by Charles Townshend, chancellor of the exchequer, stirred up tensions once again. Like Grenville, Townshend intended to reduce British taxes at home by more efficiently collecting duties levied on American trade. To do so, he tightened the administration of customs and sponsored duties on colonial imports of paper, glass, lead, and tea exported from Britain to the colonies. By imposing fees on trade, Townshend was intentionally testing whether the colonies would accept a means of raising revenue that was presented to them as a regulation of commerce.

The most widely read colonial response to the Townshend acts was the twelve *Letters of a Pennsylvania Farmer*, written by Philadelphia lawyer and politician John Dickinson beginning in December 1767. What is significant for our purposes is to see that Dickinson does not rely on natural rights arguments.

Dickinson had earlier been involved in drafting the resolves of the Stamp Act Congress. In these "Farmer's" letters, Dickinson was clearly trying to awaken his follow colonists to what he regarded as the seriousness of the new acts. Insisting they were as insidious as the earlier Stamp Acts, Dickinson urges his fellow colonists to react strenuously.

> Here then, my dear countrymen, Rouse yourselves, and behold the ruin hanging over your heads. If you Once admit, that Great-Britain may lay duties upon her exportations to us, *for the purpose of levying money on us only*, she then will have nothing to do, but to lay those duties on the articles which she prohibits us to manufacture—and the tragedy of American liberty is finished.

Dickinson further writes, "In short, if they have a right *to* levy a tax of one penny upon us, they have a right to levy a million upon us: For where does their right stop?"[6] In distinctions familiar from earlier colonial writings, Dickinson argues that "The parliament unquestionably possesses a legal authority to regulate the trade of Great-Britain, and all her colonies. Such an authority is essential to the relation between a mother country and her colonies; and necessary for the common good of all." In Dickinson's view, the colonies are not separate political entities, a position with which others such as Richard Bland and Jefferson would disagree.[7]

> He, who considers these provinces as states distinct from the *British Empire,* has very slender notions of *justice,* or of their *interests.* We are but parts of a *whole;* and therefore there must exist a power somewhere, to preside, and preserve the connection

in due order. This power is lodged in the parliament; and we are as much dependent on *Great Britain,* as a perfectly free people can be on another.[8]

While Dickinson concedes that Parliament has the right to regulate trade, he argues that the new Townshend Acts, though they imposed duties on commerce and thus masqueraded as trade regulations, were in effect really "external taxes" and therefore overstepped Parliament's power. He thus disagreed with those who thought Parliament had a right to impose such regulations as part of the power to regulate commerce. Dickinson believed it was possible to distinguish these types of regulations by discerning the intention behind the rules. Some regulations are legitimate regulations of trade that were within Parliament's rightful power. But some regulations of trade like the Townshend Acts were really an excuse for a tax and therefore overstepped Parliament's powers.

For our present purposes, it is significant that throughout his Farmer's Letters in 1767, Dickinson nowhere explicitly appeals to natural rights as a justification of colonial rights. Indeed, he barely invokes rights of any sort, even though he assumes the Townshend acts are denying American freedom. For example, he writes: *"Those* who are *taxed* without their own consent, expressed by themselves or their representatives, are *slaves."* "... Who Are a Free People? Not *those,* over whom government is reasonable and equitably exercised, but *those,* who live under a government so *constitutionally checked and controlled,* that proper provision is made against its being otherwise exercised."[9]

Here Dickinson appeals to a conception of liberty familiar from writers such as Montesquieu and Hume. Liberty arises for people out of an institutional framework that has proper checks and balances. And again:

> No free people ever existed, or can ever exist, without keeping, to use a common, but strong expression, 'the purse strings,' in their own hands. Where this is the case, *they* have a *constitutional check* upon the administration, which may thereby be brought into order *without violence....The elegant and ingenious Mr. Hume, speaking of the Anglo-Norman government...*Thus this great man,

whose political reflections are so much admired, makes *this* power one of the foundations of liberty.[10]

Is it possible to form an idea of a slavery more *compleat*, more *miserable*, more *disgraceful*, than that of a people, where *justice is administered, government exercised,* and a *standing army maintained,* At The Expense Of The People, and yet Without The Least Dependence Upon Them?[11]

These are powerful statements about liberty. But one does not find in these letters any philosophical justification of liberty or an explanation of why liberty should be protected. Is it everywhere assumed or is Dickinson hedging his bets and avoiding the question of government's origin and the validity of the social contract? That seems possible especially given Dickinson's appeal to the ideas of philosopher David Hume in the above citation. Hume was a critic of Lockean natural rights theory and argued that Locke's natural rights arguments were as much a political ideology as the divine right theory that justified kingship. In the essay "Of Original Contract," Hume had this to say about natural rights:

As no party, in the present age, can well support itself, without a philosophical or speculative system of principles, annexed to its political or practical one; we accordingly find, that each of the factions, into which this nation is divided has reared up a fabric of the former kind, in order to protect and cover that scheme of actions which it pursues.... The one party, by tracing up government to the Deity, endeavour to render it so sacred and inviolate, that it must be little less than sacrilege, however tyrannical it may become, to touch or invade it, in the smallest article. The other party, by founding government altogether on the consent of the People, suppose that there is a kind of *original contract*, by which the subjects have tacitly reserved the power of resisting their sovereign, whenever they find themselves aggrieved by that authority, with which they have, for certain purposes, voluntarily entrusted him. These are the speculative principles of the two parties...[12]

Hume is arguing here that the idea of a social contract is simply a political ideology, no more true an understanding of government than any other. Given the picture we have of the founders' embracing Locke and social contract theory, it is startling to see Dickinson appealing to Hume, a profound critic of Locke and social contract theory. We shall see in fact that the young Jefferson was also reading Hume and arguably could have been influenced by him as well before writing the Declaration. Given that Dickinson is quoting Hume, is it not possible his hesitation to evoke natural rights is based on misgivings about making those rights the foundation for his argument? We do not know.

The only time that Dickinson offers a justification of colonial rights is when he quotes the resolves of the Stamp Act Congress, which he had earlier drafted but which avoided the use of natural rights. Quoting the third resolve of the Stamp Act Congress, and referring to these resolves as the "American Bill of Rights," this is as close as Dickinson gets to offering a philosophical basis of liberty.

> III. "That it is *inseparably essential to the freedom of a people*, and the *undoubted right* of Englishmen, that No Tax‡ be imposed on them, *but with their own consent,* given personally, or by their representatives."[13]

We have no way of knowing in these letters how Dickinson grounded "the essential freedom of a people" and "undoubted right of Englishmen." Only on one occasion (Letter Seven) does Dickinson quote Locke: "If they have any right to tax us—then, whether our own money shall continue in our own pockets or not, depends no longer on us, but on them. 'There is nothing which' we 'can call our own; or, to use the words of Mr. Locke— what property have' we 'in that, which another may, by right, take, when he pleases, to himself?'"[14] This quote from Locke is apropos. Locke here is talking about the duty of people to support government with taxes. Locke makes clear in this passage that paying taxes must be with their consent, as defined by the vote of the majority. While Dickinson brings Locke's authority to bear in supporting the idea that there should be "no

4. Diverging Theories of American Rights Before Jefferson   137

taxation without consent," he does not invoke Locke's notions of social contract or natural rights.

At least at one point Dickinson seems to assume a very different source of colonial rights than his colleagues. Specifically, he assumes that the rights of the colonies were granted by Great Britain in exchange for the benefits that the colonies brought the mother country. Strikingly, Dickinson includes the right of property as a privilege conferred by Great Britain on the colonies, rather than an inherent right.

> For all these powers, established by the mother country over the colonies; for all these immense emoluments derived by her from them; for all their difficulties and distresses in fixing themselves, what *was the recompense made them*? A communication of her rights in general, and particularly of that great one, the foundation of all the rest—that their property, acquired with so much pain and hazard, should be disposed of by none but themselves*—or, to use the beautiful and emphatic language of the sacred scriptures,† "that they should sit *every man* under his vine, and under his fig-tree, and none should make them afraid."[15] [italics added]

It is striking that the colonial right to property is here described not as a natural right, but as a "recompense" or payback from Great Britain to America for the benefits that accrued to the mother country. The colonies' rights were the result of a trade or contract. No one arguing strictly from natural rights directly would ground the American right of property this way. Moreover, the religious overtones in Dickinson's essays, though not frequent, are obvious here when he invokes scripture rather than Locke or reason to prove his point.[16] In a similar vein, he also credits American freedom to Divine Providence:

> But while Divine Providence, that gave me existence in a land of freedom, permits my head to think, my lips to speak, and my hand to move, I shall so highly and gratefully value the blessing received as to take care that my silence and inactivity shall not give my implied assent to any act, degrading my brethren and

myself from the birthright, wherewith heaven itself *"hath made us free."*[*][17]

Quoting the New Testament, Dickinson appeals to freedom as a grant from God. The absence of natural rights language or at least a fully articulated rights theory in Dickinson would seem consistent with his ongoing commitment that the colonies remain part of Great Britain. Dickinson rejects any talk of the colonies as "independent states" which are part of a larger federated empire. "But if once we are separated from our mother country, what new form of government shall we adopt, or where shall we find another Britain to supply our loss? Torn from the body, to which we are united by religion, liberty, laws, affections, relation, language and commerce, we must bleed at every vein."[18] Dickinson, as is well known, would later refuse to sign the Declaration of Independence, believing in July 1776 that there was still some hope for reconciliation between the colonies and Great Britain.

We see in Dickinson, then, several impulses familiar from earlier writers who avoided natural rights language: a commitment of subordination to Parliament's authority in matters of trade, a resistance to seeing the colonies as independent political entities, and an inclination towards grounding freedom in divine appointment.

To summarize, Dickinson's Farmer's Letters in 1767 assume a free people live in a society that has checks and balances. Yet he does not appeal to natural rights explicitly to ground these rights. Instead, he appeals to the language of "birthright" and sees these rights as recompense by Great Britain to the colonies. He also emphasizes God's role in general, and when he does allude to rights, he seems to ground them in British rights that had been granted the colonists. Eight years later, we will see Dickinson rewriting Jefferson's draft of the *Declaration of the Causes and Necessity of War*, and avoiding natural rights arguments altogether again. In that case, too, we will see both a heavy use of theological and religious language, linking freedom to God's actions.

The Natural Right to Quit Society and the New Emerging Theory of the Empire

There was another conception of rights and the British Empire emerging at the end of the Stamp Act Controversy that placed the burden of emphasis on a "right to quit society." From March 7 to 14, 1766, shortly before the repeal of the Stamp Act, one of the most developed and interesting uses this type of natural rights argument made its appearance. A Virginia politician and lawyer by the name of Richard Bland gave natural rights arguments a new twist in his pamphlet *An Inquiry into the Rights of the British Colonies*.[19] Bland was an important Virginia politician, a cousin of Thomas Jefferson, and one of the early spokespersons for colonial rights in the famous Parson's Cause. Bland had also been in the Virginia House of Burgesses during the initial Stamp Act resolves, when he interestingly enough voted against them. The reasons for that vote are unknown. He would later participate in the First Continental Congress in 1774 and was a member of the revolutionary conventions in 1775 and 1776.

In this pamphlet, Bland was responding to the official parliamentary position developed by Thomas Whately in *Regulations Lately Made*, which was published in the spring of 1765. In this pamphlet, Whately argued that the Stamp Act tax was within rightful parliamentary powers because the colonies were virtually represented in Parliament and therefore could be taxed by Parliament. By "virtual representation," Whately meant that the elected officials could represent even those people in geographies or locations that did not hold elections or send elected officials to Parliament. They were, however, still "virtually" represented by the other elected officials. Bland's pamphlet was written as a refutation of that position. Although not widely read or circulated at the time, some of Bland's ideas were quoted in the *Virginia Gazette*, and the pamphlet was later published in England in 1769.[20]

Bland makes an ingenious use of natural rights that anticipates in critical ways Jefferson's own ideas in *A Summary View*, as we shall see when we take up that essay. Unlike Hopkins or Otis, Bland does not seem to have any worry at all about the "metaphysical jargon" or historical accuracy of social compact theory. He argues unabashedly from a notion of social compact and a state of nature. But as we shall see, his use of natural rights theory is quite different from anything considered thus far and points to a shift in how natural rights could be put to new use.

> Men in a State of Nature are absolutely free and independent of one another as to sovereign Jurisdiction[2], but when they enter into a Society, and by their own consent become Members of it, they must submit to the Laws of the Society according to which they agree to be governed; for it is evident, by the very Act of Association, that each Member subjects himself to the Authority of that Body in whom, by common Consent, the legislative Power of the State is placed.[21]

So far this is good, standard, natural rights theory, and Bland cites Locke, Vattel, and Wollaston as sources of this view. But now Bland adds an important twist. It is worth quoting him in full.

> But though they must submit to the Laws, so long as they remain Members of the Society, yet they retain so much of their natural Freedom as to have a Right to retire from the Society, to renounce the Benefits of it, to enter into another Society, and to settle in another Country; for their Engagements to the Society, and their Submission to the publick Authority of the State, do not oblige them to continue in it longer than they find it will conduce to their Happiness, which they have a natural Right to promote. This natural Right remains with every Man, and he cannot justly be deprived of it by any civil Authority.[22]

It is worth pondering this statement in detail as it offers both a new twist on natural rights as well as anticipates most of Jefferson's major ideas in *A Summary View*. Jefferson in later life credits Bland with having articulated key ideas early in the debate but understates the influence of Bland's essay in anticipating most of his own ideas.[23]

Although starting initially from a straightforward account of natural rights and social compact, Bland is using natural right theory in a different way than some other colonial Americans and in a way that departs from or at least reinterprets Locke. Instead of emphasizing the right to be represented in society and the right to consent, Bland emphasizes the natural right "to quit" or "retire" from society, "for their Engagements to the Society, and their Submission to the publick Authority of the State, do not oblige them to continue in it longer than they find it will conduce to their Happiness."

Locke did argue that every person at the age of maturity has the opportunity to decide whether to stay or take leave of a society. "For every Man's Children being by Nature as free as himself, or any of his Ancestors ever were, may, whilst they are in that Freedom, choose what Society they will join themselves to, what common-wealth they will put themselves under."[24] In Locke's view, reaching the age of maturity is the moment in time when individuals have the opportunity to leave their parental authority and choose which political society in which they prefer to live. "And thus the consent of Free-men, born under Government, which only makes them Members of it, being given separately in their turns, as each comes to be of Age, and not in a multitude together..."[25] When people leave society, they can start a new government "in any part of the world they find free or unpossessed."[26] Pre-Revolutionary colonial writers did not all agree on whether the American lands were free or possessed, as we have seen.

In any case, Locke is much more stringent than Bland on the grounds for leaving society once a person has signed on and explicitly consented. Locke acknowledges that a person who gave "tacit" consent to live in a society, by having property or any benefits from a particular government, can leave a society when use or benefit has been given up. "Whereas he that has once, by actual Consent, and by express Declaration given his Consent to be of any Commonwealth, is perpetually and indispensably obliged to be and remain unalterably a Subject to it, and can never be again in the liberty of the State of Nature: unless by any Calamity, the Government he was under comes to be dissolved, or else by some publick Act cuts him off from being any longer a Member of it."[27]

According to Locke, then, once an individual gives explicit consent to join or become a member of a political society, for example through an oath of citizenship, he or she cannot renounce that consent, unless the government is dissolved, some legal action puts an end to the relationship, or the government abuses its power. Locke, of course, does offer a lengthy discussion on the appropriate grounds for dissolving a government but Locke recognizes no individual "right to quit" society after explicit consent is given and certainly not for the reason of one's individual happiness.[28] On the contrary, Locke acknowledges that when one joins society, one has to conform to the wishes of the majority and thereby make a sacrifice and give up some of one's natural freedom and some of one's desires for the good of the whole.[29]

Like Locke, other prominent political philosophers in the natural rights tradition, such as Pufendorf, conclude that a person who joins a society must respect its express rules about leaving.

> But if a Man *absolutely Free*, that never knew what it was to be a *Subject* (as the *Patriarchs* and *Master of Families* of old,) or is at *present free* from any *Subjection* he had been under *before*, *voluntarily* joyn himself to any Commonwealth, it must also be determined by the *Constitutions* of that *Commonwealth*, what *Liberty* remove thence was left him. For in some *Commonwealths*, no Man is permitted to leave them without the *Express Consent* of the *Government*. In others, a Man may be allowed that *Liberty*, if he submit to certain *Impositions*; as suppose if he pay such a *Sum* of *Money*, or leave part of his *Goods* behind him.[30]

Pufendorf goes on to argue that if in such as case where society has no explicit law about leaving, custom would dictate that a person has a right to leave. Pufendorf also disagrees with Grotius, who argues that people cannot depart a society in "companies" or "great numbers." All this is to suggest that it was by no means self-evident in the natural rights tradition whether there was a "right to quit society" or a "right of expatriation," as Bland and Jefferson would suggest. Bland, and later Jefferson, are picking up one ambiguity in the tradition and extending and building upon it. But neither of them questions the philosophical foundations of their position. Neither tries to argue that in joining a political society, a person retains his or her right to quit society.

In arguing that people can quit society if it doesn't conform to their happiness, Bland anticipates Jefferson's and the Declaration's shift of emphasis from "life, liberty, and property" to "life, liberty, and the pursuit of happiness." Happiness in Bland and in the Declaration of Independence is described as a natural right. As discussed above, it was widely accepted in colonial writing before the Revolution that happiness was one way to describe "the end" or purpose of government.[31] Indeed, Locke often comes close to saying something similar, when explaining why people join society. "And 'tis not without reason, that he seeks out, and is willing to joyn in Society with others who are already united, or have a mind to unite for the mutual Preservation of their Lives, Liberties, and Estates, which I call by the general Name Property." Or again "But though Men, when they enter into Society, give up the Equality, Liberty, and Executive Power…all this to be directed to no other end, but the Peace, Safety, and publick good of the People."[32]

Why then did Bland emphasize the right to quit society for purposes of happiness? It is unclear whether Bland knew he disagreed with or was reinterpreting Locke or the natural rights tradition. But by emphasizing this natural right to quit society, rather than the right to join society, Bland, in a *tour de force*, reinterprets the debate with Great Britain, reformulating the debate over virtual representation as well as the meaning of the colonial charters and immigration. At the same time, he fundamentally reinterprets Locke, or at least takes Locke and the natural rights tradition in a new direction.

Starting with his founding assumption that each individual has a right to quit society whenever it is not conducive to happiness, Bland draws out the implications for "tacit" consent.

> This natural Right remains with every Man, and he cannot justly be deprived of it by any civil Authority. Every Person therefore who is denied his Share in the Legislature of the State to which he had an original Right, and every Person who from his particular

> Circumstances is excluded from this great Privilege, and refuses to exercise his natural Right of quitting the Country, but remains in it, and continues to exercise the Rights of a Citizen in all other Respects, must be subject to the Laws which by these Acts he *implicitly*, or to use your own Phrase, *virtually* consents to.[33]

According to Bland, the British subjects who remain in Great Britain without the right to vote are "implicitly" or "tacitly" consenting to the laws of society. One cannot say, as Thomas Whately did, that they are "virtually represented"; it is just that they have "tacitly consented" to live in British society despite their lack of representation.

The notion of tacit consent is familiar from Locke. Locke had used "tacit" consent to describe the situation where a person comes to maturity and continues to live in a society without expressly consenting to become a member of that society. But Bland applies the concept here to a new context to explain the status of nonelectors (i.e., people who are not eligible to be elected or vote). While these "nonelectors" accept the status quo and tacitly consent to live in society, this hardly proves that they are in fact represented in Parliament or that the situation is right.[34]

In language striking for its criticism of the British constitution, Bland condemns the British Constitution for failing to live up to standards of liberty and argues that "gangrene" has infected the British political system.

> If what you say is a real Fact, that nine Tenths of the People of Britain are deprived of the high Privilege of being Electors, it shows a great Defect in the present Constitution, which has departed so much from its original Purity; but never can prove that those People are even *virtually* represented in Parliament. And here give me Leave to observe that it would be a Work worthy of the best patriotick Spirits in the Nation to effectuate an Alteration in this putrid Part of the Constitution; and, by restoring it to its pristine Perfection, prevent any "Order or Rank of the Subjects from imposing upon or binding the rest without

their Consent." But, I fear, the Gangrene has taken too deep Hold to be eradicated in these Days of Venality.[35]

Having proven that there is no "virtual consent" in Britain, Bland can dismiss Whately's claims.

Bland also goes further, turning to a second ingenious use of natural rights, again derived from the right to quit society. This time he reinterprets the meaning of the emigration to America and the colonial charters and founds it on natural rights.

> I have observed before that when Subjects are deprived of their civil Rights, or are dissatisfied with the Place they hold in the Community, they have a natural Right to quit the Society of which they are Members, and to retire into another Country. Now when Men exercise this Right, and withdraw themselves from their Country, they recover their natural Freedom and Independence: the Jurisdiction and Sovereignty of the State they have quitted ceases; and if they unite, and by common Consent take Possession of a new Country, and form themselves into a political Society, they become a sovereign State, independent of the State from which they separated. If then the Subjects of England have a natural Right to relinquish their country, and by retiring from it, and associating together, to form a new political Society and independent State, they must have a Right, by Compact with the Sovereign of the Nation, to remove into a new Country, and to form a civil Establishment upon the Terms of the Compact. In such a Case, the Terms of the Compact must be obligatory and binding upon the Parties; they must be the Magna Charta, the fundamental Principles of Government, to this new Society; and every Infringement of them must be wrong, and may be opposed. It will be necessary then to examine whether any such Compact was entered into between the Sovereign and those English Subjects who established themselves in America.[36]

Instead of interpreting the migration to America as bringing British rights to the colonies, and construing the colonists to be subjects of Great Britain, Bland flips the story on its head. The immigration to America now involves instances where emigrants exercised their natural right to leave their mother country (England or elsewhere), to come together, and form new sovereign states (not "colonies"). The charters are not privileges granted by the mother country to the colonies. They are rather completely new social compacts, a kind of new Magna Carta, between two sovereign states. The compacts are between the king, the head of the empire, and each individual state (i.e., colony). And these compacts represent constitutions independent of the British one. They are, as it were, treatises between independent nations.

Here then is a "federated view of the empire" identical to what Stephen Hopkins had articulated earlier, but now with an explicit philosophical foundation: the colonies are independent states, equal to the commons of England, but sharing the king as the head of government.[37] The image is not so different from the "United States" operating under the Articles of Confederation, with each state having its own constitution and a common executive body.[38] But Bland here provides what Hopkins had not: a philosophical foundation for this vision of the empire, this time anchored in a particular reading of natural rights.

Bland does not tackle the important question of whether the settlers of America set up government "in any part of the world they find free or unpossessed," to use Locke's words. As we have already seen, the question of whether the colonies are conquered territories was one important question as the debate unfolded.[39] If these lands were not "unpossessed," Bland's whole theory of American rights would unravel.

Having argued that the colonies were independent states, Bland nonetheless seems to equivocate about the extent of Parliament's power.[40] On the one hand, he seems to concede Parliament's authority "I will not dispute the Authority of the Parliament, which is without Doubt Supreme within the Body of the Kingdom, and cannot be abridged by any other Power."[41] In the next breath, however, Bland makes it clear that this is authority based on power and not right. "I say that Power abstracted from Right cannot give a just Title to Dominion. If a Man invades my Property, he becomes an Aggressor, and puts himself into a State of War with me: I have a Right to oppose this Invader; If I have not Strength to repel him, I must submit, but he acquires no Right to my Estate which he has usurped."[42] While Bland is clear that Parliament has no authority to tax the colonies, he equivocates on the question of trade. His argument about trade rests on an argument from equity rather than right.[43] In a hopelessly confusing and difficult passage, Bland both admits and then denies Parliament's power.

> I acknowledge the Parliament is the sovereign legislative Power of the British Nation, and that by a full Exertion of their Power they can deprive the Colonists of the Freedom and other Benefits of the British Constitution which have been secured to them by our Kings; they can abrogate all their civil Rights and Liberties; but by what *Right* is it that the Parliament can exercise such a Power over the Colonists, who have as natural a Right to the Liberties and Privileges of Englishmen as if they were actually resident within the Kingdom? The Colonies are subordinate to the Authority of Parliament; subordinate I mean in Degree, but not absolutely so: For if by a Vote of the British Senate the Colonists were to be delivered up to the Rule of a French or Turkish Tyranny, they may refuse Obedience to such a Vote, and may oppose the Execution of it by Force. Great is the Power of Parliament, but, great as it is, it cannot, constitutionally, deprive the People of their natural Rights; nor, in Virtue of the same Principle, can it deprive them of their civil Rights, which are founded in Compact, without their own Consent... if the Colonists should be dismembered from the Nation by Act of Parliament, and abandoned to another Power, they have a natural Right to defend their Liberties by open Force.[44]

Jefferson was correct when he later wrote that Bland did not take his argument to its logical conclusions. Here Bland vacillates, seeing the colonists as entitled to both English rights by their compact with the king, and natural rights. While the colonists are subordinate to Parliament with respect to their liberties and privileges as Englishmen, they are not subject to Parliament with respect to natural rights or their civil rights founded in compact. Jefferson would go further than Bland in arguing that the settlers live in independent states over which Parliament lacks all authority.[45]

To summarize, Bland's ingenious use of natural rights is of interest both for the ways it follows Locke and departs from Locke at the same time. Yet his selectivity is different in emphasis than Otis's. Bland seems more comfortable with the theory of social compact, apparently having no qualms about the theory's lack of historical foundation or with the lack of sufficiently religious overtones about God's appointment. Why is this so? Bland does not say. Perhaps he simply wasn't aware or worried about these objections.

Alternatively, it may be because Bland shifts the emphasis away from the origin of government in social compact to an individual's right to leave society. Moreover, by the time that Bland writes his essay, near the repeal of the Stamp Act, it was clear that the argument from British rights alone had its own set of problems, as we have seen. Perhaps the earlier disagreements and doubts over natural rights theory and social compact had temporarily receded into the background as colonists sought other footing for their rights.

Because the colonial charters were now construed as new social compacts, rather than gifts from the king, Bland also sidesteps the question of government's theoretical origins. Since the colonial charters were historical "social compacts," as Bland suggests, they were actual empirical compacts between the sovereign and the states and thus as "real" and empirical as the British compact. The theoretical origin of government in general did not matter. But Bland had still to justify the original settlers' individual right to leave their mother country and set up new states, which the traditional Lockean theory of natural rights did not fully or at least explicitly provide.

4. Diverging Theories of American Rights Before Jefferson 149

Classic Natural Rights Arguments as Extensions of British Rights

In contrast to the "right to quit society" argument of Bland, there was a second type of natural right argument adapted to justify colonial rights. This second type of natural right argument was more prominent and arguably more classically Lockean in its concepts and language. Arguments of this type based the limitation of Parliament's power on the character and requirement of "representation" and the purposes of government. In this stream of thinking, the right to quit society did not provide the basis of colonial rights. On the contrary, the settlers were conceived of as British people who came to the Americas with their British rights and obligations. Their rights were their birthright. The limitations of Parliament's power arose, not because the colonies were independent states, but because Parliament could not inherently represent them.

A well-developed example from this stream of thought can be found in James Wilson's pamphlet, *Considerations on the Nature and Extent of the Legislative Authority of the British Parliament*, written in 1770 but not published until 1774. This essay serves as an interesting counterpoint to Bland's, though they both come to similar conclusions but by very different routes. We know that Jefferson read Wilson's essay, as he quotes from it in his political commonplace book, and there is some speculation that this essay influenced his writing of the Declaration of Independence.[46] My point here is not to argue literary dependence but to examine another type of natural rights arguments used to justify the colonists' rights.

The heart of Wilson's essay addresses the question of whether Parliament has authority over the colonies. Like Bland and Hopkins before him, Wilson arrives at the conclusion that the colonies are independent states which Parliament has no right to tax or even to regulate their commerce. But Wilson still views the colonists as subjects with allegiance and duties to the British Crown. Wilson grounds his argument, not in a right to quit society, as did Bland and as will Jefferson, but in a different kind of natural rights theory that limits Parliament's authority.

Wilson develops his argument by taking aim at the commentaries of Blackstone, the British jurist who wrote authoritative "commentaries" on the British common law in the mid 1760s. Blackstone argued that the British constitution was founded in natural rights. In Blackstone's view, the colonies were conquered territories and for that reason not subject to Parliament's supreme authority but only to the authority of the Crown.[47] Wilson agrees with Blackstone's view that there must be a supreme authority in every society, and that "by the constitution of Great Britain" the authority is vested in "the king, the lords, and commons." Wilson nonetheless adds an important qualification:

> I admit that the principle, on which this argument is founded, is of great importance: its importance, however, is derived from its tendency to promote the ultimate end of all government. But if the application of it would, in any instance, destroy, instead of promoting, that end, it ought, in that instance, to be rejected: for to admit it, would be to sacrifice the end to the means, which are valuable only so far as they advance it.[48]

> All men are, by nature, equal and free: no one has a right to any authority over another without his consent: all lawful government is founded on the consent of those who are subject to it: such consent was given with a view to ensure and to increase the happiness of the governed, above what they could enjoy in an independent and unconnected state of nature. The consequence is, that the happiness of the society is the first law of every government.[49]

In language that anticipates the Declaration of Independence and that is very Lockean in character, though Locke is nowhere quoted, Wilson begins with a very classical natural rights argument that "all men are, by nature, equal and free" and that "all lawful government is founded on the consent of those who are subject to it." Wilson then goes on to say that the consent was given "to ensure and to increase the happiness of the governed, above what they could enjoy in an independent state."

So far Wilson has not said anything to which Locke would likely have objected, though Locke does not use the term "happiness" in this way. But Wilson arguably comes closer to Locke's view than does Samuel Adams, who argued that "the first fundamental natural law also, which is to govern even the legislative power itself, is the preservation of the Society."[50] For Locke, people relinquish natural rights in order to make their lives better, not just to preserve society. Interestingly enough, Wilson does not quote Locke here at all and instead cites Jean-Jacque Burlamaqui, a natural law professor in Geneva, whose *The Principles of Natural and Political Law* was translated into English in 1763 and taught in American universities.[51] Burlamaqui is cited as the authority for the conclusion that "[t]he consequence is, that the happiness of the society is the first law of every government." What does it mean to talk about the happiness of society?

> This rule is founded on the law of nature: it must control every political maxim: it must regulate the legislature itself....The people have a right to insist that this rule be observed; and are entitled to demand a moral security that the legislature will observe it. If they have not the first, they are slaves; if they have not the second, they are, every moment, exposed to slavery.[52]

Although Wilson's use of the term "happiness" here could be leveraged to move quite far from a Lockean point of view, in fact Wilson stays very close to a traditional theory of natural rights. A large part of the essay that follows explores what it means "to demand a moral security" that the legislature abide by the rule that "the happiness of the society is the first law of every government." As the essay unfolds, it is clear that Wilson has in mind a very traditional Lockean notion of representation. He reviews the history of rules that developed to ensure that Parliament reflects and pays attention to the views of the common people. Those rules included the expectation that the members of the House of Commons live among their constituents. In this way, the legislators were personally impacted by the laws they legislated and also would have to worry about their reputations. This would not be the case if they legislated for people among whom they did not live. The House of Commons lacked such constraints when it came to the Americans.

But are the representatives of the commons of Great Britain the representatives of the Americans? Are they elected by the Americans? Are they such as the Americans, if they had the power of election, would probably elect? Do they know the interest of the Americans? Does their own interest prompt them to pursue the interest of the Americans? If they do not pursue it, have the Americans power to punish them? Can the Americans remove unfaithful members at every new election?

The answer to all these questions is "Obviously not." The inevitable conclusion is that Parliament cannot makes laws for Americans since it is not bound by "a moral security" that the legislature will heed the happiness of Americans. Here then is an extension of a familiar argument that the House of Commons cannot by definition represent Americans because of the geographic distance from the governing body.

In contrast to Bland, then, Wilson never argues that the American ancestors had a right to quit their societies and establish new political entities. On the contrary, the Americans brought their British rights with them to the new colonies:

Can the Americans, who are descended from British ancestors, and inherit all their rights, be blamed—can they be blamed by their brethren in Britain—for claiming still to enjoy those rights?

Is British freedom denominated from the soil, or from the people of Britain? If from the latter, do they lose it by quitting the soil? Do those, who embark, freemen, in Great Britain, disembark, slaves, in America? Are those, who fled from the oppression of regal and ministerial tyranny, now reduced to a state of vassalage to those, who, then, equally felt the same oppression?

In Wilson's view, the American settlers had British rights as a birthright and brought those rights with them to the new world. Rights travel with people to new lands. It is not the lands that are occupied that confer the rights on the people. The settlers did not give up those rights when they left Britain, the way Bland and later Jefferson would argue. The limit on Parliament's power, therefore, does not derive from the settlers' decision to quit their native country and found new independent states. It derives rather from a rule based on natural rights, namely, the fact that the happiness of the society must be protected. Since Americans cannot be guaranteed that the British Commons will protect American happiness, the colonies must function with their own independent legislatures.

In arguing that Americans never lost their British rights, Wilson contests the view of Blackstone that the colonies are conquered territories.

> The original and true ground of the superiority of Great Britain over the American colonies is not shown in any book of the law, unless, as I have already observed, it be derived from the right of conquest. But I have proved, and I hope satisfactorily, that this right is altogether inapplicable to the colonists. The original of the superiority of Great Britain over the colonies is, then, unaccounted for; ...we may justly conclude, that the only reason why it is not accounted for, is, that it cannot be accounted for. The superiority of Great Britain over the colonies ought, therefore, to be rejected; and the dependence of the colonies upon her, if it is to be construed into "an obligation to conform to the will or law of the superior state," ought, in this sense, to be rejected also.

Wilson sees an analogy between the status of the American colonies and the Irish, who were also not bound by an act of Parliament in England. The English legal sages exempted the Irish from the authority of Parliament because the "Irish did not send members to parliament." This, argues Wilson, "was the same with that, on which the Americans have founded their opposition to the late statutes made concerning them."

Wilson's analogy with the Irish goes beyond the limitation on Parliament's authority. Like the Irish, the Americans are still "subjects of the Crown." Being subjects of the Crown means they still have allegiance to the king and benefit from his protection:

> From this authority it follows, that it is by no means a rule, that the authority of parliament extends to all the subjects of the

crown. The inhabitants of Ireland were the subjects of the king as of his crown of England; but it is expressly resolved, in the most solemn manner, that the inhabitants of Ireland are not bound by the statutes of England. Allegiance to the king and obedience to the parliament are founded on very different principles. The former is founded on protection; the latter, on representation. An inattention to this difference has produced, I apprehend, much uncertainty and confusion in our ideas concerning the connection, which ought to subsist between Great Britain and the American colonies.

Wilson goes on to apply this same distinction to the Americans. In migrating to America the settlers never lost the status as subjects of the Crown. They never quit society. As subjects of the Crown, they are still protected by the king and still have allegiance to him.

An Englishman, who removes to foreign countries, however distant from England, owes the same allegiance to his king there which he owed him at home....Thus we see, that the subjects of the king, though they reside in foreign countries, still owe the duties of allegiance, and are still entitled to the advantages of it. They transmit to their posterity the privilege of naturalization, and all the other privileges which are the consequences of it.

Wilson's natural rights arguments ends in the "privilege of naturalization," as he explicitly calls it, and can be contrasted with the theory of Bland and Jefferson that depends on the theory of quitting society, or "expatriation," as Jefferson will later call it. Naturalization and expatriation are thus very different theoretical justifications for American rights.

Now we have explained the dependence of the Americans. They are the subjects of the king of Great Britain. They owe him allegiance. They have a right to the benefits which arise from preserving that allegiance inviolate. They are liable to the punishments which await those who break it. This is a dependence, which they have always boasted of. The principles of loyalty are deeply rooted in their hearts; and there they will grow.

If the colonies are in fact legislatively independent from Parliament, how then shall the various parts of the empire interact with each other for trade? Should Parliament not have a power above the discrete entities to regulate and coordinate trade for the good of the whole?

> How, it will be urged, can the trade of the British empire be carried on, without some power, extending over the whole, to regulate it? The legislative authority of each part, according to your doctrine, is confined within the local bounds of that part: how, then, can so many interfering interests and claims, as must necessarily meet and contend in the commerce of the whole, be decided and adjusted?

Recall that earlier colonial writers such as Stephen Hopkins and John Dickinson had acknowledged parliamentary authority on matters of trade, assuming there had to be a supreme authority regulating trade for the common good. Wilson essentially rejects this argument, arguing by analogy that just as the trade among European countries had no "superintending authority" to regulate it, so too the flow of trade among the independent parts of the empire needs no authority to manage it. Invoking a free trade philosophy, Wilson argues:

> It has been the opinion of some politicians, of no inferiour note, that all regulations of trade are useless; that the greatest part of them are hurtful; and that the stream of commerce never flows with so much beauty and advantage, as when it is not diverted from its natural channels. Whether this opinion is well founded or not, let others determine. Thus much may certainly be said, that commerce is not so properly the object of laws, as of treaties and compacts.

Wilson pictures the different parts of the empire as independent states that can let commerce develop organically with no regulation. But this freedom of trade is not itself a "natural right." It derives rather from the fact that Parliament lacks authority over the colonies. If politicians conclude that there needs to be a superintending power for economic reasons, then Wilson proposes that the king can play that role of regulating commerce. Regulation of commerce, then, is not an issue of natural rights, but of economic policy: "commerce is not so properly the object of laws, as of treatises and compacts."

The Law of God and Nature: Christian Perspectives on Natural Rights

Many discussions of natural rights arguments in colonial literature tend to ignore or downplay the allusions to God in those discussions. It is as if the religious theological language is viewed as secondary and tangential to the core rights arguments. But to make this assumption misses the doubts and reservations that the colonists have about a straightforward Lockean style natural rights account. One of the reasons they were ambivalent about natural rights theory was religious. While natural rights theory did make God central to rights theory in some critical ways, many American writers did not think it gave enough prominence to God or traditional Christian concepts and themes. For example, we have already seen doubts by James Otis that natural rights theory did not give God a sufficiently prominent role.

There was in fact a rich literature of political sermons given by Americans on election days, Thanksgiving and other occasions. These political sermons, which combine political theory with classic themes of Christian morality, sin, and redemption, are often ignored as peripheral to the development of American rights language. Some collections of American pamphlets before the Revolution do not even have any examples of these religious political sermons.[53] This stream of religious-political writing suggests another view of natural rights that developed as colonial writers attempt to think through how traditional Christian themes of sin, redemption, creation, and morality intersected with what were political ideas derived from natural rights theory. These sermons asked, "How do Christian and natural rights concepts relate to each other?" In the process of asking this question, the writers pose a number of questions that are not found in the purely political pamphlets. How is Christian morality and notions of evil related to the notion of political consent? How does the Christian story of creation relate to the idea of the State of Nature? How does the need for society relate to the Christian notion of Adam's fall from grace? How are free will and liberty related? Is society and happiness ordained by God? How can current political views of consent be reconciled with various religious monarchies that the Jews had in the Bible. Did God intend for humans to be social beings? The view of human beings, of rights, and of political society that emerges is not always consistent with a classic Lockean account. Sandoz notes that these political religious sermons:

> ...demonstrate the existence and effectiveness of a popular political culture that constantly assimilated the currently urgent political and constitutional issues to the profound insights of the Western spiritual and philosophical traditions...
>
> ...[T]he sermon authors take as their reality the still familiar biblical image of Creator and creation, of fallen and sinful men, striving in a mysteriously ordered existence toward a personal salvation and an eschatological fulfillment. They knew that these goals are themselves paradoxically attainable only through the divine grace of election, a condition experienced as the unmerited gift of God, discernible (if at all) in a person's faith in Christ, which yields assurance of Beatitude. The relationships are variously symbolized by personal and corporate reciprocal covenants ordering individual lives, church communities, and all of society in multiple layers productive of good works, inculcating divine truth and attentiveness to providential direction according to the "law of liberty" of the sovereign God revealed in the lowly Nazarene. The picture that thus emerges is not merely parochially Puritan or Calvinistic but Augustinian and biblical.[54]

We have already looked at the election sermon of Abraham Williams in 1762 as one example of this interplay of Christian and political discourse. As another example, we can consider a sermon six years later in 1768 by Daniel Shute, Harvard graduate and Congregationalist minister in Hingham, Massachusetts. The sermon is given in Boston addressing the governor, council, and House of Representatives in the annual election day sermon. What is interesting is both how natural rights concepts are clearly discernible even as they are embedded in and transformed by more traditional religious language and theological concepts. Shute makes some statements such as the following that sound remarkably Lockean in character:

> The design of mankind in forming a civil constitution being to secure their natural rights and privileges, and to promote their happiness, it is necessary that the special end of the electors in chusing some to govern the whole, should be assented to by the elected to vest them with a right to govern…[55]

Familiar themes from natural rights philosophy are evident here. But the larger framework in which this statement is embedded is quite different and dependent on a Christian religious view that fundamentally alters the landscape of what natural rights means.

Shute begins his sermon by noting that God created humans for happiness. As we have seen, the notion that "happiness" is the goal of human and social life is one that is popular in the colonial political discourse. But here it has definite religious overtones and associations.

> The communication of happiness being the end of creation, it will follow, from the perfections of the creator, that the whole plan of things is so adjusted as to promote the benevolent purpose; to which the immense diversity in his works…And every creature in the universe, according to its rank in the scale of being, is so constituted, as that acting agreeably to the laws of its nature, will promote its own happiness, and of consequence the grand design of the creator.[56]

Here human happiness is part of the grand scheme of design, and humans as well as other animals who act in conformity to their happiness therefore are acting according to the laws of nature. The notion that every being acts "agreeably to the laws of its nature" is close to a notion of instinctive behavior. Certain ordained patterns linked to the creature's nature enable each to conform to the design of the Creator and attain happiness. Happiness is not only the end of society, but the goal of all of creation.

> Agreeable hereto, all beings in the class of moral agents are so formed, that happiness will result to them from acting according to certain rules prescribed by the creator, and made known to them by reason or revelation. The rules of action, conformity to which will be productive of happiness to *such beings, must be agreeable to moral fitness in the relation of things; in perfect conformity to which the rectitude, and happiness of the creator himself consists.*[57]

Here the pursuit of happiness has a moral and religious end, while in the strictly political pamphlets and resolutions, there is no "moral theological" dimension emphasized in discussions of human happiness. But here happiness means conforming to the rules prescribed by the creator and made known through reason or revelation. If happiness involves acting religiously according to God's word, then consent to political society is not simply an individual decision, the way it is presented in Locke, but a religious act conforming to God's will and the purpose of the universe.

> Mankind may naturally have a liberty to live without civil government in the same sense that they have a liberty, i.e., a power to neglect any moral duty: But they are evidently made dependent on one another for happiness; and that method of action, which in the constitution of things, will present misery, and procure happiness to the species, on supposition of their being acquainted with it, and in a capacity of going into it, is not only wrong in them to neglect, but even duty indispensable to pursue. From hence arises their obligation to civil government as mentioned before.[58]

In Shute's perspective, it is a sin to live outside of political society. This is a dramatic deviation from Locke's classic view of the state of nature, which saw human consent as key to entering political society. If living alone is in fact a sin, then the notion of consent as understood here is substantively different than the notion presupposed by Locke. Civil government is now a moral and religious obligation. One must join society to fulfill God's law. In contrast to Locke, Shute holds that there can be no laws of God in the state of nature since that state is in fact a state of sin.

From here Shute offers a fundamental break with Lockean theory. In Shute's view, civil government does not involve a relinquishing of natural rights.

> Civil government among mankind is not a resignation of their natural privileges, but that method of securing them, to which they are morally *obliged* as conducive to their happiness. In the constitution of things, they can naturally have no rights incompatible with this; and therefore none to resign. For each individual to live in a separate state, and of consequence without civil government, is so pregnant with evil, and greatly preventive of that happiness of which human nature is made capable, that it could never be designed as a privilege to man by the munificent creator. [emphasis added][59]

Shute here contradicts Locke in some key ways. Locke had said people relinquish some natural rights when they join society. They voluntarily enter into a social contract for the benefits they see in society under government. For Shute, it is only by joining society that they secure their natural privileges. And only by joining political society do they fulfill their moral duty to God. Since living alone is evil, one cannot say that people renounce natural rights when they enter society. To say they have natural rights to live alone would be to say they have rights to live in a state of evil.

Shute also sees society as having a religious end, though he acknowledges that there should be freedom of conscience to worship as one likes:

> That public homage which the community owe to the great Lord of all; and which is equally their interest as their duty to pay, should be earnestly promoted by their rulers.[60]

Since the purpose of political society is promoting human happiness in accordance with the plan of creation, society should promote recognition of God's role.

The religious political writing in the colonies in the period before the Revolution represents an important strand of discourse that certainly weighed in on the debate with Great Britain. This stream of thought, moreover, both affirmed classic natural rights doctrines even as it changed and transformed them. It is reasonable to assume that when public documents refer to "God and nature," they are exhibiting a sensitivity to, if not an endorsement of, these kind of religious and Christian perspectives. The colonists were straddling several very different perspectives and views of natural rights that were not self-evidently compatible or would necessary lead to the same vision of the future society. These fault lines had to be papered over as the colonies came together to contest Great Britain's actions. But under the surface there were deeper divisions among the colonists in their view of rights that the public statements only hinted at but wanted to downplay.

5. *A Summary View*: Jefferson's First Major Foray into Political Writing

It was not until 1774, nine years after the Stamp Act controversy, that Thomas Jefferson, now thirty-one years old, sat down and wrote his first major political work, a pamphlet that would be published under the name of *A Summary View Of The Rights of British America*. The piece was written in preparation for the First Continental Congress, which was preparing to meet to discuss the latest set of disturbing parliamentary rules known in the colonies as the "Intolerable Acts." This Jefferson pamphlet provides a fascinating window into Jefferson's thinking only two years before he drafted the Declaration of Independence. Within a year of writing *A Summary View*, Jefferson was at work on his second major piece of political writing for the Second Continental Congress, drafting the *Declaration of Causes and Necessity of War*. In what follows, we look at these pamphlets in detail and try to place them in relationship to the various streams of thinking about rights that had developed in the nine years since the Stamp Act controversy.

Placing Jefferson against this backdrop is illuminating because there is a striking similarity between Jefferson's essay and that of his cousin Richard Bland. Whether or not Jefferson read Bland's essay at the time is not clear. But both were Virginia politicians in the House of Burgesses, and part of Bland's essay was published in the *Virginia Gazette* at the time. In any case, Jefferson's thinking very much stands in the same stream of thinking as Bland's. The major justification of rights comes from the "right to quit" society.[1]

Let's fast forward to that moment in 1774 when Jefferson is essentially recapitulating the same argument made by his older cousin nearly nine years before. Much had happened in the intervening years. The Stamp Act had been repealed, but the Declaratory Acts at the end of the Stamp Act controversy still proclaimed that Parliament had supreme authority over the colonies. A new Parliament had come to power and legislated the Townshend Acts, which set out to test the authority of Parliament over the colonies once more. The Townshend Acts suspended the legislature of New York, quartered troops in the colonies, and required the colonies to pay for them. There had been a few years of calm in 1770–1773 once the Townshend Acts were repealed. But violence had broken out again with the new restrictions on tea that were part of a new set of legislation, which the colonies dubbed the "Intolerable Acts." In the wake of these acts, momentum gathered in the colonies to convene a Continental Congress to proclaim the colonies' rights. It was in preparation for this Congress that Jefferson penned his pamphlet *A Summary View*, which was intended to be instructions to the Virginia delegates who were attending the Congress. Jefferson himself was too ill to attend the Congress but his pamphlet was sent and laid on the table before the congress. Congress, it turned out, decided on a set of resolves fundamentally different than Jefferson's views, which we shall examine below.

A Summary View

In his pamphlet, Jefferson summarizes the contentions between the colonists and Great Britain as well as the foundation for the colonies' complaints. Making essentially the same argument as Bland before him, Jefferson argues that the colonies are free and independent states who share a sovereign with England. He bases his arguments on the right to quit society.[2] Let us follow Jefferson's argument as it unfolds.

Jefferson begins by providing an overview of what he considers the responsibility of his fellow Virginia delegates to the First Continental Congress. Their responsibility is:

> to propose to the said congress that an humble and dutiful address be presented to his majesty begging leave to lay before him as chief magistrate of the British empire the united complaints of his majesty's subjects in America; complaints which are excited by many unwarrantable encroachments and usurpations, attempted to be made by the legislature of one part of the empire, upon those rights which god and the laws have given equally and independently to all.[3]

The complaints of the colonies are made to "his majesty" (not Parliament) from one legislature (those of the American "states") about the inappropriate behavior of another legislature (i.e., Parliament). Jefferson here indicates that the "settlements" are still part of the British Empire. As independent legislatures on equal footing with Parliament, they are excited by "many unwarrantable encroachments and usurpations," attempted "by the legislature of one part of the empire" on another.

Jefferson does not use the language "rights of nature" here choosing instead "those rights which God and the laws have given equally and independently to all."[4] Jefferson will use the term "right of nature" later in the essay. Here he says simply God and "the laws." Though appealing to common rights, Jefferson highlights the role of God in giving these laws, showing some disinclination to use more classical natural rights language, in contrast to writers like Wilson and others. Jefferson will end his essay as well with the emphasis on God's role in creating liberty. "The god who gave us life, gave us liberty at the same time: the hand of force may destroy, but cannot disjoin them."[5] Jefferson's writing thus resonates with the theologically oriented subtradition that ascribes liberty's origin to God even though Jefferson was likely already a deist by this point and likely did not have a personal notion of God like some of the other colonial writers previously discussed. Jefferson's statement that rights were "given equally and independently to all" anticipates the rights language of the Declaration of Independence and can be reasonably construed as a restatement of the Lockean classical idea that all individuals are created equal and independent by God and that from the equality flows the rights of each person.[6]

As discussed earlier, there is another possible interpretation of this statement. The context refers to the encroachment of the legislature on another legislature within the British Empire. Jefferson's reference to "the laws" giving rights "equally and independently to all," then, could be a reference not to individual natural rights given equally to all, but to the British common law tradition ("the laws") which gives equal rights to all political entities of the empire. This could explain why Jefferson avoids the term "nature" here. He may be referring to "the laws" reaching back into antiquity which the Americans inherited from the Saxons. This reading as we will see also fits with a possible interpretation of Jefferson's later comments.

On the Right to Quit Society

It is interesting that the first time that Jefferson refers explicitly to "rights of nature" in the essay, he does so in precisely the same way as Bland to mean the right to depart one's country. Congress should remind His Majesty:

> that our ancestors, before their emigration to America, were the free inhabitants of the British dominions in Europe, and possessed a right, which nature has given to all men, of departing from the country in which chance, not choice, has placed them, of going in quest of new habitations, and of there establishing new societies, under such laws and regulations as to them shall seem most likely to promote public happiness.[7]

Jefferson here talks of a natural right to depart a country in which one was born. The status of this privilege as a natural right was debatable as already discussed. Wilson following Blackstone held the view that an English subject could not throw off their natural born allegiance when they went to the Americas. And Locke certainly did not make the right to quit society a right under all conditions but only for individuals at maturity or those who had not explicitly consented to embrace the social compact at social maturity.[8] Jefferson does not offer any justification or source of this natural right to quit society and simply takes it for granted. In his later autobiographical reflections he will refer to this as the right of "expatriation" and he singles out this right as the main point of his essay.[9]

This right entitles people to leave the country in which they were born and to set up new societies under laws that will "promote public happiness." In contrast to Bland, Jefferson does not here refer to happiness as a "natural right," although in his first draft of the Declaration of Independence he will call "pursuit of happiness" a sacred right, a significant shift in emphasis from this essay. Here he is more in line with Locke and Wilson, seeing the end of political society to promote "public happiness," which is different from an individual's right to pursue happiness, as discussed earlier.

Jefferson does not say what he means by "our ancestors...were the free inhabitants of the British dominions in Europe." Does he mean the American ancestors were free because they were under British common law? Or were they free in some other sense? It appears Jefferson assumes they were part of the British Commonwealth, for otherwise there would be no need to justify a right to quit society. In any case, he seems to share the view of Bland that one has a right to depart a country at will, and not just at the age of majority. Jefferson thus rejects the argument of other colonial writers such as Wilson that the colonists brought their British liberties and duties with them and therefore have them as birthright. For Jefferson, the emigrants came without British rights and were never subject to Parliament's authority from the start.

To drive home the point that the settlers of the Americas had the right to settle and start new political entities, Jefferson with obvious irony argues that England was founded in the same way.[10]

> That their Saxon ancestors had, under this universal law, in like manner, left their native wilds and woods in the North of Europe,

had possessed themselves of the island of Britain, then less charged with inhabitants, and had established there that system of laws which has so long been the glory and protection of that country. Nor was ever any claim of superiority or dependence asserted over them by that mother country from which they had migrated; and were such a claim made it is believed his majesty's subjects in Great Britain have too firm a feeling of the rights derived to them from their ancestors to bow down the sovereignty of their state to visionary pretensions.[11]

Jefferson this time calls the right to leave a society "a universal law," although he still does not explain or justify it. This same law was operative in the Saxon migration to England, which Jefferson says was relatively uninhabited. Jefferson is assuming standard Whig history that attributed the birth of liberty to the Saxons who brought liberty to Britain.[12] When the Saxons exercised the right to leave their mother country and established a society in the island of Britain, no claim of sovereignty was made over them by their mother country, since they were recognized as an independent state. The same should be true of the American states. Great Britain should have no further claim over them.

On the Conquest of America

In Jefferson's view, when the settlers came to America, they found it inhabited and conquered it with their own blood, sweat and tears.

America was conquered, and her settlements made and firmly established, at the expence of individuals, and not of the British public. Their own blood was spilt in acquiring lands for their settlement, their own fortunes expended in making that settlement effectual. For themselves they fought, for themselves they conquered, and for themselves alone they have a right to hold.[13]

Jefferson diverges from Wilson (and thus sides with Blackstone) in arguing that the colonies were indeed conquered territories. But Jefferson thinks (in contrast to Blackstone) that the conquest was under the auspices of the settlers, not the Crown. It was the conquest that gave the new settlers rights to the land and to their own political entities. Jefferson here reflects the view repeated in his commonplace book that in Saxon times "upon settling in the countries which they subdued, the victorious army divided conquered lands."[14] The American political entities misnamed "colonies" were the result of a conquest and subdivision of the land. For Jefferson, the original settlers owned their land independently of the Crown in line with the "allodial" nature of land holding that Jefferson traces back to Anglo-Saxon ancestors. Thus the assumption by other colonial writers that the settlers had received their lands from the Crown is a mistake, although an understandable one in Jefferson's opinion. The colonists "were farmers, not lawyers," explains Jefferson. "The fictitious principle that all lands belong originally to the king, they were early persuaded to believe real; and accordingly took grants of their own lands from the crown." The charters, then, were not legal documents. The people mistakenly assumed the Crown owned the lands which was not the case since the settlers conquered the land without help from the Crown.

The American settlers therefore, were a new people, and the lands belonged to them through their conquest. Setting out his theory of property and rights, Jefferson argues:

> It is time, therefore, for us to lay this matter before his majesty, and to declare that he has no right to grant lands of himself. From the nature and purpose of civil institutions, all the lands within the limits which any particular society has circumscribed around itself are assumed by that society, and subject to their allotment only. This may be done by themselves, assembled collectively, or by their legislature, to whom they may have delegated sovereign authority; and if they are alloted in neither of these ways, each individual of the society may appropriate to himself such lands as he finds vacant, and occupancy will give him title.

It is interesting to note how Jefferson describes the origin of laws in the new political states that have been created through conquest. The settlers did not found a constitution based on natural rights of "life, liberty, and property." Instead, he says, they looked back to the tradition they knew best and modeled their laws after those of the country from which they came:

> That settlements having been thus effected in the wilds of America, the emigrants thought proper to adopt that system of laws under which they had hitherto lived in the mother country, and to continue their union with her by submitting themselves to the same common sovereign, who was thereby made the central link connecting the several parts of the empire thus newly multiplied.[15]

While the colonists had a natural right to leave Britain, and were entitled to the lands they conquered, they did not, in the end, look to reason or nature to devise a new compact to promote public happiness. Instead they "thought proper" to adopt the same British constitution with its liberties that reached back in time to the Saxons. In this way, Jefferson gives the impression of an unbroken liberty tradition reaching from the Saxons through Britain to America. And he does make clear that the Saxons had established "the system of laws which has so long been the glory and protection of that country."

Jefferson thus appears to endorse the view that the American emigrants became the inheritors of the liberty traditions reaching back to the Saxons, without having to invoke the natural rights of life, liberty, and property outside of that tradition.[16] He invokes only one natural right: the right to quit society. Jefferson does not quite say it this way, but the implication is that Americans are preserving Saxon liberty traditions that are being undermined in Britain, which once had been their bastion.[17]

Based on his assumption that the ancestors had a right to quit their former society and start new ones, Jefferson also redefines the relationship of the settlements to the king. Just as the settlers brought no British rights with them, so too they had no allegiance to the Crown when they conquered and settled the Americas. They were not in fact "subjects." It was only after the conquest and settlements that the emigrants voluntarily submitted themselves to be subjects of the king in order to continue their relationship with their mother country. In Jefferson's view, the king only had executive authority over the settlements because the emigrants voluntarily adopted him as their "chief officer." The clear implication is that the settlements could have chosen a different sovereign had they wanted to do so. The nature of this relationship thus constrains the king's powers over the settlements.

> And this his majesty will think we have reason to expect when he reflects that he is no more than the chief officer of the people, appointed by the laws, and circumscribed with definite powers, to assist in working the great machine of government, erected for their use, and consequently subject to their superintendance. And in order that these our rights, as well as the invasions of them, may be laid more fully before his majesty, to take a view of them from the origin and first settlement of these countries.[18]

The king should understand that he is nothing more than the chief officer whose executive role is to assist in the working of government which is established for the people's use. His executive powers are therefore circumscribed by the laws and subject to the people's "superintendance." In describing the king's role this way, Jefferson went further at this point than many other colonists, such as James Wilson, who still believed that the colonists were still bound by allegiance to the king because they had were natural-born subjects. As Wilson put it, "Allegiance to the king and obedience to the parliament are founded on very different principles. The former is founded on protection; the latter, on representation." But Jefferson abandoned this distinction arguing that the freedom to quit society meant that the emigrants had the right to quit both Parliament's authority as well as the king's sovereignty.

Somewhat ironically given the subsequent course of history, Jefferson in this essay feels that the king is not exercising enough power in the present set of circumstances. Jefferson calls on the king to more forcefully exercise his veto power: "It is now, therefore, the great office of his majesty, to resume the exercise of his negative power, and to prevent the passage of laws by any one legislature of the empire, which might bear injuriously on the rights and interests of another."[19] In Jefferson's mind, it was the role of the chief executive, the king, to keep one legislature in the empire from infringing on another legislature. The executive was the superintending power to ensure peace between the states of the empire, each of which had their own legislatures that governed them.

Given these views, Jefferson naturally interprets the colonial charters not as privileges granted by the Crown, but as the social compacts that establish new societies. And the colonies which in essence are new states appoint the Crown to be their chief officer. Toward the end of the essay he writes:

> That these are our grievances which we have thus laid before his majesty, with that freedom of language and sentiment which becomes a free people claiming their rights, as derived from the laws of nature, and not as the gift of their chief magistrate: Let those flatter, who fear; it is not an American art. To give praise where it is not due might be well from the venal, but would ill beseem those who are asserting the rights of human nature. They know, and will therefore say, that kings are the servants, not the proprietors of the people.[20]

Here Jefferson is telling the king that the Americans as a free people will not mince their words. Flattery "is not an American art." When Jefferson describes the Americans here as "a free people claiming their rights, as derived from the laws of nature," we cannot know for sure whether he is referring to general natural rights of "life, liberty, and property" or to what he explicitly calls the natural right to "depart from a society." One might argue that the difference is semantic. After all, doesn't Jefferson's natural right to depart a society imply a right to create a new society with a new social compact? And doesn't the right to quit a society rest already on the notion of a social compact that one can choose to leave? Perhaps. But many writers who affirmed natural rights never made such arguments. And Jefferson never puts it this way, nor ties together any of these background assumptions about natural rights and the right to quit society. In other words, Jefferson nowhere justifies his critical assumption that everyone has a natural right to quit society. We therefore do not know for certain whether or how Jefferson derives that right from natural rights theory. And this is the main point of Jefferson's essay, and Jefferson clearly saw this as differentiating his point of view from those of other colonial thinkers such as James Wilson and Samuel Adams, who thought the ancestors brought British rights with them to the Americas. If, therefore, we want to conclude that Jefferson is relying on a natural rights argument here and throughout, it is at the very least a very different framework than that used by other colonists who argued from natural rights, but nonetheless argued that the settlers came as British subjects and brought British rights with them to the Americas.

It is also possible that Jefferson differed even more dramatically in his understanding of natural rights. Jefferson may be assuming that the rights of individuals flow from the natural right to quit society and not from more general "natural rights" that individuals have in a state of nature. Recall that in the traditional Lockean view, individuals are created with natural rights in a state of nature and give up some of those rights to enter into and enjoy the benefits of society. That whole story of rights in the state of nature and with reference to an original social compact is noticeably absent from Jefferson's essay. Similarly, no explicit mention is made of rights to "life, liberty, and property" together, either here or in Jefferson's later Declaration of Independence. What do we make of that absence? We could assume as many of Jefferson's interpreters have that those assumptions were taken for granted in Jefferson. Yet it is possible to interpret Jefferson as holding a different theory and standing in a different subtradition. We have seen ambivalence and doubt in some writers such as Otis and Shute over the notion of an original state of nature and the idea that people ever exist outside of a social compact. Otis had argued that there was no such thing as a state of nature. And Shute had argued that people were created by God as social beings from the very beginning and that living outside society was a sin. Jefferson could be interpreted as sharing doubts about the theoretical origin of government in social compact and natural rights in a state of nature. In that interpretation,

Jefferson is avoiding any appeal to natural rights of "life, liberty, and property" that belonged to an individual in an original state of nature. Instead, Jefferson appeals to one natural right only: the right to quit the society one was born into. Jefferson nowhere explicitly justifies this right and so we can't know for certain how he would have grounded it philosophically. Perhaps, if asked, Jefferson would have appealed to an original state of nature and the fact that people entered into societies by contract. But his reticence in this area is curious. All we can tell from this essay is that Jefferson derived American rights from the original right to quit society. Since people have a right to leave society, they can set up new societies, and those societies can be governed by laws that they choose to meet their standards of happiness.

What Went Wrong?

Given that the American settlements were set up as independent states, how then, did it come to pass that American rights were usurped by Parliament? Jefferson explains it this way:

> But that not long were they permitted, however far they thought themselves removed from the hand of oppression, to hold undisturbed the rights thus acquired, at the hazard of their lives, and loss of their fortunes. A family of princes was then on the British throne, whose treasonable crimes against their people brought on them afterwards the exertion of those sacred and sovereign rights of punishment reserved in the hands of the people for cases of extreme necessity.[21]

Jefferson locates the early signs of disintegration in the activity of earlier British "princes" (e.g., the Stuart monarchy) who exerted power inappropriately "over their subjects on that side the water." Jefferson here refers to the beheading of Charles I and the Glorious Revolution of 1688 that led to the abdication of King James II. In both cases, the British people had to exert "those sacred and sovereign rights of punishment" which empowered them to remove a king. Jefferson again avoids the language of "natural rights" and prefers instead the language of "sacred and sovereign rights", language that will appear again in the early draft of the Declaration of Independence. Once again whether Jefferson grounds such rights in natural universal rights or in the sacred common law traditions reaching back to the Saxons and Magna Carta is not made explicit. If the people there in Britain had their rights usurped, "it was not to be expected that those here, much less able at that time to oppose the designs of despotism, should be exempted from injury."[22]

But it was not just the princes who abused the rights of the colonists. Parliament also began to overstep its bounds and exercised "unwarrantable encroachments and usurpations," such as taxing the Americans. Jefferson also argues that Parliament had no right to regulate commerce either. Here Jefferson goes further than did Bland and ends up with a position similar to Wilson's: the commerce of the American colonies should be free because they are independent states. Yet Jefferson suggests that the American states had consented voluntarily to some trade restrictions. Speaking about the support of Great Britain for the colonies, Jefferson writes:

> We do not, however, mean to underrate those aids, which to us were doubtless valuable, on whatever principles granted; but we would shew that they cannot give a title to that authority which the British parliament would arrogate over us, and that they may amply be repaid by our giving to the inhabitants of Great Britain such exclusive privileges in trade as may be advantageous to them, and at the same time not too restrictive to ourselves.[23]

Since the colonies were independent states, Parliament had no authority to impose trade regulations on them. What then about the trade regulations to which the colonies had acquiesced to and never protested in the past? Jefferson insists that those regulations were privileges that the new American states granted to Great Britain in repayment for Great Britain's assistance. In other words, they were essentially commercial exchanges or international agreements to which the American states had assented.

In certain cases, however, Parliament inappropriately imposed trade sanctions without the consent of the colonies.

> But that, upon the restoration of his majesty King Charles the second, their rights of free commerce fell once more a victim to arbitrary power…History has informed us that bodies of men, as well as individuals, are susceptible of the spirit of tyranny. A view of these acts of parliament for regulation, as it has been affectedly called, of the American trade, if all other evidence were removed out of the case, would undeniably evince the truth of this observation…That to heighten still the idea of parliamentary justice, and to shew with what moderation they are like to exercise power, where themselves are to feel no part of its weight, we take leave to mention to his majesty certain other acts of British parliament, by which they would prohibit us from manufacturing for our own use the articles we raise on our own lands with our own labour. By an act (3) passed in the 5th year of the reign of his late majesty king George the second an American subject is forbidden to make a hat for himself of the fur which he has taken perhaps on his own soil; An instance of despotism to which no parallel can be produced in the most arbitrary ages of British history…The true ground on which we declare these acts void is, that the British parliament has no right to exercise authority over us.[24]

Jefferson argues that the trade regulations to which the colonies have not consented are inappropriate both on the grounds of justice and because "Parliament has no right to exercise authority over us."[25] Commenting on the right of free trade, Jefferson writes:

> That the exercise of a free trade with all parts of the world, possessed by the American colonists *as of natural right*, and which no law of their own had taken away or abridged, was next the object of unjust encroachment…[26]

One might be tempted to see here an early statement linking natural rights, liberty and free trade, a popular doctrine among libertarians and "market liberals."[27] But this interpretation would be misleading. Like Wilson, Jefferson means here that the colonists should have free trade because they live in independent political states which should be able to regulate their own commerce, "as of natural right." Free trade, in other words, is like a natural right because it is a question of national and political sovereignty of a society. Yet it is not a natural right per se like the individual right to quit society. Rules of commerce are a domain that derives from the law of nations, not the law of individuals, although the former tradition was linked to the later. Jefferson is not implying here that individuals themselves have a right to economic freedom or free trade; that freedom belongs to the political states in which they live.[28] It is "as of natural right," meaning derived from the natural right that the Americans had to quit their mother country and establish independent states. The expression "as of" is thus like the expression "as derived from laws of nature," an expression Jefferson uses when speaking of rights derived from the right to quit society. This language differs from other language Jefferson used such as "possessed a right which nature has given to all men," which Jefferson uses to describe the individual right to quit society.

Is Jefferson's Theory Lockean?

Having given an exposition of Jefferson's argument, let us step back a moment to consider whether we can say that Jefferson in this context is Lockean and embraces natural rights philosophy. The answer is both yes and no. On the yes side of the ledger, one sees something that looks very much like a natural rights philosophy behind his ideas of colonial settlement and founding. Jefferson states that nature has given everyone a right of "going in quest of new habitations and establishing new society under laws and regulations as to them shall seem most likely to promote public happiness."[29] Moreover, Jefferson views the supreme ruler as a "chosen" figure who is constrained within the set of rules consented to by the people. Jefferson also alludes to the sacred right of the people to punish their rulers. These statements are all consistent with and embedded in a Lockean style natural rights view and tradition. Furthermore, Jefferson uses explicit natural rights language at various points: he refers to "a right which nature has given to all men," to "a state of nature" and to rights "derived from nature." He also calls free trade "as of natural right." In other writings at the same time, he uses similar language.[30]

But in other ways, Jefferson is not seemingly an "overt" Lockean nor a classical natural rights theorist, at least in all the same ways as others of his contemporaries. To begin with, we see nothing like the explicit statement about the nature or origin of government in social compact or an account of original rights in a state of nature as found in other writers like Wilson or Samuel Adams, to cite earlier and contemporary examples. Although there is a statement about "life and liberty" being created by God, there is no general statement anywhere in this essay about the right to "life, liberty and property." In Jefferson, the emphasis is not on the general natural rights, but on the right to quit one's society and set up a new political entity. Instead of an argument from general natural rights, there is still a reliance on what looks like a Whig historical argument that links American liberties back to British liberties and ultimately back to the Saxons liberties.

Should we argue that a Lockean and natural rights philosophy was here everywhere assumed and therefore left unstated? That is the assumption of Jefferson's biographer Malone: "Jefferson gave no general statement of the doctrine of natural rights in his *A Summary View*, but he based his whole argument on it."[31] That might be one way to explain Jefferson's essay. But the absence of a more explicitly Lockean statement about social compact or natural rights seems more studied than that. Jefferson is only explicit about the natural right to quit society and nowhere provides a justification or explanation of that right.[32] Furthermore, we see a few examples where reticence seems to guide Jefferson and an almost conscious avoidance of natural rights language. We recall that he emphasizes "God and the laws" rather than "God and Nature" and he emphasizes God's role in creating liberty, in a way reminiscent of James Otis. Moreover, in a passage that deals with the right of the British people to depose their king, and thus a context that would normally seem quite appropriate for a reference to natural rights, Jefferson avoids the language altogether:

A *Summary View*: Jefferson's First Major Foray into Political Writing 179

"A family of princes was then on the British throne, whose treasonable crimes against their people brought on them afterwards the exertion of those sacred and sovereign rights of punishment reserved in the hands of the people for cases of extreme necessity."[33] It is interesting that Jefferson here uses the word "sacred," a word that he will use again in the first draft of the Declaration of Independence. "Sacred and sovereign rights" could simply be common rights derived from the Anglo Saxons and could have religious overtones. They are not necessarily "natural rights."

To return to the question at hand, it is not entirely clear why Jefferson deemphasized the explicit language of natural rights. It is unlikely that he did so because of its "radical implications" since his essay is quite radical by the standards of other colonial writing. And we have seen that other writers, such as Wilson, arrive at exactly the same conclusions as Jefferson, but with a more explicit and classical natural rights argument. The problem of answering this question is compounded by the uncertainty about Jefferson's own thinking about Locke prior to 1774, a point I take up in some detail in a later chapter. Becker, in his classical exposition, had assumed heavy dependence by Jefferson on Locke, and others have followed Becker in this assumption. But the burning of Jefferson's library in 1770 left doubts about what was or was not in his library and when he read Locke. Garry Wills and others noted that Jefferson hardly cited Locke in his writings or even in his commonplace book before 1776.[34] This led Wills to argue that Jefferson was more influenced by Scottish Enlightenment thinkers. Others have contested that view and reasserted the claim of Jefferson's dependence on Locke. Still others have argued that even if Jefferson did not read Locke, there were ample statements of natural rights philosophy in other things that Jefferson did read. Jefferson's commonplace book, as Chinard has pointed out, included statements from Lord Kames such as the following, which make ample use of natural rights theory.

> Mutual defence against a more powerful neighbor being in early times the chief, or sole motive for joining society, individuals never thought of surrendering any of their natural rights which

could be retained consistently with their great aim of mutual defense.[35]

It also seems unlikely that Jefferson was personally worried about the religious implications of natural rights language, the way Otis and others seemed to be. Since Jefferson was himself somewhat of a deist, at least based on later writings and his early readings in Bolingbroke, it seems unlikely that he himself was worried about emphasizing a more personal view of God, although he definitely emphasizes God language much more than for example James Wilson, who never mentions God in his essay.

Or perhaps, what we see here is simply the inconsistencies in the writing of a young man who had not yet developed a fully matured philosophy that ironed out inconsistencies. While it may be impossible to know for sure why Jefferson seems reticent about using a more classical natural rights argument, we can take an educated guess inferred from his readings as a young man as evidenced in his commonplace book and literary Bible. It is arguable that Jefferson may not have completely accepted the idea that government was founded on social compact and the general rights of nature. Indeed, it is interesting that Jefferson on several occasions talks about rights from "human nature" rather than "from nature."

One example of this inclination is his statement on slavery, which anticipates a section in his first draft of the Declaration of Independence that was deleted by Congress in its editing process.

> Yet our repeated attempts to effect this [i.e., the end of slavery] by prohibitions, and by imposing duties which might amount to a prohibition, have been hitherto defeated by his majesty's negative: Thus preferring the immediate advantages of a few African corsairs to the lasting interests of the American states, and to the rights of human nature, deeply wounded by this infamous practice.[36]

"Rights of human nature" might be a different way of saying "natural rights," although it may signal something else. Rights of "human nature" lend themselves to an interpretation like James Otis's, where liberty is anchored in the nature of human beings as created by God. Recall Otis's argument that people entered into society as soon as they were created. Jefferson may be alluding to a similar notion, that rights are embedded in human nature, and not derived from the discernment of reason. Indeed, we know that Jefferson was intimately familiar with philosophers such as Henry Home (Lord Kames), who argued that moral sense was part of human nature and a direct feeling without reflection.[37]

Another example of Jefferson's tendency to both use and avoid "natural rights language" appears in his summary of why the American colonists could not accept their subjugation to British Parliament:

> One free and independent legislature hereby takes upon itself to suspend the powers of another, free and independent as itself; thus exhibiting a phenomenon unknown in nature, the creator and creature of it's own power. Not only the *principles of common sense, but the common feelings of human nature*, must be surrendered up before his majesty's subjects here can be persuaded to believe that they hold their political existence at the will of a British parliament. Shall these governments be dissolved, their property annihilated, and their people reduced to a state of nature, at the imperious breath of a body of men, whom they never saw, in whom they never confided, and over whom they have no powers of punishment or removal, let their crimes against the American public be ever so great? [emphasis added][38]

Here again is a statement that is both Lockean and not Lockean at the same time. In very Lockean language he writes that if Parliament suspends the powers of the American legislatures, the states are reverting to a state of nature. This is the only time in this essay he uses the term "state of nature" in what is a classically Lockean way to mean a state outside of political entities and rule of law. By contrast, in very non-Lockean language he argues that for the colonies to believe they are subject to Parliament's power would require them to suspend "not only the principles of common sense, but the common feelings of human nature..." There is no allusion here to reason or natural rights; the reference to common feelings may allude to the intuitionalist ethics and belief in a special moral faculty accepted by Kames with whom Jefferson was acquainted.[39]

Then, in another statement that locates sovereignty in the people, Jefferson still avoids natural rights language:

> From the nature of things, every society must at all times possess within itself the sovereign powers of legislation. The *feelings of human nature revolt against the supposition* of a state so situated as that it may not in any emergency provide against dangers which perhaps threaten immediate ruin. While those bodies are in existence to whom the people have delegated the powers of legislation, they alone possess and may exercise those powers.... [emphasis added][40]

Here Jefferson refers to "the nature of things" not natural rights and again to "feelings of human nature," in a context that would naturally lend itself to a reference to rights derived from nature. The reference to "feelings of human nature" again suggests an attempt to find a basis for the moral sense in some natural intuitionist perception that seems different than reflection through reason.[41] Whether this was because he was influenced by the Scottish Enlightenment figures, as Wills contends, or his reading in earlier classics, does not really matter. Perhaps it was both. The point is that though one can read a classic natural rights argument back into this essay of Jefferson, there are significant signs that he did not fully embrace or at least emphasize all aspects of classic natural rights theory.

Jefferson's essay, then, is seemingly a blend of natural rights and Whig historical arguments, with possible allusions to an intuitionist moral sense, in which pieces are not so neatly separable or completely harmonized. It hardly makes sense to say that Jefferson is a Lockean without qualification. He is both a Lockean and not a Lockean at the same time. Or rather he is a "bricoleur," to borrow a term of Claude Lévi-Strauss. Conrad captures this ambiguity in his reading of *A Summary View*. As he puts it, Jefferson has a "multiple, complex visions of rights... also shows that Jefferson's ideas about rights defy simple characterization; they cannot be aligned with any single 'tradition' whatsoever."[42]

It is very possible that Jefferson was not entirely conscious of all these various inconsistencies or tensions in his writing. After all, this was the first major writing foray of a young man who had not yet developed or worked out a fully consistent outlook or philosophy.[43] And in general Jefferson was not a systematic philosophical thinker.[44] So the inconsistencies may reflect both his youth as well as the fact that he was not ultimately a systematic thinker. If so, then trying to find a coherent theory of rights might be to impose a framework on this document that did not exist. The pamphlet thus combines many different strands of American pre-revolutionary discourse, not rigorously explaining their relationship to each other, or fully working out a coherent philosophical position. Other writers, such as Wilson and Adams, were doing the same thing but with different emphases.

Jefferson Looks Back

By way of summary, it is interesting to look at Jefferson's own reflections later in his life on the essay he had penned as a young man. It is interesting that, in his memory at least, the heart of *A Summary View* was an argument for "expatriation" and a theory of colonization.

> Being elected for my own country, I prepared a draught of instructions to be given to the delegates whom we should send to the Congress, which I meant to propose at our meeting. In this I took the ground that, from the beginning, I had thought the only one orthodox or tenable, which was, that the relation between Gr. Br. and these colonies was exactly the same as that of England & Scotland, after the accession of James, & until the union, and the same as her present relations with Hanover, having the same Executive chief, but no other necessary political connection; and that our emigration from England to this country gave her no more rights over us, than the emigrations of the Danes and

Saxons gave to the present authorities of the mother country over England. In this doctrine, however, I had never been able to get any one to agree with me but Mr. Wythe. He concurred in it from the first dawn of the question [sic] What was the political relation between us & England? Our other patriots, Randolph, the Lees, Nicholas, Pendleton, stopped at the half-way house of John Dickinson, who admitted that England had a right to regulate our commerce, and to lay duties on it for the purposes of regulation, but not of raising revenue. But for this ground there was no foundation in compact, in any acknowledged principles of colonization, nor in reason: expatriation being a natural right, and acted on as such, by all nations, in all ages. I set out for Williamsburg some days before that appointed for our meeting, but was taken ill of a dysentery on the road, and was unable to proceed.[45]

There are two interesting points to be made about this memory of the older Jefferson. Jefferson claims it was his view of expatriation that the other patriots differed with him on. He does not say the essay was about "justice" or about "natural rights." His own summary of the *A Summary View* dovetails well with our analysis of it, for it remembers "expatriation" as the key point of his essay.

In retrospect, Jefferson's explanation of why the other patriots rejected his argument does not seem like the full story. He suggests that his essay was too radical for many of his colleagues who "stopped at the half-way house of John Dickinson." For this reason, many commentators interpret Jefferson's essay as "ahead of its time." But here Jefferson may be overstating his case. We know that other patriots such as James Wilson also denied Parliament's right to regulate commerce but arrived at that conclusion through a different and more classical natural rights argument. Indeed, we shall see in the next chapter that the First Continental Congress, though split on the issue of trade, did end up with a position not altogether different than Jefferson's, although it rejected his philosophical assumptions. It is arguable that Jefferson's view was at least partly ignored, not just because it was more radical than others, but because he wanted to place the whole argument on the right to quit society rather than on other foundations such as representation, birthright, and rights as British citizens. As we shall see, in the debates during the First Continental Congress, there was debate about which theory of rights to use. The committee on rights considered and rejected the option to base American rights on the right to quit society.

6. The First Continental Congress and the Rejection of Jefferson's Pet Theory

The First Continental Congress in 1774 was the first time the colonies convened to unite for joint action since the Stamp Act Congress in 1765. The immediate catalyst was the Coercive or "Intolerable Acts," as the colonists called them.

The Intolerable Acts were intended by Parliament as punishments for the Boston Tea Party of 1773 and to bring the unruly colony of Massachusetts in line. The Boston Port Act in March 1774 outlawed the use of the Boston port following the Boston Tea Party. The Massachusetts Government Act (May 1774) unilaterally altered the government of Massachusetts and brought it under control of the British government. For its part, the Quartering Act in early June 1774 extended earlier legislation by requiring British troops to be housed in occupied dwellings. Finally, in June 1774, the Quebec Act enlarged Canadian territory into areas east of the Mississippi River and north of the Ohio River. The act was intended to solidify Canadian loyalty to Great Britain and seriously alarmed the colonists. The act also removed the oath of allegiance to the Protestant faith for public Canadian office, thereby making it possible for Catholics, who were the majority religion, to hold public office. For the American colonists, who equated Catholicism with "popery" and at times monarchy, this new law was worrisome. Finally, the act gave Canadians a local government that did not have an elective assembly, placing what to the colonies appeared to be a tyrannical and threatening form of government on their northern border. The colonists saw all of these acts as further ominous signs of Great Britain's larger imperial intentions against the colonies.

In response to these acts, the First Continental Congress had three objectives: to compose a statement of colonial rights, to identify specific grievances, and to provide a plan to restore those rights. The Congress met from September 5 to October 26, 1774.

On the eve of the first Congress, Thomas Jefferson had dysentery and was unable to attend. But he sent along a pamphlet (*A Summary View*) that outlined his views. As discussed in the previous chapter, Jefferson favored an argument from "expatriation," arguing that the colonists had natural rights to quit society and found new independent political entities modeled on the laws of Great Britain (which derived from ancient Anglo-Saxon law). Present also in the Congress was Richard Bland, who had beat Jefferson to the punch and made a very similar argument in 1766, eight years before Jefferson put his thoughts on paper.

But the "quit society" contingent was not the only one present. There were fifty-four other attendees from the colonies, and many other views of rights were represented in Congress. Present from Massachusetts was Samuel Adams, who had argued from a classical Lockean view of natural rights, as well as Christopher Gadsden, the representative from South Carolina, who had tried and failed to convince the earlier Stamp Act Congress to base their resolves on natural rights. There were also others present who had not favored arguments from natural rights. In attendance, for example, was Stephen Hopkins, from Rhode Island, who had earlier avoided natural rights arguments because he considered the origin of government debatable.[1] Although John Dickinson, the author of the famous *Farmer's Letters*, had not yet been elected to the Pennsylvania Assembly and could not attend the Congress, many of the delegates socialized with him and heard his views during the proceedings as well.

In short, there were a large number of attendees, many of whom had already written about and developed views on the foundation of American rights. As we shall see, one key area of deliberation was precisely the question of what foundation should serve as the basis of the colonies' rights.

Natural Rights, Expatriation, and Naturalization: The Debates of the First Continental Congress

On September 8, 1774, Congress debated the foundation of the colonies' rights. Later in life, John Adams recalled that the committee debates revolved around two points.

> Whether We should recur to the Law of Nature, as well as to the British Constitution and our American Charters and Grants. Mr. Galloway and Mr. Duane were for excluding the Law of Nature. I was very strenuous for retaining and insisting on it, as a Resource to which We might be driven, by Parliament much sooner than We were aware. The other great question was what Authority We should conceed to Parliament: whether We should deny the Authority of Parliament in all Cases: whether We should allow any Authority to it, in our internal Affairs: or whether We should allow it to regulate the Trade of the Empire, with or without any restrictions.[2]

Adams's summary years later seems to oversimplify the debate at least when compared with his diary notes of September 8, 1774, which gives much more detail about the debate. In what follows, Adams's summary of the debate is interspersed with my comments, which attempt to tease out the fuller arguments made on this day.[3] As we shall see, one point of debate concerned whether the right to quit society or the birthright of British citizens should provide the justification of American rights.

Septr. 8.Thursday. [1774]

In the Committee for States Rights, Grievances and Means of Redress.

Coll. Lee. The Rights are built on a fourfold foundation—on Nature, on the british Constitution, on Charters, and on immemorial Usage. The Navigation Act, a Capital Violation.

Here Richard Henry Lee, a Virginian and a colleague of Jefferson and Bland in the House of Burgesses, opens the discussion. In the second Continental Congress in May 1776, Lee would be the one to make the initial proposal that the colonies declare independence. Here, Lee begins by appealing to nature to complement the argument from charters and the British Constitution, and ancient privileges or "common law." As the debate unfolded on this day in September 1774, Lee will reiterate his stance that the colonies should base rights on nature in response to some of the positions of others. What is not yet clear from Lee's comments here is precisely how he understands natural rights and their relationship to the other American rights or to the status of emigration, which remains a serious matter of dispute, as we shall see.

Lee puts a stake in the ground and says that the Navigation Act is a "capital violation." By this Lee is arguing that even regulations on trade that predated 1763, and were acquiesced to by the colonies before the Stamp Act, constitute violations of American rights. This was a matter of debate among the colonists—whether they should focus solely on trade regulations since the Stamp Act or argue retroactively to earlier ones. The issue of whether Great Britain should have the right to regulate trade would become one of the contentious issues as the Congress did its business for the next six weeks.

We have already discussed various positions on trade. Jefferson had argued that Great Britain had no right to regulate trade because the colonies were independent states. Wilson had come to the same conclusion but from a different starting position: Great Britain had forfeited its sovereignty by being unable to give sufficient "moral security" or adequate representation to protect the happiness of the colonies. Wilson doubted the economic wisdom of needing to regulate trade, but if economists felt that such regulation was necessary, then the king could play that role, not Parliament. Precisely which of these positions Lee is invoking here

6. The First Continental Congress and the Rejection of Jefferson's Pet Theory

is not clear from his comments. However, he is making an implied link between natural rights and the argument that Great Britain should not have a right to regulate American trade.

This was not the first mention of natural rights during the Congress. Two days earlier, there had been a significant procedural debate over how the Congress should make decisions—whether each colony should have equal votes in Congress or whether the population or property of the colonies should count as a factor in voting. During that debate, Patrick Henry had argued that the colonies were in a state of nature:

> Mr. Henry. Government is dissolved. Fleets and Armies and the present State of Things shew that Government is dissolved. Where are your Land Marks? your Boundaries of Colonies. We are in a State of Nature, Sir... The Distinctions between Virginians, Pensylvanians, New Yorkers and New Englanders, are no more. I am not a Virginian, but an American.[4]

Known for his dramatic flair, Patrick Henry declares the boundaries between the colonies to be no longer meaningful. They had all reverted to a state of nature. The colonies were thus no longer subject to any legitimate government and needed to implement new governments with new compacts. It is important to note that this argument differs from Jefferson's. Henry is implying that the colonies are only just now entering a state of nature because Parliament overstepped its powers, whereas Jefferson had argued that the settlers had left a state of government through the act of emigration when they founded the colonies.

> Mr. Jay. It is necessary to recur to the Law of Nature, and the british Constitution to ascertain our Rights. The Constitution of G.B. will not apply to some of the Charter Rights. A Mother Country surcharged with Inhabitants, they have a Right to emigrate. It may be said, if We leave our Country, We cannot leave our Allegiance. But there is no Allegiance without Protection. And Emigrants have a Right, to erect what Government they please.

John Jay, a moderate lawyer from New York and one of the members of the Congress who would not sign the Declaration of Independence a year and a half later, concurs here that the law of nature has to be invoked. Appeal to the laws of nature, as is evident here, did not necessarily identify one as a radical or moderate in the debates, contrary to what some assume.[5] Jay made various comments in both letters he wrote during the Congress and in the debates recorded that indicate his hope for reconciliation with Great Britain, although he could foresee the possibility of reconciliation failing.[6] In the notes on the debate on September 26 about how to restore American rights, Jay is quoted as saying that "Negociation, suspension of Commerce, and War are the only three things. War is by general Consent to be waived at present. I am for Negociation and suspension of Commerce."

It is difficult to discern precisely what is Jay's position here in this debate on September 8. The terseness of his summary makes it possible to read Jay's comments in two different ways. It seems that he is appealing to the "right to quit" society argument like Bland and Jefferson. "A Mother Country surcharged with Inhabitants, they have a Right to emigrate." And therefore in his view "emigrants have a Right to erect what Government they please." In this case, the appeal to the law of Nature could refer to the right to quit society, just as Bland or Jefferson used it. Indeed, later in the debate Jay is quoted as making statements that seem to underscore this position: "I cant think the british Constitution inseperably attached to the Person of every Subject," and "I have always withheld my Assent from the Position that every Subject discovering Land [does so] for the State to which they belong."

Jay would then seem to be holding a view that emigrants have a right to quit society and if they discover new lands they can erect societies and governments that they like. On this reading, Jay's appeal to natural rights could either refer to the "right to quit society" or "the right to found new governments on principles of nature." If this reading is correct, it is significant that someone like Jay could hold a view like Jefferson and Bland and still be arguing for reconciliation with Great Britain.[7] The particular

6. The First Continental Congress and the Rejection of Jefferson's Pet Theory 193

view of natural rights, therefore, did not necessarily identify where one fell on the continuum favoring independence and strong measures.[8]

> Mr. J. Rutledge. An Emigrant would not have a Right to set up what constitution they please. A Subject could not alienate his Allegiance.

John Rutledge, a lawyer from Charleston, South Carolina, and member of the South Carolina provincial assembly, disagrees with Jay about the principle of emigration. Emigrants may *not* simply leave a country and set up whatever constitution they want. "A Subject could not alienate his Allegiance." Rutledge seems to be reiterating the legal opinion anticipated in James Wilson's essay (rejected by John Jay) that allegiance to the Crown travels with subjects wherever they go. Being "a subject" is not a quality one can alienate through emigration.

Adams's notes do not explain how Rutledge would have responded to John Jay's conclusion that "there is no allegiance without protection." Jay implied allegiance was no longer necessary because the Crown failed at its obligations. As the debate unfolds, Rutledge will take the view that American rights can be founded on the British Constitution alone and not on natural rights.

What we see in this debate in Congress as late as 1774 is that there was neither consensus on whether to base American rights on natural rights nor on the precise status of emigrants. There was no "American Mind" on the matter. The rejection of the Bland-Jefferson type position was not simply that colleagues were "in the half-way house of John Dickinson" and uncomfortable with repudiating Parliament's authority over the colonies, although that concern figured in. Jefferson was not after all at the debates in the First Continental Congress. Looking back years later, or even from Virginia, where he was home sick, that may be how it appeared to Jefferson. But what Adams's notes on the debates suggest is that there were substantive disagreements early in the Congress on the nature of emigrant rights and whether emigrants can leave behind their allegiance to the Crown and their status as a "subject" under the sovereignty of the state. If they could not, they had no right to found new political entities. At the heart of the debate was the question of whether sovereignty and allegiance travels with emigrants. This was not simply a question of natural rights, although it intersected with that question. Since so many of the members of Congress were lawyers, these were serious philosophical and legal issues that played into the larger question of how much control should the colonies cede to Great Britain as a matter of right.

> Lee. Cant see why We should not lay our Rights upon the broadest Bottom, the Ground of Nature. Our Ancestors found here no Government.

Richard Henry Lee, from Virginia, whom later John Adams describes as having "a horrid Opinion of Galloway, Jay, and the Rutledges," responds to John Rutledge's comments on immigration, arguing the colonies should appeal to natural rights which Lee here calls "the broadest bottom," meaning the most general and secure foundation.[9] Later in the debate Lee will expand on this position and say that "Life and Liberty, which is necessary for the Security of Life, cannot be given up when We enter into Society." This is a good, terse summary of the classical Lockean position.

Lee goes on here to expand on his view of the emigration, which he had not stated before: "Our Ancestors found here no government." This statement would seem to be a rejection of Rutledge's claim that emigrants cannot alienate their allegiance to the Crown.

There are two different ways to understand Lee's comments. Does Lee mean to imply, like his Virginian colleagues Bland and Jefferson before him, that the emigrants left sovereignty behind and therefore found here no governments? That is one way to read Lee's comment. But earlier in the debate Lee had said that "The Rights are built on a fourfold foundation—on Nature, on the british Constitution, on Charters, and on immemorial Usage." If Lee believes the settlers "found here no government," why would he think the colonies' rights could be founded on the British constitution and charters? Perhaps Lee also held the view like his colleagues Bland and Jefferson that the settlers set up independent states in the Americas, founded on rights from nature, and then chose to adopt the British constitution and establish charters with the King.

> ...Lee. It is contended that the Crown had no Right to grant such Charters as it has to the Colonies—and therefore We shall rest our Rights on a feeble foundation, if we rest em only on Charters—nor will it weaken our Objections to the Canada Bill.[10]

Lee, who earlier was pressing for the importance of natural rights, now rehearses doubts about arguments from charters, similar to those we have seen in earlier colonial writings. In his view, the Charters are "a feeble foundation" because the Crown never had a right to grant such charters in the first place. The view that the lands were granted to the colonies by the King alone and were never under Parliamentary control is a weak argument in his view.[11] Both sides then—those favoring an argument from charters and those favoring an argument from natural rights—view the arguments of the other side as resting on "feeble foundations."

> Mr. Rutledge. Our Claims I think are well founded on the british Constitution, and not on the Law of Nature.

Rutledge, who earlier had argued that allegiance travels with and sticks with a subject, expresses his conviction that the British constitution provides adequate grounds for the colonies' claims without an appeal to the law of nature. This view is consistent with his view of emigration. Since the émigrés cannot relinquish the sovereignty of the state, then the best way to argue for rights is from the rights that they inherited as birthright in the British constitution.

> Coll. Dyer. Part of the Country within the Canada Bill, is a conquered Country, and part not. It is said to be a Rule that the King can give a Conquered Country what Law he pleases.

Colonel Eliphalet Dyer, from Connecticut, and a member of the earlier Stamp Act Congress, raises a question about the status of a conquered country and its relationship to the Canada bill. Dyer here refers to the view that if a land is conquered, the king can set up whatever law he pleases. The point of his statement is not entirely clear. He may simply be explaining why the Crown has the right to make the new Quebec Act. But his words may have other resonances, suggesting that the king could also give whatever laws he likes to the American colonies, at least on the view like Blackstone that they had been conquered under the auspices of the Crown.

> Mr. Jay. I cant think the british Constitution inseperably attached to the Person of every Subject. Whence did the Constitution derive is Authority? From compact. Might not that Authority be given up by Compact.

John Jay returns to the heart of the debate about the status of the colonial settlers to further develop his earlier view, "Emigrants have a Right, to erect what Government they please." Now he gives a justification of this right to emigrate, a justification that was never given explicitly provided by either Bland or Jefferson. If the authority of the original constitution comes from compact, he argues, then the authority may be given up by compact.

There is an odd ambiguity in Jay's statement that goes to the heart of the question of whether the "right to quit" a society is a classical Lockean concept in the way Americans are using it. Is the renunciation of the compact an individual right or a right of the people as a whole? Neither Jefferson nor Bland addressed this question or asked about the philosophical foundation of this right. After all, according to natural rights theory, the constitution or compact derived its authority from the whole people who consented to it. Therefore one could argue that "giving up the compact" could be construed as a right of the people as a collective rather than a right of the individual. Locke certainly inclined towards the collective view, seeing the right to end the social contract as stemming from the will of the people as a whole in response to the abuse of power. And we have seen that natural rights philosophers like Pufendorf recognized that societies could set limits on emigration. Jefferson and Bland, for their part, emphasized the individual right to quit society in which chance not choice had placed them.

Jay does not explicitly take note of this question just as Bland and Jefferson had not done so either. Jay's words seem to imply a collective understanding of this right. Giving up authority "by Compact" means that some sort of collective decision had occurred to end the authority of a government. The group that created the compact had ended it. But it is possible Jay has an individual right in mind, since an individual "consents to the compact" at maturity and therefore could give up the compact, although this was not a position Locke accepted.[12] After two comments by William Livingston of Rhode Island and Roger Sherman of Connecticut that are not immediately germane to this discussion, James Duane, another lawyer from New York and colleague of John Jay, disagrees with Jay.[13]

> Mr. Duane. Upon the whole for grounding our Rights on the Laws and Constitution of the Country from whence We sprung, and Charters, without recurring to the Law of Nature—because this will be a feeble Support. Charters are Compacts between the Crown and the People and I think on this foundation the Charter Governments stand firm. England is Governed by a limited Monarchy and free Constitution. Priviledges of Englishmen were inherent, their Birthright and Inheritance, and cannot be deprived of them, without their Consent.
>
> Objection. That all the Rights of Englishmen will make us independent. I hope a Line may be drawn to obviate this
>
> Objection. James was against Parliaments interfering with the Colonies. In the Reign of Charles 2d. the Sentiments of the Crown seem to have been changed. The Navigation Act was made. Massachusetts denyed the Authority—but made a Law to inforce it in the Colony.

James Duane, another lawyer from New York and colleague of John Jay, disagrees with both Jay and Lee and seconds the view that the rights should be founded on charters and British rights "from whence we sprung" rather than natural rights which "will be a feeble Support." Although Duane and Jay disagree about the foundation of colonial rights, both would vote together for a moderate position in favor of the Galloway plan, described below. As noted before, the differences over natural rights did not necessarily result in diverging positions on moderation at this stage of the game. One wishes something more was said about why Duane thought natural rights a more feeble support than the British constitution and charters. From Duane's own notes of what he said on this day, it is clear he thinks he is elaborating a better more solid justification of rights and believes, like earlier colonial writers examined previously, that natural rights theory is a theoretical understanding of government's origin that is subject to doubt. He writes:

> It is necessary that the first point, our Rights, should be fully discussed and established upon solid Principles: because it is only from hence that our Grievances can be disclosed; & from a clear View of both that proper Remedies can be suggested and applied. To ascertain the Constitutions of the Colonies has employed the Thoughts and the Pens of our ablest Politicians. But no System which has hitherto been published is solid or satisfactory.[14]

Duane, like Hopkins and others, wants to avoid theoretical arguments about rights and "place our Rights on a broader & firmer Basis to advance and adhere to some solid and Constitutional Principle which will preserve Us from future Violations…Let it be founded upon Reason and Justice, and satisfy the Consciences of our Countrymen. Let it be such as we dare refer to the Virtuous and impartial part of Mankind, and we shall and must, in the issue of the Conflict, be happy & triumphant."

Duane rejects natural rights arguments because they lack the widespread consensus to serve as a basis of American rights. Instead, he prefers his arguments from British right to be founded on "Reason and Justice." In his view, the emigrants brought their British rights with them and those rights are inalienable. The emigrants were blessed with the Priviledges which they never meant nor were supposed, nor coud forfeit, (by removing to a distant a more remote part of the English Empire) by altering their local situation within the same Empire. The priviledges of Englishmen were inherent. They were their Birth right and of which they coud only be deprived by their free Consent. Every Institution legislative and Juridical, essential to the Exercise & Enjoyment of these Rights and priviledges in constitutional Security, were equally their Birth right and inalienable Inheritance. They coud not be with held but by lawless oppression and by lawless oppression only can they be violated.[15]

Like James Wilson earlier, Duane makes explicit the view that the emigrants never intended to give up their rights as Englishmen, and, more importantly, they could not forfeit them even if they had so desired. These rights were "birth rights" as well as "inalienable Inheritance." Parliament could not take this inheritance away from the emigrants, and the colonists are subjects of the empire and cannot renounce the sovereignty of the British legislature.

It is interesting to see the two possible objections that Duane thinks may be leveled against his position. First, he considers the possibility that his argument from British rights will be construed as an impulse towards independence. We see here that, in Duane's view, it was not only arguments from natural rights that were thought to have "radical" implications.[16] Indeed, we have seen that writers such as James Wilson did start from the assumption that the ancestors brought British rights with them, and ended up arguing that the colonies were independent states. Duane was worried that his position could be construed in the same way, and therefore he emphasizes that his view did not have to lead in that direction. What is interesting is that even those who rejected natural rights theory were still worried and defensive that their arguments would seem like calls for independence. We thus have additional evidence that the arguments for and against natural rights did not neatly align with radical and moderate leaning positions. Lee now breaks into the discussion with another comment in response.

> Lee. Life and Liberty, which is necessary for the Security of Life, cannot be given up when We enter into Society.

Lee extends his earlier emphasis on natural rights by emphasizing that basic natural rights are not alienated when we enter society. Lee's statement may be a general statement about natural rights or, given the sequential order of these notes, it could be a response to Duane's claim that emigrants are unable to forfeit their British rights.

In response, Lee makes the classical Lockean argument that natural rights are not given up when one enters society. Even if the ancestors were subject to British rights, those rights do not supersede rights of life and liberty. Therefore, the claim that the emigrants were subject to British rights does not deal with the challenge of natural rights: namely, that that sovereignty never has a right to supercede more basic rights. Here Lee sounds very much like Samuel Adams and Wilson, and less like Jefferson and Jay. But now Rutledge weighs in with the opposing view.

> Mr. Rutledge. The first Emigrants could not be considered as in State of Nature—they had no Right to elect a new King.

> Mr. Jay. I have always withheld my Assent from the Position that every Subject discovering Land [does so] for the State to which they belong.

Rutledge again reiterates the view that emigrants cannot divest themselves of all their rights and obligations. Since they are still British subjects, they cannot be in a state of nature and had no right to "elect a new King," a position diametrically opposed to Jefferson's. As we have discussed earlier, the question of allegiance to the king and subjection to Parliament's authority were two separate though related issues. Those like Jefferson, who believed the emigrants had a right to quit society, argued that the colonists were neither subject to Parliament's authority

6. The First Continental Congress and the Rejection of Jefferson's Pet Theory 201

nor had an obligation to the king. Instead they essentially elected the king as their chief officer. On this later interpretation, the compacts were not gifts under the king's authority, but "treaty-like" agreements entered into by independent states. Jay for his part reiterates the view that all emigrants do leave behind the sovereignty of the state when discovering new lands. As he said earlier, "Emigrants have a Right, to erect what Government they please." By implication this includes choosing the king they want.

The Galloway Alternative

A lengthy summary of Joseph Galloway's speech on rights appears in the next and final section of Adams's notes for this day of debate on American rights. It is worth pausing to deepen our understanding of Galloway's position both because it is somewhat cryptic here in Adams's notes but also because it represents still another alternative view of government and rights considered during the Congress. The fact that Adams provides more detailed notes on Galloway's speech, in contrast to others, perhaps signaling that Adams viewed Galloway's position as less familiar or more problematic than the others he was recording. He may not yet have understood where Galloway would be going with the philosophical principles he was beginning to outline here. Indeed, it is not even clear whether on this day Galloway tipped his hand to the views that he would argue for later in the proceedings.

> Mr. Galloway. I never could find the Rights of Americans, in the Distinctions between Taxation and Legislation, nor in the Distinction between Laws for Revenue and for the Regulation of Trade. I have looked for our Rights in the Laws of Nature—but could not find them in a State of Nature, but always in a State of political Society. I have looked for them in the Constitution of the English Government, and there found them. We may draw them from this Soursce securely.

Galloway, a lawyer from Philadelphia and friend of Benjamin Franklin, was first elected to the Pennsylvania Assembly in 1757 and remained a member until after the Revolution. Galloway is well known for ultimately becoming a British loyalist and leaving the American states in 1778. He and Dickinson had been adversaries in local politics well before the Revolution, with Galloway favoring the abandonment of a proprietary government in Pennsylvania in favor of a royal government, a view he shared with Benjamin Franklin. His growing dissatisfaction with the emerging colonial discontent is partially articulated here in the First Continental Congress.

Galloway begins his speech here by taking a swipe at most of the major positions articulated by other American writers, particularly his longtime Pennsylvanian opponent, John Dickinson, the famous author of the Farmer's Letters. "I never could find the Rights of Americans, in the Distinctions between Taxation and Legislation, nor in the Distinction between Laws for Revenue and for the Regulation of Trade."[17] Galloway finds such distinctions made by earlier writers to be nonsense. Either the colonies are under the sovereignty of Parliament or they are not. Parliament either has authority over all matters or it has none. All of these distinctions have the colonies half in and half out.

Galloway was not the only one to find these distinctions increasingly problematic. Jefferson, Wilson, Franklin, Lee, and others had by this time all come to see such distinctions as problematic. But these other men were arriving at the opposite conclusion to Galloway. Instead of arguing that the colonies should be all "out" of Parliament's sovereignty, Galloway was arguing that the colonies should be "all in." And Galloway rejected natural rights as a source for understanding colonial rights. "I have looked for our Rights in the Laws of Nature—but could not find them in a State of Nature, but always in a State of political Society. I have looked for them in the Constitution of the English Government, and there found them." Why Galloway does not find them in a state of nature is not recorded here, but it is clear that Galloway regards the sovereignty of the political entity as a key established principle of government that is being jeopardized by the theories of his colleagues.

6. The First Continental Congress and the Rejection of Jefferson's Pet Theory

In his later pamphlet published after the Congress concluded, Galloway is vicious in his characterization of the arguments used by his colonial colleagues. As he puts it there:

> In a controversy of such great moment, it is of the first importance to ascertain the standard by which it ought to be decided. This being unsettled, the merits can never be determined, nor any just decision formed. Hence it is, that we have seen all the American writers on the subject, adopting untenable principles, and thence rearing the most wild and chimerical superstructures. Some of them have fixed on, as a source from whence to draw American Right, "the laws of God and nature," the common rights of mankind, "and the American charters." Others finding that the claims of the colonies could not be supported upon those pillars, have racked their inventions to find out distinctions, which never existed, or nor can exist in reason or common sense: A distinction between a right in parliament to legislate for the colonies and a right to tax them—between internal and external taxation—and between taxes laid for the regulation of trade, and for the purpose of revenue. And after all of them have been fully considered, even the authors themselves, finding that they have conveyed no satisfactory idea to the intelligent mind, either of the extent of parliamentary authority, or of the rights of America, have exploded them, and taken new ground, which will be found equally indefensible.[18]

Galloway is biting in his critique of his colonial colleagues for failing to find a solid and uncontested standard for settling their rights. Instead they have argued from a variety of philosophically dubious foundations. We have heard this critique before. Galloway's mocking of natural rights arguments is in line with why some of the attendees at the Congress still thought natural rights a feeble foundation for their rights. So what then does Galloway found his argument on?

It is a dispute between the supreme authority of the state, and a number of its members, respecting its supremacy, and their constitutional rights. What other source to draw them from, or standard to decide them by, can reason point out, but the principles of government in general, and of that constitution in particular, where both are to be found, defined and established?[19]

It is interesting that Galloway appeals to "the principles of government in general," yet scoffs at others who talked about "the laws of God and nature" and "the common rights of mankind." What are those principles of government Galloway appeals to? They are "the principles which are essential in the constitution of all societies, and particularly in that of the British government." Galloway thus appears to distinguish "general principles" from "natural rights" or "common rights," holding a view that there are universal principles that are not "natural rights" at least in the way that others mean them. "Natural rights," then, are only one category of universal right founded on reason. But there are others.

Later in the same essay, however, Galloway does seem to rely on the conception of natural rights as when he writes that "Protection from all manner of unjust violence, is the great object which men have in view, when they surrender up their natural rights, and enter into society."[20] By "surrender up", Galloway may be invoking a Lockean view that the entrance into society means that one has renounced natural rights. Whether Galloway means the same thing here or something more is not entirely clear. But in any case, the question of natural rights is irrelevant because natural rights do not provide a justification for Americans to cast off their allegiance to Great Britain.

We shall not find it in the "laws of nature"; the principles upon which those laws are founded, are reason and immutable justice, which require a rigid performance of every lawful contract; to suppose therefore, that a right can thence be derived to violate the most solemn and sacred of all covenants; those upon which the existence of societies, and the welfare of millions depend; is, in the highest degrees, absurd.[21]

Galloway is arguing here that the right to throw off the sovereignty of Great Britain cannot be derived from natural rights. Since the laws of nature are founded on reason and immutable justice how can they be assumed to justify "violating the most solemn and sacred of all covenants" namely the original compact of a society and in particular the British constitution. The laws of nature would lead to the conclusion that there needs to obey the original contract and obey Parliament.

It appears that Galloway fundamentally disagrees with how some of his American thinkers understand the implication of the laws of nature. It is not that he denies the existence of natural rights per se. It is rather that natural rights do not provide the basis for the American rights. "I have looked for our Rights in the Laws of Nature—but could not find them in a State of Nature, but always in a State of political Society."[22] In his view "there is no position more firmly established, in the conduct of mankind, "than that there must be in every state a supreme legislative authority, universal in its extent, over every member."[23]

Here Galloway seems to be appealing to "common practice" and "universal standard" to emphasize his view that there must be a supreme legislative authority over every member. Supporting this view, Galloway cites a number of authorities including Locke, Burlamaqui, and Tully.[24] Galloway cites Locke several times to justify his views. But he does so, not because he bases his own view on Locke particularly, but because he knows that Locke carries weight with his opponents. "I shall add the opinion of Mr. *Locke*, because it has been often heretofore relied on by the American advocates, as worthy of credit."[25]

There was in fact nothing controversial in Galloway's initial position that every society needs a supreme sovereignty or that the foundation of American rights was in the British constitution. For Galloway the key issue is whether the Americans are part of the British state "or so many independent communities in a state of nature", Disagreeing with colleagues, such a Lee and Jay in the Congress and the position of Jefferson in *A Summary View*, Galloway argues that the colonies are indeed part of the British empire and not independent states. Why?

Power results from the Real Property, of the Society.

The States of Greece, Macedon, Rome, were founded on this Plan...

None but Landholders could vote in the Comitia, or stand for Offices.

English Constitution founded on the same Principle. Among the Saxons the Landholders were obliged to attend and shared among them the Power. In the Norman Period the same. When the Land holders could not all attend, the Representation of the freeholders, came in. Before the Reign of H[enry] 4., an Attempt was made to give the Tenants in Capite a Right to vote. Magna Charta. Archbishops, Bishops, Abbots, Earls and Barons and Tenants in Capite held all the Lands in England.

It is of the Essence of the English Constitution, that no Law shall be binding, but such as are made by the Consent of the Proprietors in England.

Galloway's statements on sovereignty presuppose a view that identifies the source of rights in ownership of property. According to this view, landed property was thought to be the most stable source of power for the state. The state owns land which it acquired or conquered and divides up representation based on ownership of land. Rights are founded on the ownership of property and do not inhere in individuals outside of the state. It is ownership of land that gives one a right to vote, according to Galloway's understanding of the British Constitution. The right of representation is derived not from "nature" or one's equality per se, but from ownership of land within the state's sovereignty. We recall that James Otis had earlier discussed and dismissed theories of rights founded in property.[26] Other colonial writers had rarely mentioned this theory of rights' origins. But Galloway makes this theory the basis of rights in general.

6. The First Continental Congress and the Rejection of Jefferson's Pet Theory 207

Here and in his latter pamphlet, Galloway surveys how this principle developed in Anglo-Saxon history and then remained firm in feudal law as the basis of representation.[27]

> How then did it stand with our Ancestors, when they came over here? They could not be bound by any Laws made by the British Parliament—excepting those made before. I never could see any Reason to allow that we are bound to any Law made since—nor could I ever make any Distinction between the Sorts of Laws.
>
> I have ever thought We might reduce our Rights to one. An Exemption from all Laws made by British Parliament, made since the Emigration of our Ancestors. It follows therefore that all the Acts of Parliament made since, are Violations of our Rights.
>
> These Claims are all defensible upon the Principles even of our Enemies—Ld. North himself when he shall inform himself of the true Principles of the Constitution, &c.

In these notes recorded by Adams, Galloway seems to be taking a position that the settlers were only bound to English laws made before emigration, presumably because at that stage they were owners of land under the power of the state. Galloway here suggests that the only rules binding on the emigrants were the ones in force when they left. Any law imposed on them by Parliament afterwards stepped beyond Parliament's authority. The emigration provided a dividing line, demarcating when Parliament's authority ended. This view seems to lead in the direction of thinking of the colonies as independent entities after the migration.

> I am well aware that my Arguments tend to an Independency of the Colonies, and militate against the Maxim that there must be some absolute Power to draw together all the Wills and strength of the Empire.

This is as far as Adams's notes record Galloway's speech. We do not know whether Adams broke off because Galloway revealed the trend of his analysis or because Galloway had not yet fully articulated his view. But from speeches later that month and from his essay written after the Congress, it is clear that Galloway came to a very different position.

Elaborating later on the status of the settlers, he makes it clear that the only solution to the emigrants' status is either to declare independence or set up a plan of union that would give Americans representation in their own legislature while also keeping them under British sovereignty.

On September 28, Galloway proposed a set of resolutions and a "Plan of Union" for the colonies that ironically anticipated in several respects the final Constitution of the United States. In this plan, Galloway proposed the creation of a grand council, or legislative branch, to be chosen by the representatives of the colonies. The Grand Council would act as a cross-colony legislature while each colony would retain its present constitution and powers under this legislature. The Grand Council would be presided over by a President-General who would be appointed by the king and would exercise all the legislative rights, powers, and authorities necessary for regulating and administering all the general policy and affairs of the colonies. This branch would be an inferior branch of the British legislature. The assent of both legislatures (the British and the American) would be needed for any law to go into effect.

When presenting his proposal, Galloway also had some forward looking things to say about the regulation of trade: "The Right of regulating Trade, from the local Circumstances of the Colonies, and their Disconnection with each other, cannot be exercised by the Colonies." The idea that the colonies could not regulate trade among themselves, without a neutral legislative body above them, was, ironically, one of the drivers to the United States Constitution proposed in 1787 and ultimately one of the powers eventually given to the United States federal government, for precisely the same reasons that Galloway articulates here. In his pamphlet, Galloway admitted his plan may not be perfect,

> but it is an universally prevailing opinion, that the colonies cannot be represented in parliament, I know of none other which

> comes so near to them; and it is most evident, upon a due consideration of it, that the rights of American would have been fully restored, and her freedom effectually secured by it. For under it, no law can be binding on America, to which the people, by their representatives, have not previously given their consent: This is the essence of liberty, and what more would her people desire?[28]

In this proposal, Galloway was attempting to address both the demands for American representation in the legislature while still acknowledging Parliament's sovereignty. Other similar plans had been proposed both in the colonies and in Britain itself since the Stamp Act.[29] But the delegates of the Congress were not ready for such a plan, perhaps, in part, because it may have been too conciliatory. It is likely too that Galloway's plan also partly failed because the colonies ironically were not yet ready for a cross-colony legislature of the "united states" which superseded the authority of the independent colonies themselves. That idea was still controversial ten years later, in 1787, when the debates over the Constitution were occurring. Henry Lee, for example, commented on Galloway's proposal that "We shall liberate our Constituents from a corrupt House of Commons, but thro them into the Arms of an American Legislature that may be bribed by that Nation which avows in the Face of the World, that Bribery is a Part of her System of Government."[30] At least part of the worry seems to be that there would be a supreme legislative power above the colonies themselves, which ironically did come to pass with the approval of the United States Constitution.

Galloway's plan and ideas were given significant discussion during the Congress on September 28 but was tabled for later discussion and then reconsidered and rejected again on October 22. After the Congress concluded, Galloway would go on to further develop his views of and justification of his plan. In that context, he further developed his ideas about the status of the ancestors and their rights in land.

> The lands upon which the colonies are established must be considered, as they truly are, either discovered, or conquered territories. In either case the right of property is in the state,

under the license or authority of which they were discovered or conquered. This property being vested in the state, no subject can lawfully enter upon, and appropriate any part of it for his own use, without a commission or grant from the immediate representative for that purpose.[31]

Since land confers rights, Galloway holds the position that rights travel with people if they move from one territory to another within a government. But if people leave a government's territory for the land under control of another state, they thereby become subject to that state's sovereignty. To justify this position, Galloway argues that the American colonies were discovered by Sebastian Cabot at the behest of King Henry the Seventh. The settlers brought over their rights and duties with them since they moved from one land of the British Empire to another land of the same state.[32] By contrast, Jefferson, we recall, considered the colonial lands conquered under the auspices of the settlers themselves.

To sum up, Galloway sometimes recognizes the category of natural rights, but does not think natural rights have any implication for the American situation. Instead he bases his argument on "general principles" of government which he distinguishes from natural rights. Key is the principle of sovereignty. A state has ownership over land, and it is the state that distributes rights in that land to the people who are part of it. Once individuals belong to a society, they are subject to its sovereignty, which is tied to land. Sovereignty cannot be thrown off by moving to another part of that same state's land. Because the ancestors of the colonies were in fact moving to another part of land under the sponsorship of the state of Great Britain, they are not entitled to deny the supreme sovereignty of the state but they are entitled to the rights of living on land owned by the state.

When Galloway presented his plan on September 28, it is not surprising that James Duane supported him. As discussed above, Duane held a view that was similar to Galloway's, arguing that natural rights were irrelevant and that the emigrants could not alienate their status as subjects. But it is somewhat surprising that John Jay also endorsed the

Galloway plan. After all, Jay had argued during the debate that emigrants did not bring the sovereignty of the state with them. Jay, then, must have been willing to endorse a practical solution that would attempt to avoid war, even though he and Galloway had quite different views of rights.

It is interesting to note that John Adams was still making positive statements about Galloway even after Galloway's September 28 proposal. As late as October 10, after Galloway had proposed his Plan of Union, Adams still describes Galloway in as in the class of "sensible and learned but cold Speakers."

The First American Bill of Rights

The detailed look at Adams's notes illustrates just how diverse were the colonists' views on American rights as late as 1774. It would take another six weeks before Congress would finally publish its Declaration of Rights and Grievances in mid-October.[33] On September 9, 1774, the day after the first debate on rights, "The Comee. met, agreed to found our Rights upon the Laws of Nature, the Principles of the english Constitution & Charters & Compacts; ordered a Sub. Comee. to draw up a State of Rights."[34] In this short summary from Samuel Ward's diary, we see that Congress did begin to define a position and rule out some options. First of all, Congress did decide that natural rights would be included as one of the foundations of American rights.[35] Those who were against relying on natural rights, like Duane, Rutledge, and Galloway, lost the debate. At this point, the colonies had collectively agreed to specifically name natural rights as one of their founding rights. Alongside natural rights, the Congress not surprisingly listed the English constitution, charters and compacts, acknowledging those sources of rights as well.[36] How all of these rights fit together was still ambiguous. The colonies were hedging their bets.

In fact, the endorsement of natural rights did not necessarily resolve a number of critical questions that were left open and referred to the work of committees. Conspicuously absent was any clear statement on the ancestors' status. Did the ancestors bring British rights with them to the new lands or did they set up new and independent states? In addition,

Congress had not yet resolved all the thorny philosophical questions about the nature and extent of political sovereignty, nor come to agreement on a theory of the British Empire. What was the nature of sovereignty of the state and empire, and how did it relate to natural rights? Did British sovereignty extend to the colonies and what made one expansion of land in the empire a "colony" versus a part of the core state? Was sovereignty a characteristic of the king only or of the whole British government, including the Commons and House of Lords? How did political states acquire new lands and how did the right of nations relate to the rights of individuals? These were the many philosophical and political questions touched on in the debates on September 8 and not yet resolved by the decision to endorse natural rights.

It would take the Congress up to six weeks longer, working in relative secrecy, to finally publish its Declaration of Rights and Grievances, sometime between October 14 and 18. During this six-week period, a subcommittee of twenty-four (two from each colony present and almost half of the forty-five delegates present) was appointed to deliberate on the colonies' rights and grievances, and a separate committee of twelve (one from each colony) was appointed to consider trade regulations.[37] Many of the delegates who had spoken on September 8 were included in the committee of twenty-four. Through the month of September, Congress heard subcommittee reports, endorsed the Suffolk resolves, and agreed to a nonimportation and nonexportation resolution as measures to restore American rights.[38] The Congress also debated and tabled Galloway's Plan of Union discussed above.[39]

Into October, discussion kept spilling unavoidably into philosophical and political theory. Richard Henry Lee's proposed that the colonies create militias for defensive purposes. In a debate over that proposal, Patrick Henry reiterated his view that the colonies were in a state of nature and therefore should take on the obligation to prepare and pay for their own defense.[40] John Adams also drafted a set of resolutions that proposed the creation of militias.[41] Others like Ed Rutledge, Harison, Low, and Richard Bland argued that the creation of militias would be regarded

6. The First Continental Congress and the Rejection of Jefferson's Pet Theory 213

as a provocative move on the colonies' part and belie any attempts at reconciliation.[42]

There was also significant debate on the question of whether Parliament should be allowed to regulate trade. The latter question was partly tied to the unresolved philosophical and political questions. As early as September 14, Adams wrote that he

> visited Mr. Gadsden, Mr. Deane, Coll. Dyer, &c. at their lodgings. Gadsden is violent against allowing to Parliament any Power of regulating Trade, or allowing that they have any Thing to do with Us. Power of regulating Trade he says, is Power of ruining us—as bad as acknowledging them a Supream Legislative, in all Cases whatsoever. A Right of regulating Trade is a Right of Legislation, and a Right of Legislation in one Case, is a Right in all. This I deny.[43]

The comment "This I deny" by Adams at the end implied he held the view that it was possible to grant a right to regulate trade without giving up rights in all cases. As we shall see, something like this view is articulated in the final Declaration of Rights that would be published late in mid-October. Similarly, delegates like Samuel Ward rejected various arguments that others had invoked to justify Parliament's right to regulate trade. Among others, he noted that "The Parliamt. ought not to be allowed the Regulation of our Trade for many Reasons. 1st. Because We having no Voice in their Election they are not our Representa[tive]s & consequently have no Rights to make Laws for Us in any Case whatsoever."[44]

In contrast to Gadsden and Ward, Duane, who held that the ancestors did not and could not forfeit their British rights, "has had his Heart sett upon asserting in our Bill of Rights, the Authority of Parliament to regulate the Trade of the Colonies. He is for grounding it on Compact, Acquiescence, Necessity, Protection, not merely on our Consent..."[45] There were also other delegates like Samuel Chase and John Adams who found a legitimate position between the two polar views. As Samuel Chase put it, "I am one of those who hold the Position, that Parliament has a Right to make Laws for us in some Cases, to regulate the Trade-and in all Cases where the good of the whole Empire requires it."[46]

Although John Dickinson was not present in Congress for the debates, he lived locally in Pennsylvania and was weighing in with his views as well. Visits to Dickinson are mentioned by various delegates and quite a number of times by John Adams himself. As Adams put it, "Mr. Dickinson is a very modest Man, and very ingenious, as well as agreable. He has an excellent Heart, and the Cause of his Country lies near it. He is full and clear for allowing to Parliament, the Regulation of Trade, upon Principles of Necessity and the mutual Interest of both Countries."[47]

In the end, the colonies were split down the middle on the question of trade: five colonies were for allowing Parliament to regulate trade, five against it, and two (Massachusetts and Rhode Island) divided among themselves.[48] The disagreement about trade regulation was even more pronounced than the one about natural rights, indicating that the former question was in some sense independent of the latter one.

The American Bill of Rights

During the proceedings of the Continental Congress, the Declaration of Rights and Grievances was referred to by many delegates as an "American Bill of Rights." In many ways, this declaration represents the first collective Bill of Rights of the colonies. This American Bill of Rights was finally completed and published between October 14 and 18, 1774.[49] Silas Deane, in a letter to Thomas Mumford on October 16, summarized the sentiments of many at the end of the work:

> No Resolution of any Consequence, and I dare say, you will judge, some of them so, has been pass'd in the Congress, but with an Unanimous Voice, though they have many of them taken up Days in close, & at Times, warm debate. Three capital, & ,general Objects were in View From The First—A Bill of American Rights,—A List of American Greivances,—And Measures For Redress. You will easily consider the First the most important Subject that could possibly be taken up by Us, as on the Fixing

them rightly, with precision, yet sufficiently explicit, & on a certain, and durable Basis, such as the Reason & Nature of things, the Natural Rights of Mankind, The Rights of British Subjects, in general, and the particular, & local privileges, Rights, & immunities of British American Subjects, considered in degree dis tinct, yet connected with the Empire at large. On This I say, all the Consistency at least, of Our future proceedings, in America depends, and in a great degree, the peace, & Liberty, of the American Colonies In doing this, We have proceeded with the Utmost Caution knowing how critical and important an undertaking it was, & how fatal a misstep must be, not to Ourselves only but to all posterity.[50]

As we now turn to the actual resolutions that were published, we find that Congress not only endorsed natural rights but clarified the thornier question of the emigrants' status as well as the related question on trade. Some historians represent these declarations as a kind of compromise position. And perhaps that is the right way to look at it. But given the range of views that were represented in earlier debates, the resolutions clearly take a stand on several of the critical and debated issues.[51] A compromise can imply that the final position was not coherent in its own right. Yet Congress did define a philosophically coherent position on natural rights, the settlers' status, the sovereignty of Parliament, allegiance to the king and the question of trade.

Beginning first with the list of grievances that it had worked on, the declaration provides the basis of its deliberations and rights:[52]

The good people of the several colonies…justly alarmed at these arbitrary proceedings of parliament and administration, have severally elected, constituted, and appointed deputies to meet, and sit in general Congress, in the city of Philadelphia, in order to obtain such establishment, as that their religion, laws, and liberties, may not be subverted: Whereupon the deputies so appointed being now assembled, in a full and free representation of these colonies, taking into their most serious consideration, the best means of attaining the ends aforesaid, do, in the first place, as Englishmen, their ancestors in like cases have usually done, for asserting and vindicating their rights and liberties, declare...

The first point to note is that the Congress makes its declaration "in the first place, as Englishmen, their ancestors in like cases have usually done." The language is somewhat equivocal as to whether the colonists are saying that they are protesting "as Englishmen" or protesting in the way that their ancestors, "who were Englishmen," traditionally have done. Whether intentional or not, the ambiguity reveals the heart of the question whether the Americans were still "Englishmen" or a new kind of people.[53]

Consistent with the earlier decision on September 9, the Bill of Rights articulates a fourfold basis of American rights.

That the inhabitants of the English colonies in North America, by the immutable laws of nature, the principles of the English constitution, and the several charters or compacts, have the following rights:

Resolved, N. C. D. 1. That they are entitled to life, liberty and property, and they have never ceded to any sovereign power whatever, a right to dispose of either without their consent.[54]

Here the people are called "inhabitants of the English colonies" signaling that they still see themselves as persons in English colonies. The use of the word "colonies" is significant, suggesting that in some sense they are still part of the empire, and not separate states.

The first resolve presents a classic formulation of natural rights with the entitlement to "life, liberty and property." These rights have never been "ceded to any sovereign power whatever," meaning that by entering into any social compact, individuals do not relinquish the rights to life, liberty and property. This is a point that Lee had made during the debates. But what is not yet clear is what compact these resolves are talking about? Are they referring to the British constitution, to compacts or charters, or both? In other words, what was the status of the

6. The First Continental Congress and the Rejection of Jefferson's Pet Theory 217

ancestors who came to the colonies? Did they bring English sovereignty with them, come under the auspices of charters, or create a new compact with the British Empire and king, as Jefferson had asserted?

As we shall now see, the subsequent resolves take a clear position on the thorny status of the ancestors' status. Congress sides with the view that the ancestors did not lose their British rights when they emigrated from Great Britain.

> *Resolved*, N. C. D. 2. That our ancestors, who first settled these colonies, were at the time of their emigration from the mother country, entitled to all the rights, liberties, and immunities of free and natural-born subjects, within the realm of England.

> *Resolved*, N. C. D. 3. That by such emigration they by no means forfeited, surrendered, or lost any of those rights, but that they were, and their descendants now are, entitled to the exercise and enjoyment of all such of them, as their local and other circumstances enable them to exercise and enjoy.

It is clear that by October 12, 1774, Congress had taken a position on the status of their ancestors. On that day, Samuel Ward records in his journal that Congress "Met, considered the Bill of Rights. (That relative to Statutes & that mentioning our Fathers (bringing over all the R[ights]) having not forfeited by Emigration &c, I did not like.)"[55]

Rejecting the view put forward by Jefferson, Jay, and Ward, among others, Congress sided with those who held that the colonists brought their British rights with them to America and did not forfeit them in their emigration. The "right to quit" society argument was decisively rejected. The resolves do not say whether the colonies are considered to be lands that were discovered or conquered. But it is clear that the emigration is conceptualized as a migration under British auspices, not as the founding of a new set of political states.

While the foregoing statement is a clear rejection of the "expatriation" position that had been put forward by Bland, Jefferson, and Jay, among others, the resolutions up to this point have not yet clarified the current status of British sovereignty over the colonies. If the ancestors were entitled to all their rights as natural born subjects and did not forfeit them, are they still subject to British sovereignty now?

The third resolve begins to hint at an answer to this question. The colonists are entitled to all those same rights "as their local and other circumstances enable them to exercise and enjoy." The reference to their "local circumstances" is an allusion to the argument that the colonies could not be full participants in deliberations of British Parliament due to geographical distance. This last statement thus lays the groundwork for justifying a critical and unavoidable limitation on Parliament's sovereignty which is spelled out in the next resolve.

> *Resolved*, 4. That the foundation of English liberty, and of all free government, is a right in the people to participate in their legislative council: and as the English colonists are not represented, and from their local and other circumstances, cannot properly be represented in the British parliament, they are entitled to a free and exclusive power of legislation in their several provincial legislatures, where their right of representation can alone be preserved, in all cases of taxation and internal polity, subject only to the negative of their sovereign, in such manner as has been heretofore used and accustomed: But, from the necessity of the case, and a regard to the mutual interest of both countries, we cheerfully consent to the operation of such acts of the British parliament, as are bona fide, restrained to the regulation of our external commerce, for the purpose of securing the commercial advantages of the whole empire to the mother country, and the commercial benefits of its respective members; excluding every idea of taxation internal or external, for raising a revenue on the subjects, in America, without their consent.

This resolution, which John Adams claims to have drafted, is in some sense the punch line of the whole set.[56] The resolution essentially declares that the colonies are independent states and draws that conclusion from the implications of natural rights theory.

The logic is now familiar: The ancestors were British subjects and entitled to British rights when they emigrated. But they can no longer be subject to Parliament's authority because they lack representation in Parliament and "from their local and other circumstances, cannot properly be represented in the British parliament." Not only was Congress rejecting the solution of sending representatives to England's Parliament, it was also rejecting Galloway's alternative plan, which tried to solve the problem of representation with a local legislature. Because the key requirement of natural rights for representation could by definition not be fulfilled the colonies must be independent states, legislatively speaking. This is a view of the colonies that was very similar to the one developed by James Wilson discussed earlier and differed substantially from that of Bland, Jefferson, and Jay.

While the right to representation applies to Parliament's sovereignty, the same issue does not here extend to the king's authority. As Wilson and others had noted, the matter of the king's sovereignty was separate from the extent of Parliament's authority. In this regard, the Bill of Rights recognizes a concession to "the negative of their sovereign," meaning that the colonists' legislative acts are still subject to the king's executive veto, not unlike that given to the American president later in the U.S. Constitution. The key difference, of course, was that the president was an elected official and the king was not, at least in the view of some. In this respect, the resolves do not claim that the king was "chosen," as Jefferson had claimed in his *A Summary View*, leaving the implication that emigrants were still subjects of the king and had not forfeited their allegiance.[57]

In the end, the Bill of Rights puts forward a federated view of the empire that we have seen before in Hopkins and more fully developed in Wilson.[58] The king is the head of the empire, with the colonies as independent states that are not subject to Parliament's legislative authority. Parliament's authority was limited to the people of England whom it could and did represent. This view was thus thought consistent with natural rights theory, because the representation of the people in their local legislative bodies was thought to fulfill the requirements of representation.

The resolutions also take a clear-cut position on trade. Parliament lacks *the right* to regulate trade. The colonies do "cheerfully consent" to acts of Parliament regarding trade that are "bona fide" and whose purpose is for securing the commercial advantages of the mother country and the benefits of the empire. The use of the words "cheerfully consent" is critical here. Trade is thought to be a right that inheres in independent states (not in individuals directly). Since the colonies are now conceptualized as independent entities with their own legislatures, the colonies are the decision makers. The concept here is very much like a trade agreement executed between two independent political states. It is done so for necessity and for mutual benefit. While this position still gives Parliament control over trade regulations and offers tremendous commercial benefits to Great Britain, it implies that the colonies are independent entities that have consented to that agreement. In this way, the colonies can choose to relinquish control over trade without sacrificing the natural rights of their individual members.

Some commentators imply that the resolves were a kind of compromise position, not conservative enough for Duane and Galloway, but not radical enough for Ward, Lee, and others. As I have suggested, the resolves do claim a radical position but they get there via a different philosophical route. They claim that the colonies are not subject to Parliament's authority and recognize only a "treaty-like" agreement with Parliament to control trade. It is like the United States making an agreement with Great Britain over trade regulations. Moreover, the resolves rest on a coherent philosophical position that accounts for natural rights, sovereignty, the status of emigration, and the role of trade as a right of political states. Adams and others believed that power over trade could be granted to Parliament without violating colonial rights.

It is not surprising that later in life Jefferson characterized the First Congress as landing in the "half-way house" of John Dickinson. By then Dickinson had in fact refused to sign the Declaration of Independence

6. The First Continental Congress and the Rejection of Jefferson's Pet Theory

and in retrospect seems to represent the more conservative element. But here in 1774, the matter was more complex.

While it is true that the Congress did offer Parliament control of trade and recognized the King as the head of government, this was hardly the "half-way" house of Dickinson. Jefferson's characterization is misleading for several reasons. Most importantly, Dickinson had earlier argued that Parliament had the *right* to regulate trade, whereas the resolves go further and argue that the colonies only *consented* to give Parliament the control over trade. There was a significant philosophical difference between these two positions. To say that Parliament had no right to regulate trade was a good as declaring the colonies independent states within a federated empire, a point recognized and criticized by emerging loyalists like Galloway. It was also further than Dickinson had been prepared to go in his earlier Farmer's Letters.

Furthermore, the pragmatic position that Congress did endorse was not that far from Jefferson's own position in *A Summary View*. Recall that Jefferson had also implied that the colonies could allow Parliament to regulate some aspects of trade in return for the benefits that the colonies had received. Jefferson had also envisioned was a kind of trade agreement between independent entities of one federated empire. Speaking of the assistance Britain gave the colonies, Jefferson writes in August 1774 that

> We do not however mean to underrate those aids, which to us were doubtless valuable, on whatever principles granted: but we would shew that they cannot give a title to that authority which the British parliament would arrogate over us; and that they may amply be repaid, by our giving to the inhabitants of Great Britain such exclusive privileges in trade as may be advantageous to them, and at the same time not too restrictive to ourselves.[59]

And again Jefferson:

> It is neither our wish, nor our interest, to separate from her. We are willing, on our part to sacrifice every thing which reason can ask to the restoration of that tranquility for which all must wish.

On their part, let them be ready to establish union and a generous plan. Let them name their terms, but let them be just. Accept of every commercial preference it is in our power to give for such things as we can raise for their use, or they make for ours. But let them not think to exclude us from going to other markets to dispose of those commodities which they cannot use, or to supply those wants which they cannot supply.[60]

Congress had in fact articulated a view that was surprisingly close to what Jefferson had himself espoused in his own essay only weeks before the First Congress. Consent was the basis of granting Parliament the regulation of trade. Congress indicated consent would only be given for "bona fide" laws. Jefferson had spelled out one set of criteria for identifying "bona fide" regulations.

If anything, Jefferson, looking on from afar in Virginia, might have been disappointed for another reason. His pet philosophical and political theory of expatriation had been completely rejected by his colleagues. Not only did Congress endorse the language of natural rights, which Jefferson may have been ambivalent about, but Congress rejected Jefferson's view that the ancestors left behind their rights and sovereignty when they migrated to America. Congress had arrived at a pragmatic position that was not so different from Jefferson's in the end: the colonies were independent, they had the right to regulate their own trade, and they had the right to make their own laws. But the Congress arrived there from quite different philosophical and legal suppositions. We shall see that by the second Continental Congress, Jefferson had not given up his theory of expatriation, which he was still promoting to his colleagues who had already once rejected it.

Jefferson and the Necessity and Causes of Taking Up Arms

By the time the Second Continental Congress reconvened as planned on May 10, 1775, fighting had broken out at Lexington and Concord only a short time earlier. On June 14, Congress would vote to create a Continental Army out of militias around Boston and appointed George

6. The First Continental Congress and the Rejection of Jefferson's Pet Theory

Washington as commander in chief. On July 6, 1775, the Congress published "A Declaration by the Representatives of the United Colonies of North-America...setting forth the causes and necessity of their taking up Arms." This declaration was to be read by George Washington at his arrival in the camp in Boston.[61] For many, the fighting was not yet conceptualized as a fight for independence but was viewed more like a kind "civil war" between two parties that belong to a larger whole. Although some individuals like Jefferson and Wilson already thought of the colonies as independent states, there still was a consensus among most that colonies at least owed allegiance to the King and were part of the British Empire. For most, the war was to protect colonial rights and establish the colonies' rights to independent legislatures, not yet a war to end the relationship with Great Britain completely.[62]

This time Thomas Jefferson was able to attend the Congress and was chosen to draft an early version of what became the *Declaration of the Causes and Necessity for Taking Up Arms*.[63] John Rutledge supposedly had drafted an earlier version of this document which no longer exists. This draft was reported to Congress on June 24, debated both on the twenty-fourth and twenty-sixth, and then referred back to committee, with Jefferson and Dickinson added to the committee. Jefferson wrote two versions of this declaration, the first of which he likely shared with Dickinson and on which he made some revisions, and the second which he submitted to the committee. This later version, however, was not approved by the committee, in part because Dickinson and possibly William Livingston did not agree with it. Dickinson, therefore, made a revision, substantially rewording parts of Jefferson's earlier draft. Congress itself made some minor revisions on the Dickinson draft and finally published the Declaration.[64]

For our purposes it is interesting is to look at Jefferson's view of rights (now only a year before drafting the Declaration of Independence) and to compare it with Dickinson's revision that was edited and accepted by Congress. The oft-told story is that Dickinson softened Jefferson's draft. Yet there was more than softening going on.[65] There was in fact a shift from one version of rights arguments to a different form of rights arguments.

Jefferson's preamble anticipates the Declaration of Independence in the sense that he begins by explaining that the goal is to make known to the world that the cause is "approved before supreme reason." Here is Jefferson's wording with handwritten edits represented by strikethroughs.

> The large ~~advances~~ strides of late taken by the legislature of Great Britain towards establishing ~~in~~ over the colonies their absolute rule, and the hardiness of their present attempt to effect by force of arms what by law or right they could never effect, renders it necessary for us also to ~~shift~~ change the ground of opposition and to close with their last appeal from reason to arms. And as it behoves those who are called to this great decision to be assured that their cause is approved before supreme reason, so is it of great avail that it's justice be made known to the world whose ~~prayers cannot be wanting intercessions~~ affections will ever ~~be favorable to a people~~ take part with those encountring oppression.[66]

After this preamble, the similarity to the Declaration of Independence disappears. Jefferson now turns to the discussion of the ancestors and tries to revive the line of thinking that he has proposed in his *A Summary View* a year earlier. One sees here that Jefferson had not yet reconciled himself to the position on rights that the First Congress had taken, namely, that the ancestors brought their British rights with them to the colonies. Even though Congress had spent six weeks drafting its American Bill of Rights, Jefferson is still trying to revive his theory of rights, a theory that Congress has explicitly repudiated. Jefferson's Composition Draft:

> our forefathers, inhabitants of the island of Gr. Britn. ~~harrassed~~ having ~~vainly there~~ long endeavored to bear up against the evils of misrule, left their native land to seek on these shores a residence for civil and religious freedom. at the expense of their blood, ~~with~~ to the ~~loss~~ ruin of their fortunes, with the relinquishment of everything a quiet and comfortable in life, they

6. The First Continental Congress and the Rejection of Jefferson's Pet Theory

effected settlements in the inhospitable wilds of America; they there established civil societies ~~under~~ with various forms of constitution, but possessing all, what is inherent in all, the full and perfect powers of legislation. to continue their connection with ~~those~~ the friends whom they had left ~~& loved but~~ they arranged themsevles by charters of compact under ~~the same~~ one common king ~~who became the thro whom a union was ensured to the now multiplied~~ who thus became the link ~~uniting~~ of union between the several parts of the empire.

Jefferson's Fair Copy for the committee (after input from John Dickinson)

Our forefathers, inhabitants of the island of Great Britain <~~having long endeavored to bear up under the evils of misrule~~> left their native lands to seek on these shores a residence for civil & religious freedom. at the expense of their blood, ~~with~~ to the ruin of their fortunes, with the relinquishment of every thing quiet & comfortable in life, they effected settlements in the hospitable wilds of America; ~~they~~ and there established civil societies with various forms of constitutions <~~but possessing all what is inherent in all, the full and perfect powers of legistlation~~> to continue their connection with the friends whom they had left they arranged themselves by charters of compact under ~~one~~ the same common king, who thus completed their powers of full and perfect legislation and became the link of union between the several parts of the empire.

Jefferson does not explicitly refer to a natural right to quit society in either of these versions. But in his first version he does provide a more explicit justification for emigration: The ancestors left their native land because of the "evils of misrule" and "at the expense of their blood, to the ruin of their fortunes," they created "civil societies with various forms of constitution but possessing all, what is inherent in all, the full and perfect powers of legislation." Here the right to emigrate does not sound like a "generic individual right" to pursue happiness but appears justified by the Parliament's abuse of power. Indeed, Jefferson's position here sounds much closer to a classically Lockean view of the conditions under which a person can quit a society than the view Jefferson expressed in his *A Summary View*.[67] Here the abuse of power is what generates and justifies the emigration.

We also find that the first version of the Declaration reiterates Jefferson's view that the colonies are independent political entities: the colonies "established civil societies with various forms of constitution, but possessing all, what is inherent in all, the full and perfect powers of legislation." As in his *A Summary View* almost a year earlier, we see Jefferson's disinclination to use the language of "natural rights" and "consent," although his language could be presupposing such assumptions. Why Jefferson thinks that "full and perfect powers of legislation" are "inherent in all" he does not say. And while that language could be construed as natural rights language, his avoidance of such language is consistent with the assumption that Jefferson did not resonate with such language, and may have had some reservations about natural rights theory in some respects.

Jefferson's revised version, after input from John Dickinson, changes the tone and implications to a certain degree. In the revised version, Jefferson has taken out the reference to "evils of misrule," although there is still a moral justification to the immigration since the ancestors left to find "civil and religious freedom." In this revised version, Jefferson has softened the criticism of the mother country. The colonies are still described as their own political entities with their own various forms of constitution. This time, however, Jefferson has made two significant changes that make obvious the connection to Great Britain. The emigrants wanted to continue their connection with friends they had left behind, and therefore they arranged themselves under charters of compact under the same common king. The political entities they created did not by themselves have the full and perfect powers of legislation. It was the king who "thus completed their powers of full and prefect legislation and became the link of union." In this version, Jefferson has still retained

6. The First Continental Congress and the Rejection of Jefferson's Pet Theory

his emphasis on the settlers' freedom to set up new political entities and their choice to enter into compacts with the king.

Jefferson does make one allusion to a general theory of liberty well into the body of his essay. "We do then most solemnly ~~before in the presence of~~ before God and the world declare, that, regardless of every consequence at the risk of every distress, ~~that~~ the arms we have been compelled to assume we will wage with ~~bitter~~ perseverance, exerting to their utmost energies all those powers ~~with~~ which our creator hath ~~invested~~ given us to ~~guard~~ preserve that ~~sacred~~ Liberty which He committed to us in sacred deposit, and to protect from every hostile hand our lives and our properties." This language of "sacred deposit" moves within the natural rights tradition, as does the reference to protecting "our lives and our properties." But the language has much more of the religious and theological overtones as we have seen in writers like Otis, Shute, and Jefferson's own earlier pamphlet. As noted in the discussion of *A Summary View*, Jefferson still avoids the explicit language of the natural rights tradition and favors a more religious description of liberty's origin that may resonate more with Jefferson's notion that moral sentiments are known self-evidently. We see here too the use of the word "sacred" to describe liberty, a term that Jefferson uses again in his first draft of the Declaration of Independence a year later. Compare now Dickinson's equivalent version of the ancestor story with Jefferson's.

> Our forefathers, inhabitants of the Island of GB. left their native Land, to seek ~~in the distant & inhospitable wilds of American~~ on these shores a Residence for civil and religious ~~Liberty~~ freedom. To describe the Dangers, Difficulties & Distresses ~~the Expence of Blood &~~ ~~Fortun~~ ~~Treasure~~ they were obliged to encounter in executing their generous Resolutions, would require volumes. It may suffice to observe, that, at the Expence of their Blood, to the Ruin of their Fortunes, (~~& every Prospect of advantages in their native Country)~~ without the least Charge to the Country from which they removed, ~~with~~ by unceasing Labor and unconquerable Spirit, they effected Settlements in the distant

and inhospitable wilds of America, then fill'd with numerous & warlike Nations of Barbarians. Societies or Governments, vested with perfect legislatures ~~within them~~, were formed under Charters from the Crown, and ~~such~~ an harmonious Intercourse ~~and Union~~ was established between the colonies & the Kingdom from which they derived their origin.[68]

Dickinson's version of the emigration significantly softens the implication that the colonies are independent political entities.[69] They are vested with perfect legislatures "formed under Charters from the crown." Dickinson's language eliminates Jefferson's view that the colonies acted by choice as free political entities. They came into being "under charters" as part of Great Britain. In Dickinson's language the colonies received their "perfect legislatures" as part of a grant from the Crown "from which they derived their origin." Dickinson's version, of course, still suggests that the colonies' legislatures are independent from Parliament. But the origin of those legislatures stems from an act of the king who granted charters, not the outcome of the colonists' emigration and subsequent decision to enter into compacts. This softening of Jefferson's language was not the only change that Dickinson made.

The differences continue in the body of the Declaration between the two men's versions. Writing about Parliament's usurpation of powers, Jefferson writes:

> they have attempted fundamentally to alter the form of government in one of these colonies, a form established by acts of it's own legislature, and further secured ~~to them~~ by **charters** ~~of compact with and grants from~~ on the part of the crown;[70]

In this first version, Jefferson emphasizes that charters only "further secure" the rights that were already established by the legislature of one of the colonies. Here is Jefferson's revised version after comments from colleagues:

> they have attempted fundamentally to alter the form of government in one of these colonies, a form ~~established~~ secured by

charters on the part of the Crown and confirmed by acts of it's own legislature, ~~and further secured by charters on the part of the crown;~~

Here Jefferson is pressured to treat the form of government as arising from charters from the Crown with the local legislature playing only a supporting validating role.

Dickinson takes it still further. He stresses that the form of government is not just "secured" as Jefferson wrote but "established" by charter:

> and for altering fundamentally the Form of Government ~~in one of the Colonies, a Form secured~~ established by Charter and ~~confirmed~~ secured by Acts of its own Legislature solemnly ~~and assented to~~ confirmed by the Crown.[417]

It is also clear that Dickinson did not like using the "emigration of the ancestors" as the preamble and justification of colonial rights. While Jefferson opened with the emigration as a justification of rights, Dickinson inserted a long preamble giving a quite different justification of the armed resistance and making the "story of ancestors" much less critical in the overall justification.[73]

> If it was possible for ~~Beings endued with Reason to believe, that the Divine Author of their Existence who entert feel a proper Reverence for~~ Men, who exercise their Reason in contemplating the works of Creation, to believe, that the Divine Author of our Existence, intended a Part of the human Race to hold an absolute property in & an unbounded Power over others mark'd out by his infinite ~~Mercy~~ Goodness & Wisdom, as the legal Objects of a Domination never rightfully ~~to be~~ resistable, however severe & oppressive, the Inhabitants of these Colonies ~~would~~ might ~~at least with propriety~~ with at least require from the Parliament of Great Britain some Evidence, that this dreadful ~~Authority was vested in that Body~~ authority over them has been granted to that Body. But since ~~Reflecti Considerations drawn a due Reverence~~ a Reverence for our great Creator, ~~Sentiments~~ Principles of

Humanity ~~and the Dictates of Reason have convinced the wise and good~~ and the Dictates of Common Sense, ~~have~~ must convince all those who will reflect upon the Subject, that Government was instituted to promote the Welfare of Mankind, and ought to be administered for the Attainment of that End, ~~since these generous and noble Principles have on no Part of the Earth been so well vindicated asserted and enforced as in Great Britain, the Legislature of that Kingdom hurried on by an inordinate passion for Power, of Ambition for a Power which their own most admired Writers and their very Constitution, demonstrate to be unjust; and which they know to be inconsistent with their own political Constitution~~...The Legislature of Great Britain stimulated by an inordinate ~~Passion for a Power manifestly unjust and which~~) Passion for a Power not only ~~generally pronounc'd held to be~~ unjust, but unjustifiable, but which they know to be peculiarly reprobated by the very Constitution of that Kingdom, and desperate of Success ~~in a Mode of Contest~~ in any Mode of Contest, where ~~any~~ Regard should be had to Truth, ~~Justice, or Reason, have at last appeal'd length~~ Law or Right, have at length attempted to effect their cruel and impolitic Purpose by Violence, and have thereby rendered it necessary for US to ~~change~~ close with their last Appeal from Reason to Arms. Yet however blinded ~~they~~ that Assembly may be by their intemperate Rage, ~~yet~~ we esteem ourselves bound by Obligations of Respect to the rest of the World, to make known the Justice of our Cause.[74]

The Second Continental Congress approved this preamble of Dickinson's, which changes the tone of Jefferson's original draft. Here, the opening justification of rights is not the emigration. Instead, this preamble plays up ideas that move in the natural rights tradition, ideas noticeably downplayed if not almost absent in Jefferson's version. Dickinson's somewhat convoluted language essentially argues the following: If it was possible for men who exercise their reason to believe that God intended for one people to hold absolute power over another, then the Parliament should at least show evidence that they were granted that authority. But a "reverence" for "our Creator, Principles of Humanity, and the Dictates of Common Sense" (Dickinson scratched out "Dictates of Reason" which is interesting) will convince all that government was instituted to promote the welfare of mankind. Therefore there is no need to ask Parliament what justifies its authority.

There are several interesting aspects of this language. First, Dickinson has shifted the justification of American rights away from Jefferson's emphasis on migration of the ancestors to broader principles. Second, the interplay of "reason," "reverence," "common sense," and "principles of humanity" shows that more than just reason is being invoked. And while Dickinson here articulates good natural rights ideas, it is clearly a version of natural rights that evokes and moves within the religious and theological subtradition that we have seen before. No mention is made of "natural rights" specifically. Instead, allusion is made to the divine author's "infinite Goodness and Wisdom" as the ground for believing that no people should be able to subjugate one another. This could be presupposing the classical Lockean view that people are equal because they are God's property. Yet, the language would almost have made James Otis happy in its emphasis on the theological and religious origins of freedom. This language thus avoids the question of whether government is founded at creation or created subsequently by human decision, a claim by the natural rights tradition that bothered some thinkers like Otis and Shute, as discussed. To be sure, allusions to "principles of humanity" and "dictates of common sense" could be construed as references to natural rights. But they may also suggest a source of rights in some inherent moral sense that is self-evident to "common sense." Perhaps the intervening criticisms of the American Bill of Rights after the First Continental Congress suggested that natural rights alone was not a sufficient basis for justifying American rights. And at any rate the Declaration would appeal to more theologically minded individuals who may not have been as satisfied with the Bill of Rights from the First Congress.

The religious overtones of the document are reiterated at the end of Dickinson's version in what is powerful language that was once attributed to Jefferson is now known to be Dickinson's.[75]

> Our cause is just. Our union is perfect. Our internal resources are great, and, if necessary, foreign assistance is undoubtedly attainable.—We gratefully acknowledge, as signal instances of the Divine favour towards us, that his Providence would not permit us to be called into this severe controversy, until we were grown up to our present strength, had been previously exercised in warlike operation, and possessed of the means of defending ourselves. With hearts fortified with these animating reflections, we most solemnly, before God and the world, declare, that, exerting the utmost energy of those powers, which our beneficent Creator hath graciously bestowed upon us, the arms we have been compelled by our enemies to assume, we will, in defiance of every hazard, with unabating firmness and perseverance, employ for the preservation of our liberties; being with one mind resolved to die freemen rather than to live slaves.

To summarize, we have seen that within a year of Jefferson's writing the Declaration of Independence, Jefferson and Dickinson offer their congressional colleagues two different versions of American rights. Neither of these versions of rights is what would be called a classical natural rights theory, like that adopted by the First Continental Congress and put forward by thinkers like James Wilson. Jefferson is still avoiding natural rights language and putting emphasis on the emigration of the ancestors as a justification for American rights. When he does allude to a broader conception of rights, which is buried in the body of his essay, he alludes to the "sacred deposit" provided by God and makes no allusion to reason or rights of nature. Dickinson's language moves much closer to the natural rights tradition, though he evokes the religious and theological subtradition that places emphasis on God's role in founding liberty. But Dickinson also appeals to common sense and reverence for the creator as justifications and foundation for liberty. It is arguable that Congress preferred Dickinson's version not simply because it toned down the view of the colonies as "independent" entities, but also because it provided a broader justification of rights than did Jefferson's, one closer to the Bill of Rights for which they had already fought so hard to achieve consensus in September 1774.

In any case, the point here is that while others were appealing to a classic version of a natural rights philosophy, Jefferson himself had not abandoned his argument based on emigration. Once again, Jefferson's view was essentially rejected. Instead, the Congress endorsed a quasi-religious statement of rights, influenced by the natural rights thinking to be sure, but not quite Lockean in the way that some American writers including the First Congress would have articulated it.

PART III

The Precariousness of History

7. What Do We Really Know about Jefferson on Locke?

The debate over Jefferson's knowledge of and reliance on John Locke's *Second Treatise of Government* and/or Lockean notions of political philosophy is one of those interesting historical questions that may reveal as much about the problems of historicism and history as it does about Jefferson himself. In the preceding chapters, we have looked at Jefferson's relationship to natural rights language and ideas in his major political writings. In this and the following chapter, we look back to the younger Jefferson to try to understand the place of natural rights thinking in his earlier intellectual development. The problem in a nutshell is that the evidence of Jefferson's relationship to Locke's writing is very meager in this earlier period of his life. If we set aside the Declaration and Jefferson's earlier pamphlets (*A Summary View* and *Declaration of the Causes and Necessity for Taking Up Arms*) considered already, there are only four pieces of evidence that suggest Jefferson was familiar with Locke's Second Treatise:

- an invoice from a British bookseller to Jefferson in 1769 for his purchase of twelve titles that included "Locke on government";[1]
- a famous letter to Robert Skipwith in 1771 in which Jefferson recommends books for Skipwith's library, including several of Locke's works;[2]
- one explicit citation of Locke that Jefferson jotted down in his legal commonplace book;[3] and

- several citations of Locke in Jefferson's notes on a scandalous divorce case in Williamsburg that he was preparing to argue written around November 1772.[4]

I wish to explore here not just the question of Jefferson's relationship to Locke and Lockean theory, but the larger question of history itself. This meagerness of information around what has come to be perceived as so important and interesting an issue raises fundamental questions, not just about Jefferson's intellectual background and his knowledge of Locke, but about the limitations and problems of appealing to history in deciding issues of normative significance.

There are two different and related questions at stake here, and they are both entangled in interesting ways with each other. The first is the problem of history as a humanistic discipline: what kinds of facts can be counted towards a historical interpretation and what role interpretation of those facts plays in building out a more complete understanding of a particular historical question. That question is interesting in its own right, and the ongoing discussions and debates within history about the past are often implicitly if not explicitly about such methodological questions. As we shall see, at issue is precisely the question of how to develop a context of understanding from the various pieces of information that we have at hand. Facts become meaningful in frameworks and frameworks emerge through interpretation. The precariousness of history is the subject of this and the following two chapters with the question of Jefferson's relationship to Locke as an example of the problem. I wish to show both that we have a very difficult time answering the question of Locke's influence on Jefferson, and at the same time point to some of the dilemmas of historical interpretation itself, especially as those dilemmas intersect with questions about how we wish to live.

The precariousness of history would not be such a problem, perhaps, were it not for the fact that people often appeal to history in order to settle other problems that have more immediate pertinence, including how we should resolve social debates, decide matters of law, shape our institutions, and settle other issues of ongoing concern to societies. For

Americans, this is particularly true when it comes to the documents of the founding era, although Americans are by no means unique in this way. Any religious tradition displays the same interesting tension between history and religious interpretations of the past.[5] Anything we say about the Declaration, Jefferson, and the dilemmas of history apply in very similar ways to the Bible or Jesus or any other religious source.[6] Jefferson, as the author of the Declaration of Independence, comes into particular scrutiny, not only because of his later role leading the emerging Republican Party and as president, but also because he drafted the first official document to envision the colonies as independent "united states." The Declaration was the culmination of ten years of colonial reflection, as the colonists pondered their rights and the nature of the relationship between themselves and Great Britain. Appealing to the founders' understandings is one way in which Americans want to settle debates about what American society was envisioned to be. If we can remember what the founders intended, then we can get clearer about what we should be doing today.

The precariousness of history, then, raises an interesting problem for those who want to have history settle questions of how we should live. If historians fill in gaps of knowledge and link facts together to produce coherent stories and pictures of the past, to what extent can history provide that solid fulcrum for saying what should be? And if history cannot provide the solid foundation, then what role should history play, if any, in answering the question of how we should live? I will take up these questions in detail in my final chapter and argue that history may have a role to play but not necessarily the one that is normally attributed to the discipline. Whatever role history can play should include an awareness of its precariousness as a humanistic discipline.

In this and the next chapter, I want to concentrate on the first point, showing how complicated it is to answer a very specific historical question about Jefferson's knowledge of and reliance on John Locke's *Second Treatise on Government*. The goal is to illustrate the problem of moving from available historical facts to larger interpretations, and ultimately therefore to the significance of history. In this case, the broader debate that touches down on this question of history involves particularly sensitive issues in American social policy, namely, what individual rights were envisioned as protected by the founders. And the question of Jefferson's relationship to Locke's *Second Treatise* potentially has implications for answering those questions.

To anticipate my argument, I will show that the available evidence is terribly equivocal. We can, of course, render it unambiguous. One might argue that this is one of the tasks of history and the historian. But to render any interpretation at all requires extrapolations of all different sorts to arrive at the story that we tell about Jefferson's relationship to Locke. Those extrapolations include various kinds of unexamined assumptions that we bring in, sometimes consciously, sometimes not. Matters as mundane, yet as potentially equivocal, as why a person bothers to buy a book, build a library, or jot down a reference to a book, all come into play. To even answer matters as simple as these we bring in all sorts of assumptions about the psychological motivations of actors, what they were up to and why. But too often we bring in these assumptions without knowing that we have done so. And when we bring these assumptions to the fore we see that it is by no means easy to come to a direct conclusion about Jefferson's knowledge of or reliance on Locke. The significance of that finding is the subject of my final chapter where we consider what the precariousness of history and of Jefferson's history may or may not mean.

The Facts of the Case: The Invoice, Letter, and the Citations of Locke

I begin with a brief chronology of the facts immediately relevant to our discussion. I say "immediately relevant" because I want to show that the "bare facts," whatever that might mean, are not very helpful until we start the labor of interpreting them. Indeed, the act of interpretation raises the question of what facts are relevant to the discussion and how those facts relate to each other. Any description of the facts can be claimed to be incomplete until the labor of interpretation is finished. And even then the matter is in doubt. For until we ask the questions, we do not know what facts are relevant to the answers. Or to put it another way, the first description of the facts themselves raise questions that in turn lead to other facts in ever widening circles.

Without further ado, Jefferson was fourteen in 1757 when his father, Peter Jefferson, died and left him a library of forty-two volumes on law, history, literature, and religion, one of the largest libraries in Albemarle County.[7] That library included a number of books on various topics including several volumes of Addison and of English history, a work on astronomy, some books of a geographical nature, and many maps. We know further that in 1764 and 1765, Jefferson was visiting the office of the *Virginia Gazette* newspaper in Williamsburg to buy books there during his years as a law student.

On February 15, 1764, he purchased "*Practice, King's Bench*, 2 vols. *Do Common Pleas*, 2 vols. (author not given), *Harrison's Chancery Practice*, 2 vols." On the twentieth of that month he acquired an attorney's pocket companion. On October 3, 1764, he bought William Rastell's *Collection in English of the Statues Now in Force*, which included statutes from the Magna Carta in the early thirteenth century through the reign of James I in the early seventeenth century. Then again on April 30, 1765, he bought *Virginia Laws Since the Revisal*, and then in June he purchased *Grounds and Rudiments of Law*.[8] He had access to George Wythe's library and other law books in Williamsburg. These law-oriented purchases reflect the interests and focus of a young apprentice lawyer. The *Gazette* invoices show the kind of books he thought important to own at this time in his life. But Jefferson was buying more than just law books at this point as well. It should be noted that despite the concentration on law, Jefferson was reading or at least purchasing books on other topics: Milton's *Works*, Hume's *History of England* (six volumes), Robertson's *History of Scotland* (two volumes), Stith's *History of Virginia*, Yorrick's *Sermons*, Sali's *Koran*, Bacon's *Philosophy*, and the *Thoughts* of Cicero; and this is not a complete list.[9]

We also know that by 1769 Jefferson was adding to this library. There is a London invoice in Jefferson's papers dated October 2, 1769, reflecting thirteen discrete titles that Jefferson had ordered.[10] The total of the London purchase in 1769 was £13.1, a fact that will become interesting as we proceed. "Locke on Government" is among these thirteen books he ordered. The list also includes a number of other works such as *Burlamague Le Droit Natural* (*Principles of Natural Law*) and Ellis's *Tracts on Liberty*, as well as a history of Parliament by Gordon and the works of Montesquieu.[11] A full list of the books on the invoice appears in the table below.

Invoice of September 19, 1769[12]

Item ordered	Price of items in £ sterling
Petits Jus Parliamentum C Gilt marble Leaves extra very elegant	1.4.0
Gordon's History of Parliaments 2 vol do. & do.	0.12.0
Modus tenendi Parliamentum very scarce and could not be got otherwise bound	0.4.0
Determinations of the House of Commons extra	0.7.0
Locke on Government do. & do.	0.6.0
Burlamaque Le Droit Natural do. & do. [Principals of Natural Law]	0.18.0
Ellis's Tracts on Liberty do. & do.	1.1.0
Warners History of Ireland do. & do.	0.5.0
(same author) History of Civil Wars do. & do.	1.4.0
Pettys Survey of Ireland do. & do.	0.5.0
Ouvres de Montesqieu 3 Vol do. & do.	2.12.6
Fergusons Civil Society do. & do.	0.17.0
Stewarts Political Oeconomy do. & do.	2.12.6
Paid for a Box.	0.3.0
	£13:10:0

In attempting to determine Jefferson's relationship and familiarity with Locke, Jefferson's purchase of Locke's *Second Treatise* is a significant piece of information. Earlier writers such as Carl Becker in his *Declaration of Independence* assumed direct dependence between Jefferson and Locke simply from the cadence of Jefferson's language without even having this evidence in hand.[13] Other interpreters see this invoice as weighty evidence, when considered with the wording of Jefferson's Declaration of Independence, to draw the conclusion that Jefferson had knowledge of and dependence on Locke.

Morton White, for example, argues that there was significant Lockean influence on Jefferson. White writes that

> ...we do have Jefferson's word that he was trying to harmonize the sentiments he found in books of public right like Locke's. We know that in 1769 Locke's "On Government" was ordered by him from a London bookseller along with Burlamaqui's *Le Droit naturel* and other volumes of interest to students of Jefferson's ideas, and we know that he wrote a correspondent in 1790 that Locke's little book on government, is perfect as far as it goes.

White continues:

> In the light of this evidence and of certain striking similarities of expression which go under the name of "internal evidence," there is little doubt in my mind that Jefferson read Locke's *Second Treatise* carefully before writing the Declaration and that he had been influenced by what Locke had said there, in particular by passages in which Locke *freely uses* the concept of self-evident truth.

White goes on to consider whether Jefferson was closer in philosophical orientation to Locke or others such as Burlamaqui and Hutcheson, particularly around the question of whether he accepted the notion of a moral sense that was pre-rational. Thus White leans heavily on the book purchase and "similarities in ideas" to argue for dependence and influence.[14]

While it is possible that this purchase in 1769 proves Jefferson's mastery of Locke, that is an interpretive inference. Furthermore, a number of other questions arise about that purchase of Locke's *Second Treatise*. Was there some reason Jefferson was purchasing Locke at that particular moment in 1769? Was his intent to read Locke or had he already read Locke previously when he was in college or studying law? What did the purchase of a book mean to Jefferson anyway? The only way to try to approach these questions is by trying to place that purchase in the larger context of events in Jefferson's life and in the colonies. And here we have to invoke other facts from his life and the context of colonial Virginia at the time.

Filling the Gaps in Jefferson's Story

Between the time Jefferson inherited his father's library in 1757 and purchased Locke's *Second Treatise* in 1769, Jefferson attended and graduated from the College of William and Mary (1760–62), where he studied with William Small, a Scotsman and professor of natural philosophy. After graduating from the college, he studied law with a mentor and later friend, George Wythe, a substantial figure in the founding period. At the time, Wythe was an eminent General Court practitioner and leader of the Virginia House of Burgesses, later to become a delegate to the Continental Congress in 1775, first professor of law in America in 1779, and an eventual delegate to the Constitutional Convention. Jefferson would later describe Wythe as a second father. Jefferson took his bar exam in 1765.[15] Although back in England lawyers trained at Courts of Inns, such formal training of lawyers was not yet institutionalized in the colonies. Individuals became lawyers by apprenticeship, and the length of training varied substantially. Some lawyers, like Patrick Henry, received only minimal training and learning.[16] Previously, scholars had assumed that Jefferson had a quite lengthy apprenticeship. But recent reconsiderations suggest that Jefferson started his studies with Wythe sometime after he graduated from William and Mary, probably by the fall of 1762. During that Christmas of 1762, he was studying the foundational legal work of *Coke on Littleton* back at his home at Shadwell, during which time he wrote a letter to his friend John Page reflecting his distraction from his studies and his frustrations with studying Coke. In that letter of December 25, 1762, Jefferson complains that he was distracted from study with his love for Rebecca Burwell on an occasion when he had accidentally destroyed Rebecca's picture

Being distracted by unrequited love, Jefferson was clearly finding studying difficult, and admitted not yet having seriously picked up his books at this point. The lovesick Jefferson in this letter was obviously not here thinking yet of the pursuit of happiness in political terms, but feeling like Job that there is no "such thing as happiness in this world." His mood also spilled over into doubts about the value of study, what he called "mere jargon" at this point in time. If he was studying nonstop during this period and if he was studying philosophical works, he certainly was not enjoying it, for he complained to Page about how endlessly boring and routine his days were. He stayed at Shadwell for most of 1763, partly because of a smallpox outbreak in Williamsburg, and did not return to the capital until October 1763. The few letters over that year show that Jefferson was still preoccupied with his thoughts of Rebecca. At that point he returned to Williamsburg for two years of reading of both law and possibly other subjects, mixed with observation and training in the practical aspects of being a lawyer. Jefferson was admitted to the Virginia bar in 1765.[17]

It seems there is no other direct or conclusive evidence whether Jefferson read Locke during either his two years in college or the years of his legal studies. Some biographers assume Jefferson was reading political and moral philosophy under Small or Wythe. But a careful reading of these biographers' footnotes shows that there is very little direct evidence of what Jefferson read with these two teachers. Historians and biographers are filling in gaps with speculations that often are uncertain and at times simply fanciful. Anyone reading biographies of Jefferson can see this process at work in the stories that biographers tell about Jefferson's early life and the development of his intellectual commitments. Biographers often rely on Jefferson's autobiography and letters from second decade of the 1800's more than 40 years after the events occurred. They are filling in the gaps with the later reflections of the older man.

Willard Sterne Randall's *Thomas Jefferson: A Life* is a particularly egregious example of this trend to fill in the gaps. It is worth taking a look at Randall's account for a moment to see just how detailed and certain is his reconstruction of Jefferson's study habits, though a reading of his footnotes shows just how flimsy is the evidence.

Regarding his studies with William Small at William and Mary, Randall writes, "Few men had more influence over Thomas Jefferson's youthful character formation than William Small, yet remarkably little is known about him other than that he taught at William and Mary from 1758 to 1764 and then returned to England...." With no footnote to buttress his view, Randall can confidently conclude that "Jefferson, who began to absorb from Small the ideas and the attitudes of the Enlightenment, considered him a great man, the embodiment of the spirit of Enlightenment." Again with no supporting footnote, he concludes that "From him, Jefferson first learned of Montesquieu and Molière, Voltaire, Rousseau, and Diderot."[18] He continues:

> Thanks to his tutelage under Dr. Small, he was familiar with the injunctions of seventeenth-century Scottish philosophers of the importance of mastering the law. Jefferson bought John Locke's 1693 treatise, *Some Thoughts Concerning Education*, which advised young gentleman to read works on international law and legal philosophy by Grotius and Pufendorf, two jurists very popular in Virginia. Jefferson owned Locke's Education with this much-read passage. "It would be strange to suppose an English gentleman should be ignorant of the law of his country. This, whatever station he is in, is so requisite that, from a justice of the peace to a minister of state, I know no place he can well fill without it."[19]

Randall provides no footnote to buttress this statement that Jefferson bought Locke on Education at this time let alone read the particular passage from Locke that he quotes. We do know that Jefferson recommends Locke on Education in his letter of 1771 to Skipwith, as we shall see below. By that point he clearly knew about the work.

Speaking of Jefferson's studies with George Wythe during his legal apprenticeship, Randall has this to say, again with no footnote. "Mentor and protégé habitually and interchangeably discussed natural philosophy, the law of nations, and the natural rights of man with Dr. Small and their equally learned friend, the royal governor, Francis Fauquier, at frequent intimate dinners at the Governor's Palace."[20] Randall also concludes, based on a source in 1816, that "By his college days, Jefferson was studying fifteen out of every twenty-four hours, often long after midnight."[21] And to further buttress his argument he notes that "just how rigorous and omnivorous was his self-imposed regimen can be deduced from his answer to a request from young Robert Skipwith ten years later to suggest a list of books for him to study."[22] We shall look at the Skipwith letter soon. The point here is how Randall assumes that, based on a reading list sent to Skipwith in 1771, he can infer Jefferson's study habits while in college nearly ten years earlier. While Randall's conclusions are possible, he presents them with certainty without acknowledging just how many assumptions and gaps are being filled.

Indeed, Randall and other biographers make extrapolations about Jefferson's study habits from letters Jefferson wrote to young would-be lawyers. One such letter in February 1769 was to Thomas Turpin, father of his cousin, Phillip, an aspiring lawyer.[23] Turpin had asked Jefferson to take Phillip on as an apprentice. In his reply, Jefferson turns him down, explaining that apprenticeship is not the best way to become a lawyer anyway, since apprenticeship distracts a young man from his studies.

Jefferson's thoughts about apprenticeship may reflect his own experience that apprenticeship actually got in the way of his studies. If so, then Jefferson may have had much less time to study than his biographers tend to suggest was the case.[24] Instead Jefferson recommends study and reading as the best training for the aspiring lawyer and mentions having already given Phillip a list of books to study, divided into four parts, totaling £100 sterling in estimated cost. Jefferson encourages Phillip's father to invest in the purchase of the books, rather than apprenticeship, as the best way to support his son becoming a lawyer. While Jefferson's sentiment may reflect his own experience of apprenticeship, we cannot rule out the possibility that Jefferson was also trying to find an excuse for not taking on the apprenticeship of his cousin.

Because we do not have the list of books Jefferson recommended to Phillip Turpin, commentators often place more emphasis on another

Jefferson letter to a young friend Thomas Moore, although the letter is less reliable. The original letter to Moore is missing but a revised copy is in a letter to John Minor, dated August 20, 1814.[25] We do not know when Jefferson sent the letter to Thomas Moore. In the 1814 version, Jefferson says he revised only the list of books included but not the substance of the letter in which he describes his recommended methods of study for an aspiring lawyer, including how to break up the day into different subject matters. Unfortunately, Jefferson revised the list of books in 1814 (adding books like *The Federalist*), making it difficult to readily infer from the revision what he might have recommended in 1769, although this does not stop some interpreters from doing so.[26]

Randall is typical in extrapolating from that letter to Jefferson's own study habits but he goes further and also assumes he knows what Jefferson studied.

> But the scientific regiment Jefferson outlined for Moore was not the half of his own daily labors over the books. By his own account, it only took him from eight in the morning to noontime. He believed there was a "great inequality" in the "vigor of the mind at different times of day," and he divided his day into five periods. Even before he tackled his legal studies each morning at eight, he had read "ethics, religion and natural law" for three hours "from five to eight," including Cicero, Locke's essays, Condorcet, Francis Hutcheson's *Introduction to Moral Philosophy*, and Lore Kame's *Natural Religion*. For his matinal reading, under the rubric of religion he read commentaries on the New Testament, the sermons of Sterne, Massillon, and Bourdaloue. For natural law, he read Vattel and Rayneval.
>
> After he had survived this unimaginable seven-hour morning of philosophy and law...Jefferson embarked on the third period of his day. After lunch, he read politics: more Locke, Sidney, and Priestly on government. Montesquieu's *On the Spirit of the Law*, Say's *Political Economy*, Malthus's *The Principles of Population*.[27]

Not all biographers are as ambitious, thank goodness, as Randall in filling in the missing gaps. And the amount of "gap filling" depends on part on what the purpose of the biography may be. What is obvious is that the interpretive decisions in developing the narrative are often made in the background, in some cases perhaps not obvious to the biographer.

Malone, Jefferson's most well-known biographer, also paints the picture of Jefferson as a diligent student, but is more cautious by qualifying and hedging his conclusions. Malone notes, "He followed an appallingly rigorous program most of the time, unless the sincerity of his advice to others and the entries in his own notebooks are to be doubted."[28] Or again, "If we may judge from Jefferson's own recommendation, the hours from eight to twelve in the morning, when his mental vigor was greatest, were devoted exclusively to the law. The rest of the time, except for a period of afternoon exercise, was given to allied subjects."[29]

Malone is also more cautious in assuming that Wythe gave Jefferson a philosophical program.

> Despite his deserved reputation, Wythe's intellectual interests were not so broad as his distinguished pupil's afterwards were... This moderate man may not have been disposed to attack learning on quite so wide a front. Probably he never drew up so long and formidable a list of subjects kindred to the law as Jefferson afterwards commended to the young; probably he did not expect his protégé, along with the law to study physics, ethics, religion, natural philosophy, belles-lettres, criticism, rhetoric, politics, and history.[30]

Malone, like others, quotes the much later reminiscences of Jefferson's boyhood friend John Page, who in 1850 wrote that Jefferson "could tear himself away from his dearest friends, to fly to his studies."[31] Dewey, reconsidering the available evidence, suggests that we can only really assume Jefferson followed such a rigorous discipline at his home in Shadwell from Christmas 1762 to fall 1763, when he returned to Williamsburg and was busy as an apprentice and with social commitments. We cannot conclude that Jefferson himself kept to this rigorous discipline he recommended to others nor read the list of books in the 1814 letter. Dewey, a historian with more caution, puts it this way: "In short, Jefferson's own student reading cannot be reconstructed from the advice he gave to Moore."[32]

Malone, in contrast to a biographer like Randall, is much more cautious in identifying when Jefferson formed his conceptions of rights and read Locke. Malone writes:

> The step from the study of law to that of government was so short that he could easily have taken it without any special deliberation. It would have been strange indeed if he had not given some thought to political theory and done some reading on the subject while he was inquiring so diligently into legal origins. It is reasonable to suppose, however, that his interest in general political questions was stimulated by his entrance into the House of Burgesses, when he assumed his traditional responsibilities as a public man; and unquestionably it was accentuated thereafter by his growing awareness of the fundamental problems which must be solved.[33]

In the footnote to this passage, Malone refers to the 1769 invoice for books discussed earlier and adds this comment: "In view of the scarcity of his early book lists this [1769 invoice] is an important item, but I shall not attempt to date the history of his thought so precisely." Malone thus concludes:

> Before the imperial crisis became acute in 1774–1775 and he first had occasion to present his political ideas in an important way, the doctrine of natural rights was one of his postulates. Just where he got it is a fascinating question, but one to which it seems impossible to give a specific answer. If he did not draw on John Locke in the first place but got the ideas of that noted writer secondhand, he certainly had his [Locke's] very phraseology by heart in 1776.[34]

Although Malone senses that the evidence is less than certain on Jefferson's relationship to Locke, he still ends up with a conclusion like Carl Becker assuming that Jefferson was remembering Locke's language by heart in the Declaration of Independence. The key evidence then for reliance on Locke is the Declaration itself and its cadences or what White calls "internal evidence," but nothing outside of that.

Extrapolations from the Events in Question

Biographers make extrapolations, not just about what Jefferson read and when he read it, but also about how he responded to several critical political events in Virginia from 1764 to 1770 in the prologue to Revolution. These include the Parson's Cause and Two Penny Acts (1758–1764), the Stamp Act Crisis (1764–early 1766), and the Townshend Acts (1767).[35] It is interesting just how little we know about Jefferson's reactions to these events, or what he heard or learned, and, more to the point, whether he heard Locke and natural rights invoked in these contexts.

Jefferson's letters and writings barely allude to these events before his first major writing effort in 1774. For example, on his first trip outside Virginia in May 26, 1766, Jefferson writes his friend John Page from Annapolis. It is striking that in his letter to John Page, Jefferson mentions witnessing the rejoicing that occurred in the Stamp Act repeal. But he does so only in passing and does not provide an account because "this you will probably see in print before my letter can reach you." We have no evidence of how Jefferson thought about the Stamp Act crisis itself or the meaning of that repeal. In that same letter, Jefferson does go into a bit of detail describing the workings of the Maryland assembly which he visited, clearly thinking it to be chaotic and unstructured. The fact that he visited the Maryland Assembly and found it interesting enough to comment upon in his latter to Page suggests an emerging interest in political life.

If Jefferson is already thinking seriously about politics in his early twenties, it is not self-evident from his letters. This reticence on Jefferson's part leads biographers to depend heavily on reminiscences of Jefferson much later in life, specifically in letters to Wirt in 1812, 1815, and 1816 in which Jefferson recalls the events in question.[36] We do not know, therefore, how familiar Jefferson was with the various debates and publications during these critical events. Was he a young man taking a detailed interest in political matters? For example, Jefferson was twenty-one in 1764 when Richard Bland, his cousin and senior member of the House of Burgesses, published *The Colonel Dismounted* in Williamsburg during the debates on the Two Penny Act.[37] That dispute between the local parsons and the Virginia colonial legislature anticipated several of the major issues on political and civil rights that would erupt within a few years between Great Britain and the colonies. Did Jefferson read this essay by his cousin or his subsequent essay, *An Inquiry Into the Rights of the British Colonies?* We do not know. We also do not know whether he read the widely circulating essays by James Otis such as *The Rights of the British Colonies Asserted and Proved*, in which Otis set out many terms of the debate but also raised reservations about the social contract theory of John Locke and by implication parts of natural right theory.[38] Nor do we know whether Jefferson read the essays of Rhode Island Governor Stephen Hopkins, *The Rights of the Colonies Examined*, (1765) or Maryland's Daniel Dulany's *Considerations On the Propriety of Imposing Taxes In The British Colonies* (1765). Any of these essays he could have come across during his trip north to Maryland and New York in 1766. And later, in 1767, in the wake of the Townshend Acts, we also do not know whether Jefferson read John Dickinson's famous *Letters of a Pennsylvania Farmer*, which had wide circulation in the colonies. These various essays took quite different angles on the question of colonial rights as we have seen. In short, if Jefferson read or was impressed by any of these events or writings he did not say so then and we have to speculate from his silence. The only American essay he cites is James Wilson's *Considerations on the Nature and Extent of the Legislative Authority of the British Parliament*, written in 1770 but not published until 1774, which could have influenced him in his writing of the Declaration.

To fill the gaps in the Jefferson story, biographers often turn to Jefferson's later letters and autobiography to picture Jefferson at Patrick Henry's famous speech in the House of Burgesses over the Stamp Act crisis (May 30, 1765) when he was twenty-two.[39] It is of course dangerous to rely on the later recollections of an older man, and there are some documented misrecollections that Jefferson made later in life.[40] But even if Jefferson was in fact taking in all of these events, as perhaps he was, there was no consensus yet among the colonists on the source of the colonists' rights. Neither the Virginia Stamp Act resolutions nor the resolutions of the Stamp Act Congress mentioned natural rights as a foundation of the colonies rights, in contrast to those of other colonies, such as Pennsylvania and Massachusetts.[41] In fact, at this stage Patrick Henry's resolutions in the House of Burgesses were rejected by the men that Jefferson probably emulated most, like Richard Bland and his own teacher George Wythe.[42]

The point is that as an impressionable young man, we do not know exactly what colonial pamphlets Jefferson read, what ideas he picked up from those writings or from those philosophical sources he read directly. It is possible for young people to take minimal or little interest in politics only to find that later events trigger their interest. This could be what happened with Jefferson; we cannot be sure. Even if he picked up ideas that were in the air, there were many ideas circulating about rights that were not all Lockean in origin.

In his chapter called "Disciple of Enlightenment," for example, Malone thus seems very judicious when he writes that "There is no certain way of knowing just when this apostle of freedom first wore eternal hostility against every form of tyranny over the mind of man, but there can be no doubt that by this time he was bold as well as active in the pursuit of knowledge."[43]

What Can We Infer From the Purchase of Locke on Government?

Leaving extrapolations aside and returning now to the direct evidence, we know only that Jefferson purchased "Locke on Government" in 1769. We do not know whether he had read Locke already by this time. It is suggestive that several years after admission to the bar, Jefferson is purchasing a number of political and historical works including "Locke on Government." Kimball rightfully points out that the invoice suggests a new focus for Jefferson's reading compared with what we know of his earlier book buying habits in the mid-1760's. But she overstates the case a bit when she writes that "every one of the 14 items on this bill deals with theories of government."[44] Well, not exactly. They include works of history and political economy, too, as well as some matters of legal interest. But the point is well taken that not a single law book is included in that purchase of 1769. One possibility is that now that Jefferson is finished with his legal studies, has been admitted to the bar, and has taken his seat among the House of Burgesses in 1769, he is turning to a broader range of intellectual interests. The coincidence of his entrance to the House of Burgesses and his purchase of Locke and other political and historical works is suggestive in this regard, as noted by Malone.

Evidence of just such a shift in Jefferson's reading habits does appear in his commonplace book on politics and history, as Chinard and Kimball have both pointed out.[45] In this journal, Jefferson recorded notes on law, history and politics.[46] The first 694 articles deal almost exclusively with matters of law and seem to reflect the notes of Jefferson as a legal apprentice or a young lawyer. The fact that this young Jefferson is not yet thinking politically when making these notes is evident, for example, when he passes over without comment article 231: "The laws of England do not extend to Virginia, which being a conquered country, their law is what the king pleases. Holt. Smith v. Brown and Cooper. 2 Salk. 666." By 1774 when he wrote *A Summary View*, Jefferson would take a diametrically opposed position arguing that the American lands were conquered, but by the settlers and not by the king. Here in his commonplace book, Jefferson passes over in silence the view that "their law is what the King pleases" suggesting that he was not yet rethinking political relations between the colonies and the mother country.

After the articles on legal matters (articles 1 through 694) there is a noticeable and somewhat abrupt shift in focus to other topics including readings in European history, with a particular focus on the peopling of Europe, the practices of ancient people such as the Romans, the Anglo-Saxons and the impact of the Norman Conquest. In the midst of these historical/political notes, there appears a reference to Locke's *Second Treatise on Government* which we will consider in some detail below. The question arises whether we can date this shift in focus and link the timing of the Locke citation to Jefferson's purchase of Locke in 1769? If so, then perhaps we can say something specific about how Jefferson perceived Locke in 1769?

It has been difficult to date the commonplace journal entries with any certainty. Kimball who used handwriting analysis as a guide suggests that many of the key interesting political entries belong to the same time that Jefferson purchased "Locke on Government." In fact, she suggests that the arrival of that book order is reflected in the notes that Jefferson jotted down. Speaking about the book purchase of 1769, she writes:

> As might be expected, the reading and study of these books is immediately reflected in Jefferson's commonplace book, that confidant of his inmost thoughts. The first 693 entries in this book, as we have already seen, dealt exclusively with abstracts from books on law.... With the next entry Jefferson was just turning his attention to the history of the early populations of Europe, when, his shipment of books from London arrived. He glanced through Ferdinand Warner's "History of Ireland," and noted: "The laws of the Tanistry among the antient Irish, like Alexander's will, gave the inheritance to the strongest." Then his eye fell upon Montesquieu's "Esprit des Lois." He picked it up and began devouring its words. They seemed like a revelation to him, expressing, as they did, so many of the thoughts and ideas he had more than half sensed and been mulling over these many months.... It was the first of 27 excerpts from the French philosopher which Jefferson transcribed—more than he was to devote to the work of any other writer.[47]

Regarding the purchase of Locke, Kimball says, "Among the other books that reached Jefferson in December 1769 were Locke's essays on government. Curiously enough, there is just one extract from them included in the commonplace book... It would seem that Jefferson was already familiar with the English philosopher, otherwise his words would doubtless have been as copiously transcribed as were those of Montesquieu."[48] Malone takes a similar tact: "The simplest explanation of his failure to copy much from Locke in his student notebooks is that he was familiar

256   Liberty in America's Founding Moment

with his most important ideas already. For the same reason, probably, he did not bother to copy extracts about natural rights from the writings of other prominent exponents of the theory."[49]

On Kimball's reconstruction, then, Jefferson's notes in his commonplace book reflect the arrival of his book order of 1769. And since he was already familiar with Locke, he therefore only jotted down one reference to Locke. But Montesquieu was new and fresh to him, and he jotted down twenty-seven articles of notes. On this interpretation, then, Jefferson was well acquainted with Locke by 1769.

Kimball's reconstruction of events, however, does not deal with some key questions. Why are there no notes on the other books Jefferson ordered at that same time? And why, if he had just received Warner's *History of Ireland*, would he only cite just that one sentence about the law of "tanistry" which involved the rules of succession to the kingship among the Celts.[50] Where are his notes on the other books he ordered, such as Ellis's *Tracts on Liberty*, Gordon's *History of Parliament*, or Burlamaqui's *Principals of Natural Law*?

There are also other clues that suggest a later dating than Kimball suggests. As Chinard has pointed out, based on comments that Jefferson made in his notes, it is possible to tell which entries were before 1776 and some that can likely be dated before 1774. For example, Chinard notes that that in article 750 Jefferson writes that "There are certain articles in the constitution of the Helevetic body also worthy of attention in constituting an American Congress."[51] Chinard assumes Jefferson wrote this statement "before 1776", but it seems reasonable to go further and conclude that he wrote it sometime before 1774 possibly in summer of that year when there was talk about constituting the first Continental Congress.[52] It is not possible that he wrote that statement in 1769 when he ordered his Locke, for an American Congress was not yet in the offing. In article 832, there is also a quotation from James Wilson's *Considerations on the nature and extent of the legislative authority of the British Parliament*, published in Philadelphia in 1774, suggesting that Jefferson read that essay sometime after that date, possibly after it was circulated at the First Continental Congress.[53]

Another clue appears in the middle of the quite lengthy series of citations from Montesquieu (articles 775-803).[54] Montesquieu quotations make up the largest set of citations in his commonplace book. In the middle of those notes (article 793), Jefferson comments: "This melancholy truth applies to the American colonies whose trade is so regulated by a foreign commercial power as to center all it's benefits in herself."[55] Chinard concludes that Jefferson wrote this before 1776.[56] Yet it seems reasonable to conclude he penned these words even earlier. The use of the word "colonies" here suggests Jefferson made this comment before he started describing the colonies as "states," as he did in *A Summary View* in July 1774 in preparation for the August 1 assembly of the House of Burgesses and in the early resolutions he wrote that summer in June and July 1774 in preparation for the same event. And "the melancholy truth" about American trade being regulated by a foreign commercial power was an issue of substantial debate in the First American Congress.

One other clue supports this dating. In article 747, Jefferson cites various Virginia statues related to rules governing fees to public officials. Jefferson cites the date of each statute's publication and its expiration. The last statute reads: "1772. c. 4 to continue till. Apr. 12. 1774 at which time it expired," suggesting it was written after this date. As Dewey has recently argued convincingly, entries 741-748 refer to the fee bill controversy in Virginia that erupted in May 1774.[57] Douglas Wilson has recently come to similar conclusions through handwriting analysis.[58]

To summarize, then, there is a reasonable number of clues pointing to the summer of 1774 when Jefferson made a number of these entries, including the one on Locke.

However we might be even more specific about the situation in which Jefferson was taking these notes. He may have been making these notes precisely in preparation for writing *A Summary View*. In article 749, for example, Jefferson turns his attention to the Union of Utrecht, entered into in 1579, and makes notes on how that treaty structured the relationship between different provinces and between those provinces and a central federal government. He seems to be thinking both about the relationship of various colonies to each other and possibly the role of the Continental Congress in relationship to the colonies.

In article 750, he turns to Stanyan's *An account of Switzerland* written in the year 1714. Here he remarks, "There are certain articles in the Constitution of the Helvetic body also worthy of attention in constituting an American Congress." Jefferson takes particular note of how the Helvetic unions organized themselves together for defensive purposes only. Here too his attention seems to be on how the colonies might model their relationship with one another.

In article 751, Jefferson moves on to a discussion of the northern European countries and their relationship to the Anglo-Saxons. In this context he cites a number of historical works. The importance of the Anglo-Saxons to Jefferson's argument in *A Summary View* has already been discussed. These notes are a very technical historical discussion focused on the relationship of these northern federations to Anglo-Saxon law and ultimately to the conquering of England.[39]

In Article 752, Jefferson quotes Lord Coke on laws regarding a privy-counselor, without any patent or grant, the significance of which I do not understand in the current context.

Article 753 deals with the relationship of English law to Ireland and discusses the types of laws which England can bind on Ireland and Wales and the kinds of laws over which they have their own self-jurisdiction. We know that in *A Summary View* he would argue that the relationship of the colonies to England was analogous to the relationship between England and Scotland. To summarize:

Article	Possible Dating
Articles 1-694	Mostly laws probably reflecting Jefferson as a law student or apprentice
Articles 741-748: Refers to fee bill controversy	Debate erupted in May 1774 (per Dewey)
Article 747: Reference to a statute that expired on April 12, 1774	Suggesting it was written after April 12, 1774
Article 750: Reference to how rules in the Helvetic body are relevant to an American Congress	Possibly referring to First American Congress in September 1774 (My argument)
Article 754: Discussion of how Denmark shifted from an elected to a hereditary monarchy with citation of Locke and discussion of how British monarchy is elected institution	Suggests the Locke citation occurs in the summer of 1774 as Jefferson was thinking about the role of the First American Congress and the rights of the colonies. (My argument)
Article 792: Reference in midst of Montesquieu notes to the melancholy truth applies to the American "colonies"	Likely written in summer of 1774 before Jefferson begins calling the colonies "states" as he does in A Summary View and in resolutions written that summer as discussed below. (My argument)
Article 832: reference to James Wilson's Considerations (published in 1774)	Possibly read after Wilson's essay circulated at the First Continental Congress

Based on these clues it seems possible to go further than Chinard and conclude that many of these entries (at least 747-792) were made in the period leading up to the first Continental Congress when Jefferson was thinking about or taking notes for *A Summary View*.

Jefferson's Commonplace Notes for *A Summary View*

As discussed in previous chapters, *A Summary View* was written as a set of resolutions for an August 1, 1774, meeting of the House of Burgesses, which had been disbanded back in May by the governor. The immediate catalyst for these events was news of the Boston Port Act which closed the Boston port to commerce. The act triggered a series of reactions across the colonies and news reached Virginia before May 19, 1774.[60] The House of Burgesses drafted a resolution calling for a day of fasting and prayer on May 24, 1774. The resolution spoke about the great dangers to be derived to British America...." The fast was to "implore divine Interposition for averting the heavy Calamity, which threatens Destruction to our civil Rights, and the Evils of civil War; to give us one Heart and one Mind firmly to oppose, by all just and proper Means, every Injury to American Rights."[61]

These resolutions were considered radical enough that Governor Dunmore of Virginia dissolved the House of Burgesses on May 26. Undeterred the members of the House published a declaration the next day from the "Late House of Burgesses." This declaration talked about how "security of our just, antient, and constitutional rights, have been not only disregarded, but that a determined system is formed and pressed for reducing the inhabitants of British America to slavery, by subjecting them to the payment of taxes, imposed without the consent of the people or their representatives..."[62] The declaration also called for a meeting of a congress across the colonies. "We are further clearly of the opinion, that an attack, made on one of our sister colonies, to compel submission to arbitrary taxes, is an attack made on all British America, and threatens ruin to the rights of all, unless the united wisdom of the whole be applied." The declaration calls for a congress "to deliberate on those general measures which the united interests of America may from time to time require."[63]

The declaration still uses the language of "colonies" and not "states," language Jefferson will adopt soon thereafter. Jefferson is one of the signers of this declaration but the author of this declaration is not known. On May 31, Peyton Randoph and others wrote to the Late House of Burgesses calling for a meeting on August 1 to discuss possibilities of a boycott of "nonimportation." On July 23, Jefferson and John Walker send a letter to the inhabitants of the Parish of Saint Anne calling for a day of Fasting. In it the authors present the fast as helping to "avert from us the dangers which threaten our civil rights" (not "natural rights").[64]

On July 26 Jefferson writes a series of resolves on behalf of the freeholders of Albemarle that has some significant similarities to Jefferson's *A Summary View* which he was writing at the same time, as others have noted.[65] The resolves open with the following statement: "Resolved, that inhabitants of several *states* of British America are subject to the laws which they adopted at their first settlement and to such others as have been since made by their respective legislatures, duly constituted and appointed with their own consent; that no other legislature whatever may rightfully exercise authority over them, and that these privileges they hold as the common rights of mankind, confirmed by the political constitutions they have respectively assumed, and also by several charters of compact form the crown." [emphasis mine]

The use of the term "states" rather than "colonies" here may be significant, reflecting a shift towards Jefferson's theory articulated in *A Summary View* that the settlers had conquered and set up independent states, not colonies of the Crown. Here however Jefferson has not yet invoked the "natural right to quit society" as the basis for his claim that the early settlers were not subject to either Parliament or the Crown's power. Then again on July 26 ,1774, in *Draft of Declaration of Rights* prepared for the Virginia Convention of 1774, Jefferson repeats the same claim that "We the subscribers inhabitants of the colony of Virginia do declare that the people of the several states of British America are subject to the laws which they adopted at their first settlement and to such others as have been since made by their respective Legislature duly constituted and appointed with their own consent...."[66] This one sentence is a great summary of the theory Jefferson sets out in *A Summary View*.

Given the course of events that summary of 1774, it seems very possible that Jefferson was making the notes in his legal commonplace book during the period leading up to the First Continental Congress when he undertook his first major political work, *A Summary View*, an essay intended as resolutions for the Virginia delegates' meeting on August 1, 1774. If this reconstruction is correct, then this part of Jefferson's legal commonplace book is not simply notes on general reading, but notes from very purposeful reading he was doing during the summer of 1774 for a very specific purpose: to think through his view on the status of the colonies in preparation for writing *A Summary View* and setting forth his view of rights and his ideas about how the "states" should relate to each other.

We cannot of course be sure that this reconstruction of his notebook is correct, although it seems to fit the data. If it is correct, it means that the citation of Locke in article 754 was made that very summer of 1774 when Jefferson was writing *A Summary View*, a piece of information that is important to understanding that essay as well as his relationship to Locke. This interpretation would indeed make sense of the citation of Locke, and I shall come back to that citation in some detail below.

To see how this reconstruction makes sense, consider the order of the notes Jefferson took in this section of his commonplace book. In article 750 he had already indicated he was reading about the Helvetic laws in efforts to think about an American Congress. Then in article 754 he opened up Molesworth's *History of Denmark*, skipped over the sections dealing with travel and geography, and focused on how Denmark had once been an elected monarchy and subsequently become a hereditary monarchy. In the middle of making notes on Molesworth, he interrupts his note taking and makes notes to himself proving that England has an elective monarchy and cites Locke as proof that a Parliament cannot set rules for hereditary succession. [67]

This very same issue of the "elected nature" of the monarchy was a central contention in Jefferson's *A Summary View* as we have in an earlier chapter. There Jefferson argued that the settlers had set up new states and had chosen the British constitution for their law and the British monarch as their own king. In the context of 1774, the notes from Molesworth and the citation of Locke make sense. While working on or thinking about *A Summary View*, Jefferson was pulling books off his library shelf and taking notes as he thought through his own political positions. His short quote from Warner about the Celtic rule of tanistry also makes sense in this context. Again he is pondering how different societies deal with the rule of succession.

The articles before the ones just discussed could also come from that same period in time or earlier although it is much more difficult to determine. For example, articles 718-731 deal with the relationship of a mother state to her colonies in antiquity. Article 731 deals with the origin of slavery, an institution that is also on Jefferson's mind in *A Summary View* and which Jefferson blames on the king. Article 732 deals with the origin of capital punishment which is attributed to King Edmund I. Articles 733-734 focus on feudal law and the question of whether the king has the right to give land to the people, a question that Jefferson touches on in *A Summary View* as well. Article 740 quotes Blackstone on the origin of feudal estates.[68] One possibility is that Jefferson was already thinking about the ideas that would end up in *A Summary View* before that summer of 1774, although it is difficult to tell how much earlier those earlier entries were made.

If the foregoing analysis is correct, we see that the citation of Locke does not prove that Jefferson read Locke when he first received the books he ordered from the invoice of 1769. This citation of Locke shows that Jefferson was engaged with Locke in the summer of 1774. We shall have to look for other evidence that he read and understood Locke deeply before that summer. But let us first see just how well Jefferson understood Locke while he was writing his pamphlet that summer of 1774 before the First Continental Congress.

The Locke Citation in the Commonplace Book

Interpreters of Jefferson have made much of Jefferson's citation of Locke in article 745 of his commonplace book, debating whether this citation does or does not prove his knowledge and mastery of Locke. I will argue that both sides are partially wrong (or partially right depending how you look at it). And they are partially wrong because they oversimplify Jefferson's interpretation of Locke as well as ignore the historical context in which Jefferson was taking the notes. To appreciate these points, let us first turn to the context of citation.

Article 754 in the commonplace book contains Jefferson's own notes for his argument that the monarchy of England is elective, and not hereditary. This article appears in a middle of a sequence of notes that Jefferson is making on the nature of various governments in Europe. As discussed above, I believe Jefferson was jotting down such notes during the summer of 1774 (not in 1769) as he was contemplating the First Continental Congress and the relationships between the various colonies.

Article 754 begins with a long quotation from Robert Molesworth on the history of Denmark. Jefferson skips over Molesworth's interesting introduction in which he explains the importance of travel for the education of youth and for the preservation and better appreciation of English liberty. In the style of travel literature, Molesworth explains that the exposure to other cultures helps an individual appreciate the importance of liberty and the strength of English liberty in particular. Jefferson also skips over the detailed geographical survey and customs of the people. We now have a possible interpretation of why Jefferson ignored this earlier material. He was not just reading Molesworth, but quoting passages that would serve him in making a specific argument in 1774.

The passage from Molesworth that Jefferson quotes begins by attributing the restoration of the constitutional government to the Northern nations, a classic Whig view of history. Ultimately, this would fit with Jefferson's understanding that the Anglo-Saxons had brought such constitutional ideas to England. Molesworth goes on to note that Denmark had been under an elective monarchy up until 1632 when it ended. By "elective monarchy," Molesworth means that the people could always approve the selection of a monarch, even though in practice the monarchy was often hereditary. In addition, the people always had the right to remove the King if the good of the people was not considered. Here is the quotation that Jefferson extracts from chapter 6 of Molesworth's account.

> All Europe was beholden to the Northern nations for introducing or restoring a constitution of government far excelling all others that we know in the world. It is to the antient inhabitants of these countries, with other neighboring provinces that we owe the original of parliaments, formerly so common, but lost within this last age in all kingdoms but those of Poland, Great Britain and Ireland. Denmark was till 1660, governed by a king chosen by the people of all sorts: even the boors had their voices, which king Waldemar the third acknoleged in that memorable answer of his to the pope's nuncio, who pretended to a great power over him:...The estates of the realm being convened to that intent were to elect for their prince such a person as to them appeared personable, valiant, just, merciful, affable, a maintainer of the laws, a lover of the people, prudent and adorned with all other virtues fit for government, and requisite for the great trust reposed in him; yet with due regard had to the family of the preceding kings. If within that line they found a person thus qualified, or esteemed to be so, they thought it but a piece of just gratitude to prefer him before any other to this high dignity; and were pleased when they had reason to chuse the eldest son of their former king, rather than any of the younger, as well because they had regard to priority of birth, when all other virtues were equal, as because the greatness of his patronal estate might put him above the reach of temptations to be covetous or dishonest and enable him in some degree to support the dignity of his office. But if after such a choice they found themselves mistaken, and that they had advanced a cruel, vitious, tyrannical, covetous, or wasteful person, they frequently deposed him, often times banished, sometimes destroyed him; and this either formally by making him

> answer before the representative body of the people; or if by ill practices, such as making of parties, levying of soldiers, contracting of alliances to support himself in opposition to the people's rights, he was grown too powerful to be legally contended with, they dispatched him, without any more ceremony, the best way they could and elected presently a better man in his room, sometimes the next of kin to him, sometimes the valiant man that had exposed himself so far as to undertake the expulsion or the killing of the tyrant; at other times a private person of good reputation who possibly least dreamt of such an advancement. Molesw' *Account of Denmark*. c. 4.

After quoting this passage, Jefferson interrupts his note taking from Molesworth to digress and jot down his own reflections on the elective nature of the English Crown. It is in this context in which he paraphrases and cites Locke. It seems reasonable to conclude that Molesworth's quote prompted Jefferson to digress to a related topic in which he cites Locke. Here is the digression in which Jefferson in his own words cites Locke.

> This was the antient and is the present constitution of Sweden, as it is also of Poland, in some measure: and it may certainly be deemed the present constitution of Great Britain. Acts of parl. have indeed been passed for settling the succession; but they are void in their nature; because a king, *elected by the people,* is one of the branches to whom the people have deputed the power of making laws; and they have never bound themselves to submit to any laws but such as have received the approbation of the Commons, the Lords, and a king so elected, and his being merely a delegated power, cannot be deputed to others by the whole delegates, much less by two branches of them only, to wit the Lords, and Commons. Locke. *Gov. 2 11.* The following instances of the right of electing a king by the people of England prove a right reserved to them…

Jefferson makes several claims here. First, he reiterates Molesworth's view that Great Britain shares "this antient" constitution with Sweden and to some extent Poland. Jefferson here is reflecting the view of Whig historians that there had been an original constitution that had once been in place with many of the early peoples of Europe. While this constitution was still preserved in England, it had been lost in many other countries. Like the Whig historians, Jefferson is making a historical claim about an original constitution that had been in existence in early Europe and lost under feudal law that was introduced with William the Conqueror.

It is important to realize that this notion of an original constitution is not necessarily the same idea as Locke's notion of an original social contract, although the two views can coexist and overlap. The notion of an original constitution in Europe is a historical claim about an actual contract or actual practice of government that does not necessarily depend on an argument from the law of nature or natural rights. From that perspective, the claim is historical. This is the view that Jefferson invokes here. England preserves the old constitution along with other countries like Poland and Sweden. Denmark had it but lost it. The notion of an original, primitive and better government could be justified by Locke's social contract (and Locke layered his theory on top of already existing contract theory).[69] But the two claims were potentially separable and Whigs often talked about the original contract without necessarily invoking Lockean natural rights. Jefferson here is reflecting the view that there was an original pure form of government that England and a few other countries were still preserving. As we have seen, the same view was also evident in *A Summary View*.

Jefferson then goes on to make the point that occupies him here. In England too, he claims there was always an elective monarchy. We know from *A Summary View* that in the summer of 1774 Jefferson came to the conclusion that the king of England was nothing more than an elected chief officer of the American states. On Jefferson's vision, the British Empire would share a single king, elected by each group of independent peoples, who each had their own legislature. It was thus important to Jefferson's argument that the king of England be regarded as an elected official and not a hereditary monarch. If he had been a hereditary monarch, it would have been more difficult for Jefferson to argue that the people of the Americas had chosen him as their king.

To make his case, Jefferson had to deal with the seemingly contradictory fact that Parliament had set laws of succession for the monarchy, suggesting that British monarchy was more like a hereditary rather than elective monarchy. If that was the case, had England also succumbed to the corruption of the original constitution, the way Denmark had? Was it too in danger of losing touch with its original constitution? Jefferson in fact assumes so and argues that the laws of succession are void and essentially illegal.

Jefferson's argument is very technical. He essentially argues that the king who is elected by the people is part of the legislative apparatus to which the people have "deputed" their power. It is debatable whether the king should be seen as part of the legislative or executive apparatus and some of the readings on which Jefferson took notes, such as the Treaty of Utrecht, do seem to distinguish legislative and executive roles. But let us try to follow Jefferson's logic. Since Jefferson regards the Crown as part of the legislative apparatus, he argues that the powers to decide who is king belong to the people as a whole and cannot be assigned to only a subset. Just as the legislature has to be representative of the people's wishes as a whole, so does the Crown. In other words, Jefferson is claiming that the rules on the monarchy's succession cannot be made by Parliament but must have the approval of the whole people. It is in this context that Jefferson cites "Locke 2 Gov. 2. 11" with no further comment. The Locke citation, as we shall now see, is used to buttress his argument that Parliament has no right to set rules of succession for the king.

An Oversimplification of Locke?

Interpreters of Jefferson have made much of Jefferson's citation of Locke in this context, debating whether this citation does or does not prove Jefferson's knowledge and mastery of Locke. On the one side, Garry Wills argues that Jefferson may never have read Locke's *Second Treatise*. With regard to this citation Wills writes:

There is one citation of the Treatise (not a quotation from it) in the Commonplace Book. But it is probably derived at second hand. It occurs in Jefferson's survey of government and their forms, a survey derived from multiple sources. When Jefferson assembles the evidence for grounding the authority of Kings in elections, he appends a reference to the eleventh chapter of the Treatise on legislative supremacy-which is not the same matter at all. Apparently some reference in his reading made him think this citation apropos.[70]

By contrast, Allen Jayne has argued that this reference to Locke by Jefferson proves extensive knowledge of Locke and thus provides the grounds for arguing that Jefferson was a careful and knowledgeable reader of Locke. Jayne uses this citation to justify his conclusion that parallels he finds between Jefferson's Declaration of Independence and Locke's *Second Treatise* reflect direct influence.[71] Jayne writes, "By examining the context in which the Lockean paraphrase was commonplaced, however, along with the contents of the chapter cited, it can be shown that Jefferson did cite Locke correctly and appropriately and in a manner that indicates considerable knowledge of the Second Treatise." And additionally, Jayne writes, "He was correct and appropriate in his use of Locke as authority for his argument." Jayne continues:

> It would also seem that since he knew chapter 11 of the *Second Treatise* well enough to paraphrase provisions that applied to the legality of legislation relative to the successors of elected kings, his knowledge of that chapter extended beyond those provisions and indeed to the entire work. Evidence of this may be seen in the similarity of many of the provisions of the Second Treatise with those of the Declaration which clearly shows that Jefferson not only had extensive knowledge of Locke's work but put it to use in drafting the Declaration.[72]

I believe both views are oversimplifications, for Jefferson gets Locke both right and wrong. Jefferson displays knowledge of Locke but he oversimplifies Locke and adapts Locke in a misleading and possibly incorrect way. What this oversimplification means is an interesting issue in its own right for interpreting Jefferson's relationship to Locke. Furthermore, interpreters of this citation have not paid sufficient attention to the context in which it was written since most did not realize it was made during the summer of 1774 when Jefferson was preparing his *A Summary View*.

To understand these points fully, let us look at the content in the chapter of Locke that Jefferson cites. The chapter in question deals with the limitations on the power of the legislative body. In this chapter, Locke is indeed discussing the restrictions against the delegation of powers by the legislature. In a passage that sounds like the one Jefferson is paraphrasing, Locke writes:

> Fourthly, The legislative cannot transfer the power of making laws to any other hands; for it being but a delegated power from the people, they who have it cannot pass it over to others. The people alone can appoint the form of the commonwealth, which is by constituting the legislative and appointing in whose hands that shall be. And when the people have said, We will submit to rules and be governed by *laws* made by such men, and in such forms, no body else can say other men shall make *laws* for them; nor can the people be bound by any *laws*, but such as are enacted by those whom they have chosen…the *legislative* can have no power to transfer their authority of making laws, and place it in other hands.[73]

Now on the surface this statement from Locke seems to provide a very strong support for Jayne's view that Jefferson knew his Locke well. Locke here is clearly talking about restriction on delegated powers and thus Jefferson seems to be making a very technical reference to Locke.

Before concluding that Jefferson knew Locke cold, it is important to realize that Jefferson is presupposing one particular reading of Locke here, and that there is indeed an ambiguity in Locke that could undermine Jefferson's own position. The ambiguity arises because Locke himself made it clear that the people had a right to create a government with a hereditary kingship. On Locke's account, a hereditary kingship is compatible with natural rights. Indeed, in the chapter of Locke just before the one Jefferson cites (chapter 10), Locke has a substantive discussion of hereditary and elective kingship. There (10:132) Locke makes quite explicit that hereditary monarchy is permissible if the people have founded the society that way by choice.

In other words, Locke sees hereditary monarchy as compatible with liberty as long as there is a legislature that represents the people's consent. Locke also says that if the power of the legislature was placed in any individual or institution for limited duration, then the power reverts to the people at the designated time. When that occurs, the people can change the nature of their government if they desire from an elective to a hereditary monarchy.

Reading Locke carefully in that context, one could conclude that a people could switch from an elective to a hereditary monarchy if they so chose. On that reading of Locke, an elective monarchy in England could be converted to a hereditary monarchy with the people's approval. Locke could, therefore, argue that Jefferson's historical data is irrelevant. Even if the English monarchy had been historical in the past, it need not remain so in the future. And if we asked how a society would switch from an elective to a hereditary form, it might be reasonable to assume from Locke that the legislature, which is representative body of the people, could make that decision.

Locke does not say this explicitly but it seems like one possible reading of him. On this interpretation, we could argue that Locke might have disagreed with Jefferson's reading of him and that Jefferson's citation of chapter 11 missed something important in Locke's chapter 10.

So what have we learned? One might argue that we are splitting hairs. Jefferson, after all, still seems in the right Lockean "ballpark," so to speak. He cites a chapter of Locke that is relevant to the question at hand and he seems to be paraphrasing or even interpreting it, even if another interpretation is possible. We can also conclude that shortly before writing *A Summary View* Jefferson was thinking of Locke as providing justification for the fact that elective monarchy could not be switched by

Parliament to a hereditary monarchy. And it does seem to show Jefferson was familiar enough with Locke that he could make an intelligent use of him, even if the interpretation could be disputed and did not fully or accurately represent Locke's position.

But the citation of Locke does not necessarily prove that Jefferson knew Locke by heart, for he very well could have pulled Locke along with other books off the shelf when making these notes in preparation for *A Summary View*. It also seems important to note that Jefferson turned to Locke, not for a general justification of natural rights here, but to prove a specific point of law, as he had done before in earlier legal cases, which we shall see below. He appeals to Locke because he is looking for support for the view that Parliament had no right to create laws of succession and change an elective monarchy to a hereditary one.

The worry that England might legally have changed to a hereditary monarchy might in fact have been prompted by Jefferson's reading of Molesworth. After discussing the elective nature of the Danish monarchy, Molesworth goes on to talk about how the Danish people themselves had desired to end their elective monarchy. In a long detailed account, Molesworth explains how the people's conflicts with the nobility had prompted them to ask the king to take more *power*! Molesworth's account therefore describes the situation of a people who *by choice* renounced and gave up an elective monarchy. Jefferson himself cites this part of Molesworth, though he paraphrases it. Had the English people done the same? Had they given up their elective monarchy at some point in historical time? Core to Jefferson's argument in *A Summary View* was the contention that the American states had elected their king and not inherited him.

8. Hume, Locke, and Jefferson's Early Legal Cases

The Fire, the Letter, and the Library

We have learned that Jefferson purchased Locke in 1769. A citation of Locke also appears in his commonplace book, which seems to have been made in the summer in 1774, when he was preparing his essay *A Summary View*. So how much did Jefferson know of Locke before 1774 when he cited him in his commonplace book? To answer this question, three other important facts become relevant here in trying to answer that question.

The first is the fire in 1770 that burned his mother's house in Shadwell to the ground and destroyed "almost every book."[1] On February 21, 1770, Jefferson writes to his friend John Page that "To make the loss more sensible it fell principally on m[y books] of common law, of which I have but one left, at that time lent out." Jefferson estimated the loss at about £200 sterling. Given that estimate of value, and the invoice total of books he ordered in 1769 at £13 sterling, we can surmise that the 1769 order must have represented about 6 percent of his total library, a substantial size order. Furthermore, in his letter of 1769 to the father of the aspiring lawyer Turpin, Jefferson indicates that he had given his son a list of books totaling £100 sterling, suggesting that his own library was double in size what he thought a young law student should master.

In several letters following the fire, it is clear that other friends had heard of Jefferson's devastating loss. On March 6, 1770, Thomas Nelson Sr. writes to Jefferson "extremely concerned to hear of your Loss." "As

I have a pretty good collection of Books, it will give me pleasure to have it in my power to furnish you with any you may want." The same day Thomas Nelson Jr. writes Jefferson and confirms that "You may depend on your Letter to your Bookseller being sent by the first opportunity," suggesting that Jefferson was immediately taking steps to rebuild his library. His close friend John Page also wrote to Jefferson on March 6 that "I heard of your Loss [and] heartily condole with you..." On March 9 George Wythe, his mentor and former law instructor, writes Jefferson that "You bear your misfortune so becomingly, that, as I am convinced you will surmount the difficulties it has plunged you into..."[2] By August 1773 he noted in his account book that he again had 1,256 volumes in his library, indicating he had rapidly repopulated his collection.[3]

A number of additional questions obviously arise from the fire. Was "Locke on Government" one of the books that survived or was it burned as Wills has suggested.[4] If not, did Jefferson have access and take advantage of the offer to use the library of Thomas Nelson Sr.? Should we assume that Jefferson already read Locke before he ordered it? And can we assume Jefferson reacquired Locke's work after the fire? We can only infer an answer to some of these questions by turning to a famous "Skipwith" letter that Jefferson wrote in the post-fire period.

During July 1771, one of Jefferson's friends and neighbors, Robert Skipwith, wrote Jefferson a letter requesting a list of recommended books that Skipwith should purchase for his own library.[5] It is clear from the letter that the two had had a previous conversation at Skipwith's house, which he called "The Forest," and that Jefferson had asked Skipwith to give him some guidance. He wanted "to remind you," writes Skipwith, "of your obliging promise and withal to guide you in your choice of books for me, both as to the number and matter of them."[6] Skipwith requests a list that is "suited to the capacity of a common reader who understands but little of the classicks and who has not leisure for any intricate or tedious study. Let them be improving as well as amusing and among the rest let there be Hume's history of England, the new edition of Shakespear, the short Roman history you mentioned and all of Sterne's works." Skipwith concludes that they should "amount to about five and twenty pounds sterling, or, if you think proper, to thirty pounds."

On August 3, Jefferson responds with a list of 177 discrete titles that he recommends.[7] Along with the list of recommendations, Jefferson wrote a rather lengthy letter to his friend. Briefly, Jefferson indicates that he could not comply with the request to stay within Skipwith's budget: "I sat down with a design of executing your request to form a catalogue of books amounting to about 30. lib sterl. but could by no means satisfy myself with any partial choice I could make." Jefferson continues: "...I have framed such a general collection as I think you would wish, and might in time find convenient, to procure. Out of this you will chuse for yourself to the amount you mentioned for the present year, and may hereafter as shall be convenient proceed in completing the whole."

Locke is included three times in the list of 177 titles: "Locke on government" is listed under the category of "Politicks, Trade" along with six other works in that category. "Locke's conduct of the mind in search of truth" (i.e., Locke's *An Essay Concerning Human Understanding*") is included under the category "Religion." "Locke on Education" is included under the category "Miscellaneous." Other authors whose names appear almost as often as Locke include Hume (twice); Lord Kaims, Henry Home (three times); Montesquieu (twice); Cicero (twice); and Sherlock (twice).

Does this recommended list to Skipwith tell us anything about Jefferson's perception of Locke? Well it depends. Jefferson estimates the suggested collection to cost about £107.10 in 1771. This recommended collection is therefore only about half the cost of the collection that Jefferson estimated he had lost in his fire. Interestingly enough, it is also the same estimated cost as the list of books he gave to aspiring lawyer Phillip Turnpin in 1769. Why then did Jefferson not recommend a longer list to Skipwith? Is Jefferson reflecting here his top choices? Is he whittling down his favorites based on Skipwith's desire for books suitable for a "common reader?" Is this the list that Jefferson thinks a "Virginia gentleman" should have in his library, as some interpreters put it?[8] Indeed, in explaining why there are so few books on law, Jefferson writes that "In Law I mention a few systematical books, as a knowledge of the minutiae of that science is not necessary for a private gentleman." If we analyze Jefferson's list a bit more and look at the relative weight of his categories, a number of other questions arise.

Category	Percentage
Fine Arts	57% (106 titles)
Criticism of Fine Art	4% (7 titles)
History	11% total
	"antient history" (6.8%)
	"modern history" (4.5%)
Religion	8.8%
Natural Philosophy	7.3%
Politicks, Trade	5.3%
Miscellaneous	2.8%

Why does "fine arts" comprise such a large proportion? In part, Skipwith's letter may have prompted that focus since he asked Jefferson to include those that would "be improving as well as amusing." But expanding on Skipwith's own comments, Jefferson's explanation suggests that he is in agreement with the importance of literature and wants to justify the preponderance of literature in the list. Jefferson explains his emphasis this way:

> A little attention however to the nature of the human mind evinces that the entertainments of fiction are useful as well as pleasant. That they are pleasant when well written, every person feels who reads. But wherein is its utility, asks the reverend sage, big with the notion that nothing can be useful but the learned lumber of Greek and Roman reading with which his head is stored. I answer everything is useful which contributes to fix us in the principles and practice of virtue.

This statement certainly implies that Jefferson sees more than reason as the foundation of virtue, a potentially significant statement that could align Jefferson more with the thinking of the Scottish school than with Locke on the origins of virtue.[9] As other interpreters have noted, Jefferson's view here seems very much in line with views of figures like Lord Kames, whose books were listed in the recommendations to Skipwith.

Jefferson, however, only partially follows Skipwith's instructions in drawing up the list of recommendations. Jefferson did include Hume and sermons from Sterne as well as a number of works on antient history, though it is not clear which specific short history Jefferson had earlier mentioned to Skipwith. But Jefferson left Shakespeare off the list, for what reasons it is hard to say.[10]

After fine arts, history is the next largest category (11 percent of total). The importance of history is consistent with Jefferson's commonplace book, which is filled with notes from his historical sources.[11] "Politicks, Trade," the category in which Jefferson places Locke "on government," represents only 4.5 percent of the total. We cannot necessarily conclude that this topic is less important to Jefferson, however. Jefferson offers a reason for the sparse selection of politics and trade. "I have given you a few only of the best books, as you would probably chuse to be not unacquainted with those commercial principles which bring wealth into our country, and the constitutional security we have for the enjoinment of that wealth." This statement is important because it is one of the few direct comments that we have about how the pre-1774 Jefferson thought about Locke. The only other citations of Locke by Jefferson are simple citations with a paraphrase of Locke without specific commentary as we shall see. This statement to Skipwith makes clear that Jefferson thinks that Locke, Sidney, Montesquieu, Bolingbroke, and others are among the "best in class." But the rest of the comment is a bit cryptic and can be read in different ways.

The most probable reading, in my view, is to interpret Jefferson here as slightly apologetic for including some reading that might not fit Skipwith's criteria of books "suited to the capacity of a common reader who understands but little of the classicks and who has not leisure for any intricate or tedious study." Jefferson may be acknowledging that these works are somewhat more difficult than Skipwith had bargained for, but that Jefferson thought that Skipwith "would probably chuse to be not unacquainted with those commercial principles which bring wealth into our country and the constitutional security we have for the enjoiment of that wealth." By "our country" Jefferson is referring to Virginia, as many colonial writers referred to their colonies as "their country" and indeed thought of them as independent countries. Jefferson is implying that a man like Skipwith should be familiar with basic economic principles that bring wealth to Virginia and the laws by which that prosperity is constitutionally secured. On this reading, Jefferson is saying that at least these books should be mandatory reading for even the "common reader."[12]

Following this line of analysis, Jefferson clearly views Locke and Sidney as standard knowledge of an educated Virginian gentleman of Skipwith's type. Whether Jefferson views such knowledge as quintessential for all Virginians, we cannot say. It is interesting that Jefferson portrays the knowledge of Locke and Sidney as critical for understanding the "constitutional security we have for the enjoiment of that wealth." This is the earliest direct comment we have by Jefferson on the meaning of Locke's work and presumably refers to the *Second Treatise*. From this limited comment, it is difficult to completely arrive at a full understanding of how Jefferson thought about Locke. But with Jefferson we do not have much else to go on. It is interesting that Jefferson emphasizes constitutional security and its relationship to Virginia's commercial wealth. Jefferson could be saying that Locke and Sidney provide the foundation for understanding the securities guaranteed by the British constitution, which ultimately protect individuals' rights to property and ultimately commercial wealth of Virginia and possibly even free trade, though that is going beyond the language here. Given that Jefferson had already witnessed the Stamp Act crisis in 1764–1765 and the Townshend Acts (1767), this was not just a theoretical connection. This is one way to understand Locke, by placing emphasis on the role of Lockean natural rights to protect property rights and, by extension, the economic well-being of the commonwealth. But we cannot rule out that Jefferson may be emphasizing the protection of wealth to appeal to Skipwith's own interests, rather than reflecting Jefferson's own particular reading of Locke.

Jefferson's language of "constitutional security" may be significant but can also be interpreted in more than one way. Jefferson could be alluding to the underlying rights that Locke and Sydney thought the British constitution ultimately guaranteed. It is interesting again that Jefferson again does not speak here of "natural rights," a term that he seems to have generally avoided, as we have discussed before. We thus do not know from this statement alone whether Jefferson is already thinking of a strictly natural rights justification of colonial rights or whether he would be satisfied at this point in time with arguments like those by Wilson and others that the colonists brought their British rights with them when they settled in the Americas. All we know is that Jefferson thought Locke relevant to the question of rights and commercial wealth. Jefferson's categorization of these books under the heading "Politicks, Trade" further underscores the close link in his mind between political theory and notions of trade. Of course, this may not exhaust Jefferson's understanding of Locke but it does suggest at this point in his life he that he is seeing the liberties discussed by Locke and Sidney as closely linked to the development and protection of the colonies' commercial wealth.

Stepping back a moment, the inclusion of "Locke on Government" among the best books in 1771 certainly suggests that Jefferson had at least a decent familiarity with Locke's general positions, as he viewed Locke as among the best books on the subject. Still, a number of further questions arise from the Jefferson list. How much does the list represent Jefferson's own top 177 works and how much does it reflect what he thinks is appropriate for Skipwith or a Virginia gentleman who does not want to read books that are too tedious? Indeed, Jefferson ends his letter by contrasting this suggested library for his friend to his own. "But whence the necessity of this collection? Come to the new Rowanty [Jefferson means here his own house],[13] from which you may reach your hands to a library formed on a more extensive plan." Jefferson suggests that "There we should talk over the lessons of the day, or lose them in Musick, Chess or merriments of our family companions." The contrast Jefferson makes with his own library "formed on a more extensive plan" suggests that, by 1771, Jefferson already had built back a more extensive collection than the one listed in the letter to Skipwith, and it seems likely that his own library would have included all the books in the list that he recommended to Skipwith. It seems reasonable, then, to assume Jefferson had reacquired Locke's works by this time only a year after the fire. Indeed, by 1773, his library apparently had been rebuilt to 1,256 volumes based on notes he made in his account book.[14]

There are some other points of interest about Jefferson's recommended reading list to Skipwith. A large proportion of them are from the writers in the Scottish Enlightenment. The list contains, in one form or another, twenty-eight of the 122 books that had been published by 1769.[15] Garry Wills has made much of the connection of Jefferson to Scottish Enlightenment thinkers, placing most emphasis on Jefferson's similarity to Hutcheson.[16] While this list substantiates interest in Scottish Enlightenment figures generally, it is interesting to see what is included and what is missing. In fact, Hutcheson is not even listed in Jefferson's top 177. However, it is possible that Hutcheson might have been one of those that Jefferson would have listed in an expanded list of "Politicks, Trade" had he thought fit to expand that list. Arguably, Henry Home (Lord Kames) another Scottish Enlightenment thinker, is one of the central figures in this list and several interpreters have emphasized the importance of Lord Kames writing on Jefferson.[17]

In analyzing the letter, we should not ignore the possibility that there also might have been personal motivations entangled in the recommended list of books to Skipwith, as noted by Burstein.[18] Jefferson had begun courting Martha Wayles Skelton, who was half-sister of Robert Skipwith's wife, Tibby Skipwith.[19] Jefferson may have been trying to court favor with Tibby or even Martha in his choice of books he recommended to Skipwith. When Jefferson concludes his letter and invites Skipwith to partake of his own library, he imagines the women present. "Come then and bring our dear Tibby with you; the first in your affections, and second in mine. Offer prayers for me too at that shrine to which, tho' absent, I pay continual devotion. In every scheme of happiness she is placed in the fore-ground of the picture, as the principal figure. Take that away, and it is no picture for me." How do we factor Jefferson's desire to impress

Tibby, Martha, or even Skipwith in the list of books he drew up for him? Did that shape his list of suggested reading and its emphases?

Having now pondered Jefferson's letter to Skipwith in some detail, I'd like to step back for a moment and summarize what have learned from the initial facts of the case. We might conclude that Locke was critical to Jefferson's thinking, particularly "Locke on Government." And it does seem reasonable to conclude from his letter that Jefferson regarded "Locke on Government" as mandatory reading and knowledge for an educated person in the colonies. He also viewed Locke on Education and Locke's *Essay Concerning Human Understanding* as important for the library of his friend and by implication as critical to his own library. But beyond that what else do we know?

What Does a Personal Library Tell Us?

Owning a book, and even listing it among "best of class," does not necessarily tell us how that work fits into an individual's intellectual universe and ideas. That is the problem of what to infer from Jefferson's letter to Skipwith. At stake here is the question of how an intellectual of Jefferson's sort builds up his political and theoretical commitments from the diverse books which he has read. To what extent did Locke in particular or Lockean ideas in general shape Jefferson's thinking? The letter to Skipwith had 177 titles in various categories and Jefferson implied his library was substantially larger already by 1771. Weighing the impact of each source and category of writing on Jefferson's thinking is by no means a simple task.

Interpreters of Jefferson typically go about the business of answering these questions as a matter of course in their narration often without explicitly raising the complex theoretical issue that they are inescapably resolving. But history is like that. Historians often tell the story without bringing their theoretical assumptions to the surface, if they are even aware of them at all. Intellectual historians of Jefferson, therefore, move from a book in his library to assumptions about what influenced him. There is of course no real alternative if we want to imagine how Jefferson came to write the Declaration and hold the views that he did. But the interpretive issues are far more complex than the various narratives about Jefferson often suggest. If these interpreters were questioned, they would most probably agree that they are interpreting facts, making inferences and filling in gaps. At issue, of course, is how we move from what book a person has purchased, recommends to friends and has in his library to the question of weighing influence on him and shaping his ideas. Which of his ideas came from which of the many sources he read? This is an enormously complicated issue, even today when scholars elaborately footnote their ideas. Even in such situations it is not always easy to sort out the multiple strands of influence on a particular author's work. Some interpreters of Jefferson, such as the earlier work of Koch or, more recently, Allen Jayne, have been sensitive to Jefferson's other intellectual interests and have drawn attention to the various philosophical impacts of other intellectual sources such as Bolingbroke, Kames, Sterne, Burlamaqui, Hutcheson, Montesquieu, and others.[20] Others have emphasized his interest in classical sources and literature. But the interpretive problem is still there. Sorting out which source influenced which of Jefferson's ideas is complex if not impossible to answer.

How did Locke's influence on Jefferson differ from Kames's, for example? Out of all Jefferson's ideas, how do we determine which of his readings influenced him? Which of Locke's ideas were prominent for Jefferson and which were not? Jefferson's library had sources with similar conceptions but subtle variations. For example, as Chinard pointed out, Jefferson was exposed to Lockean ideas, not only from Locke's writing, but from Jefferson's reading of Kames. For example, in the early part of his legal commonplace book, Jefferson copied the following excerpt from Kames in the middle of a long discussion of the origin of punishment (article 557):

> Man, by his very nature is fitted for society, and society by it's conveniences is fitted for man. The perfection of human society consists in that just degree of union among individuals, which to each reserves freedom and independency, as far as is consisth with peace and good order. The bonds of society where every

man shall be bound to dedicate the whole of his industry to the common interest would be of the strictest kind, but it would be unnatural and uncomfortable, because destructive of liberty and independency; so would be the enjoyment of the goods of future in common.[21]

Based on the order of the entries, Jefferson may have read this statement before he read Locke. The complexity of saying whether Locke himself, or some derivation of Locke, influenced Jefferson on particular ideas is complex, if not impossible to resolve.

To complicate matters still further, there is a dispute about how to interpret Locke among those who study Locke closely. There are theological readings of Locke,[22] readings of Locke emphasizing the link of individualism, property, and expanding capitalism,[23] readings of Locke that stress the concern with the good of the community,[24] and readings of Locke that suggest his real commitments were only hinted at but never fully explicated,[25] to name only some of the interpretations. In other words, the question of Jefferson's relationship to Locke is complicated by the fact that the very notion of "Lockean" ideas is somewhat problematic because there are multiple renditions of Locke, depending how one understands Locke.[26] In the colonies too in the decade leading to the Revolution there were competing interpretations of Lockean natural rights and some pretty significant ambivalence about various dimensions of that theory, as already discussed. Indeed, Jefferson was also reading works that were critical of straightforward Lockean views, as we shall see below.

There is further complexity in trying to sort through the impact of various disciplines on Jefferson. In the Skipwith letter, historical works represent quite a large proportion of books in his list. His letter indicates that the "Politicks, Trade" category would have been much larger had Jefferson not been sensitive to Skipwith's request for a list for a "common reader." In Jefferson's larger libraries developed over time, these two categories were both quite large and of equal size.[27] But if we may infer from Jefferson's readings in his commonplace book, citation after citation from historical works indicates his avid interest in the history of European peoples. Jefferson himself noted in 1787 that he had been an avid reader of history when he was a young man.[28]

To what extent was Jefferson's mind-set historical rather than philosophical per se? This question is itself interesting and difficult because the "Whig" historical writings that he read invoke varying political, moral and philosophical conceptions and he appears to be reading historical works to answer political questions. Indeed, whether history can be separated from political-philosophical background conceptions is itself debatable, which is one of the points of this book. Still there is a substantial difference between historical and philosophical modes of thinking and writing. Some thinkers like Hume could pull off both modes. Hume, for example, could write his philosophical works and his histories of England and the two are interrelated in complicated ways. But many thinkers and writers leaned more prominently to one mode than the other. And Jefferson's own essays never achieved that kind of theoretical philosophical style that was more obvious in other writers like James Otis and James Wilson, leading some writers to conclude that Jefferson was not philosophical, even though he clearly had an interest in philosophical works.[29] As Malone puts it, "He never did set forth his political philosophy in full and systematic form…"[30] Thus if we do not find a fully worked out and consistent set of philosophical ideas in Jefferson, this can be because he had multiple influences and because he was not a systematic thinker.

On the Possible Influence of Hume on Jefferson

In addition to the issue of weighing various disciplinary influences on Jefferson, there are books on Jefferson's recommended reading list for Skipwith that Jefferson likely read but to which interpreters seem to grant little to no weight in understanding him. One notable example is David Hume's corpus. We know Jefferson purchased Hume's *History of England* from the *Virginia Gazette* records in 1764 (before even the Locke purchase). Jefferson also lists Hume's four volumes of *Essays* and Hume's *History of England* as recommended books to Skipwith. Hume was also on Jefferson's recommended reading to Skipwith in two different categories

"Politicks, Trade" and "Religion," two of the three categories in which Locke was mentioned.[31] But one is hard pressed to find any biographers or intellectual historians who emphasize the influence of Hume on Jefferson, and many dismiss Hume citing Jefferson's negative comments later in life.[32] Randall, for example, writing about Jefferson's rigorous studies as a young lawyer draws on a letter to Horatio G. Spafford, on March 17, 1814, to conclude that "Jefferson developed an early affinity for his magisterial if tedious defense of the rights of free-born Englishmen. He came to worry that Blackstone and the Scottish philosopher-historian David Hume were making 'making tories of those young Americans whose native feelings of independence do not place them above the wily sophistries of a Hume or a Blackstone.'"[33] Kimball quotes the same passage in precisely the same discussion of Jefferson's early studies as a law student.[34]

But why should we assume that Hume had little to no influence on Jefferson and Locke had so much?[35] I raise the question of Hume, not to argue that Hume influenced Jefferson necessarily, although I think that is indeed very possible, but to point out how constructions of Jefferson under Locke's influence often sidestep complex issues in trying to sort out how intellectual minds are made.

One could argue from the evidence, for example, that there is as much evidence of Hume's influence on Jefferson as there is for Locke's. It is true that later in life Jefferson had negative things to say about Hume. But can we rule out the possibility that Jefferson's early reading of Hume shaped his thinking? On what grounds do we marginalize Hume's body of work but place Locke in the center of Jefferson's intellectual influence, if not for the Declaration of Independence in 1776? Even if it was completely clear that Locke's *Second Treatise* was the predominant influence on Jefferson for the Declaration in 1776, which I have argued is an oversimplification, we would be unable to rule out Hume's earlier influence.

It is true that Hume is never quoted extensively in Jefferson's legal commonplace book, although he does once cite Hume's *History of England* in article 751 in discussions of the Anglo-Saxons.[36] Yet the same can be said about Locke who is mentioned only once in the commonplace book, ironically not too many pages from Jefferson's only citation of Hume.

Thus the "direct" or "bare evidence" of Locke and Hume's influence is about the same. Both are mentioned in the letter to Skipwith and neither have a very prominent role in Jefferson's commonplace book. We shall see also below that Locke and Hume are both cited in the notes of one of Jefferson's legal cases in the early 1770s.

Assuming Jefferson did read Hume's essays and *History of England*, what might have influenced him? Hume's essays went through several editions in which new essays were added and others deleted as the editions changed. In his letter to Skipwith, Jefferson cites only "Hume's essays, 4 v." The four volumes of Hume's essays likely refer to the four-volume edition he published in 1750, in which he drew together his various essays. Volume 1 (1753) of this collection contains the *Essays, Moral and Political* and Volume 4 (1753– 54) contains the *Political Discourses*. Volumes 2 and 3 contain his two *Enquiries* (*Concerning Human Understanding* and *the Principles of Morals*).[37] Thus Jefferson appears to be recommending to Skipwith a large part of Hume's corpus, including Hume's reflections on politics, religion, knowledge, and history.

It is beyond the scope here to delve in detail into Hume's political philosophy or his critical relationship to Locke and to the Whig historians who wrote before. Yet we can make a few preliminary points here that are relevant to Jeffersonian scholarship. Hume fundamentally challenged many contentions in the major disciplines in which Jefferson was reading. He argued, for example, against the rationalist foundations of morals like that of Locke. And he also threw fundamental doubts on Lockean political philosophy. Because Hume is typically received as a "conservative" political thinker, a partially misleading and oversimplified understanding of Hume, there is a presupposition that Jefferson would not have been influenced by Hume.[38] As in the case of Locke, there are different interpretations of Hume's project among contemporary scholars, and so any attempt to sort through the impact of Hume on Jefferson would have to contend with the diversity of views of Hume. Still, we can pull out clear tendencies that distinguish Hume from Locke and in which Hume fundamentally critiqued Locke's political philosophy. Why should we assume that Hume's skeptical critique did not influence Jefferson?

There are many ways into Hume's corpus, and it is evident that Hume's political philosophy is closely tied into his "moderate skepticism", his critique of rationalism, and his desire to develop a human sciences.[39] Starting from Hume's political philosophy, expressed in his essays, we realize immediately we are in a different world than that of Locke. Locke, of course, had made the state of nature and "the social contract" the centerpiece and foundation of his argument about why government is constrained by the wishes of the people. In that account, humans were born into a state of nature in which they enjoyed a "natural liberty" before God.[40] But the inconveniences of life in the state of nature and the desire for benefits from social life drove people to join together into human society. In joining together they created a social contract in which they agreed to relinquish some of their rights in the state of nature in exchange for the benefits of social life. In doing so, they transferred their own rights to representative bodies that now governed and protected them by consent.

Hume throws all sorts of doubts on this rationalist account of government's origin and legitimacy. To begin with, Hume sees contract theory, the foundation of Locke's philosophy, as more like the political ideology of a faction or interest group than a true foundation of political theory. Hume writes:

> As no party, in the present age, can well support itself, without a philosophical or speculative system of principles, annexed to its political or practical one; we accordingly find, that each of the factions, into which this nation is divided, has reared up a fabric of the former kind, in order to protect and cover that scheme of actions, which it pursues…The one party by tracing up government to the Deity, endeavour to render it so sacred and inviolate, that it must be little less than a sacrilege, however, tyrannical it may become, to touch or invade it, in the smallest article. The other party, by founding government altogether on the consent of the People, suppose that there is a kind of *original contract*, by which the subjects have tacitly reserved the power of resisting

their sovereign, whenever they find themselves aggrieved by that authority, with which they have, for certain purposes, voluntarily entrusted him. These are the speculative principles of the two parties; and these two are the practical consequences deduced from them.[41]

This is an extraordinary statement by Hume. Hume calls contract theory and natural rights merely a party ideology no different in essence than the royalist theory of divine right. This view which would have had a significant impression on Jefferson had he indeed read the essay, which seems very probable given his letter to Skipwith and other evidence discussed below. Indeed, Hume's essays are scattered with provocative statements of just this sort. In Hume's view, all factions and parties advance political philosophies that justify their positions. In this sense, Hume is like an emergent social scientist who sees political philosophy itself as an activity or ideology representing particular interests groups and not "truth" that can be defended. While this led Hume to have doubts about either party's ideology, in some ways he was ahead of his time in understanding that political ideologies serve party interests.

Indeed, we have seen that other colonial writers, such as James Otis and Stephen Hopkins, did in fact have doubts about the social contract theory that may partially have been the influence of Hume if not other sources that had been critical of natural rights theory. And we have seen that Jefferson himself exhibits some ambivalence about natural rights language that could also have been influenced by doubts such as those Hume expressed.

Hume's critique of the social contract flows in part from Hume's skeptical tendencies that questioned whether any rationalist account could provide a foundation for knowledge or morals. Though Locke had already questioned the doctrine of innate ideas (in a book Jefferson recommended to Skipwith), Hume's theory of knowledge was even more skeptical, questioning the use of reason to be certain about anything. Even ideas such as "cause and effect" Hume argued could not be known for certain and seemed more like logic imposed by the human mind on sensations. Given this critique of reason, an account like Locke's that founded government on a law of nature that was discernible to reason was problematic. Indeed, there are some scholars who think that even Locke himself may have ultimately realized that he could not provide a rationalist ground for the law of nature.[42] But if that point is ambiguous in Locke, it is not in Hume. Hume clearly does not find reason to be the location of justice and other foundations of government and social life. While Hume did not end up in radical skepticism and still thought that government and allegiance to the rule of law could be justified on moral grounds, he rejected reason as the ultimate foundation for morals and government.[43] Instead he argued that moral sentiments were of two types: those resulting from immediate natural instinct in the human being, such as love of children, gratitude to benefactors and pity to the unfortunate. Others arose from a sense of obligation out of the necessities of human society and these checked natural instincts. These included regard to property, fidelity to promises. Anticipating a functionalist interpretation like those of later social scientists, Hume argues these rules arise to check individual instinct because of the benefit to society in general.[44]

In addition to his critique of reason as a foundation for knowledge and government, Hume appeals to empirical historical evidence to contest the idea of social contract. "But would these reasoners look abroad into the world, they would meet with nothing that, in the least corresponds to their ideas or can warrant so refined and philosophical a system. On the contrary, we find, every where, princes, who claim their subjects as their property, and assert their independent right of sovereignty, from conquest or succession."[45] And then shortly afterwards: "It is strange, that an act of the mind, which every individual is supposed to have formed, and after he came to the use of reason too, otherwise, it could have no authority; that this act, I say, should be so much unknown to all of them, that, over the face of the whole earth, there scarcely remain any traces or memory of it."

Here we see Hume leaning towards an empirical critique of the Lockean contract position, arguing that there is no empirical evidence of a social contract in most societies in the past and that most people do not form such a conception. We have seen that this charge against Lockean social contract was already a worry for several colonial writers, such as James Otis, Samuel Hopkins, and others in the period leading up to the Revolution. In fairness, Locke had already been aware of this possible objection and had attempted to address it.[46] But for Hume empirical evidence indicated that government in fact was not founded in social contract. "Almost all the governments, which exist at present, or of which there remains any record in story, have been founded originally either on usurpation or conquest, or both, without any pretence of a fair consent, or voluntary subjection of the people."[47] Hume thus concludes that

> It is vain to say, that all governments are or should be, at first, founded on popular consent, as much as the necessity of human affairs will admit. This favours entirely my pretension. I maintain, that human affairs will never admit of this consent; seldom of the appearance of it. But that conquest or usurpation, that is, in plain terms, force, by dissolving the ancient governments, is the origin of almost all the new ones, which were ever established in the world. And that in the few cases, where consent may seem to have taken place, it was commonly so irregular, so confined, or so much intermixed either with fraud or violence, that it can have any great authority.[48]

Reason, history and experience show us that few political societies have had an origin in consent. By contrast, Hume sees the origin of government as arising out of force and conquest. "The face of the earth is continually changing, by the encrease of small kingdoms into great empires, by the dissolution of great empires into smaller kingdoms, by the planting of colonies, by the migration of tribes. Is there anything discoverable in all these vents but force and violence? Where is the mutual agreement or voluntary association so much talked of?"[49] As we have seen already, there were in fact colonial writers who pondered the possibility that the colonies were themselves "the result of colonization" or "conquest." Blackstone had himself articulated this view in his *Commentaries* which were also on Jefferson's reading list. Jefferson himself assumed that the settlement of the American lands was a conquest. But the notion of conquest sat uneasily with the notion of a social compact. Colonial writers were conversant with the theory of government's origin in conquest and occupation and were concerned with the possible implications for their own theory of rights. And there was a healthy skepticism among some colonial writers about the origin of government in social contract.

Because Hume sees contract theory as a kind of party ideology he denies that contract theory alone embodies truth. Hume was much more willing to see both sides of the story and find positives in various forms of governments, particularly in the balanced monarchy. Comparing contract theory and the theory of divine right of kings, Hume writes that "both these systems of speculative principles are just; though not in the sense, intended by the parties." And Hume expressed significant reservations about an unrestrained democracy and saw the need for a centralized and supreme authority in government. For Hume therefore both Tories and Whigs had elements of value in their positions, but neither had the whole truth.

Holding himself somewhat above the commitments of parties, Hume did not align himself with either the Whigs or Tories and in many ways took historical views that overlapped and conflicted with both. Thus Hume's *History of England*, a book Jefferson purchased in 1764 and recommended to Skipwith, was contentious in challenging both the Whig and Tory views of history. Hume was aware that both Whigs and Tories would find fault with his *History of England*. The Whig and Tory histories diverged on many points, and Hume saw the picture in a more complicated way.

That colonial writers were reading and thinking about Hume is evident not just from Jefferson's letter to Skipwith. We saw earlier that John Dickinson in his famous Farmer's Letters (Letter XI) wrote that, "The first principles of government are to be looked for in human nature. Some of our best writers have asserted, and it seems with good reason, that government is founded on 'opinion'." Dickinson is here quoting from Hume's essay *Of the first principles of Government* in which Hume's argues that government is founded on opinion. In this essay, Hume is making an interesting argument that anticipates political and social science: what he means is that since force is always on the side of the governed, governors have nothing to support them but opinion. "It is therefore on opinion only that government is founded." What Hume is essentially arguing is that any form of government has a "world view" or ideology that makes it intelligible. In this very essay that Dickinson cites, Hume critiques Locke: "A noted author has made property the foundation of all government; and most of our political writers seem included to follow him in that particular. This is carrying the matter too far; but still it must be owned, that the opinion of right to property has a great influence in this subject."

If Jefferson thought highly of Hume, as his letter to Skipwith would suggest, it would at least be pertinent to consider whether Jefferson entertained any doubts with Hume about a social contact theory of society. As Malone himself noted, Jefferson said relatively little at any time "about the social contract which was supposed to have preceded the formation of society; when he referred to contracts or compacts he generally meant charters, constitutions, or other formal agreements of the historical sort. Even if the hypothetical prehistoric contract had been successfully challenged in his day, as it was afterwards, it is practically inconceivable that he world have surrendered his conviction that men were born to freedom and not to slavery, for with him this was a profound moral conviction."[50]

While Jefferson hardly articulates a full-blown Humean theory of government, it is as easy to argue for the influence of Hume on the early Jefferson as it is to see the influence of Locke. The evidence to support both is about the same. The point, then, is not to argue for Humean influence on Jefferson as much as argue that the strength of argument is about the same for Hume and Locke.

I briefly reviewed some of Hume's ideas that Jefferson may have encountered in order to raise the larger questions I wish to ask here. How do we know whether Hume's skepticism, and his more "social scientific" views of political ideology, did not affect the younger Jefferson? Because Jefferson wrote Lockean-like ideas in the Declaration when he was writing for a committee, can we be certain that Hume's doubts about Locke did not enter into his views of the social contract? If we see, as we do, some avoidance of Lockean terminology and natural rights arguments, may not some of this hesitation derive from Hume's doubts about Locke? Because the Lockean interpretation of Jefferson has become so powerful, it is hard to imagine Jefferson taking account of Hume. And yet if we continue to loosen and question the grip of Lockean interpretations of Jefferson, we can see that Jefferson may have entertained some reservations about the "natural rights" account of government.

The goal of this discussion of Hume, then, was to point out how complex it is to say what really shaped the mind of the young Jefferson and how problematic it is to figure out just which of the many books in his library shaped his maturing thinking.

Natural Rights in Jefferson's Early Legal Cases

There are two of Jefferson's early legal cases that make reference to Locke or invoke natural law in the period between the invoice of 1769 and the citation of Locke in the commonplace book, which we have concluded was made in 1774. In one of these legal cases, Jefferson cites Locke; in the other he does not.[51] I suggest that both of these cases are interesting and important in weighing the "Lockean" influence on Jefferson's conception of natural rights. Together both show that natural law ideas were important to Jefferson as a practicing lawyer thinking strictly about his legal cases, even if the use of natural rights here did not yet have overt political implications. Together they also show that Jefferson does not associate natural rights arguments strictly or exclusively with Locke, and indeed, did not cite Locke in the first instance in which he is known to have cited natural law. They also show that Jefferson would pull various books off his shelf for particular specific purposes as he constructed his arguments for legal cases.

The Case of the Mulatto's Grandson: Howell v. Netherland

Jefferson ranked the first of these cases, *Howell v. Netherland*, as one of the top fourteen most important legal cases before the Revolution, although that categorization may have been self-serving. The notes for the case were included in a group of important Virginia cases that Jefferson had collected. But his collection was not published until three years after his death in a volume entitled *Reports of Cases Determined in the General Court of Virginia*.[52]

Apparently, *Howell v. Netherland* was argued in April 1770, shortly after the fire at his mother's house in Shadwell and before the letter to Skipwith. The notes Jefferson had originally prepared for this case may very well have been among those to which Jefferson referred when he wrote his friend John Page complaining that the fire had destroyed notes he had made for cases pending in the spring of that year.[53]

The case involved a man named Samuel Howell who was seeking his freedom from servitude.[54] Howell was penniless when he had come to Jefferson for legal help, and Jefferson took his case for no fee.[55] Howell had originally been placed in servitude as a child because he was born to a mulatto mother during her servitude. By a 1723 Virginia law, if a mulatto woman gave birth during her servitude, the child was also to be placed in servitude for thirty-one years, the same term of service as the mother. During his period of servitude, Howell's master had sold him to another master.

Jefferson's argument makes several different points. First, Jefferson argues that if the servitude was legal in the first place, the act of selling Howell from one master to another violated the law. Second, and of more interest here, Jefferson argues that Howell should never have been made a servant in the first place. He bases his argument on two assumptions: a) the law on the books did not apply to Howell's case and b) his mother's servitude violated the laws of nature in the first place.

It is the latter claim that receives the most attention by Jefferson commentators and we shall start there, even though it is not the first point that Jefferson makes in his legal argument. Here is the passage in *Howell v. Netherland* in which Jefferson invokes natural law:

I suppose it will not be pretended that the mother being a servant, the child would be a servant also under the law of nature, without any particular provision in the act. Under the law of nature, all men are born free, every one comes into the world with a right to his own person, which includes the liberty of moving and using it at his own will. This is what is called personal liberty, and is given him by the author of nature, because necessary for his own sustenance. The reducing the mother to servitude was a violation of the law of nature: surely then the same law cannot prescribe a continuation of the violation to her issue, and that too without end, for if it extends to any, it must to every degree of descendants. Puff. b. 6. c. 3. S. 4. 9. supports this doctrine. [56]

From evidence that remains of Jefferson's early writings, this case appears to be one of the earliest if not first example in writing in which Jefferson invokes natural law concepts explicitly. Biographers therefore make the most of this case. Commenting on this case, for example, Malone writes that "Even as early as 1770, he had said publicly that under the law of nature all men are born free."[57] This statement comes at the conclusion of a paragraph in which Malone summarizes Jefferson's commitment to enlightenment ideas. "Like so many of his enlightened contemporaries, Jefferson believed that men had originally been in a state of nature; that they had then been free to order their own actions and to dispose of their own persons and property as they saw fit; that government was instituted among them in the first place by consent. In the Declaration of Independence he summarized the current doctrine in its classic American form."

Randall being more dramatic writes "His first eloquent, ingenious pleading that all men are created equal came in the case of Howell v. Netherland, which pitted him against George Wythe." After summarizing the case, Randall continues: "Even if Jefferson was on shaky legal ground, he felt he had a strong moral and philosophical position, and he pressed it boldly." "It was the first time Jefferson had spoken the words in public—'all men are born free' six years before he wrote the

Declaration of Independence."[58] Kimball for her part writes that "it was, likewise, the first expression of the ideas that had been growing in his mind, nurtured by the books he had recently acquired."[59] Dumbauld puts it this way: "In the other case argued by Jefferson, his eloquent and ingenious appeal to the law of nature, under which all men are born free, on behalf of a mulatto seeking release from servitude fell on deaf ears." In a footnote, Dumbauld comments: "In the political forum of mankind Jefferson's doctrine received a more favorable hearing when six years later in the Declaration of Independence he proclaimed that all men are created equal."[60]

It is interesting that biographers make so much of this statement by Jefferson when natural rights statements of this sort are commonplace in the literature before the Revolution and we know that Jefferson had ordered a number of philosophical works in 1769, including Locke and Sidney, among others. We would be surprised if we didn't find such statements in Jefferson's writing. And in fact the paucity of them is what is more surprising. Biographers pounce on this statement because it provides the one and nearly only foundation of the Jefferson they wish to see in the Declaration. We can understand why biographers who think of Jefferson of the Declaration embraced a pure form of natural rights and a Lockean version would rejoice in having his statement in Jefferson's 1770 legal case. There is almost no other evidence that Jefferson embraced a straightforward natural rights philosophy or a Lockean one in particular. Indeed we know that Jefferson was reading some philosophers such as Hume who were critical of natural rights.

It is true that this statement of Jefferson is a succinct statement of natural rights. But this statement on its own can't bear the weight interpreters are putting on it. It can't provide evidence alone that there is an unbroken continuity from Jefferson of 1770 and Jefferson of the Declaration in 1776.

To begin with, this is only a legal case and not a political philosophical essay. Jefferson here is appealing to ideas that he believes will help him in this specific legal case. It does not mean this represents the position he would put forward in quite this way were he articulating his own political philosophy, which was only in the process of maturing. This statement is thus context-bound. And the legal context must have some influence on how we interpret it. We shall see in the next legal case considered that Jefferson the lawyer will quote all kinds of philosophical ideas—even contradictory ones—in order to build out the foundations of an argument.

But even if this statement did represent Jefferson's own mind in 1770, we still have to be cautious in drawing a straight line from this Jefferson to the Jefferson of 1776. We have already looked deeply at Jefferson's writing in 1774 in *A Summary View* and looked at Jefferson's draft of the Declaration. I already suggested that there is evidence there that Jefferson is avoiding natural rights language at times and was possibly ambivalent about social contract ideas, like other colonial writers. I won't repeat that evidence here. To sum up this point, even if this statement concretizes Jefferson's thinking in 1770, it is still a leap to argue that Jefferson's ideas had not changed by the time he wrote the Declaration.

In any case, let's assume for a minute that this is Jefferson's own personal view in 1770. What does it tell us about Jefferson at this point in his life shortly after he purchased "Locke on Government"? Since biographers generally don't bother to provide a reading of this statement in context, they obfuscate some interesting nuances about what Jefferson is arguing here that are quite interesting and illuminating. These nuances show (1) that Jefferson is here articulating ideas about slavery that are different (and perhaps less mature) than he would espouse later, and (2) that he is not clearly a Lockean at this point. Let's look at the nuances that other interpreters pass by.

To begin with, interpreters tend to leave the impression that Jefferson here is invoking natural rights to argue against slavery as an institution (a position he will take later in *A Summary View* and his draft of the Declaration). But upon closer examination we find that Jefferson is not in fact making such an argument. The only way we realize this is if we look at the secondary citation that Jefferson provides at the end of this quote. Here Jefferson cites the work, not of Locke, but of Pufendorf. None of the biographers tend to make much of this citation and one can infer many of them may not even have looked it up. So who was Pufendorf and why does Jefferson invoke him here?

Samuel von Pufendorf (1632–1694) was a German jurist, political philosopher, and statesman. Among Pufendorf's best known works are commentaries and revisions of the natural law theories of Thomas Hobbes and Hugo Grotius, such as his 1672 *De jure naturae et gentium*, which took up and refined ideas of Hobbes and was written even earlier than Locke's *Second Treatise*. Very few biographers of Jefferson even mention the fact that Pufendorf is quoted here in support of Jefferson's position.[61] That omission helps reinforce the impression that Jefferson is a strict Lockean. It is interesting, moreover, that Pufendorf was not on the list of books purchased in 1769 by Jefferson and his notes on the case make no mention of Locke, which he had recently ordered. Pufendorf was also not on the list of recommended books to Skipwith in 1771, perhaps because Jefferson kept the category of "Politicks, Trade" to a minimum as discussed earlier. If it were not already obvious, it is clear that Jefferson was quite familiar with philosophical works that never appeared in his letter to Skipwith nor in his book invoices. We shall see that Pufendorf also figures more importantly than Locke in the second legal case in which Jefferson invokes natural law.

In the reference from Pufendorf that Jefferson cites, Pufendorf is arguing against Hobbes's theory of the origin of slavery. Hobbes assumes that slavery originates in the war of all against all. In the original condition of human kind, according to Hobbes, individuals have a relentless desire for more power.[62] Because humans are essentially equal in basic capabilities, each feels worthy of having as much as any other.[63] Since both desire the same ends, they compete and end up at odds or what Hobbes calls "enemies." In this "warre of every man against every man," there is no law and everyone has a right to make use of anything to "preserve his life against his enemyes. It followeth, that in such a condition, every man has a Right to every thing; even to one anothers bodies." For Hobbes, servitude originates in this war of all against all.

Pufendorf, in the passage cited by Jefferson, is taking up Hobbes's theory and offering another understanding of slavery's origin. The passage appears in book 6, chapter 3 of Pufendorf's *Of the Law of Nature and Nations* and is entitled "Of Despotical Power, or the Authority of the Master over his Servant." Here Pufendorf discusses at length the origin of slavery as an institution. He disagrees with the view that servitude was established by nature (i.e., the view of Hobbes). He also takes exception to those who held that the institution of servitude grew out of the phenomenon of war. According to that view, victory in war itself was a sign of divine favor. Since victors could legitimately kill their captives in war, captives had the option of preserving their lives in exchange for slavery. That is to say, enslaving another person was not right unless that person had already forfeited his right to life in the first place. In this view, the institution of servitude arose with divine approval and is part of the law of nations.

Pufendorf disagrees with both views of slavery. Instead he argues that servitude historically originated, not from war or nature, but as a voluntary contract between people of different economic classes, some of whom were materially well-off and some of whom were poor. The poor voluntarily entered into servitude to escape the conditions of their poverty. This voluntary contract thus sets the boundaries on the legitimate powers of the master over the servant. A master cannot engage in capital punishment nor sell the servant to another master because the master does not own the body or life of the servant. A master simply owns a servant's labor which is given in exchange for feeding and clothing the servant. Pufendorf argues that this form of "contract servitude" differs from and arose earlier than servitude that derived from war.

It is this notion of "contract servitiude" that Jefferson has in mind when he makes his argument about Howell, the son of a mulatto's mother. Jefferson makes several points about Howell's status that depend on Pufendorf's notion of "contract servitude." First, Jefferson argues that if the enslavement of his mother was legitimate, then Howell could not be sold to another master. This follows from Pufendorf's notion of "contract servitude." Since contract servitude is a contract for the servant's labor, and not her body, the child of her body does not belong to the master. Therefore the master had no right to sell her offspring. That is the first point Jefferson makes.

Second, Jefferson then goes on to question whether the mulatto mother should have been put into servitude. "The reducing the mother to servitude was a violation of the law of nature." We now can see that Jefferson is not saying that all slavery is a violation of the law of nature.[64] He is making the argument that the enslavement should not arise simply because a mulatto is a product of interracial sexual activity. In other words, Jefferson is *not* here calling into question the institution of slavery in general. He still assumes here with Pufendorf that "contract servitude" would be permissible. But the mulatto's enslavement had nothing to do with a contract. Jefferson, then, is arguing that miscegenation was not valid grounds for servitude. Since Howell's mother had done nothing to forfeit her rights to life nor voluntarily entered into a contract for servitude, neither Howell nor his mother should have been put in servitude in the first place. Jefferson then is arguing that Virginian laws about miscegenation violated the laws of nature.

It is thus Pufendorf's ideas about "contract servitude" that drew Jefferson's attention to these points. Jefferson expands on Pufendorf's position as follows:

> For having proved that servitude to be rightful, must be founded on either compact, or capture in war, he proceeds to shew that the children of the latter only follow the condition of the mother: for which he gives this reason, that the person and labor of the mother in a condition of perfect slavery, (as he supposes to be that of the captive in war) being the property of the master, it is impossible she should maintain it but with her master's goods; by which he suppose a debt contracted from the infant to the master. But he says in cases of servitude founded on compact, "The food of the future issue is contained or implied in their own maintenance, which their master owes them as a just debt; and consequently their children are not involved in a necessity of slavery." This is the nature of the servitude introduced by the act of 1705,

the master deriving his title to the service of the mother, entirely from the contract entered into with the churchwardens.

Jefferson here summarizes Pufendorf's views about the status of children born in slavery. In cases where the mother was enslaved through conquest, the mother's body and labor belong completely to the master. For this reason, her child is born into the status of slave as well. But in cases where servitude is founded on contract, the contract implies that the child's maintenance is included in the original contract. Since there is no debt incurred in this case between the infant and the master, the infant is not considered a slave like the mother. Jefferson's point is that the 1705 Virginia law on servitude for mulatto's implies it is of the "contract servitude" type. Otherwise, why would the law say that the church wardens get involved in negotiating the terms with the child's master? Since this is contract servitude, the child should not automatically fall into the same status as the mother.[65]

To step back for a minute to the larger point, it is certainly fair to say that Jefferson is here invoking the natural rights tradition that a person is born with personal liberty. He does so however only in a limited legal context and not yet in a political context to justify the rights of the colonies, though other writers before him had already done so. Jefferson also clearly thinks that "miscegenation" is not a valid reason to make a person a servant by the laws of nature.

Given this intimate knowledge of Pufendorf, we see that Locke alone is not the source of Jefferson's understanding of natural rights. We also see a tendency we shall see in his next legal case. Jefferson was familiar enough in detail with major philosophers such as Hume, Locke, and Pufendorf that he could find particular passages that would support very specific points of law. We cannot from here jump to any conclusion that Jefferson had embraced a specific form of natural rights theory or a Lockean specific version. Indeed, the citing of Pufendorf here, and Hume in the next case, raise the question asked earlier—how we can align Jefferson's thinking with one of these thinkers versus the other? We know only what we knew already—that Jefferson, like other colonial thinkers, had read such works and was familiar with them. In Jefferson's case, he was familiar with them in sufficient detail to find citations that supported very technical points of law.

To drive home the complexity of this question of what view of natural rights Jefferson held, we can also look at the language Jefferson used here to explain why God gave personal liberty: "every one comes into the world with a right to his person" a right given by "the author of Nature."[66] Jefferson also summarizes his understanding of why God gave people personal liberty: because it is "necessary for his own sustenance." Whose view of liberty's origin is here being invoked? Jefferson's view is arguably not Locke's, for Locke never really says why God gave people liberty.[67] Locke says that sustenance, which is the source of life, is the justification for private property, not liberty. "Whether we consider natural reason which tells us, that men, being once born, have a right to their preservation, and consequently to meat and drink, and such other things as nature affords for their subsistence..." We see here that Locke assumes that a right to sustenance comes from liberty, not the other way around. But in Jefferson a need for sustenance is the basis of liberty. As Jefferson puts it, "Under the law of nature, all men are born free...This is what is called personal liberty, and is given him by the author of nature, because necessary for his own sustenance." In Jefferson's view, ownership of one's own body is given by God so that a person can labor and provide sustenance for him or herself. In Locke's view, the right to sustenance flows from the fact that God created people with liberty and a right to preservation.

Is Jefferson aware he is reversing Locke? Is he simply forgetting what Locke had said? Does that mean he has not memorized Locke as other commentators suggest he has by 1776? Or is some other view of liberty at the back of Jefferson's mind? Is he perhaps more influenced by Pufendorf, who wrote in book II, chapter 2 of the *Law of Nature and Nations*:

> What kind of Rights attend Men in a State of Nature we may easily gather, as well from that Inclination common to all living things, by which they cannot but imbrace and practise with the

greatest Readiness and Vigour all possible ways of preserving their Body and their Life, and of overcoming all such things as seem to drive at their Destruction; as from this other Consideration, that Persons living in such a State are not subject to any Sovereignty or Command. For from the former Reflexion it follows, that Men plac'd after this manner in a Natural State, may use and enjoy the Common Goods and Blessing, and may act and pursue whatever makes for their own Preservation, while they do not hence injure the Right of the rest.[68]

Here Pufendorf seems to be deriving the idea of original liberty in nature from the fact that people like all living creatures have inherent inclinations to preserve their life and body. Jefferson seems much closer to Pufendorf in arguing that the liberties in the state of nature flow from or can be inferred from the need for preservation whereas in Locke the right to preservation flows from liberty itself. Do any of these nuances matter? Perhaps not. But they certainly show how complicated is the question of what influenced Jefferson and in doing so open up that conversation about what values and views ultimately shaped the thinking about liberty in the founding of America. They also suggest just how hard it ultimately is to say definitively what core values or positions one of our most important founders may have had. To try to say this early Jefferson embraced natural rights, or a particular Lockean view, is thus an oversimplification that supports the myth of Jefferson as committed to natural rights philosophy and perhaps a Lockean version of it.

A Messy Case of Divorce

We turn now to notes for a second legal case in which Jefferson again cites Pufendorf but this time along with Locke and Hume. This case involves a messy Williamsburg divorce scandal in 1772, and has been superbly documented by Dewey.[69] In Virginia law, like English law, divorce was not permitted without an act of Parliament. For certain types of causes, such as adultery, one could obtain the equivalent of a legal separation with the approval of an ecclesiastical court.

In 1772 Jefferson took on a case trying to obtain a divorce for Dr. James Blair of Williamsburg from Kitty Eustace, whom he had married in May 1771. The marriage apparently broke up almost immediately after the wedding, and there were recriminations on both sides. On one side were charges that Dr. Blair was "incompetent," and on the other side that Kitty "jumped out of bed and would not do anything." There were hopes of reconciliation but those were dashed when Blair found out that Kitty had written a letter accusing him of impotence.

In November of 1772, Jefferson was asked by Blair to look into divorce. But Blair then died on December 26, 1772, and his will made no provision for Kitty. By Virginia law, a wife was entitled to a life interest in a portion of her husband's property (called a dower). In November 1773, the James City County court denied Kitty's claim of her dower. The case was argued on November 3, 1773, and Jefferson, who had been retained by the state before the case reached the General Court, did not participate in the oral argument but may have helped prepare the case and made notes on the legal issues in preparation for the case. Jefferson was in court when the case was presented and made a full report.

Dewey suggests the notes were prepared between November 25, 1772 when Blair retained Jefferson and December 26 when he died. They were written at Monticello and the research was likely done in Jefferson's own library. In preparing the case, Jefferson had to contend with the fact that Virginia had no precedent for divorce and the possibility of obtaining a divorce was unlikely. There was also little chance of proving adultery. To win a divorce, Jefferson would therefore have to convince the Virginia General Assembly to follow Parliament's practice of granting a divorce by special act, but to grant it on a type of grounds that Parliament itself had not recognized.

In Jefferson's notes, one can discern the case he would have made. Locke is one of the sources that Jefferson cites and shows that by 1772 he was familiar enough with Locke to know that Locke had something to say about divorce in his *Second Treatise*. What is just as interesting and significant is the mix of other sources that Jefferson cites. The majority of sources are from Pufendorf's *The Law of Nature and Nations*. Jefferson cites Pufendorf more than twenty times. He also cites Hume, Montesquieu, and Milton. In addition to these philosophical and literary works, Jefferson also lists relevant citations from scripture.

Jefferson divides his arguments into two parallel pro and con columns. Both columns begin with notes from Hume's "Of Polygamy and Divorces," found in Hume's *Essays* (the same *Essays* Jefferson recommended to Skipwith).[70]

This essay by Hume is fascinating, complex, and ironic in its own right. Hume is essentially arguing that marriage customs should be variable by time and place and even entertains the idea that polygamy is a viable institution. Hume is also arguing that divorce should be permitted. We do not know what Jefferson thought of the larger argument or Hume's fundamental emphasis on variability of laws which today we would call cultural relativism. But it is interesting that in paraphrasing Hume's "pro-divorce" reasons Jefferson makes his own gloss. Hume wrote, "But the liberty of divorces is not only a cure to hatred and domestic quarrels: It is also an admirable preservative against them, and the only secret for keeping alive that love, which first united the married couple."[71] Here is Jefferson's paraphrase:

> Liberty of divorce presents and cures domestic quarrels. Ib.
> Preserves liberty of affection. Ib. (which is natural right).

It is interesting that Jefferson adds the words in parentheses "which is a natural right," as a gloss at the end of his paraphrase of Hume. Hume himself would not likely have justified his argument that way and we see that Jefferson is reading a "natural right" style argument into Hume, which was in fact foreign to Hume. This illustrates just how complicated it is to understand the relationship of Jefferson to his philosophical sources. When he read Hume, he assumes that Hume was making an argument from natural right, even though that was probably not Hume's intent. It is also interesting that Jefferson construed the liberty of affection as a natural right. Perhaps this is the seeds of Jefferson's later claim that pursuit of happiness is a natural right, an idea we have seen that was not shared by all natural rights theorists.

After his notes from Hume, Jefferson paraphrases Locke's comments on divorce in his *Second Treatise*.[72] Locke devoted a whole chapter to detailing how human marriage is a compact that differs from the simple propagation of animals. Both Locke and Hume were concerned with the relationship of marriage, procreation, love and ultimately the institution of marriage. In part the interest in marriage arose from larger questions about the nature of political power and whether different forms of relationships such as husband and wife or parents and children were like the power of political authority.

Locke suggests that marriage is like a compact that can be dissolved. Locke's statement is itself very convoluted and Jefferson tries to summarize and clarify Locke's meaning. Paraphrasing Locke, Jefferson writes "Since procreation, education, & inheritance taken care of, no necessity from nature of thing to continue the society longer, but it may be made at the time of contracting dissoluble by consent, at a certain time, or on certain conditions, as other compacts. Locke. 265."[73] If, as I argued earlier, the citation of Locke in Jefferson's commonplace book was from the period of 1774, then this citation represents an even earlier citation of Locke and proves that by 1772 he knew Locke well enough to remember that Locke had a chapter on marriage and a position on divorce. After citing Locke, Jefferson goes on to cite Pufendorf more than twenty times.

What seems likely from these notes is that Jefferson is pulling down relevant books from the shelf of a library and making notes for his case. More importantly, we see that Jefferson felt comfortable pulling on ideas from a wide range of sources, including Locke, but also including Hume, Pufendorf, Milton and Scripture. While in this case he is preparing a law case, and one could argue he therefore wants "all the help he can get", we see Jefferson's mind at work drawing on and knowledgeable about a wide variety of philosophical sources. While this legal argument is not about political consent, we can anticipate that Jefferson would be willing also to frame his ideas about government from a wide range of sources, and not just Locke.

To summarize the evidence of the legal cases, we see that Locke is one of source, among others, to which Jefferson turned in thinking through and justifying positions he was taking. Locke was not the exclusive source for positions related to natural law. Hume, Pufendorf, and Milton figure in as well. And Hume and Pufendorf figure in even more than Locke. But in part this is because they have more to say on the specifics of the cases that Jefferson was arguing and Locke tended to be more general and philosophical and less specific on particular social issues.

Conclusion: Does It Matter What the Declaration Means?

The answer to the question of whether it matters what the Declaration of Independence means is in some ways simple: "It depends." And the fact that we cannot give an unequivocal answer to the question points to one claim which is ultimately at stake in this book: the very question of whether the Declaration, or for that matter whether any historical document, matters is itself part of the interpretive historical enterprise and political philosophical journey of American public life. The point of this concluding chapter is theoretical: to argue that whether the Declaration matters depends on how we answer other questions about its place in history and its significance as a statement of American political philosophy. And how we answer those questions depends not only on history, but a theory of history and the relationship of history to political theory.

In making this argument, I am shifting from what has been principally a historical exercise in this book to a theoretical and philosophical one, though the two are ultimately tied together. In the historical argument, I explored whether it the pre-Revolutionary founders had a consensus on rights and in particular whether that consensus was visible in the Declaration of Independence. I argued that in fact the Declaration skirted over divergent and contested theories of rights that were present among the pre-Revolutionary founders. Many, and possibly even Jefferson, were ambivalent about certain aspects of natural rights theory and ideas about social contract in particular. Furthermore, the pre-Revolutionary colonial thinkers were not all of one mind on the question of American rights.

This conclusion I suggest is significant for the question whether history can and should serve as a foundation for political rights. For if key documents such as the Declaration have ambiguous meanings or we cannot pin down the meanings of those documents through historical analysis, then the use of historical documents for resolving political rights is thrown in doubt or at least subject to reinterpretation.

I wish now in this final chapter to turn back to this normative question that has been hovering in the background since the beginning: Does it matter what the Declaration of Independence means anyway? Or to put it another way, should the Declaration of Independence have moral and normative significance for American life? Forget for a moment that the Declaration may have had that kind of significance in the past. The matter at hand is whether that significance was and should continue to be warranted. To what extent should history or great historical documents such as the Declaration play a role in ongoing debates about political rights?

The question under discussion is interestingly enough at the heart of "social contract" theory itself. For one version of social contract political theory suggests that some original vision or agreement, "a social contract," should remain binding in some fashion upon subsequent generations in that society. In this view, the "original contract" with America should be definitive for the way later Americans live their lives. The founders' views of rights should count heavily in how we define and protect rights. This conviction that Americans should harken back to the founders' views is often based on the Declaration of Independence itself, which supposedly proves that the founders' embraced a natural rights theory. Since natural rights theory assumes that a society enters into a binding social contract upon inception, Americans must therefore pay attention to the original contract or founding view when debating ongoing political rights. This kind of argument is a kind of vicious circle. The Declaration proves the founders embraced Lockean natural rights and the foundation in natural rights in turn proves the founders' vision of society is binding upon us. But should that be?

In doubting these matters, I am pressing several separate but related issues: (1) Should American public life be bound by philosophical notions of the social contract, and in particular notions that say the founders' views matter more than others?; (2) Can history provide a vehicle for getting at the original contract and the founders' intentions anyway? These two broader philosophical questions dovetail with the more specific historical questions examined already in this book; (3) does the Declaration in particular prove the founders' embraced natural rights theory and a specifically Lockean social contract theory; and (4) does the Declaration therefore prove that those conceptions are therefore incumbent and binding on us. My answer to all these questions is "No" for a number of intersecting reasons. To tease out these reasons, it is useful to lay out a possible alternative political philosophy for contrastive purposes.

An alternative political philosophy that did not start from a foundation in natural rights could work from the assumption that we are not bound in any particular way by the views of the founders. That is, the founders' views are not inherently or by definition better than any other person or group of persons that has existed or will exist in this society. The founders in such a view were at best smart thoughtful men (and to some extent women) whose views are worth throwing into the mix of our discussion. But their views are one voice among many in the public debate about rights. They were not all-seeing or all knowledgeable. And we are no more obligated to their views then we are to yours and mine. This is a very different view of the founders' voice than typically underlies the interest in the Declaration of Independence. The return to the Declaration is often fueled by an attempt to get back to some original vision of the founding as a way to say what America really stands for and therefore how we should govern our lives today. It is a way to say that our own views and values matter less than those who originated our society. History therefore is evoked to put an end to the philosophical and moral debates that we have about how we should structure our contemporary social practices. In this manner, the founders get invoked on one side or other of the debate in trying to defend a particular position, as if knowing their views should put an end to any other moral convictions that we may have.

The Declaration in particular has often figured prominently in discussions of the founders' political philosophy. Abraham Lincoln's Gettysburg Address is, of course, the most famous example of this desire to treat the Declaration as the definitive political vision for the United States.[1] On November 19, 1863, Lincoln defined the meaning of the Civil War this way: "Four score and seven years ago our fathers brought forth, upon this continent, a new nation, conceived in Liberty, and dedicated to the proposition that all men are created equal." Lincoln was referring to 1776 and alluding to the Declaration of Independence and the Declaration's words "all men are created equal." This famous address is illustrative of many of the underlying assumptions of those who treat the Declaration as the presumptive political philosophy of the United States. Lincoln implies here that a vision of a new nation was in place in 1776, that the Declaration of Independence encapsulates the vision for the new nation and that the phrase "all men are created equal" is the centerpiece of the Declaration.[2]

Lincoln was neither the first or last to make this argument. As Philip Detweiler has shown, the Declaration was largely ignored before the 1790s in the period before the ratification of the Constitution and the emergence of the rival political parties of Federalists and Republicans.[3] If the Declaration was invoked in that period at all it was typically associated with the idea of the colonies' political independence, not its statement on individual rights. Most state constitutions drafted during the revolutionary period after 1776 did not model their language of rights after the Declaration. And the debates during the Constitutional Convention and ratification process for the most part ignored the Declaration. It was not that the earlier constitutions or the ratification process ignored rights language and concepts. But the Declaration did not figure significantly as an authoritative source of what rights should be or the language by which they should be understood.

Matters changed during the 1790s, shortly after the ratification of the American Constitution, during the political debates between the emerging Federalist and Republican political parties.[4] The two parties had rival political philosophies and approaches to government and thus fundamentally disagreed on what vision of liberty had been conceived during the Revolution. Republicans, who were the party of Jefferson, naturally turned back to the Declaration as an interpretive tool to say what American political institutions should be like and what the founders really intended by the Revolution and the move towards independence. They appealed to the Declaration's preamble and focus on rights, as well as the anti-British character of the document, as a means of chastising Federalists for abandoning the spirit of '76.

In the Republicans' view, the vision of a strong federal government articulated by then Secretary of Treasury Alexander Hamilton undermined the core values of the Revolution which had been focused on liberty and rights. Hamilton's Federalist vision of government, which he modeled after Great Britain's, was anathema to Republicans, who thought it represented a return to the corrupting institutions that were responsible for the loss of liberty under British rule in the first place. Republicans appealed to the Declaration's account of liberty to suggest that the Federalists under Hamilton's leadership were abandoning the original vision of the Revolution as it was articulated.

There were several reasons that Federalists were naturally less likely to find the vision of the Revolution in the Declaration. Not only was the document authored by Jefferson, the leader of the opposition, but Federalists like Hamilton had to contend with the anti-British rhetoric of the Declaration. Led by Hamilton's vision, Federalists had a much more positive view of the relationship with Great Britain than did Republicans, seeing economic and political ties as key to the economic growth of the newly formed United States. Hamilton's Federal banking vision which was anathema to Republicans was modeled after Great Britain's own system. The Declaration's anti-British character thus lent itself more easily to Republican ideology that favored closer ties with France rather than Britain. Similarly, the Declaration's focus on revolution also posed a difficulty for Federalists who had a more negative assessment of the French Revolution with its reputation for violence.

It is significant that the early political debate over the interpretation of the United States and the Constitution provoked an appeal to the Declaration as one of way to grasp the meaning of the founders' vision. Up until that point, the Declaration apparently did not hold such a prominent place in American imagination. It was only after debate emerged over how to interpret the new nation and its Constitution that Republican political leaders reached back to the Declaration to try to pin down the meaning of the Revolution.

In many ways, it actually would have made more sense to look for a statement of American political philosophy in the American Constitution, the document that constituted the United States officially as more than a confederation of states. But the Constitution itself is noticeably light on an explicit political philosophy. Apart from the preamble to the Constitution, there is no explicit statement of rights and no mention of natural rights in the Constitution until the Amendments.

> We the People of the United States, in Order to form a more perfect Union, establish Justice, insure domestic Tranquility, provide for the common defense, promote the general Welfare, and secure the Blessings of Liberty to ourselves and our Posterity, do ordain and establish this Constitution for the United States of America.

The Constitution's preamble is thus quite abbreviated compared to other statements of rights that we have seen, such as the resolutions of the Stamp Act Congress, the Declaration of Rights of the First Continental Congress, the Declaration of Independence, and various state constitutions in the period leading up to the Constitution. Indeed, it is partly because the Constitution lacked a more explicit statement of rights that some prominent anti-Federalists such as Patrick Henry, George Mason, and Richard Henry Lee, among others, were against its ratification creating the mounting pressure to add the Bill of Rights, the first ten amendments to the Constitution, within a year of the Constitution's ratification. Indeed, some historians argue that the promise by Federalists to add a Bill of Rights was critical to the ratification process.[5]

Of course, it is possible to argue, as Akhil Amar does, that the political philosophy of the United States is everywhere taken for granted in the American Constitution but not explicitly articulated here because it was well understood.[6] On one reading, for example, the preamble embraces a republican ideology that sees the Constitution grounded in the people and consent. Yet we know that the Constitution was debated and crafted in closed-door sessions in Philadelphia during the summer of 1787, a partial record of which is recorded in the notes of Madison which were not published until fifty years later in 1840.[7] Most points of the Constitution were debated multiple times and subject to intensive debate involving questions of political philosophy. But whether there is a single, unified political philosophy exemplified in the Constitution is arguable. In fact, many interpreters see the Constitution itself as a political compromise between competing visions of America's political philosophy and different visions of how government power and individual rights should related. That is a separate debate beyond the scope of the present study, but does intersect with the questions at hand in this study.[8]

To summarize, there were several reasons that early Republicans probably reverted to the Declaration to try to settle the issue of America's political philosophy. It was not just because the Declaration was conveniently drafted by their party leader. The Constitution itself was terse on its vision of rights and a statement on the particular balance of government and individual freedom. Since the Constitution could not self-evidently anchor the Republican view of government and in fact was explicitly created to give the federal government more power than the earlier Articles of Confederation had provided, Republicans had to find some other vehicle to anchor their view of the founding vision. The Declaration was one natural place to alight since the document was associated with the moment when the colonies declared independence. Even though there were dozens of other statements of rights before the Declaration, and some like that of the First Continental Congress, were arguably as important, the Declaration represented a consensus of the colonies on why the war with Great Britain had become a war for political independence.

The desire to invoke the Declaration and to pin down American political philosophy continues into contemporary political philosophers on both sides of the political spectrum. In the book *To Secure These Rights*, for example, Scott Gerber, argues that "it was in the Declaration of Independence that the Founders articulated the political philosophy upon which this nation is based." Gerber argues that the "principles embodied in the Declaration are not 'above' or 'beyond' the Constitution; they are at the heart of the Constitution.[9] Gerber places himself in a tradition of other scholars such as Walter Berns, Martin Diamond, Harry Jaffa, and Walter Murphy, among others, who make a similar argument. Building on the assumption that the Declaration is "the" political philosophy of America, Gerber and others go on to argue that Declaration endorsed Lockean natural rights and therefore that we can resolve questions of the American Constitution by reading John Locke. Gerber argues we can even come to clarity on complicated questions such as abortion, gay marriage, rights to terminate life, and the meaning of equality, among other heated topics. Gerber ultimately believes his methodology ends the debate between liberals and conservatives by letting Locke's natural rights resolve our questions about rights.

Gerber is not alone in giving the Declaration this kind of prominence. H. N. Hirsch, in *A Theory of Liberty*, argues that the Declaration and Locke are critical for understanding the political philosophy of this country and that the centerpiece of the founders' vision was the idea that all men were created equal. Similarly, Michael Zuckert, in *Natural Rights and the New Republicanism*, argues that the United States is unique in creating a state based on natural rights. His argument depends on seeing the Declaration as endorsing natural rights and making that philosophy the foundation of the United States. In this way, he can contrast the uniqueness of the American founding with the "Glorious Revolution" and the English constitution of 1688, which he argues were not founded on Lockean vision of natural rights. Conservative thinkers such as Randy Barrett make similar arguments, seeing natural rights as the core of the American founding. In popular accounts of the Constitution's history, such as the Wikipedia, there is a straight line from the Declaration of Independence, which is portrayed as the political philosophy of the United States, to the Constitution. The Wikipeida article begins with this statement:

> On June 7, 1776, a resolution was introduced in the Second Continental Congress declaring the union with Great Britain to be dissolved, proposing the formation of foreign alliances, and suggesting the drafting of a plan of confederation to be submitted to the respective states. Independence was declared on July 4, 1776; the preparation of a plan of confederation was postponed. Although the Declaration was a statement of principles, it did not create a government or even a framework for how politics would be carried out. It was the Articles of Confederation that provided the necessary structure to the new nation during and after the American Revolution. The Declaration, however, did set forth the ideas of natural rights and the social contract that would be at the foundation of constitutional government.[10]

As is evident now, I find the attempt to anchor an American political philosophy in the Declaration, or any historical document for that matter, to be problematic for many reasons. While that attempt was originally motivated by a Republican anti-Federalist agenda that was focused on limiting government power, it is equally problematic when adopted by more moderate or liberal thinkers. My point is that the Declaration and the founders' views are essentially as relevant or irrelevant to the nature of rights in America as are mine and yours. That is, they may be illuminating but they are not prescriptive.

The alternative view, which downplays or at least equalizes the founders' views with our own, places less emphasis on history as the source of moral and philosophical insight about what our society should be. It sees appeals to the founders' views as distractions from the core issues about what values do we want to embrace as a society and what are the rules by which we end disagreements when they arise. In this alternative political philosophy, history ceases to be a source of truth and becomes just one more perspective in the debate, but much less important than otherwise thought, especially since history is interpretive and ambiguous anyway.

On the view proposed here, the Declaration's meaning does not matter for several reasons, some of which are specific to the history of American in particular and some relevant to the nature of history in general.

To start with the specifics of American history, there are several reasons the Declaration should not be considered the summary of American political philosophy. First, as noted above, there were many different statements of rights leading up to the war with Britain and to the Declaration of Independence. As other interpreters such as Pauline Maier have already argued, it is debatable whether the Declaration itself should be "the document" that represents the founders' views. The Declaration is only one among many documents on the path towards independence. As Maier puts it, the Revolution

> is not of a solo performance or even, to extend the metaphor, a performance of chamber music with a handful of players. What I had mind was more the Boston Symphony orchestra, or, better yet, the Mormon Tabernacle Choir, a production with a cast of hundreds...I set out in short to tell the stories of Independence and of the Declaration of Independence when the Declaration was a workaday document of the Second Continental Congress, one of many similar documents of the time in which American advocated, explained and justified Independence, the most painful decision of their collective lives.[11]

The problem Maier is describing I would argue is broader than just the question of the Declaration. It is a problem that is in some sense inherent in the historical enterprise itself. It is always a problem of interpretation to say which of many documents represent the essential views of a period. In this case, which of all the statements on rights that the pre-Revolutionary and post-Revolutionary American writers produced should represent the founders' views?[12] The decision of which documents represent the founders' definitive political philosophy is itself an interpretive decision that is already caught up in some other interpretation of what matters.

The notion that the Declaration is the definitive statement or vision of the United States is problematic for several reasons. While the Declaration was the consensus statement about why the colonies were declaring independence, it was not a statement about founding of the United States. On the contrary, the Declaration was a statement justifying the political independence of the colonies as independent political states. The vision of a United States, which was achieved in the Constitution, was not yet in view at the signing of the Declaration. Indeed, the one person who came closest to envisioning a United States, Joseph Galloway, had been ignored by Congress. It is true that the Declaration did use the language of "united states" but only in the sense that it represented the common view of independent states that had been united in a common cause. There was no "United States" envisioned in the Declaration in the sense of a state that had federal powers above the state level. On the contrary, the signers of the Declaration envisioned only a union of loosely confederated states each with its own political independence. That is why the Declaration of Independence was staged to happen at the same time that Virginia announced its political independence as a political state. The Declaration is a joint statement by the colonies explaining why they each would become independent political states.

This is one reason, among others, that it is problematic to turn back to the Declaration to define what the Constitution meant or what the United States was supposed to be. Such a position ignores the fact that the Constitution was in fact a response to the problems perceived in the Articles of Confederation in the years intervening since the drafting of the Declaration. Between 1776 and 1787, the Articles of Confederation proved inadequate during the revolutionary war because they could force the independent states to take action. The Constitutional Convention took up that problem in 1787. The Declaration itself, by contrast, never envisioned a Federal government at all. Ironically, then, if one wants to see the political philosophy of the United States in the Declaration of Independence, *one should theoretically be against any form of federal government* and not just for a particular interpretation of its limited powers.

But suppose for a moment that we could agree that the Declaration is *the* political philosophy of the United States and ignore the fact that there were many different competing visions of American rights in the period leading up to the Revolution. We still have another problem. The problem, as I have argued throughout this book, is that even the meaning of the Declaration is ambiguous. The Declaration is much more equivocal about natural rights than is often thought. My argument in this book has been that the founders were not all of one mind on the question of rights. Even in the Declaration, at the moment they were declaring independence, the undercurrents of debate were still visible. Jefferson, the Declaration's author, still had a different theory of rights than the majority of colleagues in Congress. While Jefferson's own alternative view of rights was for the most part edited out of the Declaration, the Declaration is still a palimpsest through which we can see the unresolved questions of rights on which the founders' had not agreed. The Declaration simply sidesteps and skirts over the key debates over the nature of American rights. While Jefferson himself can be interpreted as standing in the natural rights tradition, there is an indication he may never have bought into key natural rights concepts such as "social contact" and may have been persuaded by Hume among others to doubt the very notion of the social contract. The evidence for these views is already provided in other chapters of this book and need not be rehearsed here again.

There are historical and interpretive reasons, therefore, not to treat the Declaration as the only statement of American political philosophy nor to think that the Declaration offers a single definitive view of what our political philosophy should be. Going further, it is therefore arguable that the notion of natural rights and social contract were not the only political philosophy at work in the American founding. Indeed, as we have seen, many of the founders had doubts about Lockean notion of social contract. Those doubts continue to be visible up into the Declaration and may lie behind Jefferson's own reluctance to explicitly endorse a social contract theory. We know Jefferson was reading Hume as well as Locke, for example. And he was therefore aware of Hume's damaging critique of Locke's social contract theory. Similar doubts about Locke's social contract theory had been voiced by others before him.

What my historical reading confirms is that the American founding was constituted by conflicting and contested views of rights.[13] There were multiple political philosophies at work and in play. If we take away any conclusion from history about how we should resolve great questions of rights, it could easily be that we work through a process of debate and disagreement from multiple points of view and agree on a process by which we achieve compromise. That position, which does not evoke a political philosophy as "the true view of the founders", is arguably more true to the founding.

It is, as I have been arguing, also more true to the nature of history as an interpretive enterprise. The desire to turn to history to put an end to moral debate is ultimately problematic because history can't bear that weight. There is an inclination in doing so to treat history as science and to forget that history, like moral debate itself, is ultimately interpretive. History is inherently ambiguous. Our views of historical periods change over time. And interpretations of particular documents like the Declaration are nearly always open to multiple interpretations. That is the nature of historical interpretation as a humanistic activity.

History, therefore, does not stand outside of or above moral debate as a kind of standard that can put to rest squabbles we have over rights. It too is embedded in an interpretive process that is subject to debate. So should America (or any country) be bound by the political philosophy of its founders? My answer is no. They had contested understandings of rights just as do we. There was not a single political philosophy of the founders. Whether Locke's natural rights or Hume's political philosophy or even Kant's should guide us today is up for grabs now just as it was then. They debated key issues of rights within the frameworks of their moral understandings. We have to do the same.

The rejection of the founders' wisdom, then, stems from an understanding of history as a limited tool by which to resolve issues of rights. This alternative view which downplays the founders' views and treats them as nothing more (or nothing less) than just some voice in the debate obviously takes leave of one notion of the social contract. For if the social contract is interpreted to mean that there is an original founding contract with society, then we cannot dismiss the founders' views or the documents which embodied their views. We are on the contrary duty bound to understand their views and vision and try to apply it to our current circumstances. Their views are more important than ours. Our role is interpretive rather than constructive. History and interpretation become the key way through which we come to understand the rules by which we should live by. On the alternative view described here, the nature of the debate is shifted away from history to the values and processes by which we come to resolution. The founders carry no particular weight in the debate. History cannot and does not put to an end to the debate on the thorny moral and political issues that face us. All we have is the political process that tries to create a set of fair rules by which we have that debate and resolve it. For some, this alternative view is perhaps worrisome since there is no foundation in the past for resolving contentious issues of today. But while that may be worrisome, it is arguably the way things really are. And what that insight does is shift the debate, not to what the founders' meant, but to the values that ultimately we want to embrace and protect.

Notes

Introduction: On Natural Rights, History, and the American Founding

1. Following Locke, they believed that people entered into society through a social contract in which they traded their freedom in the state of nature for life under society. People made this compact because life in society was preferable to life in the state of nature in which people, living without political societies, lacked protection of their lives, health, liberty and possessions. In this state of nature, there was a law of nature that was discernible to reason and to which they were subject before entering into society. But because life in the state of nature was vulnerable, people preferred to come together and relinquish some freedoms in exchange for the benefits provided by society.
2. See Zuckert, *Natural Rights*.
3. This was one of the criticisms of Locke's natural rights arguments made by his critics. For example, Hume and others criticized Locke for implying that societies historically developed through social contract. Locke himself had taken up this question in a footnote but left the ambiguity in his work, as we shall see later
4. I discuss the history of the wording in this paragraph later. See also Becker, *Declaration*, and Boyd, *The Declaration*.
5. I review this literature in more detail as we proceed.
6. I am not alone in this contention, although I have weighed in on this issue in my own writing, such as Eilberg-Schwartz, *Savage in Judaism*, *God's Phallus*, and Schwartz, "Does God Have A Body." However, as we shall see many philosophical and legal interpreters seem to assume history can provide a solid foundation for interpretation that resolves ambiguity in the matters of rights. This is evident in debates on the meaning of the Declaration and Constitution, for example.

7. For examples related to the Declaration, see Hirsch, *A Theory of Liberty* and Gerber, *To Secure These Rights*. For a general discussion of intent and the Constitution, see Rakove, *Original Meanings*, and Levy, *Original Intent*.

8. On original intent, see discussions in Levy, *Original Intent* and Rakove, *Original Meanings*.

9. In general the notion of original intent is tied up with the notion of history, since history is the vehicle through which the original intent is uncovered. In this view, history becomes a key contributor to the interpretation of the founders' intent. But some Supreme Court justices, feeling the possible dilemma of history's own limitation, try to argue that original meanings of text can be derived from their language without reference to history. See the position of Justice Antonin Scalia in *A Matter of Interpretation*, which problematically tries to ignore history but still hold onto the notion of original meaning.

10. Most modern political philosophers agree the modern critique of traditional social contract theory has been devastating and they therefore seek other philosophical foundations for rights. Critiques of Lockean social contract by Hume, Bentham, Kant and numerous others made a traditionally Lockean account of rights problematic to political philosophers. But these critiques are considered irrelevant in America if the founders' intent is binding upon us. If the founders accepted Lockean natural rights as a foundation of their social-political framework and if we as a society are bound to their conceptions, then it does not matter that Lockean natural rights are a problematic construction or that there are better philosophical foundations for understanding rights.

11. In questioning whether natural rights are or should be the source of American rights, I actually have my aim on the implied link between the idea of "original intent" and social contract theory itself, for social contract theory claims that governments should be founded in the consent of the governed as defined by an original contract that structures the meaning and intent of the original parties. In this sense, social contract theory, at least one interpretation of it, seems to rest on the notion that it possible to locate and fully excavate the original intent of the original contract. The founders' views in the original contract are the views that define the rules by which we live. In the American situation, the American Constitution is thought to be the original "social contract" whose philosophical underpinnings are expressed in the Declaration of Independence. The notion that we should be governed by the "original intent" of the Constitution, therefore, rests on and is tied tightly into the philosophy of natural rights and social contract theory.

There is, if one thinks about it, a kind of interesting circular self-fulfilling logic at work here. If the Declaration or Constitution is our original social contract and if natural rights philosophy informed the understanding of rights that was embodied in the Constitution, then America is to be governed by natural rights, even if later generations have different views. In such a view, it does not really matter whether natural rights philosophy is right or wrong. It is our philosophy of rights, whether we like it or not. I shall return to this issue in the conclusion and argue that it is indefensible based on the historical analysis in this book.

12. For a discussion of this point, see my conclusion.

13. In some sense, I see Hume as more thoughtful than Locke on this point since Hume begins to develop a social-scientific view of political philosophy which he sees as justifications and worldviews for political organizations. As we shall see, Jefferson was reading Hume and arguably was influenced by him. I discuss Hume's possible influence on Jefferson below.

14. See Eilberg-Schwartz, "Who's Kidding Whom?", *The Savage in Judai*sm, and *God's Phallus*.

15. These essays have been published online. See my www.freedomandcapitalism.com.

Chapter 1 The Declaration, Locke, and Conflicts about Natural Rights

1. The closest the Constitution comes to articulating a political philosophy is the preamble of "We the people." Of course, that statement evokes a political philosophy of republicanism and/or natural rights behind it, but it does not explicitly articulate those assumptions and one has to look to documents prior to the Constitution, such as the Federalist Papers or the debates leading up to the Constitution to excavate its political philosophy. Indeed, the fact that the Constitution did not explicitly articulate a theory of rights was one of the reasons for resistance to it. The Bill of Rights, which followed a year later, was intended to address that gap. Ironically, the Bill of Rights also does not anywhere explicitly articulate a political philosophy, though it does mention the right to life, liberty, and property in Amendment V and thereby points back to a natural rights philosophy. It is interesting that the Bill of Rights never articulates that political philosophy explicitly, especially as some of its predecessors, such as the First Continental Congress Declaration of Rights and the Virginia Bill of Rights provide an explicit statement endorsement of natural rights philosophy. Indeed, the iteration of American rights in resolutions preceding the Revolution make the absence of such statements in the Constitution and Bill of

Rights surprising. The philosophy of rights and government lying underneath the Constitution and Bill of Rights therefore has to be inferred from the diverse and sometimes contradictory writings and debates leading up to the adoption of those documents. On the discussion related to the Constitution, see Amar, *America's Constitution*. See also Gerber, *To Secure These Rights*, for an explicit argument that the Declaration of Independence serves as the principle source for the view that the founders' intent was to create a Constitution that protected natural rights. I return to this subject in the conclusion to the book.

2. I discuss this point below in the chapters that follow.

3. Carl Becker's *The Declaration of Independence* is the classic exposition of this view, although as early as the 1820s, Jefferson was noting that Richard Henry Lee had suggested he had copied it from Locke. Many other writers follow or endorse this view as discussed below in note 14.

4. This issue is actually more complex than is suggested here. In the *Second Treatise*, Locke initially argued that humans derived their inherent rights because they were the "workmanship" and hence property of God. See Locke, *Second Treatise* 2:6.

5. C. F. Adams, *Works of John Adams*, II 512. See also Becker, *Declaration*, 24, a point to which we return.

6. See Boyd, *Declaration*, 16. Becker, *Declaration*, 25.

7. See Malone, *Jefferson*, 220; Ford, *Works*, X, 343; Boyd, *Declaration*, 16; Becker, *Jefferson*, 25.

8. Becker, *Declaration*, 24-25.

9. Boyd, *Declaration*, 15-16.

10. Ibid., 17.

11. Ibid., 24.

12. Malone, *Jefferson* I, 221; Petterson, *Jefferson*, 90. For similar views, see also Carey, "Natural Rights" 49.

13. Maier, *American Scripture* (135) for a similar view. Maier articulates the same position in writing that "The sentiments Jefferson eloquently expressed were, in short, absolutely conventional among Americans of his time."

14. The classic argument is by Becker, *Declaration*. See also Friedenwald, *Declaration*, 197-201; Chinard, *Jefferson*, 72; Carey, "Natural Rights," 47; Maier, *American Scripture*, 138; Jayne, *Jefferson's Declaration*. Gerber, *To Secure These Rights*, 22, writes that "Virtually no student of American political thought denies that the Declaration of Independence is an expression of natural-rights political philosophy." Jayne, *Jefferson's Declaration*, gives a more complex and in my view more accurate picture of Jefferson by arguing that he was influenced by multiple philosophical sources including Bolingbroke, Lord Kames, Locke

and others. But in my view Jayne still overemphasizes the importance Lockean influence on Jefferson. For my particular reservations about Jayne's argument, see note 29.

15. Becker, *Declaration*, 27.

16. An excellent summary of these various arguments is found in Ganter, "Pursuit of Happiness." See Becker, *Declaration*, 108; Chinard, *Commonplace Book*, 39-44; and Chinard, *Jefferson*, 72-73.

Carl Becker initially noted the similarity of Jefferson's language in the Declaration to James Wilson's pamphlet *Considerations* but assumed both were still Lockean. Chinard recognized that passages from Wilson's pamphlet were actually copied by Jefferson into his own commonplace book, proving that at some point Jefferson had read Wilson's essay. Chinard then raises the question of whether "Mr. Becker's statement that the lineage is direct (Jefferson copied from Locke and Locke quoted Hooker) now calls for some reservations. It becomes quite possible that Jefferson remembered not only Locke, but also Wilson, who quoted Burlamaqui, who drew his inspiration from Locke." Based on a chronological analysis, Chinard argues that Jefferson copied from Wilson sometime in 1776, but Chinard cannot determine if it was before or after drafting the Declaration, which would affect whether Jefferson can be assumed to have relied on Wilson's language in writing the Declaration itself. As Chinard notes, the whole relationship of Jefferson's dependence on Wilson's language in his pamphlet is made more puzzling by the fact that Jefferson did not copy into his Commonplace book the passage of Wilson that is so close to his own in the Declaration but copied the passage before and after it. Why would Jefferson not copy the very language of Wilson that is so similar to his own in the Declaration?

A possible answer to Chinard's puzzle is provided by the interpretation given of Jefferson in chapters to follow. In my view, Jefferson never heartily adopted a natural rights perspective, a point that ironically Chinard himself seemed to understand at times, at least when commenting on Jefferson's *A Summary View*. On this view, Jefferson copied precisely the passages from Wilson that interested him, and skipped those that did not interest him, namely those dealing with natural rights. He copied the passage before and after because those were of more interest to his line of thinking. As I discuss below, Jefferson and Wilson had fundamentally different views of American rights. As will become evident below, I disagree with Becker's conclusion that "Mr. Wilson's theory of the relations of the colonies to Great Britain was essentially the same as that which we find in the Declaration of Independence" (Becker, *Declaration*, 113, 115).

328 Liberty in America's Founding Moment

17. On the claim that Jefferson was dependent on George Mason's *Virginia Bill of Rights*, see John C. Fitzpatrick's, *The Spirit of the Declaration*, 2-3; Chinard, *Jefferson*, 74; and Maier, *American Scripture*, 104, 126, 134. Boyd, *Declaration*, 22, suggests that "it was scarcely possible that Jefferson could have escaped a conscious or unconscious reliance on two notable Virginia Documents of the preceding weeks." And Chinard wrote that "Jefferson had expressed the American mind, but he had above all expressed the mind of his fellow Virginians." See also Malone, *Jefferson*, 221, who notes the similarity to Mason's language and suggests that Jefferson could have been influenced by it. Pittman, *George Mason,* provides one of more incisive arguments in favor of Jefferson's reliance on Mason's Bill of Rights.

18. I am endebted to Zuckert, *Natural Rights*, for the characterization of this stream of thought as a "republican synthesis." The key writers who fall into this category are Bernard Bailyn, *Ideas*, Gordon Woods, *Creation*, and J. G. A. Pocock, *Machiavellian Moment*. See also the assessment of Locke's influence in America in Dworetz, *Unvarnished Doctrine*; Huyler, *Locke in America*; Jayne, *Jefferson's Declaration*. For others who side with the Lockean hypothesis, see Zuckert, *Natural Rights*, Gerber, *To Secure These Rights*, and Jayne, *Jefferson's Declaration,* Harmowy, "Jefferson and the Scottish Enlightenment."

19. See Maier, *American Scripture*, for an account that emphasizes the Declaration's relationship to the English Declaration of Rights. For a contrasting view, see Zuckert, *Natural Rights*.

The debate provoked by Garry Wills, *Inventing America*, does and does not belong in this category. Wills argued that the Lockean interpretation of the Declaration was overstated (a point with which I agree) but he then argued that Jefferson was dependent on the writers of the Scottish enlightenment, such as Lord Kames, Adam Ferguson but particularly Francis Hutcheson. Harmowy, "Jefferson and the Scottish Enlightenment" argues that Wills is incorrect and that Jefferson is "Lockean." But for important criticisms of Harmowy's argument, see Varga, et al., "Communications." My own view follows Wills in arguing that the Declaration should not be taken as a straightforward "Lockean" document but I diverge from Wills by not trying locate the specific source of Jefferson's thinking instead seeing Jefferson as trying to stay true to his own theoretical perspective (wherever that may have come from) while also meeting the expectations of the Second Continental Congress.

20. See Zuckert, *Natural Rights*, who presents a comprehensive view of how Locke's theory differed from other theories of the seventeenth century such as those of Grotius and Pufendorf and how Locke's reception came to dominance after the Glorious Revolution. See also Dworetz, *Unvarnished Doctrine*,

who argues that the republican synthesis has underestimated the importance of Locke. Gerber, *To Secure These Rights* (28), argues that the Declaration of Independence was ignored by those favoring the republican synthesis and constitutes significant evidence of the influence of Locke.

21. Carey, "Natural Rights" (49), for example, writes that "there cannot be much doubt of Jefferson's claim that the document's 'authority rest[ed]...on the harmonizing sentiments of the day.'" When Carey explains what this means, he adopts the commonly accepted view that social contract theory and Locke's depiction of the conditions of the state of nature were widely accepted. Carey does recognize that there were conflicting view of rights in the period before the revolution but he tends to see these as all details in the tradition of social contract theory. My own view emphasizes the disagreements and thus argues that there was not such a monolithic tradition as previously assumed and that the Declaration's harmonizing of sentiments is actually smoothing over and hiding these disagreements. See also Gerber, *To Secure These Rights* (31), which says "the harmonizing sentiments of the day were those of Locke."

22. See Conrad, "Putting Rights Talk," who has applied a similar perspective to the reading of Jefferson's *A Summary View*. In part II of this study, I look at the diverging view of rights from the Stamp Act through the First Continental Congress. For others who anticipate this position but do not develop it as fully see Carey, "Natural Rights," 48. Carey notes that "not all contract theories were exactly alike: differences existed over the context and source of the natural law, as well as over the character of rights." But Carey conflates Jefferson's view with a standard social contract view and concludes that "In sum...the language of the Declaration itself, illustrates the veracity of Jefferson's claim that the Declaration itself was but an expression of the American mind."

23. For those who make this point, see Becker, *Declaration* (18), who says that the Declaration is "solely" or "chiefly" concerned with a theory of government but elsewhere (ibid., 203) says that the "primary purpose" was "to convince a candid world that the colonies had a moral and legal right to separate from Great Britain." Amitage, *Declaration*, makes one of the strongest arguments linking the Declaration to the Law of Nations tradition and Vattel. See also Carey, "Natural Rights," and Detweiler, "The Changing Reputation."

24. See Amitage, *Declaration*, for a strong statement of this position. Carey, "Natural Rights," 63, also provides the interesting interpretation that the equal rights mentioned refer not to individual rights but corporate rights of "one people."

25. Vattel, *Law of Nations*, VI.

26. See Detweiler, "The Changing Reputation," for an account of the early reception of the Declaration.
27. Vattel has an excellent introduction to this issue in his *Law of Nations*.
28. I discuss this in detail below in the following chapters.
29. This view of Jefferson is articulated in his *A Summary View*, which I analyze in much more detail below in Chapter 5. As noted there, I disagree with those writers who think Jefferson's *A Summary View* articulates a classic natural rights philosophy that is "Lockean." See Malone, *Jefferson*, v. I, 184; and Ward, *Politics of Liberty*, 352. Becker, *Declaration*, never even asks the question of whether Jefferson's *A Summary View* represents a Lockean or natural rights perspective and simply assumes that it does. Becker, (ibid., 116-119), thus summarizes Jefferson's *A Summary View* but never asks whether Jefferson's view there is consistent with his argument that Jefferson endorsed a Lockean natural rights view (because he simply assumes that is the case).
30. For a discussion of the relationship of Bland's and Jefferson's pamphlets see my discussion below in Chapter 4 and 5.
31. See Colbourn, *Lamp of Experience*; Chinard, *Jefferson*, 49; and Ellis, *American Sphinx*, and my discussion in Part II.
32. See R. G. Adams, *Political Ideas, 15-18*, on various conceptions of the British Empire among the American colonists and particularly on the notion of a commonwealth of nations. Adams identifies three major views of the empire (dependence, federated state, and commonwealth of nations or league of states). Adams argues that the colonists moved from a view of the colonies as dependent to a view of the empire as a league of nations.

The notion of a league or commonwealth of nations meant that various dominions of the empire were independent states with their own legislatures rather than subordinate political entities to Parliament and England. On this view of the commonwealth, the Crown served to link the various parts of the empire together serving as a common executive branch and therefore attending to the issues that were "intra-state." The notion of a commonwealth was endorsed eventually by John Adams, Benjamin Franklin, James Wilson, and Thomas Jefferson. Because they all shared such a view, R. G. Adams tends to conflate their views at times, as do other interpreters. But R. G. Adams recognizes that there were different paths of reasoning that led to each to the view of a league of nations, a point I will explore below. Jefferson, Wilson, and Adams all arrive at view of a commonwealth of nations in different ways. The fact that they arrived there through different theoretical assumptions is important to the understanding of what the Declaration does and does not declare.

33. Jefferson does not appear to ponder the question of whether the settlers came from many European countries, possibly because he wanted to emphasize that the American settlers inherited the Anglo-Saxon political tradition.
34. See Jefferson's own account in Ford, *Complete Works*, I: 15.
35. I take up this question in much more detail in my analysis of Jefferson's *A Summary View* below, 178.
36. See my discussion below of the debate on natural rights in the First Continental Congress, see p. 207ff.
37. See below, Chapter 5.
38. See below, Chapter 6.
39. I discuss in more detail in my analysis of Jefferson's *A Summary View*. See also Reid, *Authority of Rights* (133), who notes that terms like "contract" and even "original contract" also belonged to the common law tradition.
40. See my discussion below, Chapter 6.
41. See J. G. Adams, *Political Ideas* (29-36), for a survey of various individuals in the colonies and England who proposed adding American representatives to Parliament as a solution. See also Woods, *Creation* (162-196), on the debate about the nature of representation.
42. On the debate about virtual representation, see Woods, *Creation* (162-196), and my discussion below in chapter 3. Early Doubts about Natural Rights Before the Revolution."
43. Some have also noted Jefferson's alternative view in *A Summary View* but have not always drawn the implications relevant to the Declaration. This is discussed below in Chapter 5. *A Summary View*: Jefferson's First Major Foray into Political Writing.
44. Boyd, *Papers*, I: 191. See my account and analysis below, in Chapter 6.
45. See my discussion of Jefferson's version of the *Declaration of the Causes and Necessity of Taking Up Arms*, in Chapter 6.
46. The contrary view that held that allegiance followed or "stuck to" a subject was put forward by the Stamp Act Congress, James Wilson and, during the First Continental Congress, Rutledge and Duane, among others. As John Duane put it in his notes for debate, "The priviledges of Englishmen were inherent They were their Birth right and of which they coud only be deprived by their free Consent." The First Continental Congress endorsed this view in its *Declaration of Rights* in 1774.
47. See Woods, *Creation*, 197-226.
48. See Woods, *Creation*, 197-226 on ideas of blended government among the colonists.

49. Jefferson in *A Summary View* (129) wrote that "It is now therefore the great office of his majesty, to resume the exercise of his negative power, and to prevent the passage of laws by any one legislature of the empire, which might bear injuriously on the rights and interests of another."

50. Hume articulated similar views and we shall see Jefferson was also reading Hume. For a discussion, see below, in Chapter 8.

51. I'm following Jefferson's spelling in this quotation.

52. Jefferson, *A Summary View*, 129.

53. Wilson, *Considerations*.

54. James Harrington is one seventeenth century thinkers who emphasized rights arising out of property ownership. Americans were familiar with the theory. James Otis, in *The Rights of the British Colonies Asserted and Proved*, for example, mentions this theory in his review of the theories of government. Similarly, Galloway bases his view on rights arising from property during the First Continental Congress debates. Galloway states that "Power results from the Real Property, of the Society" and argues that is the founding assumption of many states. See John Adams, "Notes on Debates" in *Letters of Delegates*, Letter 23, also discussed below 203. David Hume also held the view that often possession was the source of government, and we shall look at evidence below that Jefferson had read Hume.

55. See for example the discussion in Reid, *Authority of Rights*, 118 on the intersection of the "migration" issue and the question of whether America was conquered or settled. I disagree with Dworetz, *Unvarnished Doctrine* (47) who minimizes the question of conquest with respect to looking at the use of natural rights in the colonial writing.

56. Jefferson, *A Summary View*, in Boyd, *Papers*, I, 129.

57. Jefferson, ibid., 133.

58. Blackstone, 1. Bl Com. 106. 107.

59. See Jezierski, "Parliament or People," on the relationship of Blackstone and Wilson's legal theories from a theoretical perspective, although there is no discussion there of this particular disagreement.

60. Vattel, *Law of Nations*, 100. Originally written in French in 1758 it was translated into English in 1759. James Otis, for example, mentions Vattel in *The Rights of the British Colonies* (July 1764).

61. Blackstone, 1 BL *Com. 106, 107*.

62. Thompson, *Revolutionary Writings*, 121. See also Taylor, *Papers*, I: 315ff for the essay by Adams and background on Adams's role in drafting this essay and in the debate with Governor Thomas Hutchinson.

63. Thompson, *Revolutionary Writings*, 120.

64. The claim is made by among others Becker, *Declaration*, 96-97 and Morgan, *Stamp Act*, 87. For a discussion, see my discussion in Chapter 3.
65. See below chapter 3.
66. See, for example, Locke, *Second Treatise*, 8:100 and in particular 16:175. Here Locke offers several different responses to the objection that not all societies developed through a social contract. First, he argues that the evidence of the social contract is often lost in early history because by the time people kept records they had passed the stage of entering the contract. Second, he argues that there were historical societies in which consent is evident, such as Rome, Venice, and Sparta. But Locke also ponders the possible criticism that there were no convincing historical examples of the social contract. On this possibility he parenthetically writes that "(though at best an argument from what has been, to what should of right be, has no great force) one might, without any great danger, yield them the cause." Here Locke is saying that what has been true historically has no great value for what should of right be, separating the historical from the moral claim, which is based on reason. Many modern interpreters emphasize this last dimension of Locke (Laslett, *Locke*, 93; Dunn, *Locke*, 49; Becker, *Declaration*, 65), which was not the dimension of Locke that was most prominent to the American colonists.

Indeed this is just a parenthetical statement here and does not seem like Locke's primary conviction. When he wraps up he summarizes by again appealing to both reason and history: "But to conclude, reason being plain on our side, that men are naturally free, and the examples of history shewing, that the governments of the world, that were begun in peace, had their beginning laid on that foundation, and were *made by consent of the people*, there can be little room for doubt, either where the right is, or what has been the opinion, or practice of mankind, about the *first erecting* of governments." (Locke, *Second Treatise*, 8:104). For an extended discussion see Schohet, "The Family and Origins." I also discuss this issue again in Chapter 3, note 29.
67. See my discussion below, in Chapter 3.

Chapter 2: Jefferson's Declaration of Independence

1. Boyd, *Papers*, I, 277-284
2. Boyd, *ibid.*, 283.
3. Boyd, *ibid.*, 284.
4. See Boyd, (*ibid.*, 284) for the dating of the essay. Boyd citing Keller also notes the similarity between the views expressed here and Jefferson's earlier *A Summary View* and *Declaration of the Causes*.

5. JCC IV, 342

6. Maier, *American Scripture*, 37. Rakove, *The Beginnings* (21-62), suggests the language equivocated to some degree. Colonies that had government "sufficient to the exigencies of their affairs" did not have to engage in constitution making, enabling the more radical states to progress faster than the more moderate ones.

7. Adams wrote to his wife that "Great Britain has at last driven America to the last step." Quoted in Boyd, *Declaration*, 18.

8. For a discussion of the context in which Jefferson wrote these drafts, see Boyd, *Papers*, I: 329-337, 345; Boyd, *Declaration*, 22; Maier, *American Scripture*, 48; Hazelton, *Declaration*, 147. Boyd, *Papers* (345) suggests the possibility that Jefferson had made notes even before returning to Congress in anticipation of the need for a constitution.

9. See Boyd, *Papers*, I 384, who disagrees with the previously held view that Jefferson's draft arrived too late to have any measurable impact on the Virginia constitution.

10. See Boyd, *Papers* (I: 332) and Boyd, *Declaration* (22-23), for the insight that the draft of the Virginia Constitution should be viewed as the documentary history of the Declaration of Independence. I am, however, going further than Boyd and arguing that the first draft of the Virginia Constitution should be viewed as Jefferson's actual first "Declaration of Independence" and one that most closely adheres to his own views.

11. Confirmation of this view is found in a letter in 1825. Jefferson wrote "the fact is that that preamble was prior in composition to the Declaration, and both [the Declaration and the Virginia Constitution] having the same object, of justifying our separation from Great Britain, they used necessarily the same materials of justification: and hence their similitude." Quoted in Boyd, *Declaration*, 23.

12. Maier, *American Scripture*, 47.

13. An exception is Maier, *American Scripture*, 128, who also notes that Jefferson did not add a preamble originally to his own theory of independence. Maier even comments that the Committee of Five may have asked Jefferson to add the section. But Maier does not draw the conclusions which I do, namely, that this preamble was not in keeping with Jefferson's own views.

14. For arguments that Jefferson read Mason's essay, see Pitman, "George Mason."

15. See Maier, *American Scripture* (51-55) on the *English Bill of Rights* being a model for the Declaration of Independence. See also Zuckert, *Natural Rights*, who argues that the English Declaration did not rely on Locke's natural rights philosophy.

16. Boyd, *Papers*, I: 347.

17. Lee's resolution is available online: http://www.yale.edu/lawweb/avalon/lee.htm.
18. Jefferson and Adams's own account of why Jefferson was selected differ and have been discussed on numerous occasions. See Boyd, *Declaration*, 20-21, Hazelton, *Declaration*, 141, Maier, *American Scripture*, 99-100.
19. There is a conflict between Jefferson's and Adams's memories of how much consultation occurred between Jefferson and the Committee or between Jefferson and Adams and Franklin in particular. Boyd, *Declaration* (22) concludes that there likely was a discussion and Jefferson, though he challenged the fact that there was a "subcommittee", never denied the fact that there was a discussion on the subject. Boyd speculates that Committee of Five likely discussed the codification, arrangement, amplification and emphasis to be given. Maier, *American Scripture* (100-103) also emphasizes that Jefferson likely consulted with the Committee or at least some of its members on several occasions.
20. Boyd, *Declaration*, 24.
21. Peterson, *Jefferson* (89) also uses the word "smuggle" to describe Jefferson's attempt to get his views in the Declaration.
22. Compare the fair version prepared for the Committee of Five (Boyd, *Papers*, 426) with the "Rough Draft" version after Congress made its changes (Boyd, *Papers*, 318). Boyd, *Declaration*, 34 attributes these changes to Congress but passes over this deletion without attributing to it much significance.

For a discussion of the history of the evolution of the text, see Boyd, *Papers*, I, 413-17 and Boyd, *Declaration*, 26-33, as well as Becker, *Declaration*, 135-193. Eighty-six changes were made to the original draft that Jefferson wrote and Congress cut out about 25 percent. Adams and Franklin made a much smaller set of changes during their review before the committee submitted its copy to Congress. Although the rough draft contains the whole history of the changes made in the Declaration as it went through its revisions, it is possible to see the state of the text at various points in its evolution. John Adams copied an early version, before the fair copy was created by the Committee of Five. This Adams version already contains some changes that may have come from Adams's and Franklin's suggestions

23. Jefferson recounts the now famous story of how he was sitting next to Benjamin Franklin "who perceived that I was not sensible to these mutilations." Franklin told Jefferson that he avoided drafting papers for public bodies precisely to avoid such heavy editing. To illustrate, Franklin then told him a humorous story of an apprentice hatter who created a public sign that read "John Thompson, Hatters, makes and sells hats for ready money." But when he submitted it to his friends for comments, they eliminated nearly all the words

as unnecessary. By the end of the review session, the sign was reduced to "John Hatter" with a figure of a hat only. See Becker, *Declaration*, 208; Ford, *Works*, X, 120; Hazelton, 179.

24. Quoted in Boyd, *Declaration*, 20.

25. Becker, Declaration, 209; Boyd, *Declaration*, 33, Maier, *American Scripture*, 148.

26. Becker, *Declaration*, 211. Becker thus assumes that the Declaration of Independence still reflects Jefferson's theoretical perspective, namely, the view that the ancestors created independent states and voluntarily joined the empire.

27. Boyd, *Declaration*, 36. Maier, *American Scripture* (148) portrays Congress's editing job here as reducing Jefferson's overlong attack on the British people. But she seems to sense that something more is going on but without drawing out the full significance: "Out went his claim that the Americans had settled the country without any British help; the remaining assertion that 'we reminded them of the circumstances of our emigration and settlement here' then became more justifiable. From the beginning of the conflict, the colonists had insisted that in coming to America their ancestors had yielded none of the right of Englishmen. That could be construed as reminding British people of the "circumstances of our emigration." Maier thus does not fully draw the conclusion that a significant dispute over the matter of rights is being played out here and that the rewrite raises precisely doubts about what theory of rights the Declaration is endorsing.

28. Becker, *Declaration*, 115, writes: "If, therefore, the first Continental Congress did not adopt the theory of British American relations which we find in the Declaration, it was not because the theory was a novel one. In 1774 it was familiar doctrine to all men."

As proof Becker cites Jefferson's *A Summary View*. Becker, however, makes the mistake of assuming the Declaration reflects Jefferson's view and therefore draws the conclusion that the Declaration does not reflect the same theory as that published in the Declaration of Rights published by Congress in 1774.

In my reading, by contrast, the changes made by Committee and Congress moved Jefferson's original draft to a place where it aligned with the Declaration of the First Congress. Furthermore, Becker also misses the fact that Wilson and others had a different view than Jefferson in *A Summary View*, not giving sufficient detail to the disagreements which I have pointed out above. Becker writes: "Mr Wilson's theory of the relationship of the colonies to Great Britain was essentially the same as that which we find in the Declaration of Independence." The reason Becker draws this conclusion is because he sees no differences between the view of Jefferson and Wilson. On my reading, however, Jefferson and Wilson fundamentally disagreed. The First Continental Congress espoused a view like Wilson's. Jefferson wrote the first draft of the Declaration trying to slip his theory back in. But after it was edited out, the Declaration is ambiguous because it does not explain the foundation of the settlers' rights at all and leaves equivocal whether it represents a view like Wilson or like Jefferson.

29. See Boyd, *Papers*, I, 427, and 319, for the fair copy prepared for Committee of Five and for the rough draft with changes by Congress.

30. Becker, *Declaration*, 171. Boyd argues that Jefferson's *Notes of Proceedings* is not a later recollection but is much closer in time than other interpreters had thought. See Boyd, *Papers*, I, 299-309.

31. That is not the only reading possible since the resolution is itself ambiguous whether it is declaring the colonies to be states at the moment of the declaration or treating them as states that were already in existence.

32. Becker, *Declaration*, 210.

33. Quoted in Hazelton, *Declaration*, 178.

34. I am here following Becker's reconstruction of the early draft based on the Adams's copy of the Declaration. Becker, *Declaration*, 141, 160. See also Boyd, Papers, I, 315 and 423.

35. Boyd, *Declaration*, 31 identifies these changes as resulting from the Committee work.

36. Becker, *Declaration*, 198.

37. Maier, *American Scripture* (132) also notes that "a people" was consistent with Jefferson's theory in *A Summary View*.

38. Becker, *Declaration*, 144

39. In *America Declares Independence*, Dershowitz (75) makes a great deal of Jefferson's use of the language "the laws of nature & of nature's god." Dershowitz sees this as evidence that Jefferson embraced a deist view of God and religion. In the deist tradition, Jefferson saw God as an abstract creator God of reason but not as a personal being with whom one could have a personal relationship. Dershowitz suggests this is why Jefferson did not choose more traditional theological language. On this basis, Dershowitz then explains "another challenging question" of how "Jefferson persuaded his colleagues—first, those on the committee appointed to draft the Declaration, and second, those in the Congress who eventually approved it—to accept his un-Christian and anticlerical references to "Nature's God" and "Creator" in place of the more orthodox reference to "Almighty God," "Jesus," or simply "God." Dershowitz' answer is that the majority on the committed (Franklin, Adams, Livingston) were deists or Unitarians.

I am sympathetic with Dershowitz' general argument against those who read very traditional Christian conceptions into the Declaration. I think that is wrong too. But Dershowitz provides an overly simplified view of Jefferson's position and the complicated ways in which colonial writers brought religious and natural rights language together. Some writers like James Wilson did not invoke God at all in his pamphlet *Considerations*. But Jefferson was among those who felt comfortable invoking God as he did in *A Summary View* and *Declaration of Causes*. In both of these cases, moreover, Jefferson used more traditional God language without any reference to "nature's god" as found here in the Declaration. It is only here that he invokes the God of Nature. I suggest that Jefferson adopted more natural rights oriented language in the Declaration precisely because he was writing for the committee who expected him to lay out a statement of natural rights. When left to his own inclinations, as in *A Summary View* or the *Declaration of Causes*, Jefferson favored more straightforward references to just "God." At what point Jefferson came to hold deist views of religion is itself an interesting question. All of Dershowitz's quotes illustrating Jefferson's deist type views come from later in his life. But as a young man Jefferson was clearly reading deist oriented literature, as evident in his commonplace book, though he did not adopt the language of "nature's god" in his earlier writings.

To further complicate matters, there is a complex relationship between more traditional Christian theological and covenantal language and the natural rights tradition that I discussed below in Chapter 4. There were various ways in which American colonial writers tried to bring together more traditional covenantal and theological conceptions with the natural rights language. If anything, the Declaration was trying to straddle those conceptions, speaking simultaneously to more traditionally theologically minded Christians and those oriented to more deist type language. Congress added two additional references to God in revising Jefferson's earlier draft.

40. I thus disagree with those who project back from the Declaration the emphasis on natural rights into Jefferson's earlier writings.
41. See, for example, Boyd, *Declaration*, 36.
42. Becker, *Declaration*, 21, 203-204.
43. Becker, *Declaration*, 203-204. Boyd, *Declaration* (36) also recognizes that the Declaration assumes no connection between the American colonies and Parliament but misses the fact that there was substantial disagreement on how that relationship had ended. In eliminating Jefferson's theory, Congress left equivocal which theory was the foundation of that rejection of Parliament's power.
44. Becker, *Declaration*, 204.

45. Ibid., 142, 161.
46. See the reference in *A Summary View*, and Boyd, Papers, I, 123. For the reference in the draft of the Declaration, see Boyd, Papers, I, 317.
47. This was the case for example in the Stamp Act resolutions and in the writing of Samuel Adams, see below in Chapter 3.
48. See Zuckert, *Natural Rights*, for a particularly helpful discussion explaining how the Whigs relied on the common law tradition of "inherent rights" before the rise to prominence of Locke.
49. Becker tends to treat these changes as simply literary improvements of Jefferson and not necessarily substantive changes.
50. This philosophical perspective of Jefferson has been emphasized by Koch and by Wills.
51. Becker, *Declaration*, 144.
52. See, for example, Schlessinger, "Lost Meaning;" Ganter, "Pursuit of Happiness," Part II; Maier, *American Scripture*, 134, Maier follows the view that Jefferson was trying to be more economical in his writing style than Mason and "sacrificed clarity of meaning for grace of language." Ganter cites dozens of passages from Locke's *Essay* and other philosophical sources that use the expression "pursuit of happiness." Becker doesn't even comment on Jefferson's use of the term happiness.
53. Maier, *American Scripture*, 134.
54. Otis, *Rights*, in Bailyn, *Pamphlets*, 425.
55. See Chapter 1, note 17.
56. Maier, *American Scripture*, 134.
57. Ganter, "Pursuit of Happiness" Part II, also mentions the Bland parallel, but he simply lists this one among many rather than as a unique source of insight for understanding Jefferson's position.
58. Jensen, *Tracts*, 112–113. Bland cites Wollaston in a footnote as a source of this view, though Locke says something quite similar about a child taking on the laws of a country when the child inherits the property from his father. See Locke II 73 and 120.
59. See my discussion below, in Chapter 5.
60. See Boyd, *Declaration*, 27-28 for a summary. Boyd prefers Jefferson as the source of change, while others attribute the change to Adams or Franklin. Boyd's tentative conclusion is that Jefferson presented the draft to Adams first, who made only one correction, and then presented it to Franklin for his corrections. However, Boyd (ibid., 30) also notes that Jefferson submitted his rough draft to Adams twice and therefore it is difficult to know which of these changes reflect Jefferson's own changes or were based on the suggestions of Adams.

61. Boyd, *Declaration* (31) attributes these changes to the committee.
62. See my discussion below, in Chapter 3.

Chapter 3: Early Doubts About Natural Rights Before The Revolution

1. See, for example, Reid, *Authority of Rights*; Maier, *American Scripture*; Morgan, *Stamp Act Crisis*. I discuss some of this literature below.
2. See accounts in Bailyn, *Pamphlets*, 356, and Morgan, *Stamp Act*.
3. Morgan, *Stamp Act* (54-74) has an excellent analysis of what was on Grenville's mind.
4. See Bailyn, *Pamphlets*, 508, 516.
5. The early consensus that Parliament had a right to regulate commerce of the empire but not tax the colonies foreshadows in interesting and complex ways the later debates over federal and state powers in the debate over the ratification of the constitution. There is a huge irony in the fact that colonists thought Parliament had no right to tax them but later gave such rights to federal powers.
6. The Rhode Island assembly commissioned the drafting of a remonstrance against the renewal of the Molasses Act. The document was written by the governor who based it on the earlier document of the Boston merchants called the State of Trade. See Bailyn, *Pamphlets*, 358, and Jensen, *Tracts*, 3-4.
7. An example of another pamphlet that argues strictly in economic terms, see *Considerations Upon The Act of Parliament* in Bailyn, *Pamphlets*, 361-377.
8. Jensen, *Tracts*, 7.
9. Ibid., 7.
10. Ibid., 12.
11. An interesting partial exception is the New York Petition to the House of Commons written on Oct. 18, 1764. This petition does evoke Lockean natural rights and does link freedom of commerce to liberty. But it does so in the context of recognizing that Parliament retains the authority "to model the Trade of the whole Empire, so as to subserve the Interest of her own." "But a Freedom to drive all Kinds of Traffick in a Subordination to, and not inconsistent with, the *British* Trade; and an Exemption from all Duties in such a Course of Commerce, is humbly claimed by the Colonies, as the most essential of all the Rights to which they are intitled, as Colonists from, and connected, in the common Bond of Liberty with the uninslaved Sons of *Great-Britain*." See Morgan, *Prologue*, 9, 11.

12. Bailyn, *Pamphlets*, 358-59.
13. Morgan, *Stamp Act*, 33.
14. In his *Regulations Lately Made* (1765), Thomas Whately argues that "Duties laid for these Purposes, as well as for the Purposes of Revenue, are still Levies of Money upon the People. The Constitution again knows no Distinction between impost Duties and Internal Taxation and if some speculative Difference should be attempted to be made, it certainly is contradicted by Fact." Quoted in Morgan, *Prologue*, 20.
15. The Sugar Act, April 5, 1764. Quoted in Morgan, *Prologue*, 4-5.
16. See note 11 above where New York does frame the response to the Stamp Act in terms of rights.
17. Bailyn, *Pamphlets*, 379.
18. See, for example, John Dickinson's "The Late Regulations Respecting the British Colonies." December 1765. In Bailyn, *Pamphlets*, 659-691 and discussed below.
19. For Hopkins, *Rights*, see Bailyn, *Pamphlets*, 499-521. A shortened version is also available in Jensen, *Tracts*, 41-62.
20. Hopkins, *Rights*, quoted in Bailyn, *Pamphlets*, 516.
21. Hopkins, *Rights*, quoted in Bailyn, *Pamphlets*, 507.
22. Dulany, *Considerations*, quoted in Bailyn, *Pamphlets*, 634. For background on Dulany, see Bailyn, *Pamphlets*, 599-607.
23. The fact that the origins of government were veiled explains why so much of colonial writing emphasizes "the end" or purpose of government in contrast to "the beginning" of government. Be that as it may, the "end of government" can only be justified if there is some theory as to anchor that view of government. Emphasizing the end of government does not really provide a ground for justifying that end as opposed to other ends of government.
24. Hopkins, *Rights*, quoted in Bailyn, *Pamphlets*, 507.
25. Hopkins, ibid., 516. Jensen, *Tracts*, 54.
26. Hopkins, *Rights*, quoted in Bailyn, *Pamphlets*, 508.
27. See Zuckert, *Natural Rights*, 49-118.
28. Hopkins does not specify whose alternative theories he has in mind here. We can speculate that it could have been Harrington and possibly Hume.
29. Locke asks about the historical evidence of the state of nature and social compacts (*Second Treatise* 2, 15, p. 277). He writes: "To those that say, There were never any Men in the State of Nature; I will not only oppose the Authority of the Judicious *Hooker*,...But I moreover affirm, That all Men are naturally in that State, and remain so, till by their own Consents they make themselves Members

of some Politick Society; And I doubt not in the Sequel of this Discourse, to make it very clear."

Locke then takes up the question again (*Second Treatise*, 8, 100, [Laslett, *Locke*, 333-334]) where he discusses the origin of political societies. "To this I find two Objections made. *First, that there are no Instances to be found in Story of a Company of Men independent and equal one amongst another, that met together, and in this way began and set up a Government. Secondly, 'Tis impossible of right that Men should do so, because all Men being born under Government, they are to submit to that, and are not at liberty to begin a new one.*" Locke gives a number of answers. First he says that it is no wonder that we have no accounts since the nature of that condition in a state of nature drove people very quickly into society and do not leave a record of that stage. Secondly, Locke then points to certain societies such as Rome and Venice which he regards as examples of states that came together through social compact. But it is clear that Locke's argument does not simply rest on the need for historical examples. He also bases it on what's right. "For if they can give so many instances out of History, of Governments begun upon Paternal right, I think (though at best an Argument from what has been, to what should of right be, has no great force), one might, without any great danger, yield them the cause." The parenthetical clause here is interesting because Locke argues that history is essentially irrelevant for what is right. He then continues to show that history is only one part of his argument: "But to conclude, Reason being plain on our side, that Men are naturally free, and the Examples of History, shewing, that the *Governments* of the World, that were begun in Peace, had their beginning laid on that foundation, and were *made by the Consent of the People*; There can be little room for doubt, either where the Right is, or what has been the Opinion, or Practice of Mankind, about the *first erecting of Governments.*" Locke clearly sees that his argument can have a foundation in reason and what's right, even apart from any historical proof of a state of nature. See also my discussion in chapter 1, note 66.

30. Laslett, *Locke* (93), puts it this way: "When men think of themselves as organized with each other they must remember who they are. They do not make themselves, they do not own themselves, they do not dispose of themselves, they are the workmanship of God. ...To John Locke this was a proposition of common sense, the initial proposition of a work which appeals to common sense throughout. It is an existentialist proposition...and it relies not so much on the proved existence of a Deity as upon the possibility of taking what might be called a synoptic view of the world, more vulgarly a God's–eye view of what happens among men here on earth. If you admit that it is possible to look down on men from above, then you may be said to grant to Locke this initial position.

John Rawl's work is the most well known example of providing social contract theory a theoretical and non-historical grounding in an 'original position.'"

31. For a discussion of Hume's influence among American colonial writers, for example, see Spencer, *David Hume*. I discuss Hume's critique in my discussion of Jefferson's reading habits in Chapter 8.

32. It is beyond the scope of the present essay to look at the "religionizing" of Locke. Locke was clearly "religious" in the sense that he assumed natural rights were embodiments of God's law and in assuming that scripture and reason were compatible. But Locke is also the beginning of, and catalyst for, the great deist critiques of the early eighteenth century. Those critiques used reason to attack and undermine traditional notions of Revelation and ultimately lead to a new understanding of Christianity, religion, and scripture. Locke himself did not take as radical a view as more critical deists such as Matthew Tindal and John Toland. But he did lay part of the foundation for this critique of traditional religion. For an account of the Deist critique, see Manuel, *The Eighteenth Century*, and Eilberg-Schwartz, *The Savage*.

33. Otis, *Rights*, in Bailyn, *Pamphlets*, 423.

34. Ibid., 419-420. De Vattel develops an extensive understanding of the rights and duties of nations based on natural rights philosophy.

35. Otis, *Rights*, in Bailyn, *Pamphlets*, 422.

36. See Bailyn, *Pamphlets*, 524-530.

37. Howard, *Halifax Letter*, in Bailyn, *Pamphlets*, 535.

38. Hopkins, *Rights*, in Bailyn, *Pamphlets*, 507.

39. Hopkins, *Rights*, in Bailyn, *Pamphlets*, 509.

40. See the discussion of the Stamp Act Congress below in this Chapter.

41. This comment appeared in the London *General Evening Post* on August 20, 1765 and reprinted in the *Newport Mercury*, October 28, 1765. Cited in Morgan, *Prologue*, 97.

42. Hopkins, *Rights*, quoted in Bailyn, *Pamphlets*, 509.

43. Ibid., 511.

44. Ibid., 512. Fitch makes a similar claim. Hopkins also writes that "These with all other matters of a general nature, it is absolutely necessary should have a general power to direct them; some supreme and overruling authority with power to make laws, and form regulations for the good of all, and to compel their execution and observation. It being necessary some such general power should exist somewhere, every man of the least knowledge of the British constitution will be naturally led to look for, and find it in the Parliament of Great Britain."

45. Hopkins, *Rights*, quoted in Bailyn, *Pamphlets*, 518-519. Jensen, *Tracts,* says Otis and Steve Hopkins come out with early positions that Parliament is not completely sovereign but then retract those positions after the attack by the gentleman at Halifax.
46. Fitch, *Reasons Why*, in Bailyn, *Pamphlets*, 395.
47. Hopkins, *Rights*, in Bailyn, *Pamphlets*, 519.
48. See Merrill p. xxvi. "In effect, Hopkins was groping toward the conception of the British Empire as a commonwealth containing equal and independent legislatures, and yet one in which matters of a general nature had to be deal with by a supreme legislature."
49. Howard, *Halifax Letter*, in Bailyn, *Pamphlets*, 534.
50. Actually, at one point Hopkins does say something that sounds like this but he says it after he has already said that Parliament has authority and right to regulate commerce. "Indeed, it must be absurd to support that the common people of Great Britain have a sovereign and absolute authority over their fellow subjects in America, or even any sort of power whatsoever over them" (Bailyn, *Pamphlets*, 519). Here Hopkins is making his argument that the House of Commons does not have power over the colonies as part of his hub and spoke view of the empire.
51. Howard, *Halifax Letter*, in Bailyn, *Pamphlets*, 537.
52. The quotes are from Howard, *Halifax Letter*, in Bailyn, *Pamphlets*, 537-538.
53. Background on Soame Jenyns can be found in Bailyn, *Pamphlets*, 600.
54. Jenyns's essay can be found at http://odur.let.rug.nl/~usa/D/1751-1775/stampact/object.htm.
55. Writing about how political decisions should represent the entire people, Locke (Second Treatise 8:92, 332) writes: "But such a consent is next impossible ever to be had, if we consider the Infirmities of Health, and Avocations of Business, which in a number though much less than that of a Commonwealth, will necessarily keep many away from the publick Assembly. To which if we add the variety of Opinions, and contrariety of Interests, which unavoidably happen in all Collections of Men, the coming into Society upon such terms, would be only like Cato's coming into the Theatre, only to go out again. For where the majority cannot conclude the rest, there they cannot act as on Body, and consequently will be immediately dissolved again."
56. The Cato letters in the early eighteenth century further develop the notion of representation arguing that "representatives...will always act for their country's interest; their own being so interwoven with the people's happiness, that they must stand and fall together. See Gordon and Trenchard, "Cato

Letters." Letter 24: "Of The Natural Honesty Of The People, to Consult Their Affections and Interest."

57. Otis, *Rights*, in Bailyn, *Pamphlets*, 423.
58. Ibid., 423.
59. Ibid., 425. In anchoring rights in human nature and sociability, Otis comes closer to the theory of rights of Grotius more than Locke but he only mentions Grotius once in his essay and not in a very favorable light.
60. See for example Otis, *ibid.*, 434.
61. Ibid., 436-7. Speaking of the natural rights of the colonies Otis writes that "those who expect to find anything very satisfactory on this subject in particular or with regard to the law of nature in general in the writings of such authors as Grotius and Pufendorf will find themselves much mistaken. It is their constant practice to establish the matter of right on the matter of fact:... The sentiments on this subject have therefore been chiefly drawn from the purer foundations of one or two of our English writers, particularly from Mr. *Locke*, to whom might be added a *few* of other nations; for I have seen but a few of any country, and of all I have seen there were not ten worth reading."
62. It is problematic to simply characterize Otis as a Lockean as Morgan does: "Otis, while acknowledging the supremacy of Parliament, argued in terms derived from Locke that Parliament ought not to violate the nature rights of the subject."
63. Otis significantly contradicts his own theory later in the essay. After arguing essentially that there is no state of nature and no consent or social compact, he writes, "I say men for in a state of nature no man can take my property from me without my consent" taking for granted the notion of a state of nature. Otis, "Rights," 447.
64. On Locke's *Second Treatise* being aimed in part at Filmer's *Patriacha*, see Laslett, *Locke*, 67-92.
65. Otis, *Rights*, in Bailyn, *Pamphlets*, 423.
66. Ibid., 423.
67. See Zuckert, *Natural Rights*, who emphasizes this distinction between Locke and Grotius.
68. On the deist debates and changing view of religion in the eighteenth century, see Manuel, *The Eighteenth Century Confronts the Gods*, and Eilberg-Schwartz, *The Savage*.
69. Abraham Williams, "Election Sermon," 5.
70. Ibid., 6.
71. The closest Locke comes to assigning this to God is the following passage: "God having made Man such a Creature, that, in his own Judgment, it was

not good for him to be alone, put him under strong Obligations of Necessity, Convenience, and Inclination to drive him into *Society,* as well as fitted him with Understanding and Language to continue to enjoy it." While this sounds like Otis, it is different. Locke here is explaining people's social inclination and in particular their desire to marry which he sees as the origin of the first societies. But Locke distinguishes these forms of social inclination from political societies. As Locke says "each of these, or all together, came short of as we shall see, of political society, if we consider the different ends, ties, and bounds of each of these" (Locke II 7, 77 in Laslett, 318). In Locke's view, God drives people to be social beings, but humans choose whether or not to enter political organizations.

72. Williams, "Election Sermon," 7.
73. Otis, *Rights*, in Bailyn, *Pamphlets*, 425.
74. Ibid., 424.
75. The colonists tend to ignore important philosophical questions in splitting the question of government's "end" from its "beginning." For the "end" or "purpose" of government has to be grounded in some moral theory. If the colonists did not have agreement on government's origin, then on what basis did they agree on "its end"? The fact is the colonists had different and competing theories of where such rights came from and therefore concentrated on agreement about what those rights were ("the end of government") rather than moral source of those rights.
76. Otis, *Rights*, in Bailyn, *Pamphlets*, 444.
77. There was some understanding that the rights of "men" posed a particular issue for women, children and blacks. Locke and Otis both raise the question of women's place in the original contract and in natural rights. Abigail Adams sensed the discrepancy in a letter to her husband, John Adams, raising the question of women's rights as a problem of liberty.
78. Otis, *Rights*, in Bailyn, *Pamphlets*, 443.
79. Ibid., 454.
80. Otis, *Vindication*, in Bailyn, *Pamphlets*, 545-579.
81. Morgan, *Prologue*, 46-49. For an excellent analysis of Patrick Henry's original resolves and the charge of treason, see Morgan, *Stamp Act*, 95-106. There are two or three other resolves that may have been proposed by Patrick Henry that did not get approved by the House of Burgesses, one of which may have been the basis for the accusation that he was speaking treason. But none of these includes a claim from natural rights. See Morgan, *Stamp Act*, 95-98. There was a fifth resolve that was apparently expunged from the records that was found in Patrick Henry's papers that may have contained the expunged resolution:"Resolved Therefore that the General Assembly of this Colony have

the only and sole exclusive right and Power to lay Taxes and Impositions upon the Inhabitants of this Colony and that every Attempt to vest such Power in any other Person or Persons whatsoever other than the General Assembly aforesaid has a manifest Tendency to destroy British as well as American Freedom."

82. See Morgan, *Prologue*, 48. Online: http://www.history.org/History/teaching/tchcrvar.cfm.

83. See Morgan, *Prologue*, 50-54 for the Rhode Island and Maryland resolves.

84. Morgan, *Stamp Act*, 109.

85. See Morgan, *Prologue*, 62-63 and online. http://www.constitution.org/bcp/dor_sac.htm.

86. Morgan, *Stamp Act*, 113.

87. Ibid., 113.

88. Ibid., 113-114.

89. Morgan, *ibid.*, 118 notes this as well.

90. Morgan, *Prologue*, 51-52.

91. For the Massachusetts Resolves, see Morgan, *Prologue*, 56-59.

92. It is true that the expression "law of God and Nature" which is so common in the American colonists writing during this period, appears in Locke's *Second Treatise*, but much less frequently than the simpler expression "Law of Nature." Although Locke himself clearly presupposed a God who created nature and embedded law in nature which was self-evident to reason, Locke prefers the term "law of nature" throughout his *Second Treatise*. Indeed, Locke's political discourse in the *Second Treatise* was light on theological justifications and Scriptural interpretations at least compared with the American political sermons. To be sure, Locke also wrote a more theologically oriented exposition of liberty in his *First Treatise of Government* as an exercise of rejecting Filmer's theory of divine right. In his *Second Treatise*, which is his classic exposition of natural rights theory, religious and theological language are noticeably secondary and illustrate just how far an exposition natural rights can move from classic Christian concepts and language. The American political sermons were pulling that discourse back in, if not remaking it in their Christianizing of political theory. Use of the expression "God and nature" appears in Locke, *Second Treatise*, 60 (here a quote from Filmer), 66, 142, 168 and 195. The expression "law of nature" appears much more frequently (approximately 55 times) throughout the *Second Treatise*.

93. Jensen, *Tracts*, xxxiii, also notes that the Connecticut resolutions had boldly asserted the right of revolution. He notes that "Stephen Hopkins in 1764

had fumbled with the idea that each colony was a separate part of the king's dominion."

94. *Massachusetts Gazette*, December 19, 1765. See, *The Avalon Project*. Online: http://avalon.law.yale.edu/18th_century/ct_resolutions_1765.asp. Morgan, *Prologue*, 54 lists a different set of resolutions in October of that month.

95. Meier, *Resistance to Revolution*, 81-85 indicates that the formal organization of a "Sons of Liberty" resistance occurred in December 1765.

96. See Morgan, *Prologue*, 114-117 for these published statements. No mention is made of natural rights in the Connecticut statement on January 13 1766, and in that of the New York Sons of Liberty on January 11, 1766. The New Jersey Sons of Liberty statement on February 25, 1766 refers to our "indubitable rights." The Sons of Liberty of Connecticut and New York published a joint agreement. They declare allegiance to King George III "and with the greatest cheerfulness they submit to his government, according to the known and just principles of the British Constitution, which they conceive to be founded on the eternal and immutable principles of justice and equity, and that every attempt to violate or wrest it, or any part of it, from them, under whatever pretence, colour or authority, is an heinous sin against God, and the most daring contempt of the people, from whom (under God) all just government springs.

Chapter 4: Diverging Theories of American Rights Before Jefferson

1. See Dewey, *Thomas Jefferson Lawyer*, 1-17. Dewey challenges an understanding of Malone, *Jefferson*, Vol. 1, 95, Chinard *Jefferson*, 38, and others on when Jefferson was admitted to the bar.
2. Malone, *Jefferson*, Vol. 1 97-98.
3. Becker, *Declaration*; Morgan, *Stamp Act Crisis*.
4. Jensen, Becker, and Morgan tend to reify the notion of "natural rights" as one argument, rather than seeing the various different strands and varieties of natural rights arguments. Some of the strands are more Lockean than others, and some are more religious than others.
5. Lewis, *A Summary View*, 39, makes a similar distinction distinguishing the Adams/Wilson view, which held that the colonists had never been released from the king's rule from the Bland/Jefferson view that they had quit society. But Lewis then mistakenly claims that the Bland/Jefferson view was a "more direct appeal to the ultimate source of sovereignty—natural law." (40). In my view, Wilson and Adams's views are more classically Lockean in character than the Bland/Jefferson view.

6. Dickinson, "Letters," in Jensen, *Tracts*, 127-163. See Letter II, Jensen, *Tracts*, 138. The second quote is from Letter VII, not published in Jensen's edition. Online: http://oll.libertyfund.org/?option=com_staticxt&staticfile=show.php%3Ftitle=690.
7. Ibid., 133.
8. I disagree with Becker, *Declaration* (96-97) who cites Dickinson's statement here as the foundation for the idea that the Americans and British were two different peoples. I read Dickinson as making exactly the opposite argument, arguing that the colonies are parts of a whole and subject to British sovereignty for commerce. Jensen, *Tracts*, xli, comes to the same reading of Dickinson here.
9. End of Letter VII.
10. Letter IX. Jensen, *Tracts*, 147.
11. Ibid., 154-155.
12. Hume, "The Original Contract," 199.
13. Letter IV. Jensen, *Tracts*, 141
14. See Locke, *Second Treatise*, 11:140 which deals with the responsibility of people to pay taxes towards government. Dickinson's only other reference to Locke is in a quote he cites approvingly of Lord Cambden at the end of Letter 7.
15. Letter V. Not quoted in Jensen. See online, Dickinson, *Empire and Nation*, http://oll.libertyfund.org/?option=com_staticxt&staticfile=show.php%3Ftitle=690.
16. This is a theme that reappears in Dickinson's later rewrite of Jefferson's *Declaration of the Causes and Necessity of War*, examined below.
17. See Letter III. Not quoted in Jensen. See online, Dickinson, *Empire and Nation*, http://oll.libertyfund.org/?option=com_staticxt&staticfile=show.php%3Ftitle=690. The quotation indicated by the asterisk in the original is from the New Testament, Galatians 5:1.
18. Letter III. Not quoted in Jensen. See Dickinson, *Empire and Nation*, http://oll.libertyfund.org/?option=com_staticxt&staticfile=show.php%3Ftitle=690.
19. Background on Bland can be found in Jensen, *Tracts*, xxxiv-xxxvi.
20. See Jensen, *Tracts*, 108-126. On Bland's background, see ibid., xxxiv-xxvi.
21. Jensen, *Tracts*, 112. Bland's footnote "2" refers to "Vattel's Law of Nature. Locke on Civil Govern. And Wollaston's Rel. of Nature."
22. Jensen, *Tracts*, 112 – 113. Bland cites Wollaston in a footnote as a source of this view, though Locke says something quite similar about a child taking on the laws of a country when the child inherits the property from his father. See Locke, *Second Treatise*, 73 and 120.

23. Jefferson's reflection on Bland is cited in Jensen, *Tracts*, xxxv and Ford, *The Works*, IX 474.
24. Locke, *Second Treatise*, 6, 73, Laslett, *Locke*, 315, 116.
25. Locke, *Second Treatise*, 117, Laslett, *Locke*, 347.
26. Locke, *Second Treatise*, 121, Laslett, *Locke*, p. 349. As discussed earlier, the question of whether the lands of North America were "free or unpossessed" is an issue as the colonists and their Great British critics debate whether the Americas were discovered or conquered and what implication those facts have on the establishment of American rights.
27. Locke discusses tacit and explicit consent in *Second Treatise* II 8, 121 and 119 (Laslett, *Locke*, 349). Locke distinguishes those who give explicit consent to membership from those who give tacit consent. If you give tacit consent, by acquiring property in a country or inheriting property from one's father, then you have tacitly agreed to live by the laws of that political entity. But once you give up that enjoyment, you can quit and move on. It is only by explicit consent according to Locke that one becomes a subject or member of the commonwealth. But once you become a member, you cannot leave.
28. Locke, *Second Treatise* II 211-243 discusses reasons for dissolution of a government.
29. For a review of this issue in Locke, see Schwartz, "Liberty Is Not Freedom."
30. Pufendorf, *Of the Law of Nature and Of Nations*, Book VIII:Xi
31. See my discussion above in Chapter 2. We have seen and will see other examples of such sentiments in this essay in the writing of Wilson, Jefferson, and Shute. See also Schlesinger, "Pursuit of Happiness," for other examples. Schlesinger, however, misses the fact that the idea that government is for the happiness of society is different than the idea of individuals having a natural right to happiness.
32. Locke, *Second Treatise*, 9:123, 131. It might be fair to characterize Locke as saying that people join society for reasons of happiness, though this is not the way Locke put it. But this is different than saying that each individual has a natural right to promote individual happiness and may leave society when it will no longer "conduce to their Happiness, which they have a natural Right to promote." Locke would have been more comfortable describing the pursuit of happiness as one of the reasons people relinquish their natural rights to join society, rather than a way to describe the rights they have in nature before joining society, or the rights they have to justify quitting society. Calling "promotion of Happiness" an inherent right, as Bland does here, and as Jefferson does in the Declaration, would not likely have been language with which Locke

would have been comfortable. Locke does use "pursuit of happiness" in his *Essay Concerning Human Understanding* in a lengthy discussion of free will. But Locke nowhere calls pursuit of happiness a "natural right."

33. Jensen, *Tracts*, 113.
34. On Locke's use of tacit consent, see Locke, *Second Treatise*, II 119, 73.
35. Jensen, *Tracts*, 114.
36. Jensen, *Tracts*, 116-117.
37. For a useful discussion of this notion of a federated empire see Adams, *Political Ideas*.
38. Of course, the big difference today is that the states are subordinate in many ways defined in the Constitution to the federal laws. The vision here, by contrast, is of no legislative branch that is between the states and the executive branch which supervises the whole.
39. Wilson argues that the colonies were not conquered territories. Jefferson, by contrast, argues they were conquered territory.
40. This is probably what Jefferson meant when he wrote that Bland did not drive to the logical conclusions.
41. Bland, "An Inquiry," in Jensen, *Tracts*, 118.
42. Ibid., 121.
43. Ibid., 122.
44. Ibid., 122. Bland here makes a distinction between natural rights and civil rights, arguing that if natural rights are violated people have a right to rebel but if civil rights are violated, the people should first complain and try to rectify the situation through peaceable means.
45. Silas Downer, James Wilson, and Thomas Jefferson, articulating a similar image of the colonies as independent states, will go further and use the same theory to argue that Parliament also lacks authority to regulate trade. But Jefferson and Wilson get there by different routes as we shall see. See also my discussion on the debate on trade during the First Continental Congress, in Chapter 6.
46. For a discussion see Chinard, *Jefferson* and *Commonplace Book* as well as Ganter, "Pursuit of Happiness."
47. This view of conquest incidentally is consistent with Locke's own understanding of conquest.
48. Wilson, *Considerations*, online.
49. In Wilson's text, footnote 3 appears here in which Wilson quotes Burlamanqi. The footnote reads "The right of sovereignty is that of commanding finally—but in order to procure real felicity; for if this end is not obtained, sovereignty ceases to be a legitimate authority. 2. Burl. 32, 33."

50. Jensen, *Tracts*, 239. Locke includes security of the society as only one reason for consenting to government but he also includes other reasons.

51. Ganter "Pursuit of Happiness," 12 reviewing Chinard's work provides an excellent summary of how Wilson's reliance on Burlamaqui was ignored by Carl Becker in *Declaration of Independence*, when he implied that Jefferson read Wilson and both were relying on Locke. As noted earlier, there were multiple various summaries of Locke's that the colonists read in addition to Locke himself. And therefore any particular Lockean idea may have had multiple sources. The interesting issue in asking how Lockean were the colonists was not whether they were reading Locke per se, but whether they endorsed Lockean views, to what extent, and if they did how did they use those arguments.

52. In the ellipsis of this quote, Wilson has a footnote "4" which refers to Blackstone: "4 The law of nature is superior in obligation to any other. 1. Bl. Com. 41."

53. Jensen, for example, does not include any political sermons for example in his collection.

54. Sandoz, *Political Sermons*, 4-5.

55. Shute, "Election Sermon," in Hyneman and Lutz, *American Political Writing*, 117-8.

56. Ibid., 110.

57. Ibid., 110.

58. Ibid., 116.

59. Ibid., 116.

60. Ibid., 119.

Chapter 5: *A Summary View*: Jefferson's First Major Foray Into Political Writing

1. For a similar conclusion, see Lewis, "A Summary View," 72.

2. I disagree with those writers who think Jefferson's *A Summary View* articulates a classic natural rights philosophy. See, for example, Malone, Jefferson, v. I, 184, Ward, *Politics of Liberty*, 352. Others have come to the same conclusion as I have. See Lewis, Liberty, 352, Peterson, *Thomas Jefferson*, 73-74, and Chinard, *Jefferson*, 47-51.

Chinard perhaps says it most explicitly. Speaking about Jefferson's own reflection on *A Summary View* and the centrality of expatriation, Chinard writes, "Jefferson had reached that conclusion, not from following a certain line of abstract reasoning, but after studying the history of the Green colonies in Stanyan, and the history of the Saxon settlement of Great Britain in many authors, as may be seen in his 'Commonplace Book', and as he was soon to reaffirm the doctrine of expatriation as the fundamental principle on which rested all the claims of the American colonies." Lewis, "A Summary View," also sees quitting society as central to Jefferson and provides a good summary. But I disagree with Lewis in seeing *A Summary View* making an affirmation of individual rights and in articulating a theory of a balance of powers, thus anticipating the later American Constitution.

3. Jefferson, "A Summary View," In Boyd, *Papers*, I:121.

4. See Lewis, "A Summary View," 46 who interestingly enough quotes Jefferson as writing "God and 'the laws of nature,'" indicating the desire and inclination to read "natural rights" into Jefferson's statements though Jefferson avoided the term here.

5. Boyd, *Papers*, 135.

6. See Locke, *Second Treatise*, 2:6. Locke writes that "The state of nature has a law of nature to govern it which obliges every one: and reason, which is that law, teaches all mankind, who will but consult it, that being all equal and independent, no one ought to harm another in his life, health, liberty, or possessions: for men being all the workmanship of one omnipotent, and infinitely wise maker…"

7. Boyd, *Papers*, 121.

8. See Peterson, *Thomas Jefferson*, 73, for a similar conclusion. See also my discussion of this issue earlier in the discussion of Richard Bland. A number of other interpreters have commented on the centrality of the "right to quit society" to Jefferson's own view. However, none of these writers have drawn the same conclusions that I have for understanding of the Declaration of Independence, as is developed here. See Lewis, *Liberty*, 352, Peterson, *Thomas Jefferson*, 73-74, Chinard, *Jefferson*, 47-51, and Ellis *American Sphinx*, 36-38 and Maier, *American Scripture*, 112.

Chinard perhaps says it most explicitly. Speaking about Jefferson's own reflection on *A Summary View* and the centrality of expatriation, Chinard writes that "Jefferson had reached that conclusion, not from following a certain line of abstract reasoning, but after studying the history of the Greek colonies in Stanyan, and the history of the Saxon settlement of Great Britain in many authors, as may be seen in his 'Commonplace Book', and as he was soon to reaffirm the doctrine of expatriation as the fundamental principle on which rested all the claims of the American colonies." Lewis, "A Summary View," also sees quitting society as central to Jefferson and provides a good summary. But I disagree with Lewis in seeing *A Summary View* as making an affirmation of individual rights and in articulating a theory of a balance of powers, thus anticipating the later American Constitution. Finally, Ellis, *American Sphinx*, 36-37 also notes the centrality of expatriation argument to Jefferson's theory and the dependence on the Whig view of history. Ellis tends to put a psychological interpretation on Jefferson's interest in this position and links this with Jefferson's romantic interest in an idyllic time, a "once upon a time" view of history that posted a "romantic endorsement of a pristine past, a long-lost time and place when men had lived together in perfect harmony without coercive laws or predatory rulers."

Jayne, *Jefferson's Declaration*, 51-55, by contrast, is one of the few interpreters to explicitly argue that Jefferson's "right to emigration", as he calls it, is influenced by Locke.

To prove this, Jayne quotes Locke:

> For there are no Examples so frequent in History, both Sacred and Prophane, as those of Men withdrawing themselves, and their Obedience, from the Jurisdiction they were born under, and the Family or Community they were bred up in, and setting up new governments in other places: from when sprang all that number of petty Common-wealths in the Beginning of Ages, and which always multiplied as long as there was room enough. (Locke, *Second Treatise*, 8,15)

This statement of Locke certainly sounds like an endorsement of the right to quit society. However, there are several problems with Jayne's assumption of a *direct* Lockean influence over Jefferson on this particular issue and they point to some of the larger problems in Jayne's analysis overall in my view.

First, Jefferson never quotes the passage from Locke that Jayne cites, and never attributes the right to quit society to Locke, though Jefferson does call it a natural right. The identification of parallel ideas does not provide enough evidence of dependence especially when there are other possible sources of the idea.

Second, because Jayne looks only at Jefferson, and not earlier colonial writers, he does not seem aware that Jefferson's own Virginian colleague, Richard Bland, had made a similar argument about the right to quit society, at the time of the Stamp Act Crisis. Jefferson's argument and language is very similar to Bland's, and Jefferson could just as easily have gotten the idea from Bland or other sources. Indeed, this raises what I consider to be one of the most significant problems with Jayne's analysis: he assumes parallels between Jefferson and Locke mean the influence was direct from Jefferson's knowledge of Locke. But in this case, as in others, there were other sources from which Jefferson could have picked up the ideas and even language. This is one of the problems in saying whether something is "Lockean" in nature or direct from Locke. A parallel in other words does not mean dependence.

Third, even if Jefferson were reading Locke and basing his theory on Locke, it is important to realize that Jefferson disagreed with other colleagues such as James Wilson about the basis of American rights. The discussion about whether Jefferson read Locke or adopted Lockean ideas thus misses the important fact that other applications of Locke were invoked by colonial writers that differed from Jefferson's. And these thinkers disagreed on precisely this point of whether the settlers were free men when they came to the colonies or British citizens. It is this disagreement over rights that is often missed in discussion of Jefferson's views in relationship to Locke.

Fourth, Locke's view is actually quite a bit more complex than the single passage quoted by Jayne to prove that Locke endorsed the right to emigration. Locke in fact did not think that a person always had an unqualified right to leave a society. There were conditions in which a person gave up that right. If Jefferson had a complex understanding of Locke, as Jayne suggests, then he might have realized that Locke's view was more complicated than the "right to quit society." The fact that Jefferson didn't acknowledge that complexity either shows that he did not have a complex view of Locke, contrary to Jayne, that he had not read Locke very thoroughly, or that he chose to ignore Locke's more complex view, all of which are more interesting claims than Jayne's assumption of an "unambivalent" adoption of Locke.

The complexity of Locke's position becomes apparent when we take a deeper look at Locke's thoughts on the conditions in which a person may quit their society. One of Locke's central contentions was that a child was not obligated to adopt the country or political allegiance of his parents. At maturity, young adults had the choice to leave a country in which they were raised. Their parents' political allegiance was not an inherited obligation of the children. A man "*cannot*, by any *compact* whatsoever, *bind his children or posterity*: for his son, when a man, being altogether as free as the father, *any act of the father can no more give away the liberty of the son*, then it can of any body else:" (*Second Treatise*, 8 § 116). "It is plain, then, by the practice of governments themselves, as well as by the law of right reason, that *a child is born a subject of no country or government.*" (*ibid.*, 8 § 118)

At maturity, a young adult can choose which political entity to join. But Locke distinguishes between two types of consent (ibid., 8, §119). As long as the young adult only *tacitly* consents to live in a country, for example, by accepting the inheritance or possession of the father's property, the young adult may still choose to leave the country later, as long as the young adult leaves the property behind. Locke notes that the father often used rights in land, which was owned by the political entity, as a way to bind his children to the political allegiance of the country in which they lived. But Locke emphasized that the young adult ultimately had the freedom to choose whether to accept the land on the conditions of living in that state or to leave the political entity in which he had been raised. If the young adult took possession of the land that belonged to the father, then that child had given *tacit consent* to live under the laws of that country. However, and this is the point that Jayne never mentions, if after maturity, a young adult explicitly consents to join a community, there is no longer a right to quit society. Once explicit consent is given to join a political society, an individual renounces his or her right to leave that society.

As Locke put its it, not too far from the quote that Jayne cites:

> so that whenever the owner, who has given nothing but such a tacit consent to the government, will by donation, sale, or otherwise, quit the said possession, he is at liberty to go and incorporate himself into any other common-wealth; or to agree with others to begin a new one, in vacuis locis, in any part of the world, they can find free and unpossesesd: whereas he, that has once, by actual agreement, and any *express* declaration, given his *consent* to be of any common-wealth, is perpetually, and indispensibly obliged to be, and remain unalterably a subject to it, and can never be again in the liberty of the state of nature; unless, by any calamity, the government he was under comes to be dissolved; or else by some public act cuts him off from being any longer a member of it. (ibid., 8 § 121)

Locke's concern in the passage is to make clear that the child's political allegiance is not determined by the father's because a child is not the property of the father. This was a critical part of Locke's argument for several reasons. First, it gave him an explanation for why Filmer's argument about the divine right of kings was wrong. Filmer had argued that children are their father's property and therefore were subject to their father's authority. In this way, the divine right of kings was "natural" since Filmer argued it could be traced back to the original father's (Adams's) authority over his children.

Locke disputes Filmer's view and makes the authority of the father over the child one key place of disagreement. The authority of the father over the child is not a political type of authority (ibid., 1 § 2) but only a temporary responsibility that a man (and woman according to Locke) have for a child. A child is not a free person in the same sense as an adult, however, because he or she have not yet matured and reached the age of reason, which is the requirement of liberty. Thus a child is born with the rights of liberty that only become fully activated at maturity, the age of reason. At maturity a child can decide which commonwealth to join. "Common-wealths themselves take notice of, and allow, that there is a *time when men* are to *begin* to act *like free men,* and therefore till that time require not oaths of fealty, or allegiance, or other public owning of, or submission to the government of their countries." (ibid.,, 6 § 62). Similarly "foreigners" cannot become full members of a society simply by living in a society. "Nothing can make any man so, but his actually entering into it by positive engagement, and express promise and compact." (ibid., 6 § 122)

Having now understood Locke's distinction between tacit and explicit consent and the implications for the right to quit society, we can return to the quote that Jayne cites from Locke concerning the multiplication of commonwealths in early times. Jayne cites this quote as evidence that Locke endorsed the right to quit society. This quote appears in a context in which Locke is replying to what he takes to be a criticism of his social contract theory. His critics, says Locke, argue that if all people are born under government, how can there be multiple different commonwealths? Wouldn't there simply be one government? The same problem, answers Locke, arises on the view of Filmer who believed Adam was the original father and monarch. If you assume the child is under the political authority of the father, then there should be one monarchy and not many commonwealths. By contrast, Locke argues that on his own view we can explain this diversity of governments. At maturity people have the right to leave their society. This explains the fact that there are multiple commonwealths in the early history of humanity.

But if we probe deeper into Locke's view of the earliest societies, we find that Locke assumes that the early political allegiances often involved tacit consent. The reason for this is that the earliest societies were extensions of the patriarchal family. In early history, children found it easier to live under their father's rule as they had been accustomed to his authority. Therefore, the first societies were patriarchal with the father as the political leader. In these early societies, the children tacitly consented to let the father rule because it was a natural extension of the family. "Thus it was easy, and almost natural for children, by a tacit, and scarce avoidable consent, to make way for the *father's authority and government*" (ibid., 6, § 75). Thus the natural *fathers of families*, by an insensible change, became the *politic* monarchs of them too: and as they chanced to live long, and leave able and worthy heirs, for several successions, or otherwise;

so they laid the foundations of hereditary, or elective kingdoms, under several constitutions and mannors..(ibid., 6, § 75). "Yet it is obvious to conceive how easy it was, in the first ages of the world, and in places still, where the thinness of people gives families leave to separate into unpossessed quarters, and they have room to remove or plant themselves in yet vacant habitations, for the *father of the family* to become the prince of -it; he had been a ruler from the beginning of the infancy of his children: and since without some government it would be hard for them to live together, it was likeliest it should, by the express or tacit consent of the children when they were grown up, be in the father, where it seemed without any change barely to continue." (ibid., 6, § 74).

Now the significance of this understanding is that Locke assumes the multiplicity of commonwealths occurred because families spread across the earth into the vacated land. These early political societies had developed organically, with the children tacitly consenting to the political leadership of the patriarchal father. The early multiplication of governments is thus consistent with the view Locke held that people can quit society only when they have given tacit consent to be bound to it. Thus, "whether a family by degrees grew up into a commonwealth, and the fatherly authority being continued on to the elder son, every one in his turn growing up under it, tacitly submitted to it, ... (ibid., 6, § 110). Thus Locke's picture is that there were many families without explicit political structures that spread across the world or combined with other families to form the original governments. Many if not most of these early societies were natural and did not involve the explicit consent that would characterize more advanced societies that were not familial in nature. When societies were more complex and land was not as abundant, explicit consent would be required to become "perfect" members of such socities. (ibid., 6, § 110112.

Jefferson shows no awareness of any of this complexity in Locke's thinking, despite Jayne's insistence Jefferson had an "extensive understanding" of Locke. Thus either Jefferson did not read Locke carefully, did not read Locke at all, or simply was simplifying a part of Locke to serve his own pragmatic interests are all possibilities that arise Thus while one might argue that the right to quit society is Lockean, we have no evidence in fact that Jefferson got the idea from Locke directly. He may just as well have gotten the idea from Richard Bland.

Jayne assumes that Jefferson had a comprehensive view of Locke's Second Treatise from one citation of Locke in Jefferson's political commonplace book. I deal with that citation and its meaning below in Chapter 7.

9. Quoted in Ford, *Complete Works*, 14. See also Chinard, *Jefferson*, 49-51 who also emphasizes expatriation as the core idea of Jefferson's pamphlet and the idea that Jefferson thought was original.

10. See Colbourn, *Lamp of Experience*, for an overview of the use of Saxon history in American rights arguments.

11. Boyd, *Papers*, 121-22.

12. Colbourn, *Lamp of Experience*, outlines the ways in which rights were thought to derive from the Anglo Saxons and how this view was used in colonial writings.

13. Boyd, *Papers*, 122. I disagree with Lewis, "A Summary View," who sees this as a statement of individual rights.

14. Chinard, *Jefferson*, 49.

15. Boyd, *Papers*, 122-23.

16. Jefferson could be construed here as standing in the common law tradition and seeing the rights of Americans as inherited from the tradition extending back to Saxon times. See Colburn, *Lamp of Experience*, for an account of this common law view.

17. On the view that Britain was corrupting the liberty tradition, see for example, Woods, *Creation*, 28ff.

18. Boyd, *Papers*, I:121.

19. Ibid., I:129.

20. Ibid., I:134.

21. Ibid., I:123.

22. Ibid., I:123.

23. Ibid., I:122.

24. Ibid., I:124.

25. I disagree with Conrad in arguing that the main point of the pamphlet is to make an argument from justice.

26. Boyd, *Papers*, 123 and 124.

27. See Schwartz, "Why Market Liberals."

28. The law of nations was sometimes based on natural rights assuming that the political entities were like individuals and the relations between nations should be like the relations between individuals. See, for example, Vattel's *Law of Nations*, which was quoted by some colonists such as Bland and others.

29. Boyd, *Papers*, 121.

30. See Jefferson's "Resolutions on the Freeholders of Albemarle County" dated July 26, 1774 in Boyd, *Papers*, 117 and Conrad who draws attention to the parallels between this statement and *A Summary View*. In Chapter 7,

I suggest that Jefferson's notes in his Commonplace Book were in preparation for writing *A Summary View*.

31. Malone, *Jefferson*, v. I, 184.

32. See my comment in note 2 above on this topic.

33. Boyd, *Papers*, I:123. Later in life, Jefferson does cite Locke as one source of inspiration for his views in the Declaration of Independence (see Boyd, *The Declaration*, 16). But Jefferson also claimed he looked at no specific source while writing the Declaration. See my earlier discussion of this point, 27ff.

34. Wills, *Inventing America*, 167-180.

35. See Chinard, *Commonplace Book*, 19.

36. Boyd, *Papers*, 130.

37. Koch, *Philosophy of*, 17. See Chinard, *Commonplace Book*, 19. Jayne, *Jefferson*, xxx.

38. Boyd, *Papers*, 126.

39. Koch, *Philosophy*, 15. See also Peterson, *Thomas Jefferson*, 54-55.

40. Boyd, *Papers*, 132.

41. Koch, *Philosophy*, 17, notes this dimensions of Jefferson's thinking in his early writings and letters. He notes that Jefferson was influenced by Kames who views the moral sense as based on direct feeling without reflection.

42. Conrad, "Putting Rights Talk," 261 and 255, and Peterson, *Thomas Jefferson*, 45-46, makes this point in general that Jefferson was not a systematic thinker. See also Chinard, *Jefferson*, 31, who makes the same point. For a contrary view, see Koch, *Jefferson*, xi-xiv.

43. Contrast this essay with the first essay of Alexander Hamilton, for an explicit appeal to natural rights theory that was fully consistent with a classic Lockean view of natural rights.

44. On the view that Jefferson was not a systematic philosopher, see comments note 42 above.

45. See Ford, *Complete Works*, I:14.

6: The First Continental Congress and the Rejection of Jefferson's Pet Theory

1. See my earlier discussion of Hopkins in Chapter 3.

2. The Adams Papers are published electronically online by the Massachusetts Historical society. See http://www.masshist.org/DIGITALADAMS/aea/. Extracts from Adams's autobiography can also be found in Charles Francis Adams, *The Works*, 374 and in Butterfield, *Diary*, 3:309. Letters of Delegates

to Congress are published online as well by the Library of Congress (http://memory.loc.gov/ammem/amlaw/lwdglink.html) and by the University of Virginia http://etext.lib.virginia.edu/toc/modeng/public/DelVol01.html. Adams's *Notes on the Debates* http://www.masshist.org/DIGITALADAMS/AEA/cfm/doc.cfm?id=D22A are published there as well. An excellent overview of the First Congress can be found in York, "The First Continental Congress." See also Taylor, *Papers*, 144-150 for a good summary of John Adams's role during the Congress.

3. John Adams's *Notes on the Debates* (Letter 23) are available online at the Library of Congress (http://memory.loc.gov/cgi-bin/query/r?ammem/hlaw:@field(DOCID+@lit(dg00123))) or at Adams's historical records. Also available in Charles Francis Adams, *The Works of John Adams*, 370. I have been unable to find any other detailed commentary on Adams's notes for this day that tries to explicate the positions of the speakers.

4. *Letters of Delegates*, Letter 9, Sept. 6.

5. Becker, *Declaration*, tends to associate the turn to natural rights with the radicalization of the positions towards Great Britain. Similarly Jensen, *Tracts*, liii-lvi, writes that "The Congress was deadlocked for weeks over a declaration of rights. The popular leaders insisted that it should be based on the 'law of nature.' The conservatives quite understandably opposed a foundation which had never been defined and which would allow every man to interpret its meaning for himself. They argued that American rights should be based on the colonial charters and the English constitution."

While some of the delegates who favored more outspoken positions did favor natural rights (such as Lee), others embraced natural rights but were not as radical (e.g., Jay who was present and Wilson who was not). The position on natural rights did not perfectly align with the position on the continuum between conservative, moderate and radical. See also chapter 6, note 16.

6. According to Adams' *Notes of Debates*, on September 6 (Letters of Delegates, Letter 9), during the debate on how the colonies should vote in the Congress, Jay said that "Could I suppose, that We came to frame an American Constitution, instead of indeavouring to correct the faults in an old one—I cant yet think that all Government is at an End. The Measure of arbitrary Power is not full, and I think it must run over, before We undertake to frame a new Constitution." And again in a letter on September 24 Jay to John Vardill (Letters of Delegates, Letter 90) Jay hopes for a good end but clearly has doubts. For background on John Jay see Morris, *John Jay*. I have not yet been able to find anyone who is surprised that Jay holds a natural rights view and one like Jefferson but is a

moderate in the convention with regard to taking steps towards war, separation and on issues like the Galloway plan.

7. There is at least one difficulty with this reading of Jay's position. First, if he thinks emigrants have a right to quit society, then why does he say it is necessary to recur to the British Constitution at all? Wouldn't the British Constitution be irrelevant? It is conceivable that he holds a position like Jefferson that the ancestors chose to model the new society after the old one and entered into compacts with the king and adopted the British constitution by choice. On this view, the constitution is endorsed by consent, but is not mandated by the fact that the colonists are born subjects. But that view is not stated here and would have to be inferred. And second, on this reading, Jay would be understood to be arguing that the states are already independent entities, which would make it somewhat surprising that he favored reconciliation by supporting the Galloway Plan.

Another possible but, in my view, less plausible reading suggests Jay is taking a position more like that of James Wilson examined earlier. On this understanding, Jay is saying that the ancestors like all people have rights both from nature (life, liberty, and property) and as subjects of the British Empire. As emigrating subjects they brought those British rights with them. Now Jay considers a possible objection. "It may be said We leave our Country, We cannot leave our Allegiance." On this view, the ancestors carry their status as subjects with them and still owe allegiance to the king, if not the common law. But Jay reasons in a way similar to Wilson: "there is no Allegiance without Protection." Allegiance is only an obligation when the Crown offers protection. Since by implication the Crown did not offer sufficient protection, the obligation of allegiance is terminated. Therefore "emigrants have a Right, to erect what Government they please." On this reading of Jay, then, the ancestors do *not* have a natural right to quit society and leave behind the sovereignty of that country. Instead they bring their rights and duties with them when they emigrate. But because the Crown has not protected them, their obligations to their mother country are ended and they have a right to set up governments as they see fit. The later right is not a "natural right" of emigration per se, like Jefferson and Bland suggest, but the outcome of the Crown's failure to offer protection. The failure of the sovereign power to adhere to its obligations ends its jurisdiction over the ancestors and puts them in a state of nature. Since the Crown fell short of its duties, the obligations of the colonies to the Crown are suspended.

Either of these readings are possible, although the first reading seems to fit better with Jay's emphasis on the rights of the emigrants. What is interesting is that on either of these readings Jay endorses natural rights and seems to hold the view that the colonies are independent states, though he clearly held out the hope of reconciliation with Great Britain. We shall see a similar ambiguity in the interpretation of other delegates' statements who favor natural rights. The ambiguity in the natural rights camp meant there was a least two different and not necessarily compatible natural rights arguments being invoked.

8. York, "First Continental Congress," 365, note 32, makes this point as well. Interestingly, Bland himself who was at the Congress, but is not quoted that often in the notes of the debates, voted against Henry's amendment calling for the colonies to develop militias. See Silas Deane's diary of October 3, *Letters of Delegates*, Letter 122.

9. See John Adams's diary for October 11, *Letters of Delegates*, Letter 156, and Butterfield, *Diary*, 2:151.

10. I skipped the statement by Pendleton as not relevant to the particular discussion here on natural rights.

11. For a version of this argument, see for example John Adams's argument in his response to Thomas Hutchinson in January to March of 1773. A discussion of Adams's role and contribution can be found in Taylor, *Papers*, 309-315.

12. See my discussion of Locke's and Pufendorf's positions in my earlier discussion of Bland in Chapter 4.

13. Mr. Wm. Livingston. A Corporation cannot make a Corporation. Charter Governments have done it. K[ing] cant appoint a Person to make a Justice of Peace. All Governors do it. Therefore it will not do for America to rest wholly on the Laws of England.

Mr. Sherman. The Ministry contend, that the Colonies are only like Corporations in England, and therefore subordinate to the Legislature of the Kingdom. The Colonies not bound to the King or Crown by the Act of Settlement, but by their consent to it. There is no other Legislative over the Colonies but their respective Assemblies. The Colonies adopt the common Law, not as the common Law, but as the highest Reason.

14. See John Duane, "Speech to the Committee on Rights." Letter 26. *Letters to the Delegates*.

15. Ibid, "Speech."

16. Becker, *Declaration*, is a writer who implies by his narrative that the turn to natural rights occurred as a way to justify independence. But as discussed already, and as evidenced again in Duane's comments, there was no perfect correspondence at this point between natural rights arguments and various degrees of radicalism.

17. Dickinson was not present at the First Continental Congress until October 17 when after he was elected to the Pennsylvania Assembly. See Samuel

Ward's diary for October 17, Letter 184, *Letters of Delegates*, and Silas Deane on October 16, Letter 180. But Dickinson met with and socialized with many of the delegates during the convention (See note 47 below).

18. Galloway, *Candid Examination*, in Jensen, *Tracts*, 352.
19. Ibid., 353.
20. Ibid., 377.
21. Ibid., 365-6.
22. See Adams, *Notes on Debates*, In *Letters of Delegates*, Letter 23 and in Butterfield, *Diary*, 2:128-31.
23. Jensen, *Tracts*, 353.
24. Galloway cites this list in his speech in congress on September 28, *Letters of Delegates*, Letter 105 (also in Butterfield, *Diary*, 2:141-44) and in his *Candid Examination*, 353-355. Citations of Locke appear in *Candid Examination*, 362, 364, 368.
25. Galloway, *Candid Examination*, 362.
26. See pp. 127ff.
27. Galloway, *Candid Examination*, 378ff.
28. Ibid., 393.
29. On other plans proposed before Galloway's, see R. G. Adams, *Political Ideas*.
30. *Letters of Delegates*, Letter 105.
31. Galloway, *Candid Examination*, 358.
32. Ibid., 360.
33. Between October 14 and October 18. According to JCC I:63, on October 14 the resolutions were published on that day. But based on notes of John Adams and Samuel Ward it appears discussion continued beyond October 14. See York, "First Congress," 359.
34. See Samuel Ward's Diary on September 9, *Letters of Delegates* (Letter 33).
35. Jensen, *Tracts*, liii-lv, makes it seem like the debate over natural rights continued throughout the congress, which is not correct. That issue was resolved on September 9 after the first debate.
36. Reid, *Authority*, makes this point repeatedly about the diverse view of rights. Reid, however, does not look historically at the unfolding of these ideas in their political context.
37. North Carolina delegates arrived late on September 14 (York, "First Congress," 358). Georgia had decided not to send delegates because of unrest on its borders with Creek tribes and fear of losing British support.
38. The Suffolk resolves were a set of resolutions put together by Suffolk County which contained the city of Boston. These resolves were fairly

inflammatory and took a position that was arguably more radical than the resolves which the Congress published. See York, ("First Congress," 367) who notes that the Suffolk resolves seemed to presuppose that the colonies had "elected" the king but that it was not clear that everyone in Congress was endorsing that implication of the resolves.

39. A nice overview of the events and unfolding debate is provided in York, "First Congress." An account of Adams's role is available in Taylor, *Papers*, vol. 2, 144-150. Accounts of John Jay's activity is provided in Morris, (*John Jay*, 133-139), although no notice is made here of the fact that Jay holds a view like Jefferson but is a moderate.

To provide a brief overview, during this six weeks, Congress appointed a subcommittee of twenty four (i.e., two from each colony) to "to ascertain Our Rights, enumerate the Violations of them, & recommend a proper mode of Redress" (Silas Deane to Elizabeth Deanne, *Letters of Delegates*, Letter 29). On this committee were many of those who had spoken on September 8, including the two Adams cousins (Massachusetts) Hopkins and Ward (Rhode Island) Jay and Duane (New York), Galloway (Pennsylvania), Lee (South Carolina), Lynch and J Rutledge (Virginia). Another subcommittee was appointed of twelve delegates "to examine & report the several statutes, which affect the trade and manufactures of the colonies." (Silas Deane, Letter 29). The larger committee on rights reported back to the general committee on September 14. The smaller committee on trade provided its report on September 17 (JCC 1:29, 40-41).

On September 16, a day John Adams referred to as one of the "happiest day of his life", (*Letters of Delegates*, Letter 56, Butterfield, Diary, 2:134-35), Congress expressed unanimous support of the Massachusetts colony by endorsing the Suffolk resolves, a set of strong statements made against the Intolerable Acts by the leaders of Suffolk county in which Boston is the major city. The resolves promised to boycott British imports and curtail exports, support a colonial government in Massachusetts free of royal authority until the Intolerable acts were repealed and urged the colonies to raise a militia of their own.

Through the end of September the committee continued to meet and carried on deliberation of the specific grievances it wanted to declare. It first decided to limit consideration of grievances about regulations made since 1763 rather than revisit the more troublesome question of regulations that the colonies had acquiesced to prior to that date (See JCC for September 24). Then on September 26, Congress approved the nonimportation of goods from Britain and Ireland as one means to restore American rights. And on September 30 Congress voted against exporting raw goods for manufacture.

On September 28, in the midst of considering the ways to restore American rights, Galloway introduced his Plan of Union discussed earlier. Galloway's plan offered both an alternative philosophical position but also a supplemental course of action to the nonimportation agreement. After substantial debate, Galloway's plan was ordered to "lie on table" and to be discussed at a later point and Congress carried on with heated discussion regarding nonexportation. More detail on the deliberations of Congress can be found in York, "First Congress," and in Taylor, *Papers*, 2: 144ff.

40. October 3, *Letters of Delegates*, Letter 122.
41. *Letters of Delegates*, Letter 113.
42. October 3, *Letters of Delegates*, Letter 122.
43. See John Adams's diary, *Letters of Delegates*, Letter 46 and Butterfield, *Diary*, 2:133-34. My interpretation is consistent with Taylor's, *Papers*, 2:147 interpretation of Adams's comment.
44. See Samuel Ward's Notes for a Speech in Congress on October 12, 1774, *Letters of Delegates*, Letter 165.
45. See John Adams's Diary, October 13, *Letters of Delegates*, Letter 166, and Butterfield, *Diary*, 2:151-52.
46. See Adams's *Notes of Debates* on October 6, *Letters of Delegates*, Letter 134.
47. A visit by John Adams with Dickinson is recorded on September 12 (Letter 39) (Butterfield, 2:132-33), as does Treat Paine on the same occasion (Letter 41). After dinner on September 20 (Letter 75), Adams's group went and found a group of colleagues including Dickinson and notes that "Mr. Dickenson was very agreable." And that "Our Regret at the Loss of this Company was very great." Adams notes dining with Dickinson on September 21 (Letter 80). On September 24 (Letter 87) Adams writes that: "Mr. Dickinson gave us his thoughts and his Correspondence very freely." On September 25 (Letter 95), Adams writes: "I spent yesterday Afternoon and Evening with Mr. Dickinson. He is a true Bostonian." On September 28, (Letter 104), Adams comments that Mr. Dickinson was present at dinner that evening. On October 1 (Letter 115b) Adams notes being present at the election of the State House when Mr. Dickinson was chosen as a representative. Adams notes on October 3 (Letter 121) that "Mr Dickinson…will make a great Weight in favour of the American Cause." On October 7 (Letter 138, see also Butterfield, *Diary*, 2:149), Adams writes to his wife about the elections in the Pennsylvania Assembly and the election of Dickinson, along with Mifflin and Thompson, "as a most compleat and decisive Victory in favour of the American Cause. And it [is] said it will change the Ballance in the Legislature here against Mr. Galloway who has been supposed to sit on the Skirts of the American Advocates." On October 13 (Letter

166), Adams again notes dining with Dickinson. Interestingly, he also makes some notes that day about the debates on regulating trade.

Adams was not the only one to visit with Dickinson. Thomas Cushing (Letter 127) on October 4 writes to his wife that he has passed her letters to Dickinson. On September 19 (Letter 70) On September 23 (Letter 85) Silas Deanne "dined with Celebrated Pensylvania Famer alias Mr. Dickinson." George Read writes to his wife that he dined with Dickinson a second time.

48. October 12, *Letters of Delegates*, Letter 166.
49. See note 33 above.
50. *Letters of Delegates*, Letter 180.
51. Jefferson himself looking back retrospectively presents the declarations of Congress as a compromise in the "half-way" house of John Dickinson. John Adams for his part later in life claimed in contrast to Jefferson that the declarations of the First Congress anticipated everything in the Declaration. I believe John Adams's view is more accurate as well shall see.

Becker, *Declaration*, 115-116, 119, follows Jefferson and views the results of the Congress as a compromise and takes Jefferson's view that the Congress could not take the leap far enough. "The Congress, in framing its declaration, was in the nature of the case less concerned with the logical coherence and validity of the statement which it made, than with making such a statement as would be acceptable to the greatest number of Americans, and at the same time best adapted to win concessions from Great Britain. If therefore the first Continental Congress did not adopt the theory of British American relations which we find in the Declaration of Independence, it was not because the theory was a novel one." And then again: "If the first Continental Congress did not, in respect to the theory of American rights, occupy the lofty ground of Mr. Jefferson, neither did it take the lower ground of Mr. Dickinson; it seems, on the contrary, to have stood midway between these two positions, inviting every man to take which of them he found most comfortable."

There are two points to be made about Becker's characterization. First, Becker is wrong that the statement of the First Congress "did not adopt the theory of British American relations which we find in the Declaration of Independence" as already noted in my discussion of that document. Ironically he turns to Jefferson's *A Summary View* to prove that the view of the empire embodied in the Declaration of Independence was well known by 1774, implying that Jefferson's view in *A Summary View* is the one shared by the Declaration of Independence, which it is not. On the contrary, I argued earlier that the Declaration of the First Continental Congress does hold the same theory as the Declaration of Independence but that neither are the same as Jefferson's in *A Summary View*.

The first Congress unequivocally rejected Jefferson's (and Jay's) view that the ancestors left their rights behind when they emigrated. And by doing so, Congress favored the view of natural rights like that put forward by Samuel Adams and James Wilson, among others. It was this later view that was reflected in the Declaration of Independence and not Jefferson's pet theory.

What about Becker's second assertion that the resolutions of the First Continental Congress were a "compromise"? It depends what one means by a "compromise." There are at least two different meanings of a compromise: (1) a something intermediate between different things or (2) a settlement of differences by mutual concessions. There are different implications of both views of a compromise.

It is true that the position articulated by Congress did not represent the views of either extreme and therefore did not satisfy everyone. But it did represent the views of some (such as John Adams). And the Congress did go quite a ways in defining a position on American rights that saw the colonies as independent states. The Congress adopted a natural rights argument (against those who were against using natural rights). Furthermore, Congress rejected the argument of Jefferson and Jay that emigrants had left their rights behind. Instead, Congress argued that Parliament had no rights to make any legislation whatsoever including trade regulations, implying that the colonies were independent states.

I tend to agree, therefore, with Jensen, *Tracts* (iv) that what he calls the "popular leaders" won a sweeping victory. York, "First Congress" (355) also offers a helpful perspective, that delegates were trying to figure out what they could say without being backed into a rhetorical corner and precipitating the war they were trying to avoid.

52. See JCC I:64-73 for October 14, http://memory.loc.gov/cgi-bin /query/ r?ammem/hlaw:@field(DOCID+@lit(jc00132)):#0010076.

53. The word "Englishmen" interestingly enough appears to have been absent in an earlier draft (the so-called Sullivan Draught). The earlier draft reads "And whereas the good people of these Colonies, justly alarmed....do, in the first place, (as their ancestors in like cases have usually done,) for vindicating and asserting their rights and liberties, declare—..." Note that the same sentence in the draft is without the word "Englishmen" inserted. The insertion now makes the resolutions appear to be emphasizing that the delegates are not just following their ancestors but acting "as Englishmen."

This draft was originally identified as the work of John Sullivan but was later identified to be in the handwriting of John Dickinson and may have been his work. Dickinson did not appear in Congress until October 17. For a discussion see the notes in *Letters of Delegates* (Letter 171, notes).

54. There are some versions published on the Web that have the word "foreign" instead of "sovereign." As far as I can tell these are simply interesting mistakes. "Foreign" would imply that the colonists viewed Parliament as a "foreign" government, which some delegates may have felt, but likely would not have voiced in such a way. The official versions published by JCC has the word "sovereign" as does the official Library of Congress publication Hutson, *A Decent Respect*, 53. For examples of this mistake, see *The University of Chicago* "The Founder's Constitution" (http://press-pubs.uchicago.edu /founders/documents/v1ch1s1.html) and the Yale University Avalon Project, http://www.yale.edu/lawweb/avalon/resolves.htm

55. October 12, *Letters of Delegates*, Letter 164.

56. On October 13 there was substantial debate on the question of trade as noted by John Adams in his diary for that date *Letters of Delegates* (Letter 166). This may be in relationship to the fourth resolve that was specifically debated on October 14. In his diary, Samuel Ward in his (*Letters of Delegates*, Letter 174) writes "Met, pursued the Subject, adopted a Plan founded on Consent." Though the editorial notes there suggest that this was a statement about the declaration of rights in general it seems to me to be a particular statement about the fourth resolution on trade, namely, that they reached agreement to take a position on trade based on consent, which is what the resolve essentially says. Thus, it is possible that by October 14 the decision to base trade on consent was already made.

In his autobiography, John Adams reminisces that he was asked by Rutledge to try his hand at this resolution to attempt a compromise between the disputing parties. He writes that after he drafted a version "I believe not one of the committee was fully satisfied with it; but they all soon acknowledged that there was no hope of hitting on any thing in which we could all agree with more satisfaction." Congress then reviewed it and "the difficult article was again attacked and defended. Congress rejected all amendments to it, and the general sense of the members was, that the article demanded as little as could be demanded, and conceded as much as could be conceded with safety, and certainly as little as would be accepted by Great Britain; and that the country must take its fate, in consequence of it." See Charles Francis Adams, *Works*, Vol. 2, 373-377.

The position of this resolution is consistent with Adams's own view that he expressed when jotting down notes about Gadsden's view of trade, with which he disagreed. For Adams's view on Gadsden's comment, see *Letters of Delegates*, Letter 46 and in Butterfield, *Diary*, 2:133-34.

If my interpretation of Ward's comment is correct, Congress reached consensus on October 14 about taking the position that the colonies "consent" to trade. It is also interesting and suggestive that Adams says nothing about drafting this resolution in his Diary where he is typically pretty open. Indeed, oddly enough on October 14, he doesn't even mention being in Congress and instead talks about his visit to see Dr. Chevott and his "Skelletons and Wax Work." One might have thought had he drafted the resolution and it was presented on the fourteenth, he might have mentioned it. On October 16, Adams does mention that he "staid at Home all day. Very busy in the necessary Business of putting the Proceedings of the Congress into Order" (*Letters of Delegates*, Letter 179). On October 16, the same day that Adams is at home, Silas Deane writes to Thomas Mumford (Letter 180) that "the General Heads are agreed on."

For other discussions of Adams's role, see York, "First Congress," Charles Francis Adams, *Works*; Becker, *Declaration*. Taylor, *Papers*, 149 notes that the view that the colonies were independent states is not a new position for Adams and was reflected in Adams' response to Governor Hutchinson in early 1773. There Adams was articulating the view that the colonies were annexed lands, and that as annexed lands, the authority over them was at most given to the Crown, not to Parliament. Through Charters, the Crown had given authority over those provinces to local governments and did not hold any executive or legislative power over them. The colonies were then under the allegiance to the Crown but not within the realm. For Adams's essay, see "Two Replies," 121.
57. See also John Dickinson's Draft Address to the King on October 22 (*Letters of Delegates*, Letter 195), which affirms the American's loyalty and faithfulness to the king.
58. Discussion of a federated view of empire in R. G. Adams, *Political Ideas*.
59. Boyd, *Papers*, vol. 1, 122.
60. Ibid., 135.
61. For background on the Declaration, see JCC Vol. 2: 128 note 1 for July 6, 1775.
62. See, for example Maier, *American Scripture*, 3-46.
63. The official declaration was debated paragraph by paragraph and approved on July 6, 1775. See JCC 2:128. See also Boyd, *Papers*, Vol 1, 187-192 for background on the writing of this document.
64. See the analysis of Boyd, *Papers*, vol. 1: 190-191.
65. Boyd, *Papers*, I:191 does a good job of bringing out some of the differences and contesting the view that Dickinson simply softened Jefferson's essay.

Boyd notes that Jefferson's view here is a forthright statement of the view from *A Summary View*. Boyd however fails to note the irony that Jefferson would be putting forward this view after the First Continental Congress had rejected it in its Bill of Rights.

66. Boyd, *Papers*, I: 193.
67. See my earlier discussion of Bland and Jefferson's position, 154.
68. Boyd, *Papers*, I: 205-206.
69. I disagree somewhat with Boyd, *Papers*, (I:191) who suggests that "it would be too much to say that Dickinson categorically rejected Jefferson's theory of imperial relations; it appears to be closer to the truth to say that he softened the blunt expression of it, partially obscuring the meaning in doing so." I don't believe Boyd has gone quite far enough. On my reading, Dickinson rejected Jefferson's "quit society" theory and reverted back to a position much closer to that of the First Congress when he said "Societies or Governments, vested with perfect legislatures within them, were formed under Charters from the Crown, and such an harmonious Intercourse and Union was established between the colonies & the Kingdom from which they derived their origin."
70. Boyd, *Papers*, I: 195.
71. Ibid., 200.
72. Ibid, 207
73. See Boyd's account.
74. Ibid, 204-05.
75. Ibid, 190.

7: What Do We Really Know about Jefferson on Locke?

1. Boyd, *Papers*, I:34. By "Locke on Government" Jefferson is referring to Locke's *Second Treatise on Government* and probably also to Locke's *First Treatise*. The list of the titles is discussed below. In these lists of books, I distinguish titles from volumes. Titles refers to a discrete title that Jefferson lists that could include multiple volumes such as "Gordons History of Parliaments 2 vol."
2. Boyd, *Papers*, I: 74-75.
3. Chinard, *Commonplace Book*, Article 754, 214. The subtitle of this book is misleading. Chinard calls it "A repertory of his ideas on Government." The actual contents of the book are much broader than ideas of government and include legal history, history of the peopling of Europe, as well as some ideas on government, particularly those of Montesquieu.
4. Dewey, *TJ Lawyer*, 57-72.

5. See my own discussion in this area, in Eilberg-Schwartz, *The Savage*, "Who's Kidding Whom?" and in Schwartz "Does God Have a Body?." The problem of the relationship of history to sacred religious interpretation is an interesting question in all religious traditions.

6. One of the modern problems for Christianity was the problem of "the historical Jesus." There is an interesting similarity between that debate and the debates over the "truth" about Jefferson's life, that would be worthy of an essay. In fact the question of what could be known historically versus through revelation emerged as a central question in the study of religion in the modern period and in many ways shaped the modern study of religion itself.

7. Malone, *Jefferson*, I:32-33; Peden "Jefferson's Libraries," 266. A typewritten inventory of Peter Jefferson's will is available at the University of Virginia.

8. Malone, I:103, Kimball, *Road to Glory*, 83, Randall, *TJ: A Life*, 67, Peden, "Jefferson's Libraries," 267 Randall, *TJ: A Life*, 66-67, Dewey, *TJ Lawyer*, 13. Reproduced in William Peden, Thomas Jefferson: Book-collector (ms. Dissertation, UVA, app. H.) and summarized in Peden, "Jefferson's Libraries." Colbourn, *Lamp of Experience* (267), is somewhat misleading in conflating the 1769 invoice purchases and the library left to Jefferson by his father Peter Jefferson.

9. Kimball, *Road to Glory*, 83, 213, Dewey, *TJ: Lawyer*, 14. Malone I:103.

10. The invoice is reproduced in Boyd, *Papers*, I:34.

11. "Ellis's Tracts on Liberty" apparently refers to Anthony Ellys, "Tracts on the liberty, spiritual and temporal, of protestants in England Addressed to J. N. Esq; at Aix-la-Chapelle," published in the mid-1760s.

12. Boyd, *Papers*, I:34.

13. Becker actually had multiple inconsistent views of the relationship of Jefferson to Locke and not all of them were direct dependence.

14. White, *Philosophy of Revolution*, 65.

15. I am here following Dewey, *TJ Lawyer*, in his reconstruction of Jefferson's legal education. Others assume he took his bar in 1767.

16. See Randall, *TJ: A Life*, 46 on Inns of Court.

17. See Dewey, *TJ Lawyer*, for a discussion which questions the date of 1767 assumed by many biographers as date when Jefferson passed the bar.

18. First two quotes from Randall, *TJ:A Life*, appear on page 38, the third on page 40.

19. Randall, *TJ:A Life*, 45.

20. Randall, *TJ:A Life*, 53.

21. Randall, *Ibid.*, 40 citing in a footnote the following: "(17 F. W. Gilmer, c 1816 quoted in Francis Walker Gilmer, 350)."
22. Randall, *TJ:A Life*, 40.
23. For the Turpin letter, see Boyd, *Papers*, I:23. On the discussion of the Moore letter, see Dewey, *TJ Lawyer*, 15 and for the original, see Ford, *Writings*, 9:480-85. In my volume of Ford, it appears in vol. 10:190.
24. See Dewey, *TJ Lawyer*, 15 on the same point. See Chinard, *TJ*, 15-16 who cautions on a similar point.
25. See note 23 above.
26. See Randall, *TJ: A Life*, 56; Malone I, 67; Dumbauld, *TJ and the Law*, 5-6. See caution by Dewey (*TJ Lawyer*, 15-16) on this point.
27. Randall, *TJ: A Life*, 56. In support of this statement Randall cites the letters to Turpin and Moore.
28. Malone, I:67.
29. Ibid., I:69.
30. Ibid., I:69.
31. Ibid., I:58.
32. Dewey, *TJ Lawyer*, 15.
33. Malone, I:173.
34. Ibid., I: 175 citing Becker for evidence of Jefferson's dependence on Locke. So Malone recognizes the limits of knowing when and how Jefferson picked up the notion of natural rights but still accepts Becker's conclusion that by the time he wrote the Declaration Jefferson was using Lockean cadences.
35. See Bailyn, *Pamphlets* (293-299) for discussion of the Two Penny Acts. I've discussed the Stamp Act Crisis and Townshend Acts in earlier sections.
36. See Ford, *Works*, IX: 339-45, 475-76, X: 59-60; Malone I:91.
37. See Bailyn, *Pamphlets*, 301-353.
38. See my earlier discussion in Chapter 3.
39. Malone I: 91; Randall, *TJ:A Life*, 77; Kimball, *Road to Glory*, 192-93.
40. See, for example, Dewey, *TJ Lawyer*, 9-17.
41. See my earlier discussion, in Chapter 3.
42. Malone I: 93.
43. Malone I: 101.
44. Kimball, *Road to Glory*, 210.
45. Chinard, *Commonplace Book*, 7-12, Kimball, *Road to Glory*, 210.
46. It is somewhat misleading to call the commonplace book "a Repertory of His Ideas on Government," as it includes a bulk of legal material and historical material as well. By this characterization, Chinard, like Kimball, stresses the presence of political ideas and downplays the historical character of the sources,

although a number of the historical works touch on the history of various political institutions.
47. Kimball, *Road to Glory*, 210.
48. Ibid., 214.
49. Malone I: 175
50. The laws of tanistry refer to laws by which the king or chief of the clan was elected by family heads in full assembly. He held office for life and was required by custom to be of full age, in possession of all his faculties, and without any remarkable blemish of mind or body. At the same time, a tanist, or next heir to the chieftaincy, was elected, who, if the king died or became disqualified, at once became king.
51. Chinard, *Commonplace Book*, 205.
52. I develop this point in more detail below.
53. Greene, *Companion to American Revolution*, xxx.
54. Chinard, *Commonplace Book*, 257-296.
55. Ibid., 8, 284.
56. Ibid., 8.
57. Dewey, *TJ Lawyer*, 16, 94-106.
58. Wilson, "Early Notebooks."
59. Chinard, *Commonplace Book*, 210.
60. Boyd, *Papers*, I: 106.
61. Ibid., 105.
62. Ibid., 107.
63. Ibid., 108.
64. Ibid., 116.
65. Ibid., 117 and Ford, *Works* (I: 418) note similarities of the resolutions to *A Summary View*.
66. Boyd, *Papers*, I: 119.
67. I shall come back to this citation in detail below.
68. Chinard, *Commonplace Book*, 191 notes without apparently understanding the full importance of his insight that "The same ideas, expressed almost in the same words, will be found in *A Summary View of the rights of British America*."
69. On the relationship of these two different notions of contract, see Zuckert, *Natural Rights*, 49-76.
70. Wills, *Inventing America*, 173.
71. Ibid., 173.
72. Quotes from Jayne, *Jefferson's Declaration*, in order, 41, 45, 46.
73. Locke, *Second Treatise*, 11:141.

8: Hume, Locke, and Jefferson's Early Legal Cases

1. Boyd, *Papers*, I 33-34
2. All of these references are cited in Boyd, *Papers*, I:37-38.
3. Malone, I:127, Chinard, *Commonplace Book*, 2.
4. Wills, *Inventing America*, 174.
5. There are two different variant spellings of the name: Skipwith or Shipwith.
6. Boyd, *Papers*, I: 74-75.
7. Boyd, *Papers*, I: 78-80. An online version is available at the The Online Library of Liberty, http://oll.libertyfund.org/?option=com_staticxt&staticfile=show.php%3Ftitle=755&chapter=86018&layout=html&Itemid=27.
8. See, for example, Sher, *The Enlightenment and the Book*. 504.
9. See Koch, *Philosophy*, 15-22. Jayne, *Jefferson's Declaration*, 62-86
10. Interestingly enough Shakespeare is not in Jefferson's later library either. See "Jefferson's Libraries," 270.
11. In Jefferson's later library, history is one of the largest categories about the same size as politics and trade. See Peden, "Jefferson's Libraries."
12. The only problem with this reading is that some of the books in other categories such as Hume are by no means easy to read either. There is another way of reading Jefferson's comment, although I think the first is more probable. Jefferson may be implying that Skipwith is already acquainted with the commercial principles and principles of constitutional security. In this interpretation, Jefferson is assuming Skipwith already knows quite a bit more about the commercial principles and constitutional security than the list of books that Jefferson is recommending for his library. "I have given you a few only of the best books," writes Jefferson, "as you would probably chuse to be not unacquainted with those commercial principles...." In other words, the list Jefferson recommends constitutes what a library should have and does not exhaust what Skipwith already knows.
13. See Burstein, *Inner Jefferson*, 29. "Rowanty" was the name of an old Indian village by which Skipwith referred to his own home. Jefferson here is expressing camaraderie with Skipwith in calling his own home by the same name.
14. See note 3 above.
15. Sher, *The Enlightenment and the Book*. 504.
16. Wills, *Inventing America*, 229-239.
17. Wilson, "Jefferson's Library."

18. Burstein, *Inner Jefferson*, 26-29.
19. Boyd, *Papers*, I 75, Kimball, *Road to Glory*, 24, Malone, I: 433
20. Koch, *Philosophy*; Jayne, *Jefferson's Declaration*.
21. For the citation, see article 557 in Chinard, *Commonplace Book*, 99. For Chinard's statement about Kames, see page 19.
22. Dunn, *Locke*.
23. Macpherson, *Possessive Individualism*.
24. See Schwartz, "Liberty Is Not Freedom."
25. Zuckert, *Natural Rights*.
26. Dworetz, *Unvarnished Doctrine*, makes a similar point.
27. Peden, "Jefferson's Libraries," 269-272.
28. Ibid., 269. McDonald, "Founding Father's Libraries," 3, is misleading in my view in claiming that colonial writers were not seriously reading theoretical philosophy, based on the readings of figures like Jefferson, Otis, Adams, Wilson, and others. I do agree with McDonald's point however that there were differences in political views among the founding generation.
29. Conrad, "Putting Rights Talk," 261 and 255; Peterson, *Thomas Jefferson* (45-46) makes this point in general that Jefferson was not a systematic thinker. See also Chinard, *Jefferson* (31) who makes the same point. For a contrary view, see Koch, *Jefferson*, xi-xiv.
30. Malone I: 173.
31. Based on letters later in life, Randall, *TJ:A Life* (58) also notes that Jefferson lent Hume on the *History of England* to Patrick Henry. See TJ to William Wirt, Aug. 5, 1815 in Ford, *Writings*, 9:476.
32. White, *Philosophy*, for example does not consider Hume's influence on Jefferson at all.
33. Randall, *TJ:A Life,* (56 and note 15 on page 603) citing a letter in Lipscomb & Bergh, *Writings of TJ*, 14:85; Peden (269), citing the letter to William Duane, on August 12, 1810, notes that Hume was among those modern historians "whom Jefferson hated for his outspoken support of the Stuarts and Toryism but admired for his charm and felicity of style."
34. Kimball, *Road to Glory*, 79, 214.
35. For a reassessment of Hume's impact in the colonies, see Spencer "David Hume and America." See also Wilson "Jefferson vs. Hume" who also challenges the notion that Jefferson was antagonistic to Hume as a young man. Wilson, however, may not go far enough. Wilson focuses on the specific question of Jefferson's perception of Hume's *History of England* as it related to his views of the Anglo-Saxons. Wilson does not take note of the fact that Jefferson also recommended Hume's essays to Skipwith and thus does not consider whether

Hume's political philosophy, with views of the social contract or the origins of government could have shaped Jefferson's view. It is the latter contention that I take up.

36. Chinard, *Commonplace Book*, 210.
37. For the history of the versions of publications, see Miller, "David Hume."
38. For an outstanding overview of how Hume's political and philosophical views intermeshed, see Miller "Philosophy and Ideology." For a good discussion of how Hume's History of England have been re-received in recent scholarship, see the good summary piece by Okie, "Ideology."
39. See Miller, "Philosophy and Ideology."
40. I realize I am simplifying some very complicated issues in Lockean scholarship in this brief summary. There are debates, for example, over whether Locke ultimately abandoned the attempt to ground the discernment of the Law of Nature through reason or whether he ultimately turned to religious revelation as the source of knowledge about the Law of Nature. Some interpreters emphasize that Locke's theory depends on a belief in God and a traditional notion of a revealing God. It is also debatable how much Locke bases the rights of the individual to life on his "workmanship argument" that we are all the property of God. The fact that there are diverging readings of Locke is one of the problems of saying that Jefferson is Lockean, for the question arises which of the many versions of Locke are we talking about. For some of these debates, see Dunn, *Locke*; Aarsleff, "State of Nature"; Aschcraft, "Faith and Knowledge"; Zuckert, *Launching Liberalism*, 25-56; White, *Philosophy*, 1-74.
41. Hume, "Of The Original Contract," 199-200 in Hume, *Essays*.
42. See discussion in chapter 1, note 66.
43. I am here following Miller, "Philosophy and Ideology."
44. See Hume, "On Original Contract" 204, in Hume, *Essays*.
45. Ibid, 201.
46. See my discussion of this point earlier in chapter 1, note 66.
47. Hume "Of The Original Contract" 201, in Hume, *Essays*.
48. Ibid., 202.
49. Ibid., 201.
50. Malone, I:175-176
51. Dewey, *TJ Lawyer*, 57-72 does a wonderful job outlining the circumstances of the case concerning divorce.
52. See Ford, I:470-481. For discussions of the case see, Kimball, *Road to Glory*, 93; Randall, 134; Dumbauld, *TJ and the Law*, 75, 83-84.
53. See Randall, *Jefferson*, 134 on the fire and notes.

54. See notes about the circumstances of the case in Ford, *Works*, I: 470-481.
55. I am relying on Randall here, who indicates that Jefferson made a note in his account book that he would not take a fee for the case.
56. Ford I: 475.
57. Malone I: 175
58. Randall, *TJ: A Life*, 145, 147.
59. Kimball, *Road to Glory*, 93.
60. Dumbauld, *TJ and the Law*, 214 note 86.
61. Randall, 147, copies a lengthy quote from Jefferson but completely excises the reference to Pufendorf. Malone makes no mention of the Pufendorf quote. Kimball is an exception. She does note that Jefferson cited Pufendorf.
62. See Hobbes, *Leviathan*, Chapter 11.
63. Ibid., Chapter 13.
64. Randall, *TJ: A Life*, 144 cites Jefferson's autobiography indicating that Jefferson tried to emancipate slaves in the Virginia House of Burgesses when he was first elected in 1769 but failed.
65. Jefferson makes a number of other arguments to prove that inheritance of the mother's status as a slave is against the law of nature, for example by arguing that a child should get the status of both the father and mother and this creates contains a contradiction where the father is free and mother a slave. See also Ford, *Writings*, I:476
66. See Schwartz, "Liberty Is Not Freedom" for a discussion. Contrast Locke, *Second Treatise*, 2:6 with 5:27. See Zuckert, *Natural Rights*, 216-223 who argues that Locke favors the latter view that people have self-ownership, a right over their own body and person. As I have argued, however, there is no contradiction here. In 2:6 Locke says that people are the property of God. But in 5:27 he says every person has a property in his own person. "The *labour* of his body, and the *work* of his hands, we may say, are property his." On my reading Locke thinks only the labor belongs to the person but not their own body, which explains why according to Locke people cannot take their own lives.
67. In one chapter, Locke says that liberty flows from the fact that people are the workmanship of God and therefore the property of God. To harm another person would therefore be damaging God's property. In another chapter, Locke argues that individuals have property in their own body and therefore no one else has a right to that person's labor but him or herself (Locke, *Second Treatise*, 5:27). For a discussion of whether these two views conflict, see Schwartz, "Liberty and the Public Good" note 2 and a contrary view in Zuckert, *Natural Rights*, 239-246.

68. Pufendorf, *Law of Nature and Nations*, Book II, Chapter 2, 82.
69. Dewey, *TJ: Lawyer*, 57-72.
70. Hume, "Of Polygamy and Divorce", in Hume, *Essays*, 85-88.
71. Ibid., 87
72. Locke, *Second Treatise*, 7:81
73. Dewey, *TJ Lawyer*, 67.

Conclusion: Does It Matter What the Declaration Means?

1. See Garry Wills, *Inventing America*, xiii-xxvi.
2. See Garry Wills, *Inventing America*, xiii-xxvi.
3. Detweiler, "Changing Reputation."
4. See Elkins and McKitrick, *Age of Federalism*.
5. On the history of the Bill of Rights, see Akil, *America's Constitution*.
6. For such a view see Amar Akil, *America's Constitution*, 5-53.
7. See Levy, *Original Intent*, 1-7 and Madison, *Notes*.
8. See Levy, *Original Intent*.
9. Gerber, *To Secure These Rights*, 2-3.
10. See http://en.wikipedia.org/wiki /History_of_the_United_States_Constitution (September 2009).
11. Maier, *American Scripture*, xviii.
12. I take this theoretical problem to be at the heart of Foucault's work in arguing that it is impossible to define a specific origin of a historical moment.
13. My own line of thinking dovetails with others who have made similar arguments such a Reid, *Authority*, and Bailyn, *Ideological Origins*. I have tried to trace this more specifically in relationship to Jefferson and the Declaration than either Reid or Bailyn, in hopes of showing that even the Declaration can't anchor the view of a univocal view of rights.

References

Aarsleff, Hans, 1969. "The State of Nature and the Nature of Man in Locke," 99-136. In *John Locke: Problems and Perspectives*. Ed. John W. Yolton. Cambridge: Cambridge University Press.

Adams, Charles Francis, ed. 1865. *Works of John Adams, Second President of the United States*. With A Life of the Author. Vol. II. Boston: Little, Brown and Company.

Adams, John, 1774. *Notes on the Debates*. (Letter 23). In *Letters of Delegates to Congress*. Available online. *Library of Congress* http://memory.loc.gov/cgibin/query/r?ammem/hlaw:@field(DOCID+@lit(dg00123)) . Also available in Charles Francis Adams, *The Works of John Adams,* 370 and in Adams's historical records http://www.masshist.org/DIGITALADAMS/AEA/cfm/doc.cfm?id=D22A

___, 1775. "Novanglus." In Jensen, *Tracts*, 297-340.

___, 1776. "Thoughts on Government." In *The Revolutionary Writings of John Adams*. Ed. C. Bradley Thompson. 2000. Indianapolis: The Liberty Fund, 286-293.

___, 1961. *Diary and Autobiography of John Adams*. Ed. Lyman Henry Butterfield, et. al., 4 vols. Cambridge, Mass: Belknap Press of Harvard University.

___, 2000 [1773]. "Two Replies of the Massachusetts House of Representatives to Governor Hutchinson." In *The Revolutionary Writings of John Adams*. Ed. C. Bradley Thompson. Indianapolis: The Liberty Fund.

Adams, Randolph Greenfield, 1922. *Political Ideas of the American Revolution*. Britannic-American Contributions to the Problem of Imperial Organization 1765-1775. Durham, N.C.: Trinity College.

Aschcraft, Richard, 1969. "Faith and Knowledge in Locke's Philosohy." 194-223. In *John Locke: Problems and Perspectives*. Ed. John W. Yolton. Cambridge: Cambridge University Press.

Amar, Akhil Reed, 2005, *America's Constitution: A Biography*. New York: Random House.

Amitage, David, 2007. *The Declaration of Independence: A Global History*. Cambridge, Mass.: Harvard University.

Bailyn, Bernard, 1992. *The Ideological Origins of the American Revolution*. Cambridge: Mass.: Belknap Press of Harvard University.

Bailyn, Bernard, Editor, 1965. *Pamphlets of the American Revolution*. 1750-1776. Vol. 1. Cambridge: Mass: Belknap Press of Harvard University.

Becker, Carl L., 1922. *The Declaration of Independence*. New York: Vintage Books.

Bland, Richard, 1766. *An Inquiry into the Rights of the British Colonies*. In Merrill Jensen, ed. *Tracts of the American Revolution* 1763-1776. Indianapolis: Hackett Publishing Company.

Bland, Richard, 1764. *The Colonel Dismounted*, 301-350. In Bailyn, *Pamphlets*.

Blackstone, [ ] [1840]. *Commentaries on the Laws of England*. Ed. John Bethune Bayly. London: Sunders and Benning. The Avalon Project.

Online: http://www.yale.edu/lawweb/avalon/blackstone/introa.htm#4

Boaz, David and Edward H. Crane, 1993, "Introduction: The Collapse of the Statist Vision." In *Market Liberalism: A Paradigm for the 21st Century*. Ed. By David Boaz and Edward H. Crane. Washington, D.C.: Cato Institute, 1-20.

Boyd, Julian, ed., 1999 [1945?]. *The Declaration of Independence*. The Library of Congress.

___, ed., 1950. *The Papers of Thomas Jefferson*. Volume 1. Princeton: Princeton University.

Burstein, Andrew, 1995. *The Inner Jefferson: Portrait of a Grieving Optimist*. Charlottesville, University of Virginia.

Carey, George W. 2005, "Natural Rights, Equality, and the Declaration of Independence." *AveMaria Law Review*. 3:1, 45-67.

Chinard, Gilbert. 1929. *Thomas Jefferson: The Apostle of Americanism*. Boston: Little, Brown and Company.

___, 1926. *The Commonplace Book of Thomas Jefferson*. Baltimore: The John's Hopkins Press.

Conrad, Stephen A. 1993. "Putting Rights Talk in Its Place: *The A Summary View* Revisited", 254-281. In *Jeffersonian Legacies*. Ed. Peter S. Onuf. Charlottesville: University of Virginia.

Colbourn, Trevor. 1965. *The Lamp of Experience: Whig History and the Intellectual Origins of the American Revolution*. Indianapolis: Liberty Fund.

Cushing, Harry A., ed. *The Writings of Samuel Adams*. Volume I. 1764-1769. York: G. P. Putnam's Sons, 1908. Ebook version at Fictionwise.com.

Dershowitz, Alan. 2003. *America Declares Independence*. John Wiley & Sons.

Detweiler, Philip F. 1962. "The Changing Reputation of the Declaration of Independence. the First Fifty Years." *William and Mary Quarterly* (3rd. Ser.) 19 557, 558-65

Dewey, Frank L, 1986. *Thomas Jefferson Lawyer*. Charlottesville: University Press of Virginia.

Dickinson, John, 1765. *The Late Regulations Respecting The British Colonies*, 659-691. In Bernard Bailyn, *Pamphlets Of the American Revolution*. 1750-1776. Vol. 1. Cambridge: Mass: Belknap Press of Harvard University.

_____. *Empire and Nation: Letters from a Farmer in Pennsylvania*. The Online Library of Liberty. http://oll.libertyfund.org/?option=com_staticxt&staticfile=show.php%3Ftitle=690

Dulany, Daniel, 1765. "Considerations On the Propriety of Imposing Taxes In The British Colonies," 599-657. In Bernard Bailyn, *Pamphlets Of the American Revolution*. 1750-1776. Vol. 1. Cambridge: Mass: Belknap Press of Harvard University.

Dunn, John, 1984. *Locke*. Oxford: Oxford University.

_____, 1969. "The politics of Locke in England and America in the eighteenth century." In *John Locke: Problems and Perspectives*. Ed. John W. Yolton. Cambridge: Cambridge University Press.

Daumbald, Edward, 1978. *Thomas Jefferson and the Law*. Norman: University of Oklahoma Press.

Dworetz, Steven M., 1990. *The Unvarnished Doctrine. Locke Liberalism, and the American Revolution*. Duke University: Durham.

Dworkin, Ronald. 1978. *Taking Rights Seriously*. Cambridge, Mass.: Harvard University.

Ellis, Joseph, 1998. *American Sphinx: The Character of Thomas Jefferson.* New York: Vintage Books.

Elkins, Stanley and Eric McKitrick, 1993. *The Age of Federalism: The Early American Republic, 1788-1800.* Oxford: Oxford University.

Eilberg-Schwartz, Howard, 1990. *The Savage in Judaism: An Anthropology of Israelite Religion and Ancient Judaism.* Bloomington: Indiana University.

____, 1987. "Who's Kidding Whom?: A Serious Reading of Rabbinic Word Plays," *Journal of the American Academy of Religion* 55:4 (1987), 65-78.

____, 1994. *God's Phallus.* Boston: Beacon Press.

Epstein, Richard A, 1995. *Simple Rules for a Complex World.* Cambridge, Mass: Harvard University.

____, 1998. *Principles for a Free Society: Reconciling Individual Liberty with Common Good.* Cambridge, Mass: Harvard University.

____, 2003. *Skepticism and Freedom: A Modern Case for Classical Liberalism.* Chicago: The University of Chicago.

Edwin J. Feulner Jr, 1998. *The March of Freedom: Modern Classics in Conservative Thought.* Dallas: Spence Publishing Company.

Ferling, John, 1977. *The Loyalist Mind. Joseph Galloway and the American Revolution.* Pennsylvania State University.

Fitch, Thomas, et al., 1765. *Reasons Why The British Colonies In America Should Not Be Charged With Internal Taxes,* 379-403. In Bernard Bailyn, *Pamphlets of the American Revolution.* 1750-1776. Vol. 1. Cambridge: Mass: Belknap Press of Harvard University.

Fitzpatrick, John C. 1924. *The Spirit of the Declaration.* New York: Houghton, Mifflin.

Ford, Paul Leicester, ed., 1904. *The Works of Thomas Jefferson.* Vol. 1. New York: G. P. Putnam's Sons.

Friedman, Milton, 1982 [1962]. *Capitalism and Freedom.* Chicago: The University of Chicago Press.

Friedman, Milton and Rose D, 2003 "Foreword". In *The Legacy of Milton and Rose Friedman's Free to Choose:Economic Liberalism at the Turn of the 21st Century.* Proceedings of a conference sponsored by the Federal Reserve Bank of Dallas, October 2003. Published online at www.dallasfed.org/research/pubs/ftc/index.html.

Friedenwald, Herbert, 1974 [1904]. *The Declaration of Independence.* New York: De Capo Press.

Ford, Paul Leicester, ed., 1904. *The Works of Thomas Jefferson.* Vol. 1. New York: G. P. Putnam's Sons.

Galloway, Joseph, 1775. *A Candid Examination of the Mutual Claims of Great Britain and the Colonies*, 350-399. In Jensen, *Tracts*.

Ganter, Herbert Lawrence. "Jefferson's 'Pursuit of Happiness' and Some Forgotten Men." *William and Mary College Quarterly*. Part I. 2nd Ser. 16:3 (July 1936), 422-434. Part II 16:4 (Oct 1936) 558-585.

Gerber, Scott. 1995. *To Secure These Rights: The Declaration of Independence and Constitutional Interpretation.* New York: New York University.

Gordon, Thomas and John Trenchard. 2005. *Cato's Letters.* 4 Vols. 1720-1723. Published by Liberty Fund, Inc. The Online Library of Liberty.

Greene, Jack P. and J.R. Pole, 2000. *Companion to American Revolution.* Malden: Mass: Blackwell Publishers.

Hamilton, Alexander, 1775. *The Farmer Refuted. The Works of Alexander Hamilton.* Vol. 1.The Online Library of Liberty. Liberty Fund. 2005, 51-128.

Hamilton, Alexander, 1774. *A Vindication of the Measures of Congress.* In *The Works of Alexander Hamilton.* Vol. 1. The Online Library of Liberty. Liberty Fund. 2005, 19-49.

Hamowy, Ronald, 1979. "Jefferson and the Scottish Enlightenment: A Critique of Garry Will's *Inventing America: Jefferson's Declaration of Independence.*" WMQ. 3rd Series. 36:4 (October). 503-523.

Hayek, F. A., 1994 [1944]. *The Road To Serfdom.* Chicago: The University of Chicago Press.

____, 1960. *The Constitution of Liberty.* Chicago: The University of Chicago Press.

Hazelton, John H. *The Declaration of Independence: Its History.* New York: Dodd, Mead and Company. 1906

Hertz, Gerald, 1911, "Bishop Seabury." *The English Historical Review.* Vol. 26 No. 101, 57-75.

Hirsch, H. N., 1992. *A Theory of Liberty: The Constitution and Minorities.* New York: Routledge.

Hobbes, Thomas, 1998 [1651]. *Leviathan.* Ed. J. C. A. Gaskin. Oxford: Oxford University.

Hopkins, Stephen, 1765. *The Rights of the Colonies Examined*, 499-521. In Bernard Bailyn, *Pamphlets of the American Revolution.* 1750-1776. Vol. 1. Cambridge: Mass: Belknap Press of Harvard University.

____, 1764. *An Essay on the Trade of the Northern Colonies*, 3-18. In Bernard Bailyn, *Pamphlets of the American Revolution.* 1750-1776. Vol. 1. Cambridge: Mass: Belknap Press of Harvard University.

Howard, Martin, 1765. *A Letter From a Gentleman At Halifax.* 523-543. In Jensen, Merrill, 1966. *Tracts of the American Revolution 1763-1776.* Indianapolis: Hackett Publishing Company.

Hume, David, 1987 [1777]. *Essays Moral, Political, Literary.* Ed. Eugene F. Miller Indianapolis: Liberty Fund 1987. Online: http://oll.libertyfund.org/EBooks/Hume_0059.pdf

Hutson, James, 1975. *A Decent Respect to the Opinions of Mankind. Congressional State Papers 1774-1776.* Washington: Library of Congress.

Huyler, Jerome, 1995. *Locke in America.* Kansas: University Press of Kansas.

Hyneman, Charles S. and Donald S. Lutz, 1983. *American Political Writing during the Founding Era.* 1760-1805. Indianapolis: Liberty Press.

Jayne, Allen. 1998. *Jefferson's Declaration of Independence. Origins, Philosophy and Theology.* University Press of Kentucky.

JCC. Journals of the Continental Congress. 34 vols. 1774-1789. Ed. W. C. Ford. Library of Congress, 1904-1937. Online: http://memory.loc.gov/ammem/amlaw/lwjclink.html

Jefferson, Thomas. 1774. *A Summary View.* In Boyd, *Papers*, Vol. I 121-186. See also http://www.yale.edu/lawweb/avalon/jeffsumm.htm

____. 1775. *Declaration of the Causes and Necessity for Taking Up Arms.* In Boyd, *Papers*, Vol. I, 193-204.

____. 1776. *Refutation of the Argument that the Colonies Were Established at the Expense of the British Nation.* In Boyd, *Papers*, Vol. I, 277-284.

Jensen, Merrill, 1966. *Tracts of the American Revolution 1763-1776.* Indianapolis: Hackett Publishing Company.

Jezierski, John V., 1971. "Parliament or People: James Wilson and Blackstone on the Nature and Location of Sovereignty." In *Journal of the History of Ideas*. 32:1 (Jan. - Mar), 95-106.

Kallich, Martin and Andrew MacLeish, 1962. *The American Revolution Through British Eyes*. Evanston, Ill.: Row, Peterson and Company.

Kimball, Marie, 1943. *Jefferson: The Road to Glory*. 1743 to 1776. New York: Coward-McCann, Inc.

Koch, Adrienne, 1942. *The Philosophy of Thomas Jefferson*. New York: Columbia University.

Kurland, Philip B., and Ralph Lerner, eds.. *The Founders' Constitution*. Chicago: University of Chicago Press, 1987. Online: http://press-pubs.uchicago.edu/founders/

Laslett, Peter. 2002. *Locke: Two Treatises of Government*. Cambridge: Cambridge University Press.

Letters of Delegates to Congress, 1774-1789. Ed. Smith, Paul H., Gerard W. Gawalt, Rosemary Fry Plakas, et al. Volume 1, August 1774-August 1775. Electronic Text Center, University of Virginia Library. http://etext.lib.virginia.edu/toc/modeng/public/DelVol01.html

Leonard, Daniel, 1774-75. "Massachusettensis." In Jensen, *Tracts*, 277-349.

Levy, Leonard, 1988. *Original Intent and the Framers' Constitution*. Chicago: Ivan R. Dee.

Lewis, Anthony, 1948. "Jefferson's A Summary View as a Chart of Political Union." *William and Mary Quarterly*. 3rd Series. 5:1 (January) 34-51.

Lipscomb, Andrew Adgate and Albert Ellery Bergh, 1905.*The Writings of Thomas Jefferson*. Thomas Jefferson Memorial Association.

Locke, John, 2002 [1690]. *Two Treatises of Government*, Ed. By Peter Laslett, Cambridge: Cambridge University Press.

Maier, Pauline. 1997. *American Scripture*. New York: Vintage Books.

Macpherson, C. B., 1962. *The Political Theory of Possessive Individualism: Hobbes to Locke*. Oxford: Clarendon Press.

Malone, Dumas. 1948. *Jefferson and His Times: Jefferson the Virginian*. Vol. 1. Boston: Little, Brown and Company.

Manuel, Frank, 1959. *The Eighteenth Century Confronts the Gods*. Boston: Harvard University.

McDonald, Forrest, "A Founding Father's Library." *Online Library of Liberty*. Liberty Fund. Online: http://oll.libertyfund.org/index.php?option=com_content&task=view&id=176&Itemid=259

Miller, David, 1981. *Philosophy and Ideology in Hume's Political Thought*. Oxford: Clarendon Press.

Miller, Eugene F., 2005. "Foreword." In *David Hume: Essays Moral Political, Literary*. Online Library of Liberty. Online: http://oll.libertyfund.org/EBooks/Hume_0059.pdf.

Morgan, Edmund S. Ed., 1959. *Prologue to Revolution*. New York: Norton.

____, . and Helen M. Morgan, 1962. *The Stamp Act Crisis: Prologue to Revolution*. Chapel Hill: The University of North Carolina.

Morris, Richard B. ed., 1975. *John Jay: The Making Of A Revolutionary*. Unpublished papers 1745-1780. San Francisco: Harper and Row.

Manuel, Frank, 1959. *The Eighteenth Century Confronts the Gods*. Boston: Harvard University.

Morris, Richard B, 1975. *John Jay: The Making of A Revolutionary*. New York: Harper & Row.

Madison, James, 1987. *Notes off Debates in the Federal Convention of 1787. Reported by James Madison*. W. W. Norton & Company.

Okie, Laird, 1985. "Ideology and Partiality in David Hume's History of England." *Hume Studies*. (April) 11:1, 1-32.

Otis, James. *The Rights of the British Colonies Asserted and Proved*. 1764. In Bailyn, *Pamphlets* Vol. 1.

Otis, James, 1765. *A Vindication of the British Colonies*, 545-579. In Bailyn, *Pamphlets* Vol. 1.

Paine, Thomas Paine, 1776, "Common Sense." In Jensen, *Tracts*, 400-446.

Peden, William, 1944. "Some Notes Concerning Thomas Jefferson's Libraries." *William and Mary Quarterly*. 3rd Series. 1:3 (July), 265-272.

Peterson, Merrill D. 1970. *Thomas Jefferson and the New Nation: A Biography*. New York: Oxford University.

Pittman, R. Carter, 1951. "George Mason and the Rights of Men." Originally published in *Georgia Bar Journal* 13:4 (May). Published http://rcarterpittman.org/essays/Mason/George_Mason_and_the_Rights_of_Men.html

Pocock, J. G. A., 1975. *The Machiavellian Moment: Florentine Political Thought and the Atlantic Republican Tradition*. Princeton University Press.

Pufendorf, Samuel von, 2005 [1672]. *Of the Law of Nature and Nations*. Translated from the Latin. Oxford.

Rakove, Jack. *The Beginnings of National Politics*. Baltimore. John Hopkins Press.

Randall, William Sterne, 1993. *Thomas Jefferson: A Life*. New York: Henry Holt and Company.

Rawls, John 1971. *A Theory of Justice*. Boston: Belnap Press of Harvard University.

Reid, John Phillip, 1986. *Constitutional History of the American Revolution: The Authority of Rights*. Madison: University of Wisconsin.

Sandoz, Ellis, ed., 2005. *Political Sermons of the American Founding* Era, 1730-1805. Vol. 1. The Online Library of Liberty. Online: http://oll.libertyfund.org/?option=com_staticxt&staticfile=show.php%3Ftitle=1878

Sher, Richard B. 2006, *The Enlightenment and the Book*. Scottish authors & Their Publishers in Eighteenth-Century Britain, Ireland, & America. Chicago: University of Chicago.

Schlesinger, Arthur M. "The Lost Meaning of 'The Pursuit of Happiness.' *The William and Mary Quarterly*, 3rd series. 21:3 (July 1964), 325-327.

Schochet, Gordon J. 1969. "The Family and the Origins of the State in Locke's Political Philosophy.", 81-98. In Yolton, Ed. *Locke, Problems and Perspectives*.

Schwartz, Howard I. 2007. "'Liberty is not Freedom To Do What You Like': How Notions of Public Good Constrain Liberty In John Locke and the Early Liberty Tradition." Online: http://www.freedomandcapitalism.com. April 2007.

Schwartz, Howard I. 2007. "Why 'Market Liberals' Are Not 'The True Liberals' or Who Really Inherits the Liberty Tradition Anyway?" First published March 2007. Online http://www.freedomandcapitalism.com. April 2007.

____, . "What Color Tie Do You Vote For?: Or Is Economic Freedom Part of Liberty? A Critique of Milton Friedman's Capitalism and Freedom." Online: http://www.freedomandcapitalism.com. January 2007.

____, . 2010. "Does God Have a Body? The Problem of Metaphor and Literal Language In Biblical Interpretation." *Bodies, Embodiment and Theology of the Hebrew Bible*. Ed. S. Tamar Kamionkowski and Wonil Kim. New York: T&T Clark.

Schute, Daniel, 1768. "An Election Sermon." In Charles S. Hyneman, and Donald S. Lutz, *American Political Writing*.

Sidney, Algernon. 1988. *Discourses Concerning Government*. (1698). The Liberty Fund. Online Library of Liberty. Online: http://oll.libertyfund.org/EBOOKs/Sidney_0019.pdf.

Simmons, John. 1999. "Locke's State of Nature." In *The Social Contract Theorists*, 97-120 Ed. Christopher W. Morris. New York: Rowman & Littlefield Publishers.

____, 1999. "Political Consent." In *The Social Contract Theorists*, 121-142. Ed. Christopher W. Morris. New York: Rowman & Littlefield Publishers.

Spencer, Mark G. 2005. *David Hume and Eighteenth-Century America*. Rochester: University of Rochester.

Sunstein, Cass, 1997. *Free Markets and Social Justice*. Oxford: Oxford University.

Taylor, Robert J., et Al., 1977. *Papers of John Adams*. Belknap Press of Harvard University.

Thompson, C. Bradley, ed., 2000. *The Revolutionary Writings of John Adams*. Liberty Fund. Indianapolis.

Vattel, Emmerich de, 1797 [1758]. *Law of Nations or the Principles of Natural Law Applied to the Conduct and to the Affairs of Nations and of Sovereigns*. London: G.G. and J Robinson. Paternoster-Pow.

Varga, Nicholas, Gilman Ostrander; 1980. Ronald Hamowy. "Communications" WMQ 3rd Series. 37:3 (July), 529-540

Walzer, Michael,1983. *Spheres of Justice: A Defense of Pluralism and Equality*. New York: Basic Books.

Ward, Lee, 2004. *The Politics of Liberty in England and Revolutionary America*. Cambridge: Cambridge University Press.

White, Morton, 1978. The Philosophy of the American Revolution. New York: Oxford University Press.

Wills, Garry. 1978. *Inventing America. Jefferson's Declaration of Independence*. Garden City, N.J.: Doubleday.

Williams, Abraham, 1762. "An Election Sermon," 3-19. In *American Political Writing during the Founding Era*. 1760-1805. Ed. Charles S. Hyneman and Donald S. Lutz. Indianapolis: Liberty Press.

Wilson, Douglas L., 1985, "Thomas Jefferson's Early Notebook." *The William and Mary Quarterly*. 3rd series 42:4, 434-452.

____, 1992-93. "Thomas Jefferson's Library and the Skipwith List," *Harvard Library Bulletin*, New Series 3:4 (Winter), 56-72.

____, 1989. "Jefferson vs. Hume." *The William and Mary Quarterly*. 3rd Ser. 46:1 (Jan.) 49-70.

Wilson, James. *Considerations on the Nature and Extent of the Legislative Authority of the British Parliament*. In *Collected Works of James Wilson*. Vol. 1, 21-38. Online Library of Liberty. 2007.

Woods, Gordon, 1969. *The Creation of the American Republic*, 1776-1787. New York: W. W. Norton.

Wynne, Mark A, 2003. "Free to Choose". In *The Legacy of Milton and Rose Friedman's Free to Choose: Economic Liberalism at the Turn of the 21st Century*. Proceedings of a Conference Sponsored by the Federal Reserve Bank of Dallas October 2003, 3-17. Online: www.dallasfed.org/research/pubs/ftc/index.html.

Yolton, J. W., ed., 1969. *John Locke: Problems and Perspectives*. Cambridge: Cambridge University Press.

York, Neil L. "The First Continental Congress and the Problem of American Rights." *The Pennsylvania Magazine of History and Biography*. Vol. CXXII, No. 4 Oct 1988

Zuckert, Michael P. 1994. *Natural Rights and the New Republicanism*. Princeton: Princeton University Press.

____, 2002. *Launching Liberalism*. Kansas: University of Kansas.

About the author

Howard I. Schwartz, Ph.D. (formerly Howard Eilberg-Schwartz) is both a business executive and an award-winning independent scholar whose work examines the relationship of religion, history, and the theory of the human sciences. A Guggenheim fellow and winner of the American Academy of Religion award for Academic Excellence, Schwartz has written a number of books pondering the ways in which the study of religion, history, and theory come together to produce understandings of the past and of our cultural myths. In *The Savage in Judaism*, Schwartz explored the ways in which our understanding of Western religions rests on a distinction between savage and higher religions and how that presupposition shaped the history of our understanding of monotheistic religions. In *God's Phallus and Other Problems for Men and Monotheism*, Schwartz explores the problems raised for men by the fact that God is imagined as masculine. Schwartz is also editor of *People of the Body* and co-editor of *Off With Her Head,* with Wendy Doniger. Before leaving academia, Schwartz taught at Stanford, Indiana and Temple Universities. For the last ten years, he has been a business executive in a public software company. For more information on the author, you can visit his website: www.freedomandcapitalism.com or email him: hsaccount@yahoo.com.

Made in the USA
Charleston, SC
07 April 2011